NEW ESSAYS ON FICHTE'S LATER JENA *WISSENSCHAFTSLEHRE*

SPEP Studies
in Historical Philosophy

General Editors David Kolb
        John McCumber

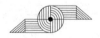

NEW ESSAYS ON FICHTE'S LATER JENA *WISSENSCHAFTSLEHRE*

Edited by

Daniel Breazeale
and Tom Rockmore

Northwestern University Press
Evanston, Illinois

Northwestern University Press
Evanston, Illinois 60208-4210

10 9 8 7 6 5 4 3 2 1

ISBN 0-8101-1864-5 (cloth)
ISBN 0-8101-1865-3 (paper)

Library of Congress Cataloging-in-Publication Data

New essays on Fichte's later Jena Wissenschaftslehre / edited by Daniel Breazeale
and Tom Rockmore.
    p. cm.—(Studies in phenomenology and existential philosophy)
    Includes bibliographical references.
    ISBN 0-8101-1864-5 (cloth : alk. paper)—ISBN 0-8101-1865-3 (pbk. :
alk. paper)
    1. Fichte, Johann Gottlieb, 1762–1814. I. Breazeale, Daniel. II. Rockmore, Tom,
1942– III. Series.
B2848 .N475 2002
193—dc21   2002003347

Contents

List of Abbreviations   vii

Introduction
On the "Later Jena *Wissenschaftslehre*," 1796–1799   ix
Daniel Breazeale

Part I. Essays on the *Foundations of Natural Right,* 1796–1797

The Deduction of Intersubjectivity in Fichte's *Grundlage des Naturrechts*   5
Klaus Brinkmann

Fichte's Theory of Punishment: "Out-Kanting" Kant in Criminal Law   18
Jean-Christophe Merle

The "Deduction of the Individual": Fichte's Efforts to "Complete" the
Jena *Wissenschaftslehre*   28
Hans-Jakob Wilhelm

The Displacement of Recognition by Coercion in Fichte's *Grundlage des
Naturrechts*   47
Robert R. Williams

The "Subtle Matter" of Intersubjectivity in the *Grundlage des Naturrechts*   65
F. Scott Scribner

Part II. Essays on the *Wissenschaftslehre nova methodo,* 1796–1799

Toward a Completion of German Idealism: Fichte's Transition from his
Grundlage der gesammten Wissenschaftslehre to the *Wissenschaftslehre
nova methodo*   83
Johannes Brachtendorf

First Steps: Lessons on Becoming a Philosopher from the Early Chapters
of the *Wissenschaftslehre nova methodo*   101
Janet Roccanova

The Individuality of the I in Fichte's Second Jena *Wissenschaftslehre,*
1796–1799   120
Günter Zöller

Reflection and Feeling and the Primacy of Practical Reason in the Jena
Wissenschaftslehre   140
C. Jeffery Kinlaw

The Unity of Philosophy in Fichte's *Wissenschaftslehre nova methodo,*
1798–1799   157
Angelica Nuzzo

Fichte's Philosophical Fictions   175
Daniel Breazeale

Intellectual Intuition, the Pure Will, and the Categorical Imperative in the
Later Jena *Wissenschaftslehre*   209
Yolanda Estes

Part III. Essays on the *System of Ethical Theory,* 1798

Fichte's Reformulation of the Categorical Imperative in the
Wissenschaftslehre nova methodo and *Das System der Sittenlehre*   229
Arnold Farr

The Severity of the Moral Law in Fichte's *Science of Ethics*   248
Lon Nease

Part IV. Essays on Various Topics

Idealism and the Ground of Explanation: Fichte and Schelling, 1794–1797 261
Steven Hoeltzel

Fichte, Jacobi, and the Atheism Controversy   279
Curtis Bowman

The Place of Aesthetics in Fichte's Early System   299
Claude Piché

The Place of the *Vocation of Man* in Fichte's Work   317
Ives Radrizzani

Fichte, Representation, and the Copernican Revolution   345
Tom Rockmore

Notes on Contributors   359

Abbreviations

BWL   *Ueber den Begriff der Wissenschaftslehre* (1794)

EPW   *Fichte: Early Philosophical Writings,* ed. and trans. Daniel Breazeale (Ithaca, N.Y.: Cornell University Press, 1988)

FTP   *Fichte: Foundations of Transcendental Philosophy (Wissenschafts-lehre) nova methodo,* ed. and trans. Daniel Breazeale (Ithaca, N.Y.: Cornell University Press, 1992)

GA   *J. G. Fichte-Gesamtausgabe der Bayerischen Akademie der Wissenschaften,* ed. Reinhard Lauth, Hans Gliwitzky†, and Erich Fuchs (Stuttgart-Bad Cannstatt: Frommann-Holzboog, 1964 ff.)

GNR   *Grundlage des Naturrechts* (1796–1797)

GWL   *Grundlage der gesammten Wissenschaftslehre* (1794–1795)

IWL   *Introductions to the Wissenschaftslehre and Other Writings,* ed. and trans. Daniel Breazeale (Indianapolis: Hackett, 1994)

SS   *System der Sittenlehre* (1798)

SW   *Johann Gottlieb Fichtes sämmtliche Werke,* ed. I. H. Fichte, eight vols. (Berlin: Viet and Co., 1845–46); rpt., along with the three vols. of *Johann Gottlieb Fichtes nachgelassene Werke* (Bonn: Adolphus-Marcus, 1834–35), as *Fichtes Werke* (Berlin: de Gruyter, 1971)

VWL   *Versuch einer neuen Darstellung der Wissenschaftslehre* (1797–1798).

WLnm[H] *Wissenschaftslehre nova methodo* ("Halle Nachshrift," 1796–1797)

Wlnm[K] *Wissenschaftslehre nova methodo* ("Krause Nachschrift," 1798–1799)

Introduction

Daniel Breazeale

Though the term *Wissenschaftslehre* is often taken to designate a specific book (usually the *Foundations of the Entire Wissenschaftslehre* of 1794 to 1795), Fichte actually coined this term as the name for his general philosophical standpoint or overall system, and thus as a synonym for "transcendental idealism" or "transcendental philosophy." He arrived at his distinctive conception of philosophy in the winter of 1793 to 1794, while he was living in Zurich, and began articulating it publicly in the lectures he delivered during his first year at the University of Jena (1794–95). These lectures were soon published under the title *Foundations of the Entire Wissenschaftslehre*.[1]

As their full title indicates, these lectures were intended only as a presentation of the first or "foundational" portion of an "entire" system, which would include not just "first philosophy," but also philosophy of nature, political philosophy (or philosophy of law or "natural right"), ethics, philosophy of religion, and aesthetics.[2] Even as he was completing his lectures on the *Foundations*, he was simultaneously extending his first principles and outlining a modest transcendental philosophy of nature in his 1794 to 1795 lectures published as *Concerning the Distinctive Character of the Wissenschaftslehre with Respect to the Theoretical Faculty*.[3]

As a consequence of the violent turmoil provoked by Fichte's efforts to help abolish the student fraternities that dominated student life at Jena, he was forced to cancel his lectures for the summer semester of 1795 and to take refuge in a nearby country estate,[4] where he devoted himself to developing a transcendental social and political philosophy "in accordance with" the general principles of the *Wissenschaftslehre*. This new "philosophy of law" was first publicly articulated in a course of lectures Fichte began delivering in the winter semester of 1795 to 1796 and continued in subsequent semesters. These lectures were published, in two parts, in 1796 and 1797, as *Foundations of Natural Right according to the Principles of the Wissenschaftslehre.*[5]

Far from being a mere systematic appendage to his initial presentation of the first principles of his system, Fichte's treatise on *Natural Right* begins with a recapitulation of those first principles, a recapitulation that also suggests a certain revision and expansion of the same, inasmuch as Fichte now argues that mutual recognition of and by free, individual subjects is just as much a "condition necessary for the possibility" of self-consciousness as are any of the categories and structures "derived" in the *Foundations of the Entire Wissenschaftslehre.* According to some scholars, these differences are sufficient to warrant a distinction between Fichte's "first Jena *Wissenschaftslehre*" and his "second" or "later Jena *Wissenschaftslehre,*" with the latter beginning only a year after Fichte's arrival in Jena, though others might argue that this distinction is not really clear until a year later, when Fichte commenced his lectures on *Wissenschaftslehre nova methodo.* For the purposes of this volume, however, the later Jena *Wissenschaftslehre* will be taken to commence with the *Foundations of Natural Right,* and several of the essays included in the present collection—including those by Klaus Brinkmann, Jean-Christoph Merle, Hans-Jakob Wilhelm, Robert Williams, and Scott Scribner—are devoted to the latter. These five essays convey some idea of the breadth and striking originality of Fichte's social thought during this period, the profound influence of which upon subsequent thinkers, such as Hegel, is still not fully appreciated.

Meanwhile, Fichte's reservations concerning the adequacy, and indeed, the intelligibility, of his original, 1794 to 1795 presentation of the first principles of his philosophy continued to grow. These reservations led him, in the winter semester of 1796 to 1797, to set aside his earlier *Foundations of the Entire Wissenschaftslehre* and to draft an entirely new presentation of the first principles of his system, "just as if I had never worked it out at all and as if I knew nothing about the old presentation."[6] Though the full title of these new lectures was "The Foundations of Transcendental Philosophy (*Wissenschaftslehre*) *nova methodo,*" they are usually referred to simply as the *Wissenschaftslehre nova methodo,* or as the "*Wissenschaftslehre* of 1796 to 1799," since Fichte repeated these lectures in the winter semesters of 1797 to 1798 and 1798 to 1799. The text, or rather the surviving transcriptions of the text of these new lectures on the foundations of the *Wissenschaftslehre,*[7] is the central document upon which any distinction between the "earlier" the "later" Jena *Wissenschaftslehre* must be based.

Though Fichte never wavered in his insistence that the underlying "spirit" of the two presentations was the same (just as later he insisted that the philosophy he propounded after his arrival in Berlin was really the same as the one he had propounded in Jena), the differences between the external form (or "letter") of the *Foundations of the Entire Wissenschafts-lehre* and the *Wissenschaftslehre nova methodo* are striking and dramatic. Gone entirely is the earlier attempt to begin with three "first principles," each of which is supposedly derived from a principle of formal logic. Instead, the *Wissenschaftslehre nova methodo* begins with a straightforward directive or "postulate": "Construct the *concept of the I* and observe how you accomplish this."[8] Gone, too, is the familiar division between "the-oretical" and "practical" parts of the *Wissenschaftslehre,* along with any attempt to treat theoretical and practical reason independently of one another. Instead, the new presentation begins with an assertion of the systematic inseparability of the theoretical and practical activities of the I and claims to demonstrate that "theoretical and practical philosophy are united."[9]

These and other, equally striking, differences between the *Wis-senschaftslehre nova methodo* and the *Foundations of the Entire Wissenschafts-lehre* have often been interpreted as evidence of a real advance in Fichte's conception of his own project during his first years at Jena, and not merely as external features of a new method of presenting the same material. This point, however, remains disputed and is closely related to a larger and much older dispute concerning the alleged "unity of the *Wis-senschaftslehre,* " not only during Fichte's Jena period, but over the entire course of his career. With the recent publication, often for the first time, of reliable editions of the texts of Fichte's many later, unpublished ver-sions of the *Wissenschaftslehre,*[10] this issue has again come to the forefront of Fichte research, though no consensus has emerged. As before, some contemporary interpreters follow Fichte himself in emphasizing the un-derlying unity of his thought and the unbroken continuity of his intellec-tual development, whereas others profess to find substantive, systematic differences between, for example, the philosophical writings of the Jena period and those of the Berlin, Erlangen, and Königsberg periods. It is often maintained, for example, that, after 1800, the *Wissenschaftslehre* takes a "turn toward the absolute" that is not only not anticipated in the writings of the Jena period, but is incompatible with the spirit of the same. It is also possible, as is evidenced by the present volume, to introduce finer-grained distinctions between, for example, the "early" and "later" Jena *Wissenschaftslehre,* or between the *Wissenschaftslehre* of 1804 to 1805 and later versions of the same.

Important as the question of the "unity of the *Wissenschaftslehre*" may be to contemporary scholars, it was not a question that exercised Fichte's contemporaries, beyond, perhaps, the narrow circle of his immediate students and listeners. With the exception of the short and extremely enigmatic *General Outline of the Wissenschaftslehre* of 1810,[11] the sole presentation of the first principles of the *Wissenschaftslehre* to be published during Fichte's own lifetime remained the very first one, *The Foundations of the Entire Wissenschaftslehre* of 1794 to 1795. This circumstance helps to explain the remarkable gap between the conventional or received view of Fichte's philosophy, which has long been based almost exclusively upon the 1794 to 1795 *Foundations,* and the very different— and, on the whole, far more interesting and plausible—interpretations of the *Wissenschaftslehre* that dominate contemporary research on Fichte, most of which is concerned with one or another version of the "later *Wissenschaftslehre.*"

Many of the essays that follow reflect the current preoccupation of scholars, both in Europe and in North America, with one of these versions in particular, namely, the *Wissenschaftslehre nova methodo,* a text that remained virtually unknown until well into the middle of the twentieth century, but which has been the object of intense scrutiny in recent decades. The distinctive riches and insights of the *Wissenschaftslehre nova methodo* are explored in the essays by Johannes Brachtendorf, Janet Rocannova, Günter Zöller, Jeffery Kinlaw, Angelica Nuzzo, Daniel Breazeale, and Yolanda Estes. These seven essays represent the most sustained and multifaceted English language discussion to date of the distinctive character of Fichte's first revised presentation of the foundations of his philosophy, and they suggest why so many among the younger generation of scholars consider the *Wissenschaftslehre nova methodo* to be among Fichte's greatest intellectual achievements.

Fichte, too, was pleased with this version of the foundational portion of his new system, and, in 1797, he began to revise his lectures on *Wissenschaftslehre nova methodo* for serial publication in the *Philosophical Journal,* of which he was then co-editor, under the general title *An Attempt at a New Presentation of the Wissenschaftslehre.*[12] Following the publication of two long introductions and the first chapter of the *New Presentation,* however, Fichte abruptly discontinued further work on this project and was swept into the "Atheism Controversy" that eventually led to his dismissal from his professorship at Jena in the spring of 1799. A year after his arrival in Berlin he made a final attempt, in the fall and winter of 1800, to revise his lectures on *Wissenschaftslehre nova methodo* for publication, but this effort too was quickly abandoned.[13]

There is, however, much more to the "entire *Wissenschaftslehre*" than the foundational or first portion of the same, and the "later Jena *Wissenschaftslehre*" therefore comprises more than the lectures on *Wissenschaftslehre nova methodo* and the *Foundations of Natural Right*. The most important systematic addition to the *Wissenschaftslehre* during Fichte's later Jena years is unquestionably the *Sittenlehre* or *System of Ethical Theory according to the Principles of the Wissenschaftslehre*, which he published in 1798, once again on the basis of prior lectures on this topic.[14] The *System of Ethical Theory* is, in fact, an essential systematic counterpart to and continuation of the *Wissenschaftslehre nova methodo*. In this remarkable text, Fichte erects a complete system of moral philosophy on the basis of the concept of the determinate "pure will" first derived in the *Wissenschaftslehre nova methodo*. Though Fichte's Jena-period ethical theory has not received as much attention as his early political philosophy or his writings on the foundations of his system, it is equally original and, in some ways, even more radical. The contributions by Arnold Farr and Lon Nease to the present collection indicate the distinctive character and originality of Fichte's bold transformation of Kantian ethics, as well as some of the philosophical problems associated with such "hypermoralism."

Though Fichte promised that the "complete *Wissenschaftslehre*" would include a new aesthetics, he actually wrote very little on this topic, and much of what he does have to say must be extracted from occasional essays and passing comments in other treatises. This relative scarcity of textual evidence makes Claude Piché's achievement, in his essay "The Place of Aesthetics in Fichte's Early System," all the more remarkable.

A final systematic division of the *Wissenschaftslehre* that Fichte touched upon during his later Jena years was the philosophy of religion. In this case, however, most of his remarks on the subject are to be found not in his lectures, but in a series of popular and polemical writings. Ironically, he had announced lectures on the philosophy of religion for the summer semester of 1799, but by then he had been publicly accused of atheism and dismissed from his teaching position. As is well known, this charge was provoked by certain remarks contained in a brief essay, "On the Basis of our Belief in a Divine Governance of the World,"[15] that Fichte published in the *Philosophical Journal* in the fall of 1798, in reply to an essay by F. G. Forberg in the same issue of that journal. In response to the public outcry produced by his and Forberg's articles, Fichte published several pamphlets and articles in which he not only defended himself against the charge of atheism and tried to clarify the boundaries of philosophy, theology, and religion, but also sought to convey some of the essential rudiments of a transcendental theory of religion "in accordance with the principles of the *Wissenschaftslehre.*" This embryonic philosophy of religion as well as the dramatic events and circumstances of the atheism controversy are dealt with in Curtis Bowman's contribution to this collection.

Though the Atheism Controversy certainly overshadowed the others, it was by no means the only "controversy" in which Fichte was embroiled at the end of his Jena period. His conflict with Jacobi, for example, though originally provoked by Jacobi's contribution to the Atheism Controversy, in the form of an "open letter" to Fichte in which Jacobi first raised the famous charge that philosophy leads to "nihilism," also generated an important public exchange concerning the ambitions and limits of philosophical speculation and the general relationship between the standpoints of philosophy of "life." Despite his considerable intellectual debt to Jacobi, Fichte devoted his final months in Jena and much of his first year in Berlin to a series of "popular" responses to Jacobi, first in *The Vocation of Man* and then in the *Sun-Clear Report.* Though written in Berlin, *The Vocation of Man* can be plausibly interpreted as the final and crowning achievement of Fichte's "Jena period," as is admirably demonstrated by Ives Radrizzani's contribution to this collection.

Another conflict that began to simmer during the end of Fichte's Jena period was of a more purely "theoretical" character and concerned his differences with his erstwhile disciple, Schelling, regarding the nature and limits of transcendental philosophy. Fichte was deeply suspicious of the latter's efforts to expand the legitimate domain of philosophical speculation into the realm of full-blown, a priori *Naturphilosophie,* which Schelling himself viewed as a necessary, "objective" counterpart and complement to Kant and Fichte's "subjective" transcendental philosophy. Though the conflict between Fichte and Schelling did not break into the open until the early 1800s, it is fully and somewhat poignantly apparent in the correspondence between the two men during the late 1790s. As Steve Hoeltzel shows in his contribution to this collection, the conflict between Fichte and Schelling concerning the ultimate ground of philosophical explanation is not without relevance to current discussions concerning the nature and limits of philosophy. In addition to the many essays exploring specific texts and systematic subdisciplines of the later Jena *Wissenschaftslehre,* this collection also includes others—for example, Tom Rockmore's essay "Fichte, Representation, and the Copernican Revolution"—that deal with more general Fichtean themes, albeit within the larger context of Fichte's later Jena writings.

Though each of the twenty essays collected in this volume is of considerable interest in its own right, the whole is even greater than the sum of its parts. Taken collectively, these essays provide a much-needed introduction to Fichte's thought during the period 1796 to 1799, a period when he was at the height of his philosophical influence. Jena, during this same period, was the undisputed capital of the new revolution in German philosophy, and Fichte was the unchallenged leader of the same. For Fichte, this was indeed a "triumphal era," a period when the *Wissenschaftslehre* was still widely hailed as the most advanced and successful systematic reformulation of the transcendental project initiated by Kant and first carried forward by Maimon and Reinhold. Yet Fichte's popular triumph as a philosopher proved to be short-lived. Never again, following his flight to Berlin, would he commit himself to philosophical speculation with the self-confidence and generous optimism that he displayed in these writings. And never again would he enjoy the widespread influence and recognition from other philosophers that he enjoyed at Jena.

Because of its historical influence and fateful "reception" by the immediately following generation of thinkers, the *Foundations of the Entire Wissenschaftslehre* will always remain one of Fichte's best known philosophical works. This, however, does not imply that it is the "best," the most profound, the most original, or the most successful presentation of his philosophy. If the recent past is any guide, then much later versions of the *Wissenschaftslehre* (for example, those of 1804 or that of 1807) are likely to receive even closer attention in the future, particularly from those who are suspicious of the strongly practical (that is, political and ethical) character of the works of the Jena period and are attracted to the more contemplative or religious dimension of Fichte's later thought.

Yet one can argue that it is neither the "first" nor the "later" *Wissenschaftslehre* that has the most to offer contemporary philosophers, but rather the version that lies between these two extremes and is presented in the writings of Fichte's later Jena period. As it happens, these include some of Fichte's most accessible and successful philosophical works. Moreover, all of the major texts of this period—the *Foundations of Natural Right, Wissenschaftslehre nova methodo,* and *System of Ethical Theory*— share a similar vocabulary and presentational strategy and are inspired by the same radical, self-confident spirit. They also offer readers an unparalleled insight into Fichte's overall *system* of philosophy: the *entire Wissenschaftslehre,* and not just another presentation of the first principles or foundations of the same.

It is to these same writings that one might most readily turn in order to demonstrate Fichte's continuing *relevance* as a philosopher. His sophisticated analysis, in the *Wissenschaftslehre nova methodo* and the *System of Ethical Theory,* of the structural connection between finite self-consciousness and free agency is an example of a line of argument that is obviously relevant to contemporary discussions of "consciousness" and "subjectivity." Another example, this time of Fichte's relevance to contemporary political and social thought, is provided by his innovative effort, in the *Foundations of Natural Right*, to defend human rights as conditions for mutual recognition by free subjects and to show that individual subjects must recognize others, and hence restrict their own freedom, in order to recognize themselves, and hence affirm that same freedom.

Many other interesting parallels between certain features of Fichte's philosophy of the later Jena period and contemporary thought are explored in the essays that follow, many of which indicate specific contributions that Fichte might make to contemporary philosophical discussions. Yet the general tone of these essays is not uncritical. If Fichte is to be taken seriously as a philosopher, then his ideas must not only be sympathetically understood within the context of their own era; they must also be critically scrutinized within the context of our own.

Taken collectively, these essays not only make a strong case for the originality and continuing significance of the later Jena *Wissenschaftslehre*, but can also serve as a general introduction to the study of the same. Anyone who wishes to know why a growing number of contemporary students and scholars are paying attention to the *Wissenschaftslehre* and who wishes to understand the basis for the contemporary renaissance of interest in classical German idealism in general, and in the philosophy of Fichte in particular, would do well to read the essays collected in this volume. The image of the *Wissenschaftslehre* that emerges here is not the familiar commonplace of textbooks in the history of philosophy. Instead, the Fichte one encounters here is a far more interesting, complex, and, above all, *challenging* thinker, a deeply original philosopher who still has much to say to independent and unprejudiced readers.

Notes

1. *Grundlage der gesammten Wissenschaftslehre*, translated by Peter Heath as *Fundamental Principles of the Entire Science of Knowledge*, in Fichte, *The Science of Knowledge*, ed. Peter Heath and John Lachs (Cambridge: Cambridge University Press, 1970), pp. 87–286.

2. See the "Hypothetical Division of the *Wissenschaftslehre*" in Part III of the 1794 *Concerning the Concept of the Wissenschaftslehre* (pages 133–35 in *Fichte: Early Philosophical Writings*, ed. and trans. Daniel Breazeale [Ithaca, N.Y.: Cornell University Press, 1988], henceforth abbreviated as *EPW*), as well as the "Deduction of the Subdivision of the *Wissenschaftslehre*" (pages 467–74 in *Fichte: Foundations of Transcendental Philosophy (Wissenschaftslehre) nova methodo*, ed. and trans. Daniel

Breazeale [Ithaca, N.Y.: Cornell University Press, 1992], henceforth abbreviated as *FTP*).

3. *Grundriss des Eigenthümlichen der Wissenschaftslehre in Rücksicht auf das theoretische Vermögen*, in *EPW*, pp. 242–306.

4. For details concerning this and other events during Fichte's years in Jena, see "Fichte in Jena," *EPW*, pp. 1–49.

5. *Grundlage des Naturrechts nach Principien der Wissenschaftslehre*, trans. Michael Baur, ed. Frederick Neuhouser (Cambridge: Cambridge University Press, 2000).

6. Letter to K. L. Reinhold, 21 March 1797 (*EPW*, p. 417).

7. Fichte's own manuscript of his lectures on *Wissenschaftslehre nova methodo* was not discovered among his literary remains, and thus, for more than a century, this version of the *Wissenschaftslehre* was known only by hearsay and from the revised extracts published in the *Philosophical Journal*. In the twentieth century, however, several detailed student transcriptions of Fichte's lectures on *Wissenschaftslehre nova methodo* were discovered. The first of these, the anonymously transcribed "Halle transcript," was published by Hans Jacob as "Wissenschaftslehre nach den Vorlesungen von Hr. Pr. Fichte," in *Nachgelassene Schriften*, vol. 2 (Berlin: Junker und Dünnhaupt, 1937), pp. 341–611. This text received very little scholarly attention, however, until 1978, when it was re-edited and republished by José Manzana, Erich Fuchs, Kurt Hiller, and Peter Schneider in the monumental new Critical Edition of Fichte's works published under the auspices of the Bavarian Academy of the Sciences (IV/2: pp. 1–267 in *J. G. Fichte-Gesamtausgabe der Bayerischen Akademie der Wissenschaften*, ed. Reinhard Lauth, Hans Jacob, and Hans Gliwitzky [Stuttgart-Bad Cannstatt: Frommann-Holzboog, 1964ff.], henceforth abbreviated as *GA*).

In 1982, Erich Fuchs discovered a second complete transcript of the *Wissenschaftslehre nova methodo*, this one by C. K. F. Krause, and quickly published it as *Wissenschaftslehre nova methodo. Kollegnachschrift Chr. Fr. Krause 1798–99* (Hamburg: Felix Meiner, 1982; second, corrected ed., 1994). This version is also included in *GA*, IV/3: 323–525. Fuchs also discovered a third, fragmentary transcript from 1796 to 1797, "WL nova methodo Nachschrift Eschen," published in *GA*, IV/3: 151–96. For further details, see the editor's introduction to *FTP*, pp. 1–49.

8. *FTP*, p. 65.

9. *FTP*, p. 86.

10. The different presentations of the *Wissenschaftslehre* include:

a. *Über den Begriff der Wissenschaftslehre* (1794; *GA*, I/2: pp. 107–67) + *Grundlage der gesammten Wissenschaftslehre* (1794–1795; *GA*, I/2: pp. 249–451) + *Grundriss des Eigenthümliche der Wissenschaftslehre in Rücksicht auf das theoretische Vermögen* (1795; *GA*, I/3: pp. 141–208).

b. *Wissenschaftslehre nova methodo* (1796–1799; *GA*, II/2: pp. 17–267 and IV/3: pp. 151–96, 323–525) + *Versuch einer neuen Darstellung der WL* (1797–1798; *GA*, I/7: pp. 183–281).

c. *Neue Bearbeitung der Wissenschaftslehre* (1800–1801; *GA*, II/5: pp. 331–402) + *Sonnenklarer Bericht* (1801; *GA*, I/7: pp. 183–268).

d. *Darstellung der Wissenschaftslehre* (1801–1802; *GA*, II/6: pp. 129–324) + ["Zur Ausarbeitung der Wissenschaftslehre"] (1801; *GA*, II/6: pp. 51–103).

e. "Vorlesungen der W.L. im Winter 1804" (January—March 1804; *GA*, II/7: pp. 66–235).

f. "Die *Wissenschaftslehre*" (II. Vortrag im Jahre 1804; April—June 1804; *GA*, II/8: pp. 2–421).

g. "3ter Cours der W.L. 1804" (November—December 1804; *GA*, II/7: pp. 289–368).

h. "4ter Vortrag der *Wissenschaftslehre*—Erlangen im Sommer 1805" (June–September 1805; *GA*, II/9: pp. 179–311).

i. "*Wissenschaftslehre*, Königsberg" (1807; *GA*, II/10: pp. 111–202).

j. "*Wissenschaftslehre* 1810" (*GA*, II/11: pp. 203–392).

k. *Die Wissenschaftslehre in ihrem allgemeinen Umrisse* (March 1810; II: pp. 693–709 in *Johann Gottlieb Fichtes sämmtliche Werke*, ed. I. H. Fichte, eight vols. (Berlin: Viet and Co., 1845–46).

l. "Wissenschaftslehre 1811" (*GA*, II/12: pp. 143–299).

m. "Die Wissenschaftslehre 1812" (*Johann Gottlieb Fichtes nachgelassene Werke*, ed. I. H. Fichte [Bonn: Adolph-Marcus, 1834–35], vol. 2, pp. 315–492).

n. "Die Wissenschaftslehre 1813" (Spring 1813; *Johann Gottlieb Fichtes nachgelassene Werke*, ed. I. H. Fichte [Bonn: Adolph-Marcus, 1834–35], vol. 2, pp. 1–86).

o. *Wissenschaftslehre* 1814 (still unpublished).

11. *Die Wissenschaftslehre in ihrem allgemeinen Grundriss*, translated by Walter E. Wright as "The Science of Knowledge in its General Outline," *Idealistic Studies* 6 (1976): pp. 106–17.

12. *Versuch einer neuen Darstellung der Wissenschaftslehre* (1797–98), pp. 1–118 in Fichte, *Introductions to the Wissenschaftslehre and Other Writings (1797–1800)*, ed. and trans. Daniel Breazeale (Indianapolis: Hackett, 1994), henceforth abbreviated as *IWL*.

13. "Neue Bearbeitung der W.L. 1800," *GA*, II/6: pp. 331–402.

14. *Das System der Sittenlehre nach den Principien der Wissenschaftslehre.* Though a new English translation by Günter Zöller and Daniel Breazeale has been announced as forthcoming from Cambridge University Press, the only complete English translation of this important text remains A. E. Kroeger's very unreliable (as well as unreadable) *The Science of Ethics as Based on the Science of Knowledge* (London: Kegan Paul, Trench, Trübner, 1798).

15. "Ueber den Grund unsers Glauben an eine göttliche Weltregierung" (1798), English translation in *IWL*, pp. 142–54.

NEW ESSAYS ON FICHTE'S
LATER JENA
WISSENSCHAFTSLEHRE

ESSAYS ON THE *FOUNDATIONS OF NATURAL RIGHT,* 1796–1797

The Deduction of Intersubjectivity in Fichte's *Grundlage des Naturrechts*

Klaus Brinkmann

The originality of Fichte's grounding of the community of right in a principle of mutual recognition as it is presented in the *Grundlage des Naturrechts* has long been recognized.[1] Nothing comparable existed prior to the publication of the *Naturrecht* in 1796 and 1797, which appeared, incidentally, a few months ahead of Kant's *Metaphysics of Morals,* with its Doctrine of Right. As Reinhard Lauth and others have pointed out, Fichte conceived of the idea of a necessary complementarity of humans as early as 1794 in the *Vocation of the Scholar.*[2] However, the development of an argument with which to back up the doctrine of mutual recognition had to await the *Naturrecht.*[3] In this work, Fichte attempts to demonstrate, first, that the individual self-consciousness can become conscious of its freedom for self-determination only through another self-consciousness, and second, that between all rational beings there exists necessarily a relationship of mutual recognition of the other's freedom without which a community of right would not be possible. In what follows I shall refer to the former as Fichte's principle of intersubjectivity and the latter as his principle of reciprocal, or mutual, recognition. The two are not always clearly distinguished, although such a distinction is in order.[4]

The principle of mutual recognition presupposes that of intersubjectivity but is not identical with it. Indeed, one of the issues I would like to explore is whether the transition from the one to the other is as unproblematic as is commonly assumed.

5

Fichte's intersubjectivity principle can be interpreted as an attempt to overcome the atomistic view of the isolated individual who is essentially self-contained and complete *prior to* his entering into any relationships with other individuals.[5] Fichte's argument for grounding the community of right in an intersubjectivity principle is unique in that it builds on a dialectic which makes the other an indispensable condition for the consciousness and the actualization of my own freedom.[6] This Fichtean proof of intersubjectivity is clearly the model for similar deductions or derivations in Schelling's *System of Transcendental Idealism* (1800) and Hegel's *Phenomenology of Spirit* (1807). In either case, the copyright is Fichte's alone, whatever the improvements or corrections made to the proof in these later theories. From the point of view of philosophical theory, the claim contained in Fichte's intersubjectivity principle, viz. that I cannot be myself without being related to another self, is a revolutionary one. As far as I am aware, before Fichte the thought that another self is presupposed by my own self-consciousness had not even been thought, let alone had a proof proposed in its defense. Whether we look to Aristotle's treatment of friendship in the *Nicomachean Ethics* or to Kant's so-called *humanitas*-formula of the categorical imperative, nowhere do we find a hint of deriving one's identity as a self on the basis of, instead of prior to or independently of, the relationship with another self. Aristotle's holistic approach, according to which the whole is prior to the parts, and thus the community prior to the individual, is primarily supported not by a principle of intersubjectivity but by reference to the priority of the organic whole over its parts. And even though friendship *(philia)* is said to constitute the essential bond among citizens, obviously no transcendental argument in Aristotle backs up this claim.[7] In short, Fichte deserves the praise accorded him both in defining the principle itself and in attempting a proof thereof.

Things are slightly different, in my view, with regard to the principle of mutual recognition. To be sure, this principle is again based on a heretofore unknown dialectical argument that relies on the idea of a mutual limitation of my sphere of freedom of action over against the other's sphere such that both limit their spheres jointly through an act of self-determination. The coexistence of a plurality of free agents is here brought about through reciprocal *self*-limitation.[8] Not only does the other limit my sphere of freedom or I his, but I limit my sphere of freedom in order to open up a sphere of freedom for the other. In this way, Kant's principle of right is no longer merely a dictate of reason, but an a priori condition for the other's being or becoming a practical agent. By contrast, in almost all of the preceding tradition, the individuals are externally constrained to respect each other's freedom through the imposition of limits by a third party precisely because the other's freedom does not enter as a constitutive moment into my own freedom but limits it only negatively. His freedom is not mine, and mine is not his. That is to say, we do not actually share in a common freedom. Indeed, this approach famously led Hobbes to argue that the individual's sphere of freedom of action could not be secured without the threat of retaliation credibly issued by a third party. For Fichte, this is equally true, but only trivially or contingently so. What Fichte realized was that the obligation to respect the other's freedom must be anchored in the individual's own freedom, that is, in his obligation to limit his own sphere of freedom for the sake of, rather than merely in contradistinction to, the other. In acting, the other must already have taken my own freedom into account.[9]

Nonetheless, the principle of the necessary mutual recognition of one another's freedom is at least as old as Hobbes's argument for the transition from the state of nature to the civil state. In this respect, Fichte can claim to have discovered the only convincing strategy for the proof of the principle of reciprocal recognition though not the discovery of the principle itself. He has made clear, however, that the coexistence of free agents and their interaction presupposes as an a priori condition the idea of a *community of individuals* that, from a transcendental point of view, is prior to these individuals. A "we" here undergirds and grounds the freedom of the individual I. As Fichte puts it in *Naturrecht:*

> The concept of individuality is . . . a reciprocal concept, i.e., it is such
> that it can be thought only in relation to another thinking [being] which
> conditions it while being the *same* thinking with respect to its form. This
> concept is possible in every rational being only insofar as this being
> is posited as being completed only through another. The concept is
> therefore never *mine* alone; . . . [it is] a communal concept in which
> two consciousnesses are united. . . . Through this concept a *community* is
> determined [or established].[10]

Despite the general agreement about the significance of Fichte's intersubjectivity principle and its groundbreaking role in the history of philosophy, there has been considerable criticism with respect to Fichte's actual achievement. I will mention only two such criticisms, that offered by Robert Williams in his book *Recognition* and the almost dismissive treatment Fichte's version of the principle of intersubjectivity receives at the hands of one of its foremost proponents. I am referring here to Vittorio Hösle and his comments on Fichte in his *Hegels System.*

Following an excellent discussion of both the significance of Fichte's intersubjectivity principle and the issues it raises, Robert Williams concludes that Fichte in a sense throws away, or in any case does not really make the best use of, the principle when it comes to grounding the community of right and the political realm. For one thing, Fichte does not, Williams claims,[11]

> develop his theory of rights concretely out of intersubjective recognition. In fact, recognition plays no role in accounting for the social and historical genesis of right. Moreover, individual acts of recognition do not play any role in securing right in Fichte's theory of the state, and Fichte allows that recognition may be bypassed altogether. [Ultimately,] intersubjectivity and *Anerkennen* are not only obscured and buried by other overriding concerns, they are ultimately superfluous for the concepts of right and social ethics.

I tend largely to agree with this assessment.[12] Hösle for his part concedes that Fichte was the first in modern times to attempt a proof of intersubjectivity. However, he goes on to remark critically that, ultimately, intersubjectivity plays only a subordinate role for Fichte and that it merely serves the function of being an indispensable element in the constitution of the finite I, which in the final analysis is Fichte's sole aim. Even in the early *Sittenlehre* of 1798, everything is geared toward the realization of the freedom of the individual I, which is construed atomistically by Fichte.[13] Later in the book, Hösle downplays Fichte's discovery even further by arguing that Fichte's early approach suffers from the fundamental weakness that it makes finite subjectivity the point of departure of his intersubjectivity proof. It would therefore be wrong to make too much of the doubtlessly groundbreaking Fichtean statements such as "Man becomes man only among men" or "If there are to be men at all, there must be several of them" (both statements being taken from the *Naturrecht*).[14]

Hösle's judgment seems excessively harsh. Fichte not only attempts to provide justification for the claim that the individual is dependent for the realization of his freedom on a community of free rational beings, he also makes it clear, in the *Vocation of the Scholar*, that the true destination of man is to form a community with others in which they jointly strive for moral perfection.[15] On the other hand, Lauth probably goes too far when he asserts that Fichte's community of right represents an interpersonal I (*Moi interpersonnel*).[16] This reads back into Fichte more of a Hegelian conception of a "we" that is I and an I that is "we" than seems warranted.[17] Hegel's concept of a community of free agents requires an exponent of subjectivity distinct from and logically prior to the individuals, which Hegel refers to as a universal substance that is subject and that, in the case of the state, can have an individualized exponent in the form of a head of state. In the case of Hegel's more abstract community of right at the beginning of the *Philosophy of Right,* that exponent of subjectivity is right itself as the universal substance of the will of the individuals. Characteristically, such an exponent of subjectivity is missing in Fichte's account of the community of right. This community remains an association based on reciprocal albeit necessary recognition and thus without a supraindividual identity. It is therefore not a surprise that when Fichte proceeds to found civil society the institution of a government as guarantor of individual freedom is derived in a contractarian fashion.[18] This, however, does not detract from the fact that a genuine intersubjective community of right precedes civil society as its ideal prefiguration.

The critical issue I wish to raise, however, is whether the transition from the first appearance of the principle of intersubjectivity in the *Naturrecht* to the establishment of the relationship of reciprocal recognition between free rational beings is as unproblematic as it is normally taken to be. Can we really move from the so-called summons of the other which establishes intersubjectivity to the relationship of mutual recognition which grounds the community of right? I will briefly summarize Fichte's argument to the extent that it is relevant to my purpose. I start with the First Proposition (*Erster Lehrsatz*).

Self-reflexive activity is the nature of the rational being. In a finite being, however, that is, in an individual self-consciousness, this self-reflexive activity must be limited. It can be so limited by the self's theoretical intentionality (*Weltanschauung*), which finds itself determined by objects.[19] As opposed to its theoretical intentionality, in which it is determined by the object and hence not free, the I is practical intentionality or efficacy with regard to objects. *Qua* efficacy, however, it is not self-reflexive; its activity, as Fichte puts it, does not return into itself. In other words, in being practical, the self must be more than merely a mechanistic cause. Since to be self-reflexive is its original character and nature,[20] the individual self must be an efficacy which determines itself freely to be efficacious (*freie Selbstbestimmung zur Wirksamkeit*), that is, to work on and transform objects.[21] This characteristic of Fichte's presocietal agent highlights the fundamental nature of the original self-consciousness, which, Fichte tells us, is to be a practical I: "Willing is the essential nature of reason. . . . The practical capacity [*das praktische Vermögen*] is the innermost root of the I to which everything else may then be attached."[22]

The object of the I's efficacy must be posited as something existing independently of the practical I, as a "system of objects."[23] The independence of the world of objects can thus be deduced as a necessary condition of individual practical self-consciousness. With this, Fichte has prepared the stage for the crucial step in the argument introducing the intersubjectivity principle in the Second Proposition *(Zweiter Lehrsatz)*.[24] To be able to relate itself to an object of its efficacy, the rational being must attribute efficacy to itself. Conversely, to attribute efficacy to itself, the self must have posited an object. Since the object is posited as determined in and of itself instead of by the self, this object cannot be posited in and through the very same act in which it is also posited as the object of its efficacy. However, since at any given moment the object must be posited simultaneously as both determined in and of itself and as determinable through the self—for only in this way can there arise a finite practical self-consciousness—but cannot be so posited in one and the same act by the self, Fichte concludes that the self must become an object for itself, because only then is what is to be determinable through its efficacy also something posited by itself. Thus the crucial point is to explain how the self can become an object for itself *qua* determinable through itself.[25] Neither in its immediate practical nor in its immediate theoretical intentionality does it have itself for an object. Therefore it can become an object for itself only through another self, which issues a summons to it to determine itself to self-determination *(eine Aufforderung. . . , sich zu einer Wirksamkeit zu entschliessen)*.[26] In other words, the self must become the addressee of an ought directed to itself from outside of itself—and which, for that reason, can issue only from another rational being.

If nothing else, this proof is extraordinarily ingenious. (It is also a prime example of Fichte's "dialectical" method, which differs significantly from Hegel's in that it stops short of Hegelian double negation and thus avoids the problem of a possible violation of the principle of noncontradiction. This, however, would be a topic for a different paper.) It demonstrates that the individual self could not realize its potential for self-determination, and thus could not *be* its true self, without the help of another self. And yet, as welcome as such a proof may be, its immediate result also raises a serious problem. For what is being proved is that *the realization of freedom presupposes a free rational being*. And this must lead to either regress or *petitio*. Furthermore, it raises the question of how we move from the summons to the community of free beings. For it would seem that the situation of the summons is one of inequality or asymmetry in which one is called upon to realize his freedom by someone who has already realized his freedom—how else could he summon the other to actualize his freedom? The community of right, on the other hand, is a community of individuals who stand in a symmetrical relationship of equality to one another: One concedes to the other exactly what the other concedes to the former. Now it might seem that already in the situation of the summons the summoned concedes to the one who summons him exactly what the latter concedes to the former—and that is precisely what Fichte, ignoring the asymmetry of the situation, takes for granted in the further development of his argument. However, this would mean turning a blind eye on the fact that the summoned is *not* the equal of the summoner. For the summoned self, the summoner sets a standard to which the summoned ought to conform. Fichte tries to argue that the summoned is free to respond to the summons any which way—taking it to heart, ignoring it, or rejecting it.[27] But clearly, if the summoned reacts in a way which does not *heed* the summons, *he will not actualize his freedom,* that is, he will not become free, and the summons will have been in vain. But for the summoned to heed the summons is nothing but to prove himself to be the summoner's equal, that is, to have already realized his freedom. In this case, the summons will become redundant. Since this cannot be, the asymmetry is a structural feature of the summons.

Consequently, if we hold on to the idea of the summons being a necessary condition, we must admit that there will be either regress or *petitio:* regress, if we assume that the summoner must himself have been summoned; *petitio,* if we merely presuppose the actual freedom of the summoner as a fact. And this in turn would mean that in the sequel of the proof the community of the free and equal has *not* been derived as a condition of the possibility of a free self-consciousness. Now Fichte himself admits that the problem of a regress needs to be addressed. The summons to free self-determination or free activity *(Aufforderung zur freien Selbsttätigkeit)* is nothing but the expression of the fact that humans need to be educated to become humans, that is, to become genuinely free. Precisely because the proof must be universally valid, he says, the question must be raised at some point, who educated the first human couple?[28] This is another way of asking: Who summoned the summoner? Fichte's answer, as is well known, is that "a spirit" took care of this initial education (Fichte makes it clear that his reference here is to the Old Testament),[29] an explanation Fichte seems to find perfectly satisfactory.

Against the above charge of a regress it has been argued that the existence of an actually free self-consciousness in the shape of the summoner must be accepted as a "transcendental fact," that is, a fact that must be presupposed as an a priori condition of the possibility of freedom.[30] And indeed, Fichte himself describes the summons as a "necessary condition of self-consciousness" and as a "necessary fact."[31] Thus it would seem that the transcendental conditions for the realization of freedom are all in place before the summons is issued and that its actualization would only depend on the contingent presence of a summoner. To this I would respond, first, that unless we have a satisfactory explanation of how the summoner actualized his own freedom prior to the summons, Fichte's proof will be vulnerable to the charge that his necessary fact might prove to be a transcendental illusion, that is, the mere postulate of a necessary contingency.[32] The addressee of the summons is, we might say, free potentially but not yet actually, whereas the summoner is free actually. Since, therefore, the summoner represents the condition for the possibility of *actual* freedom, this presupposes an actually free summoning individual. The freedom of the actually free summoning individual cannot, for obvious reasons, have been derived from the position adopted by the *Wissenschaftslehre* (henceforth abbreviated WL). It can only have been postulated outside and independently of the self-positing I. I admit that this is what makes the interpretation of the summoner as a "necessary fact" so appealing. But second, to postulate a necessary fact is simply to acknowledge, albeit *à contre coeur,* the limitations of the transcendental project of the WL. Let me elaborate.

To begin with, for the notion of a necessary fact to make sense at all we must indeed assume that what is meant by it is a transcendental fact, that is, an a priori condition of some kind. I doubt, however, that a transcendental fact can serve as a substitute for a transcendental condition. Interestingly, Fichte, in the Second Introduction to the *Wissenschaftslehre,* strongly objected to having Kant's thing-in-itself interpreted as a transcendental fact. There he argued that the "Kantians" misrepresented Kant's meaning when they took the thing-in-itself to be some kind of transcendent object needed to fulfill the function of affecting the subject's sensibility. He called this the "crudest dogmatism," diametrically opposed to Kant's idealism.[33] Instead, Kant's thing-in-itself was to be regarded as "something which we merely append *in thought* to appearances, according to laws of thought that call for demonstration, and were demonstrated by Kant, and which we are *obliged* to append, according to these laws."[34] In other words, the concept of the thing-in-itself is nothing but an *epistemic condition* and does not entail an ontological commitment. If that were not so, the thing-in-itself would be a transcendent, that is, metaphysical, entity.

But note that a transcendental fact cannot just be a transcendental *epistemic* condition. It must be more than that; indeed, it must designate a contingent fact the existence of which is postulated for transcendental, explanatory reasons. However, unlike the existence of the world of appearance, a transcendental fact can only be postulated, not posited, while the world of appearance cannot be postulated, but only posited. Indeed, Fichte has the ego *posit* the world of experience as one that is being *experienced* as not having been posited, as we saw earlier. There is no problem with positing something as not having been posited, since the positing ego as transcendental agent is distinct from the empirical ego.

Obviously, such a positing is necessary precisely because an empirical reality that had not been posited through a transcendental act would again make necessary the acceptance of a metaphysical thing-in-itself. Things are, however, quite otherwise with a transcendental fact, which is what is here under discussion. A transcendental fact is one that *cannot have been posited at all*, not even as not having been posited by the empirical self. Its existence can only be *postulated*, like the Kantian postulates of the immortality of the soul and the existence of God as necessary a priori conditions of the possibility of the highest good.[35] Philosophers may have reasons to postulate such transcendental facts. Kant explains his reasons at length, as does Schelling in his late philosophy when he insists that the unfathomable fact of God's existence (the primordial "That") precedes all questioning as to what He is. However, such a postulate is inconsistent with Fichte's original program, for it transforms a purely epistemic into an ontological condition, which cannot have been posited by the absolute I.

This interpretation seems to be contradicted by the radical idealism of Fichte's early *Wissenschaftslehre*. One of Fichte's original goals was arguably to overcome the need for postulates through the conception of an absolute ego. Hence it would at first blush seem to be improbable that Fichte would want to introduce the idea of a transcendental fact into the foundations of the WL. And yet, his characterization of the summons as a "necessary fact" can only be interpreted as referring to such a transcendental fact. In other words, Fichte here does indeed postulate the summons; he does not and cannot deduce or derive, that is, posit it, for a transcendental fact can only be understood as not being capable of being posited at all. To put it differently, Fichte here attempts to substitute a transcendental fact carrying an ontological commitment for a transcendental epistemic condition that does not. I would submit that, if this is correct, Fichte's procedure here is inconsistent with the fundamental principles of the WL. It is possible even, and in my view very likely, that this internal inconsistency drives Fichte's successive transformations of the WL.[36]

Now it has been argued that the intention to introduce transcendental facticity into the very foundations of the WL was present from the very beginning of Fichte's project; witness the presence of such a facticity in the notorious *Anstoß*. In the debate about the status of the *Anstoß*, I believe that, given the textual evidence, one must side with those who claim that the *Anstoß* constitutes an ontological given beyond the positing powers of the ego, whether one believes the *Anstoß* to originate from an aspect of the absolute ego that is different from the transcendental (positing) ego or whether one holds that the *Anstoß* falls entirely outside the (positing) absolute ego.[37] However, it should be clear that the acceptance of the *Anstoß* as a transcendental fact is at variance with the idea of a self-grounding of the absolute ego itself. It may very well have been the case that as he progressed Fichte realized more clearly that the initial project of the WL needed to be modified or revised. He should have acknowledged from the start, however, that the *Anstoß* can neither be an element within nor without the absolute ego without violating the original conception of transcendental idealism with its radical immanentism and the self-positing of the ego. For either the *Anstoß* derives from inside the absolute ego, and then the ego is to that extent not absolutely self-positing, or it derives from something outside the absolute ego, and then the ego is no longer absolute. As indicated above, I believe that the realization of this fact motivated Fichte's continuous reformulation of the original project of the WL up to its final revision in the late writings.

That the compatibility of the *Anstoß* doctrine with the idealism of the 1794 WL constitutes at least a matter of serious doubt was pointed out early on by Hegel. His comment on the *Anstoß* in the *Science of Logic* is worth quoting in full:

> It may well be that the infinite obstacle [*Anstoß*] of Fichte's idealism has no underlying thing-in-itself, so that it becomes purely a determinateness in the ego; but for the ego, this determinateness which it appropriates and whose externality it sublates is at the same time *immediate*, a *limitation* of the ego, which it can transcend but which it has in it as an element of indifference, so that although the limitation is in the ego, it contains an *immediate* nonbeing of the ego.[38]

What Hegel contends here is that even if the *Anstoß* originates from within the ego itself, it nonetheless indicates an element of irreducible alterity that cannot be reconciled with the immanentism of the initial project of the WL. I would only add that the same can be said to hold true for the doctrine of the summons.

Assuming that my skeptical observations have some validity, rather than being explained, the actuality of freedom remains presupposed. More specifically, all that Fichte's argument can really claim to have shown is that a community of mutually recognizing individuals must be presupposed for freedom to become actualized. The possibility of such a community can only be postulated, not posited.[39] There may be reasons to affirm the necessity of an irreducible facticity or alterity. If so, it was arguably not Fichte's aim to demonstrate that necessity through an argument by default. He clearly did not mean to show that *because* a purely immanent deduction of intersubjectivity had to fail we have no other option than to accept an extra-subjective principle. In other words, Fichte did not purposefully *design* his intersubjectivity proof with a view to demonstrating the limitations of the standpoint of immanentism that eventually comes up against a summons or an *Anstoß*. If so, neither the necessity to accept a principle of alterity nor the community of reciprocal recognition have been successfully derived.

Notes

1. See Reinhard Lauth, "Le problème de l'interpersonnalité chez J. G. Fichte," in: *Archives de Philosophie* 25 (1962): pp. 325–44; C. K. Hunter, *Der Interpersonalitätsbeweis in Fichtes früher angewandter Philosophie* (Meisenheim am Glan: Anton Hain, 1973), p. 8.

2. Hunter, *Der Interpersonalitätsbeweis in Fichtes*, pp. 11–14. See also Lauth, "Le problème de l'interpersonnalité," p. 330: "la conception de l'interpersonnalité est aussi ancienne que celle du point de vue de la W.-L. en général. Nous la trouvons déjà traitée pour la première fois, quoique sans être encore développée, dans la *Bestimmung des Gelehrten* de 1794." This, however, raises the not insignificant problem of why, then, the very idea of interpersonality is absent from the *Wissenschaftslehre* (henceforth abbreviated as *WL*) of 1794, and especially from its third part dealing with the foundation of the practical sphere. For a discussion of this issue, see Robert R. Williams, *Recognition: Fichte and Hegel on the Other* (Albany, N.Y.: SUNY, 1992), pp. 52–54.

3. Lauth, "Le problème de l'interpersonnalité," p. 336.

4. See, however, Hunter, *Der Interpersonlaitätsbeweis in Fichtes*, where such a distinction is made in terms of a proof of interpersonality in the wider and in the narrower sense, or of prededuction (*Vordeduktion*, p. 35) and genuine deduction of interpersonality (*eigentlicher Interpersonalitätsbeweis*, p. 93).

5. For a problematization of this view, see Richard Schottky, "La *Grundlage des Naturrechts* de Fichte et la philosophie politique de l'Aufklärung," in *Archives de philosophie* 25 (1962): pp. 441–83.

6. Fichte, *Grundlage des Naturrechts*, SW III, section 3 (*Zweiter Lehrsatz*).

7. Aristotle, *Politics* I 2, 1253a19, and III 9, 1280b39–40.

8. *SW* III, pp. 42–47.

9. Cf. ibid., p. 46.

10. Ibid., pp. 47–48.

11. Williams, *Recognition*, p. 64.

12. Williams also objects that Fichte's concept of mutually recognized freedom represents a "negative concept of intersubjectivity and/or community" only, because it requires the individuals to "restrict their own freedoms." In this way, the other is construed as "a limitation of freedom, rather than as its enhancement or ethical elevation" (pp. 63–64). I believe that this assessment gives too little weight to Fichte's explicit statements that mutual recognition of each other's freedom

implies the idea of honoring the other's nature as a free rational agent. According to Fichte, I limit my sphere of freedom not because the other would likely resist or fight my intrusion on his, but because I respect the other and in limiting my freedom deliberately make room for his without, however, prescribing what the other can or cannot do with his freedom. This seems to me to be a positive notion of intersubjective freedom. It may well be that the mutually conceded spheres are in fact materially empty and that, therefore, Fichte neglected to formulate a contentful notion of individual freedom. This, however, does not mean that his concept of individual freedom is merely negative.

13. Vittorio Hösle, *Hegels System* (Hamburg: Felix Meiner, 1988), p. 41 n. 51.

14. Ibid., pp. 379–80 n. 85.

15. *SW* VI, 332.

16. Lauth, "Le problème de l'interpersonnalité," p. 336.

17. *Hegel's Phenomenology of Spirit*, trans. A. V. Miller, foreword by J. N. Findlay (Oxford: Clarendon Press, 1977), p. 110.

18. *SW* III, section 17.

19. Ibid., sections 17–18.

20. Ibid., section 19: "ursprünglich und ihrem Wesen nach."

21. Ibid.

22. Ibid., section 21.

23. Ibid., section 24.

24. Cf. ibid., sections 30ff.

25. Ibid., sections 32–33.

26. Cf. ibid., section 33.

27. Cf. ibid., sections 33–34.

28. Ibid., section 39.

29. Ibid., sections 39–40: "Ein Geist nahm sich ihrer an." For Hösle, this admission of a possible regress is enough to dismiss Fichte's whole intersubjectivity theorem out of hand: see Hösle, *Hegels System*, p. 380 n. 85.

30. See Williams, *Recognition*, p. 60.

31. *SW* III, section 35.

32. I would like to note that Williams himself seems to remain somewhat skeptical with regard to the consistency of Fichte's proof. There exists, he says, a tension between two requirements the proof needs to satisfy, viz. "the transcendental-idealist-constitutional, and the realistic descriptive" requirement (p. 63). I doubt, however, that the phenomenological-descriptive element that Williams rightly points out as lacking in Fichte's account can serve as a *substitute* for the missing transcendental link.

33. "Second Introduction to the Science of Knowledge," *J. G. Fichte: Science of Knowledge with First and Second Introductions,* ed. and trans. Peter Heath and John Lachs (Cambridge: Cambridge University Press, 1982), p. 56.

34. "Second Introduction," p. 55.

35. See Kant, *Critique of Practical Reason*, AA V 122.

36. This assumption seems to be borne out by Johannes Brachtendorf's superb study of the permutations that Fichte's conception of the WL underwent

from the early 1794 *Grundlage* until its 1812 version. According to Brachtendorf, Fichte first eliminated the residual realism *(Rest-Realismus)* of the 1794 WL in the 1798 to 1799 *Wissenschaftslehre nova methodo* but afterward abandoned the absolute character of the ego in order to replace it by a quasi Neo-Platonic metaphysics of the absolute: see J. Brachtendorf, *Fichte's Lehre vom Sein: Eine kritische Darstellung der Wissenschaftslehren von 1794, 1798–99 und 1812* (Paderborn, München, Wien, Zürich: Ferdinand Schöningh, 1995), pp. 177–8, 233–6, 302.

37. For a good recent discussion of the epistemological status of the *Anstoß*, see again Williams, *Recognition,* pp. 57–59. I agree with Williams—against Edith Düsing's *Intersubjektivität und Selbstbewußtsein* (Köln: Dinter, 1986)—that the summons and the *Anstoß* share the same theoretical status of "transcendental fact."

38. *Hegel's Science of Logic,* trans. by A. V. Miller, foreword by J. N. Findlay (London: Allen and Unwin; New York: Humanities Press, 1976), p. 397.

39. I cannot, therefore, be quite as positive in my assessment of the success of Fichte's deduction as is Peter Baumanns in his recent comprehensive study of Fichte's philosophy, titled *J. G. Fichte: Kritische Gesamtdarstellung seiner Philosophie* (Freiburg, München: Karl Alber, 1990). Baumanns apparently has no problem with Fichte's deduction of intersubjectivity at all:

> Abhängigkeit der Natur vom Ich und Abhängigkeit des Ichs von der Natur sind zur transzendentalphilosophischen Vermittlung aufgegeben. Sie ist möglich nach Fichte im Rückgang auf das Phänomen der Aufforderung (das damit in seiner eigenen Vernünftigkeit deduziert, bestätigt wird). . . . Damit ist das "Wir" als Bedingung des "Ich" (die Intersubjektivität als Bedingung der Individualität . . . deduziert. (p. 121)

Needless to say, like Baumanns, I agree with Fichte's aims; my skepticism concerns the success of the supporting theory.

Fichte's Theory of Punishment: "Out-Kanting" Kant in Criminal Law

Jean-Christophe Merle

A popular dichotomy in legal philosophy opposes the theory of retribution to the so-called utilitarian theory of punishment. The utilitarian approach is characterized by its aim to promote collective utility by the use of measures designed to deter, prevent, threaten, or improve detrimental actions. As is well known, the retribution theory has been upheld by Kant and Hegel, who had joined to it a vociferous critique of the utilitarian theory of punishment, directing it not only against Bentham and the predecessor of Utilitarianism, Beccaria, but also against theories of natural law such as Pufendorf's, and even against Fichte.[1] Beccaria is particularly selected for stringent criticism. The critique is divided into three main points: first, the "oversympathetic sensitivity of an affected humanitarianism *(compassibilitas)*"[2] is counted against him. The second change is that Beccaria tries to justify the state's authority to penalize by deriving it from the original contract. Since nobody is willing to submit to punishment, and the contract is an expression of the general will, the state would have no grounds to legitimate its penal actions. The third objection is to the overriding appeal to collective utility. Collective utility does not follow from the right to use coercion against a criminal,[3] but from the intent to ensure the happiness of the people, that is, it follows from paternalistic reasoning. Kant buttresses this criticism with his appeal to the categorical, universally valid, imperative of law. In addition, the appeal to collective utility does not consider the relation between the crime committed and the punishment to be meted out. As we shall see, it is this problem that compels Kant to introduce his version of a retribution theory. (Hegel adopts a similar position in the chapter on "abstract right," and even though later, in section 218 of his *Philosophy of Right,* he gauges sentencing according to the "menace to civil society," he does not attempt to integrate or harmonize the relevant passages of the abstract right chapter with this text concerning the "administration of justice" [*Rechtspflege*]. Since the text from the section on the administration of justice hardly argues normatively, I will, in the course of my interpretation of rules, stress the passage from the section on abstract right.)

Now, the critique of Beccaria's arguments seems as superficial as is the identification of his position with that of Fichte (for this, see Hegel and many others).[4] While Beccaria and Fichte indeed share the same premises concerning the right to use coercion, they nonetheless draw different conclusions from them. This is primarily due to Fichte's commitment to a form of Kantianism, a form which proceeds from the categorical imperative of law and is therefore antithetical to utilitarian theories. In what follows, I would like to demonstrate not only Fichte's Kantianism, but, moreover, that Fichte's theory "out-Kants" Kant by retaining his intentions while eliminating a contradiction at the heart of Kant's theory.

The Right of Coercion and the Right to Punishment: Kant's Error

Fichte does not dispute that the principle of retribution is just. In the second edition of his *Attempt at a Critique of all Revelation,* Fichte sees a motive for moral action in what he calls "the just" (*das Rechte*), the necessary correspondence and commensurateness of merit and happiness— that is, in God as an infinitely rational creature. There is, writes Fichte in his *Foundation of Natural Right,* "no dispute whether *a murderer* is unjustly treated when he must forcibly lose his life." Then Fichte adds, "but an entirely different question needs to be answered, namely, whence derives the right of any mortal whatsoever to assume the position of moral world ruler and apply the law—the criminal's own—to the offender; it was this merely legal problem that *Beccaria* had in mind."[5] This is the problem of the authorization of punishment, which Kant attempted to derive directly from the state's own authority to use coercion.

The state's authority to use coercion can itself be derived from the general right to coercion that every human being enjoys and may make use of in the event that his or her *jus perfectum* is violated. In this case, the freedom of another human being is restricted:

> Now everything unjust is an obstacle to freedom according to universal
> laws . . . [t]hus: if a certain use of freedom is itself an obstacle to freedom
> according to universal laws (i.e., unjust), then any coercion directed
> against said obstacle is in harmony with freedom according to universal
> laws; this follows from the principle of contradiction.[6]

In natural right theories, this is precisely the case with regard to self-
defense *(Notwehr)*. The right to use coercion is conferred upon the state,
for the state is obliged to guarantee the rights of its citizens. According
to Kant and Fichte, every individual has the right to have his or her
rights guaranteed. Fichte concludes, further, that everyone has the right
to compel fellow citizens to enter into a legal community or to force them
out of it.

Once we accept this justification of the use of force, we can then ask
what are the means of coercion at our disposal? Coercion serves to *obstruct*
injustice, and it can be exercised in three different ways. The first, and
frequently forgotten, way is for the sake of prevention. Fichte calls it the
contract of protection (which, incidentally, only together with the *contract
of union* and the *contract of submission* constitutes the state's right to use
coercion): all citizens carry the obligation to protect the rights of their
fellow citizens in the event of their violation. Doubtlessly, the contract
of protection prevents a great deal of crime, for it acts as a deterrent.
The second way of exercising coercion is for the purpose of defense:
successfully preventing a crime the moment it begins to take place. The
third way does not become relevant until the crime has already occurred,
and it then serves to cancel an injustice already committed. Examples of
this last way of exercising coercion are the return of a stolen object or
the restitution of a stolen sum. Only this last means constitutes a form of
retribution: the criminal must return the object or reimburse the victim
for his or her losses.

Yet there are times when reimbursement is not possible, and even
when it is possible, it is generally held to be unequal to the crime. When
the criminal is forced to return the stolen object, the original distribution
of property is restored. The claims of the victim are thus completely
fulfilled; those of the legal community, however, are not. At this level,
it is not the distribution of property but the guarantee that citizens'
rights be protected that must be addressed. This becomes clear when
we see that the criminal is not just condemned to undo the damage but
is also condemned to *punishment* (here Fichte's distinction between the
person who acts rashly or recklessly and the person who acts according
to "a selfish will lusting after other person's goods" is quite common
in the tradition.[7] Despite compensatory measures, the fact of the crime

cannot be erased. I will return to this point. The exemplary case in which recompense is not possible is murder. Retribution, however—the death of the murderer—*is* possible.

Thus we can see that retribution has nothing to do with the restoration of acceptable legal relations. But if it is so independent of this possible basis of justification, then the question arises of how Kant justifies the application of the principle of retribution in determining the severity of sentencing. The Kantian—and later Hegelian—argument has two sides: it proceeds negatively at first, laying down negative conditions; then it introduces the principle of retribution. (A) The categorical legal imperative is subject to the universal criterion of morality, namely, universalizability. According to one of the several versions of the categorical imperative, I should always act in such a way that I treat others never as means but always as ends. The categorical legal imperative does not permit punishment to serve as a means toward the prevention or deterrence of the crime, or toward the improvement of the criminal. Otherwise, the criminal would be degraded to a mere instrument of collective legal security. Even less does the categorical legal imperative permit the punishment to serve collective utility: it is, for example, forbidden "to preserve the life of a criminal sentenced to death in the case of his agreeing to be the object of dangerous medical experiments, from which he might happily emerge, so that the medical practitioners might gain instruction beneficial to the community."[8] (B) Now, it is only in a second step that Kant introduces and grounds the principle of retribution. Because of the above considerations concerning the categorical legal imperative, Kant is compelled to find a principle that does not fundamentally regard human beings as means to a higher end. The principle of retribution is related to the legal community not by making it an end to which all actions are subordinated, but rather only insofar as it takes its bearing on particular violations of law in that community in order to determine the appropriate punishment ("whatever evil you inflict on another through no fault of their own, you inflict upon yourself").[9]

Two remarks are necessary with regard to steps A and B in the above argument: first, with regard to the demand that the criminal be seen as an end in itself, we may remark that this demand in no way excludes the possibility of his or her being treated as a means as well. The legal community is defined as the coexistence of external freedoms, so that the citizens are never only seen as means toward the end of the community's welfare. But the criminal has violated the laws of this community. Thus the possibility remains open that the criminal be treated as both means and as end: as a means, insofar as the punishment is intended to restore the state's guarantee to protect its citizens' rights; and as an end, insofar as the punishment can render an improvement in the behavior of the criminal. As a consequence, Kant's transition from A to B, to wit, to the conclusion that retribution is the only punishment theory capable of treating the criminal as an end, is dubious at best.

Indeed, the doubtfulness of this transition from A to B is confirmed in other domains of Kant's theory. An especially grave consideration is that the categorical imperative does not provide for a theory of retribution. The principle of universalizability, according to which the criminal's maxims are to be applied to the criminal herself or himself, provides only a criterion of morality, but not a maxim for realizing the highest good. But let us assume that the categorical imperative simply demanded the principle's application. Even if retribution is considered just, as is the case with Kant and in Fichte's *Attempt at a Critique of All Revelation,* it nonetheless does not necessarily belong in the law. For according to Kant himself, justice consists of both *jus strictum,* law in the strict sense, and *equitas,* fairness; and fairness expressly does not belong in the law.[10] Who may then demand retribution? Obviously the victim may do so, but only insofar as she or he asserts the right to have stolen property be returned or compensated for. On the basis of its authorization to use coercion, the state can only demand the security of its citizens by demanding that the laws be followed. Kant, however, defines the right to punishment as "the right of the commander over his subordinate to impose *pain* on him as a consequence of his crime."[11] As such, pain is not defined as compensation or as a means of maintaining collective security. Therefore, the state is not entitled to impose this pain. At best only the conscience of the criminal herself or himself could demand retribution, as Hegel will later argue.[12]

The difficulty is fundamentally this: on the one hand, Kant rejects for the sake of the exclusive validity of the retribution principle the treatment of the crime as both an end *and* as a means, although the right to prevent injustice—the right to coercion—requires such treatment; on the other hand, Kant wants to derive the state's right to punishment directly from its right to use coercion. Indicative of this second horn in Kant's dilemma is the following passage, in which the principle of retribution mysteriously falls in abeyance: "There can be no penal law which accords a person the death penalty who, in the case of a shipwreck, stands with another on a plank where both face mortal danger, and then shoves this other person off in order to save himself," because "such a penal law (could) not have the effect it intends, for the threat of harm that is still uncertain (the death penalty leveled by the judge) cannot prevail over the fear of the harm that is certain (drowning). Thus the deed . . . is not to be judged as noncriminal *(inculpabile),* but as unpunishable *(impunibile).*"[13] Now, if the principle of retribution were rigorously applied, then the survivor would have to be condemned to death, even though it would certainly not have a deterring effect. The fact that Kant brings up the lack of effect a death penalty would have in this case demonstrates that penal law aims not only at retribution, but also at deterrence by way of coercion.

Two solutions to this problem are conceivable. First, we could hold onto the principle of retribution and lose the state's right to exercise punishment. Accordingly, penal law ought not exist. Or, second, we could hold onto penal law and support it with the general right to use coercion. Just how the right to punish can be grounded in the right to use coercion still needs to be demonstrated.

Fichte's Justification of Penal Law

Beccaria[14] and Fichte both emphasize the impossibility of preventing all criminality before it takes place as well as the impossibility of acting as though no crime had been committed. If these points are taken seriously, then it will be clear that no state can succeed in preventing all crime by means of the right to use coercion. *Punishment is implemented because the right to use coercion does not in all cases suffice to deter criminality.* If the right to coercion does not work, then the guarantee for the citizens of their rights is no longer valid; rather, these rights become violated. Since the recognition of rights must be mutual, the citizens are *eo ipso* no longer obliged to recognize the rights of an offender: the innocent citizens no longer share a pact with the offender, who is thereby excluded from the state. The state thus stands in the same relation to the excluded member that two individuals in the state of nature would have to one another.

This relation can take two forms, both of which were already given in the original state of nature: each person can compel the other to enter into a legal community, or to keep their distance. The second possibility—the banishment of the criminal into the desert—remains at this point in Fichte's train of thought a merely theoretical case. For, on the one hand, the wrongdoer could not actually desire such a cruel fate. On the other hand, as Fichte writes, "the state is just as concerned with the preservation of its members—but *only if* its main purpose is compatible with such preservation—as is each individual citizen concerned not to be declared without rights every time some crime is committed."[15] Thus, Fichte explains, the state is concerned that "the whole [community] is given the opportunity of keeping those citizens whose usefulness outweighs their harmfulness."[16] Unfortunately, Fichte fails to explain what he means by "usefulness" *(Nützlichkeit);* he only speaks of "all cases in which public security could be maintained." I would like to suggest a minimalistic, not utilitarian, interpretation of the meaning of this word. "Usefulness" means nothing other than (1) that the probability of recidivism is not greater than the probability that other citizens will commit a crime; and (2) if the danger *is* greater, then the situation will at least achieve a balance at a later time. The usefulness under discussion is nothing other than the mutual usefulness of the citizens in upholding the contract of protection. The criminal is thus not subordinated to an arbitrary end.

Hence, nothing different is expected of the offender than is expected of the other citizens in Fichte's theory: all are potential, not actual sources of danger. The legal community must assume from the outset that every human being poses a potential threat; it must defend itself by means of the state's authority to use coercion *(Zwangsbefugnis).*

Thus, in the above case where the risk of recidivism is low, the offender is allowed to remain a normal citizen without further complication. This applies, for example, to the person who acts rashly: the payment of compensation acts to deter a relapse. In the other case, where the expectation of recidivism is higher than the expectation of criminal behavior among other citizens, as in the case, for example, of the person who acts "selfishly lusting after other person's goods," the state is allowed to introduce a special condition into the contract founding civil society. The condition is *punishment:* the relation the state has to the criminal is regulated by the so-called contract of atonement *(Abbüßungsvertrag).*

Fichte's recommendation for punishment is imprisonment lasting until the prisoner is "improved," that is, until he or she poses as little threat to the community as any other citizen.

The balance of the discussion thus far is that Fichte's theory of punishment meets two demands raised by Kant, but which Kant implicitly considered contradictory: first, that penal law be derived from the general right of coercion, which means that when the right to coercion is insufficient to deter crime, then penal law may step in. As such, it is a continuation of the right to coercion that serves to ensure legality for everyone. In contrast to the passive character of the right to use coercion, which is effective as a virtual threat, penal law is a kind of *active* right to coercion. Penal law is thus able to function as a guarantee of the categorical legal imperative: the coexistence of external freedoms according to law. Second, penal law is not enacted without the consent of the criminal, who can decide in favor of punishment or exclusion from the community. Should she or he opt for punishment, she or he may one day again enjoy civil liberty. Considered in this light, the criminal is treated as an end in himself or herself. In addition, penal law is in accord with the categorical imperative. Only the principle of retribution is subtracted from the Kantian inheritance, because the principle was accepted only as a result of a simplification: instead of Fichte's reading of the imperative as "never treat other persons *merely* as means, but always *also* as ends," Kant interpreted it along the stricter lines: "never treat other persons as means, but only as ends." The punishment still depends upon the infliction of pain as a means of restoring collective security, but it is determined as minimal pain, for it is to cease upon improvement of the criminal and is justified as the lesser evil compared with a life spent outside the legal community.

Fichte agrees with Hegel against Beccaria that the punishment is not to be considered a form of evil perpetrated on the prisoner. Fichte disputes the claims made by Beccaria and the utilitarian school of thought that punishment is a means of collective deterrence or prevention.

Fichte's stance has an unexpected and for many a surprising consequence. Similar to the theory of retribution, Beccaria also calls for a kind of proportional relation between crime and punishment: "the more the crime harms the public welfare, the harder the obstacles must be. There is thus meant to be a commensurability between criminal acts and their punishment."[17] But Beccaria grounds his reasoning in the deterrence such commensurability is meant to enforce. In Fichte's theory, commensurability is at best a secondary consideration. Let us see what happens in the case of a murder. Fichte lays down a term of imprisonment for a nonnegligent, unpremeditating murderer, which should last until he or she has improved. For premeditated murder, there is no punishment, since it cannot be expected of the prison guards to watch over such a dangerous human being; however, should someone volunteer to guard the prisoner, then a punishment is possible. Otherwise the murderer must be banned from the community. If he nevertheless remains within state territory, and the citizens of that state feel potentially threatened by his presence, then they or the police are entitled to shoot him down like a dangerous animal.

Fichte's rather pragmatic argumentation on this point is not very convincing and is even a bit repellent. We are today in a position to know that appropriate security measures can be taken with respect to such threatening criminals. The improvement of these criminals simply takes much longer. In the end, we may ask ourselves which kind of punishment would be appropriate for cases of merely negligent murder. If the negligence is not systematic and recurrent, then either an acquittal or obligatory training in morality to increase the murderer's moral attentiveness would suffice, although Fichte does not go into details here.

The pickpocket, however, would certainly not get off so easily. In these judgments, Fichte shows none of the "oversympathetic sensitivity of an affected humanitarianism" that Kant wrongly reproached Beccaria with, but rather the rigorous application of the Kantian right of the state to the use of coercion.

Of course, I do not hold Fichte's theory of punishment to be the last word in the theory of penal law. Its main defect is the problem of its application, which entails more difficulties than do the other theories. In order to apply Fichtean penal law, one needs to know not only the circumstances of the murder, but also the intentions of the murderer and his or her soundness of mind. But even after the conclusion of the criminal proceedings, the intentions and the soundness of mind of the criminal would have to be reinvestigated, for otherwise the risk of the criminal's committing another crime cannot be compared with that of the rest of the civil population. Such punishment, as the English say "at the pleasure of her majesty," requires reliable, nonpartisan, and verifiable criteria in order to prevent abuse of the system, especially on the part of high-handed authorities.[18]

In conclusion, I would like to point out how the Fichtean theory is both more Kantian and more liberal than its competitors. It is Kantian, because, in contrast to utilitarianism, it heeds the categorical imperative. It is more Kantian, because only Fichte succeeds where Kant failed in actually deriving the penal law from the right to use coercion in conjunction with the categorical legal imperative. It is more liberal, because Fichte's theory of punishment demands less pain and more effectiveness than Kantian legal theory, thereby also better respecting each person's freedom. However, it still needs to be investigated whether the difficulties of applying Fichte's theory do not also conceal such risks of abuse that the theory could in the end be ethically disqualified. If this is indeed the case, then preference would have to be given to one of the other theories—perhaps to Kant's second best solution.

Notes

1. G. W. F. Hegel, *Philosophy of Right,* ed. A. W. Wood and trans. H. B. Nisbet (Cambridge: Cambridge University Press, 1991), section 100n.

2. Immanuel Kant, *The Metaphysical Elements of Justice,* trans. John Ladd (Indianapolis: Bobbs-Merrill, 1965), Gen. Note, section 49, E, p. 335. Hereafter abbreviated as *MEJ.*

3. Ibid., section D, p. 232.

4. I would like to call attention to an excellent article, the focus of which, however, is different from the one adopted here: V. Hösle, "Was darf und was soll der Staat bestrafen? Überlegungen im Anschluß an Fichtes und Hegels Straftheorien" [What is the state permitted and what is the state obligated to punish? Reflections on Fichte's and Hegel's theories of punishment], in V. Hösle, ed., *Die Rechtsphilosophie des deutschen Idealismus* (Hamburg: Meiner, 1989), pp. 1–55.

For further references to Fichte and Beccaria, see: J. M. Carbasse, "Le droit pénal," in *Dictionaire de philosophie politique,* eds. Ph. Reynaud and S. Riles (Paris: P.U.F., 1996), pp. 314–19, esp. p. 318; and H. Verweyen, *Recht und Sittlichkeit in J. G. Fichtes Gesellschaftslehre* (Freiburg: Alber, 1975), p. 131. Among other critiques inspired by Hegel, but without reference to Fichte's relation to Beccaria, is R. Zaczyk, *Das Strafrecht in der Rechtslehre J. G. Fichtes* (Berlin: Dunker and Humblot, 1981); Zaczyk, however, misses Fichte's *specifically legal* point.

5. *GNR,* sect. 20 (*SW,* III, pp. 251–52).

6. Kant, *MEJ,* Intro., section D, 232.

7. See Fichte, *GNR* (*SW,* III, pp. 253–54).

8. Kant, *MEJ,* Gen. Note, section 49E, 332.

9. Ibid.

10. Ibid., Appendix to Intro., section I, 234.

11. Ibid., section 49, E, 331.

12. Hegel, *Philosophy of Right,* 12, section 100.

13. Kant, *MEJ,* appendix to Intro. II, 235.

14. Cesare Bonesana di Beccaria, *On Crimes and Punishments* [*Dei Delitti e Delle Pene*], trans. H. Paolucci (Indianapolis: Bobbs-Merrill, 1963), section VI.

15. Fichte, *GNR* (*SW,* III, pp. 251–520).

16. Ibid.

17. Beccaria, *On Crimes and Punishments,* section VI.

18. This problem will be addressed in a forthcoming publication; see J.-Ch. Merle, *Droit de contraindre et droit de punir de Kant à Hegel* (forthcoming).

The "Deduction of the Individual": Fichte's Efforts to "Complete" the Jena *Wissenschaftslehre*

Hans-Jakob Wilhelm

I
n August 1795, along with the final installment of his *Grundlage der gesammten Wissenschaftslehre,* Fichte sends a letter to Friedrich Heinrich Jacobi in which he declares: "My *absolute I* is obviously not the *individual;* offended courtiers and irritated philosophers have explained me in this way, in order to accuse me of a practical egotism. But *the individual must be deduced from the absolute I.*"[1] This he promises to do without delay in the *Naturrecht.* By deducing and acknowledging the "practical standpoint" Fichte promises to reconcile his philosophy completely with common sense, not only with regard to the latter's requirement of "individuality," but with regard to its "realism" and its belief in the existence of God as well. Fichte tells Jacobi that he is utterly convinced of the uniformity of their philosophical views, and in particular he cites Jacobi's novel *Allwill* as evidence. The two prominent features of the *Grundlage* that Fichte mentions in the letter—the principle of the "absolute I" and the related doctrine that the sensible content of experience is actually produced by a "productive imagination"—are of course those features notorious for resisting acceptance by common sense. And yet, Fichte seems to suggest, in the end his *Wissenschaftslehre* will turn out to be just as appropriate and effective a vehicle for saving the truths of "sound human understanding" *(gesunder Menschenverstand)* as Jacobi's philosophical novel can claim to be.[2]

Did Fichte succeed in substantiating his claim? A clue to the answer may be found in statements Fichte makes in March or April 1799 in a manuscript—originally intended for publication, but never published in Fichte's lifetime—written in the context of the so-called "Atheism Dispute." Responding to the popular complaint that in his system God is apparently not the creator, the preserver, the ruler of the world, that there is no providence, Fichte tells his "dear good nonphilosophers" that the entire distinction, according to which God in one sense is not and in another sense is the creator, does not exist for them. This distinction is intended exclusively for philosophers. It is just that he, Fichte, has not yet gotten around to addressing the person at the standpoint of common sense with whom, he claims, he never had any dispute. If people wait but a short while, however, this philosopher will come around to their side of the table, respect their point of view, and admit that they are right.[3]

But in the so-called "Fragment," which Fichte appended to letters to Reinhold and Jacobi on 22 April and which is composed of several excerpts from the last mentioned piece, Fichte basically has the same message for his philosophical colleagues. Philosophy is like an anatomical dissection. Just as one must kill the living body, in order to get to know it, so one must leave the standpoint of life, in order to describe and comprehend common consciousness just as it is. It is just that at this point in time he has not yet finished the composition of the entire body, that is, he has not yet completed the philosophical description of ordinary consciousness. And so his philosophical colleagues must be patient and await the following installment of his system, in case they do not know how to supply the continuation themselves.[4]

Now in 1799, however, Fichte seems much less optimistic than in 1795 about the prospects for such a completion. At least he tells his colleagues what not to expect from it. There will always remain a basic antithesis between philosophy and life. A point of union between the standpoints of the two "is just as impossible as grasping the X, which lies at the basis of the Subject-Object or I" with which the *Wissenschaftslehre* begins.[5]

Given that the *Naturrecht*, which, according to Fichte's original claim of 1795, was supposed to fulfill his promise to Jacobi, had already appeared in 1796,[6] the historical record of Fichte's pronouncements on the issue of the "deduction of the individual" or the "completion of the *Wissenschaftslehre*" provides the following complex picture. In 1795 Fichte promised that he would reconcile the *Wissenschaftslehre* with common sense in a work that, as it turned out, was published a year later. Yet in 1799 he still promises his "dear good nonphilosopher" as well as his fellow philosophers such a reconciliation, although now he admits to the latter that in a certain sense such a reconciliation can never be achieved. If we add to this the fact that from 1800 onward (following his involuntary departure in 1799 from the Jena university) Fichte's thought took a decisive turn away from the project of the *Wissenschaftslehre* in its early, "Jena" form, we must wonder whether by 1799 Fichte had perhaps begun to recognize a certain limitation of his early position.

Fichte's treatment in 1799 of the relationship between philosophy and ordinary consciousness by means of the image of eventually walking around to the other side of the table, in order to give ordinary consciousness its due, can be read in two ways. On the one hand, it could mean that Fichte would come around to speak to common sense, if we can personify it, on its own terms, and explain the situation to it. On the other hand, the image could also suggest that, rather than seriously engaging common sense, he would treat it as some people treat their children, by saying, "These are adult things that you don't understand" and "Your situation is explained by the fact that you are not adults yet, and this is why, instead of coming over there myself, I will send the nanny to educate you." The continuation of the passage leaves no doubt but that the latter reading is the correct one. Fichte says that it is contrary to the purpose of this philosophy to communicate with the human being *qua* human being. It is only in the scholar, as educator and leader of the people, especially as *Volkslehrer*, that the theorems of the *Wissenschaftslehre* become practical, and then only as a pedagogical rule, not for the purposes of communication.[7] In the end this passage leaves no doubt but that, as far as Fichte was concerned, the only way of dealing with the person at the standpoint of common sense was by means of the politics of education. I purposely say "politics" because I think that Fichte is serious about training a class of *Volkslehrer* whose mandate it is to mediate between the standpoint of philosophy and the ordinary standpoint, by "raising" the person from the latter to the former.

In light of the historical record then, my thesis regarding Fichte's "deduction of the individual" is this: the early *Wissenschaftslehre* terminates in the pragmatics of education as a way of dealing with the individual. The concrete historical individual, which Fichte said he wanted to account for just as much as Jacobi did, remains something of a surd in Fichte's early system, an entity that in an important sense escapes philosophical comprehension. In this paper I want to support this thesis philosophically.

Before I begin I should address a certain objection. One might think that in the above passage Fichte is only expressing the fairly uncontroversial view that philosophical ideas are not readily communicable to the public at large, something that could be said to hold true of many, if not of all, philosophical theories. And so it might be held that nothing particularly embarrassing is contained in Fichte's acknowledgment. This would be a good objection, except that *Fichte's* problem has to do with the fact that his "absolute I" "obviously does not" refer to the individual, whereas "I" in its ordinary usage does. Granted that a particular philosopher's inability to articulate her or his ideas in a way that the ordinary person could understand is not necessarily indicative of a *philosophical* problem with her or his position, my point is that, for *Fichte*, an inability to account for the genuinely person-referring use of "I," that is, an inability to account for the individual, would constitute a *philosophical* embarrassment.

To begin, I should briefly state what I think is the demand or claim that ordinary consciousness makes with regard to the use of "I." This requirement simply says that "I" refers to the one who uses it, that it picks out the person who utters it from among other persons. This reference of "I" to the individual person is immediate and secure. It does not rely on any special knowledge of who I am or what I have experienced but works simply by virtue of established human practice. I could be a total amnesiac and would still be referring to myself, if I used "I."[8] The question with regard to Fichte is whether ordinary consciousness can recognize itself in this way in any of the occurrences of "I" in Fichte's system. To put it differently: we have a well established practice amongst ourselves guaranteeing that whenever we have a user of "I" in a thought or an utterance, we also have a reference and the correct reference. Mastering this practice means participating in a communal life in which we treat each other as persons. With his doctrine of the "primacy of practical reason," Fichte offers us an account of the conditions that make for moral life. The doctrine of the primacy of practical reason says that rational action is itself the basis of all cognitive or "theoretical" capacities. Fichte recognizes of course that moral life is lived as the life of individuals. Stated in terms of Fichte's deductions: the "I" cannot posit itself as "knowing" unless it posits itself as "practical," and it cannot posit itself as practical unless it posits itself as "individual." A mind-independent world that is *known* can exist only for the *acting* being, but the acting being must be one that recognizes itself to be limited, not merely "theoretically," by a world of mere objects, but "practically," by being confronted with other rationally acting individuals. Fichte's doctrine of the *Aufforderung* states that in order to be conscious of itself, the "I" must posit itself as limited in response to a "call" from what, if self-consciousness is to be actualized, it necessarily posits as another rational being outside of itself. From the highest philosophical abstraction of the "absolute I" the *Wissenschaftslehre* must finally rejoin our ordinary practice, where "I" refers to, or picks out, an individual person from among others. Our question is whether it can succeed at this task.

Roughly stated, Jacobi's critique of philosophy was that in its search for universal conditions of knowledge or of moral action, philosophical reflection tends to divorce itself from actual existence. Yet philosophers, even though they might in fact be dealing only with conceptual possibilities, do not refrain from making existential claims based on their findings, and thus end up substituting a fake reality—one that in fact merely satisfies the requirements of a philosophical reflection bent on system-building—for the one that is present to us in immediately lived experience. That is to say, due to systematic exigencies, philosophy distorts or falsifies what is revealed in the course of actual experience. But Jacobi held that reason was precisely to be found in the particularities of lived experience; at least such experience constitutes an irreducible aspect of reason, one that is irretrievably lost in the abstraction of philosophical systems. Jacobi's solution is to stop philosophizing, at least in the sense of building metaphysical systems, and to engage in the study of "history" instead. Jacobi said that his purpose as a writer was to "display *as scrupulously as possible* the way humanity is, whether explicable or not."[9]

Emphasizing the realism manifest in lived experience, Jacobi chose the medium of the philosophical novel, in order to be able to describe, albeit in a fictional setting, life as it is actually experienced. "Reason" was to be found at the level of the actions or interactions of actual individuals. Reason is seen as rooted in a context where an "I" encounters an "other," a "Thou." In this interaction the "I" becomes aware of itself and recognizes itself as limited precisely to the extent that it acknowledges the reality of the other. And the characters of Jacobi's philosophical novels, although not actual individuals themselves, nonetheless possess enough "individuality" such that we can identify ourselves with them. As readers of the novel we are invited to participate, as it were, in the dealings that its characters have with each other, and indeed it is only on the condition that we thus participate—that we commit and spend actual life-energy in this fictional setting—that the novel can succeed artistically, and that Jacobi can get his message across philosophically. On this conception, there is thus a continuity between history and philosophy, between lived experience and philosophical reflection. And this continuity allows philosophy to be descriptive. Yet it is a continuity that is achieved precisely through the interpolation of a certain "distance." Jacobi gets his message across because we recognize the setting as fictional, and yet we existentially commit ourselves to it. The philosophical novel is the vehicle for a truth we live every day but which, just because it is so fundamental, we need to put at a distance, so to speak, in order to make it visible. The point of this procedure, however, is to avoid putting the truth at such a distance that we cannot identify with it as individuals.

Fichte, of course, did not write any such quasi-historical philosophical novels, but in at least two places he refers to his *Wissenschaftslehre* as a "pragmatic history of the human mind."[10] It seems that Fichte wanted to prove Jacobi wrong about the possibility of systematic philosophy by inventing a new type of philosophy that would satisfy Jacobi's requirements. I want to ask, why precisely was Fichte drawn to Jacobi's idea of a "history" in the first place, and why did he construe his philosophy as a "pragmatic history"? From the writings I referred at the outset we know that still in 1799, embroiled in the atheism dispute, Fichte insists that his philosophy is merely descriptive of views ordinarily held, that he has no dispute with "sound human understanding." And where he talks about the fundamental antithesis between philosophy and life Fichte tells us that, in order to represent life as it truly is, the *Wissenschaftslehre* requires that one transpose oneself at a distance from the standpoint one ordinarily occupies.[11] Ultimately, our question is whether the distance that the *Wissenschaftslehre* demands is perhaps so great that we cannot recognize ourselves in it. But for now we must see what it was about the philosophical problems Fichte inherited and originally responded to that made the Jacobian reference to "life" seem attractive.

Fichte's move in what he took to be the general direction of Jacobi must be seen in the context of his response to a certain quasi-Humean skepticism that Salomon Maimon had resurrected within the confines of Kant's transcendental philosophy. I must briefly state the point of Maimon's skepticism, in order to motivate Fichte's idea of philosophy as a "pragmatic history of the human mind" as a response to it.

Maimon reflected on the implications for the task of the Transcendental Deduction of Kant's requirement that in addition to being thought by the understanding an object must also be given in sensible intuition. In experience the active or spontaneous faculty of understanding must meet some resistance or it must encounter an "other," in order to issue in knowledge. That is to say, in addition to a reflective or conceptual moment there must be an intuitive or existential moment in the generation of knowledge.

Now Maimon in effect capitalized on a certain conception of the nature of sensible experience that Kant had inherited from his predecessors to show that, on Kant's premises, the transcendental deduction of the categories, that is, the argument that experience is necessarily structured by certain basic concepts, could achieve far less than Kant had hoped it would achieve. Maimon argued that on Kantian grounds one could not assume an object or a "thing" outside of consciousness as the cause of the sensible representation. In fact, sensation is an original *presentation* rather than a representation. *Qua* original *presentation,* sensation "represents nothing outside of itself."[12] The fact that ordinarily we take it to be a *re*-presentation of an object outside of consciousness is due to an illusion of the imagination.[13] Maimon bases his reasoning on the fact that "sensation" is supposed to be the "passivity" that constrains the "activity" of "thought." Conscious empirical thinking of the kind needed for genuine *re*-presentation requires both "thought" and "sensation," "activity" and "passivity" *in combination.*[14] Hence Maimon takes "sensation" *as such,* or as regarded *in isolation* from "thought," to be an ideal quantity, which through a diminution of consciousness we can forever approach but never "reach," that is, of which we can never actually be conscious.[15] Considered as something independent of thought, Maimon would seem to suggest, "sensation" might as well be considered a "thing-in-itself." The original encounter, that is, the "presentation" rather than the "representation," is one that necessarily escapes reflective retrieval just because we must assume it to occur before the onset of consciousness. Consequently he holds that Kant's transcendental deduction can at most show the applicability of the categories to *ideal* experience or to objects that are constituted by the intervening activity of the imagination, leaving entirely open the possibility that the course of *actual* experience may not be categorically determined at all.[16]

As I indicated, this reasoning depends on a certain received assumption that sensible experience consists of simple, undifferentiated "impressions," states of consciousness that intrinsically bear no relation to anything outside themselves. Of course one might dismiss as "subjectivist" this assumption and claim instead that consciousness even *qua* consciousness already transcends itself toward an object that is distinct from or irreducible to mere consciousness. This was a line that at times seems to have been pursued by both Jacobi and Reinhold, and I think it is a line worth pursuing. But this is not the direction Fichte takes. Rather, following Maimon's lead, Fichte firmly closes consciousness in its theoretical sense into its own circle, a circle that Jacobi shunned, describing it as "magic."[17] If we gave up the idea of transcending consciousness theoretically and instead found some other way of accounting for the realism of common sense, Fichte suggests, we can safely grant a role to the imagination in the constitution of "objects" without this constituting a deception, hence without the skeptical implications that Maimon saw.[18] Fichte's reconstrual of philosophy as "pragmatic history of the human mind" undercuts Maimon's skepticism by situating "experience," as the philosophers had understood it, in a wider context of "action." To effect this radical realignment, Fichte draws on that aspect of Kant's philosophy that characterizes reason as "practical," and, as a precondition for being practical, as autonomous and free.

With his "pragmatic history" Fichte is concerned to construe constraints on reason that are consistent with its characteristic freedom. Fichte's main adversaries in the pursuit of his project are the "dogmatists" or "so-called Kantians."[19] These are philosophers who have not appreciated Maimon's lesson and who continue to believe that starting from mere "facts of consciousness" one can transcend consciousness and claim a "thing-in-itself" outside of consciousness to be the source of the content of experience. Fichte argues that this idea of a constraint is incompatible with the characteristic freedom of the "I." Instead of treating the "I" as "I," such an approach would treat it merely as another "thing." This is where Jacobi's reference to the ordinary, acting and interacting, individual comes into play. The individual engaged in action gives witness to the kind of constraint that is appropriate to freedom. If one could maintain that reason is fundamentally practical, then one can perhaps accommodate the idea of a "theoretical" constraint, which has given philosophers so much trouble, by attributing it to a limited perspective within the larger or "absolute" perspective. The acting individual already gives witness to the fact that reason is fundamentally practical. Fichte's pragmatic history of the human mind wants to give philosophical expression to this truth. The kind of constraint that is manifest to the acting individual is not "sensation" but "feeling."[20] A feeling of constraint, of course, takes the committed energy of the subject into account: one can feel constrained only in light of one's sense of freedom. "Sensation," on the other hand, is a constraint regarded merely from an artificially limited perspective: a perspective that abstracts from our "practical" nature. Whereas "feeling" has a phenomenological reality, "sensation" as such is merely a theoretical entity, as Maimon had already said. Thus what Fichte has to say in the "theoretical" part of the *Grundlage der gesammten Wissenschaftslehre* about the productive imagination as the source of the content of experience only makes sense within the larger context of the "pragmatic history of the human mind."[21]

Like Jacobi, Fichte wants to begin with actual existence and from there, following a certain procedure, set out to describe it. The crucial difference lies in the procedure. Fichte requires the performance of a special "act" of abstraction or *Tathandlung* in order to ascend to the proper standpoint of philosophy. Even though the "feeling," attributed to the individual at the level of ordinary life, is the adequate expression of constraint, Fichte maintains that in order to give a transcendental account of the necessary concepts of experience, one cannot remain at the level of ordinary life. In fact, he sees a partial and unreflective attachment to the standpoint of common sense at the root of the dogmatism of the "so-called Kantians." Rather, one must abstract from the "individual" and its standpoint in "ordinary human understanding" and ascend to the standpoint of the absolute "I."[22] Paradoxically, one must leave the standpoint of life and experience precisely in order to remain faithful to lived experience. This absolute "I" is the theoretical counterpart *in philosophy* to the practical "feeling" possessed by individuals *in lived experience*. Appropriate constraints are to be deduced by taking the freedom of the "I" as the starting point and "observing" how one must "think" the "I," if this "I" is to become conscious of itself. The "pragmatic history of the human mind" is an account of the genesis of "constraint" as a "history of freedom."

The theoretical part of the *Wissenschaftslehre* is a part of that "history," but one that is shown to proceed from too narrow a conception of its own starting point. What turns out to be insufficient is the idea of an "I" as a detached "observer" who is constrained by "sensation." Thus the "history" cannot be developed further without the assumption (in the practical part) of a new and more comprehensive conception of the starting point. This more comprehensive conception will recognize constraint as a "feeling," and "feeling" is a conception of constraint in which the subjectivity of the "I" is explicitly implicated.

As a precondition for entering the *Wissenschaftslehre*, Fichte requires that the individual abstract from itself *qua* individual and grasp itself as pure intention. The "act" or *Tathandlung* that the philosopher is required to perform is not a "deed" considered as a "deed" that *is done* (that is, it is not a "fact" or a *Tatsache*); rather, it refers to the very *doing of* the "deed." Philosophical talent consists in the ability to "catch oneself in the act."[23] This effort to grasp oneself as pure or undifferentiated "activity" *(reine Agilität)* ends in failure, and in this failure the "I" encounters a limit. But this limit is not an "other," outside of the activity—it is simply the breakdown of activity. Where "I" was expected, there is suddenly a loss. But a loss is an encounter. When the "I" or "freedom" intent on knowing itself suddenly loses itself, that is, when there is suddenly "Not-I," the "I" is shocked. Fichte calls the "event" an *Anstoß*, a word that can mean "offense" as well as "impact." The point that Fichte is making is that the constraint on the activity of the "I" is already contained within the energy animating the "I" in its search for self-knowledge. Release that energy, or set the "I" free, and the constraint will appear. The "I" is scandalized to discover that it fails in its drive to grasp itself as pure intention. In response to this failure, the "productive imagination" supplies a sense-content that the "understanding" must apprehend as if it were "given." But the "supply" is contained in the "demand": a sense-content that is "given" is understood in Fichte's theory as the "remainder" that arises when a "thinking," intent on knowing itself completely *qua* pure, self-active thinking, recognizes its failure. As Fichte explains to Jacobi:

> What is the speculative standpoint for, and with it the whole of phi-
> losophy, if not for life? If humanity had never tasted this forbidden
> fruit, it could dispense with all of philosophy. But it is implanted in it
> to behold that region beyond the individual, not only in a reflected light,
> but immediately; and the first who raised a question concerning the
> existence of God broke through the limits, shook humanity in its deepest
> foundations and set it into a conflict with itself which has not yet been
> settled, and which can only be settled by boldly advancing to the highest
> point from which the speculative and the practical viewpoint appear as
> one. We began to philosophize out of wantonness and thereby forfeited
> our innocence; we saw our nakedness, and ever since we philosophize
> out of need for our salvation.[24]

In keeping with this myth, we could say that in Fichte's theory "sense-
content" is the fallout of the falling out of humanity with itself.

With the *Anstoß* the "I" takes the rupture of its activity to be a rupture of its knowledge-drive. From the presumption of being able to attain
"absolute knowledge" we derive a "determination in general," namely,
the fact that knowledge is necessarily knowledge of something limited.
In the theoretical part of the *Wissenschaftslehre* we witness the "I" trying
to posit itself by regarding itself as determined through the "Not-I." But
Fichte's point is that, although from the theoretical standpoint we can
derive the necessity of a "determination *in general,*" we cannot thus derive
a "determination *in its determinacy.*" The attempt to do so on theoretical
grounds is just the dogmatism of the so-called Kantians.[25]

The question of how we get from a "determination in general" to
actual "determinations" must be answered in the practical part of the
Wissenschaftslehre. It can only be answered when we have realized that
"knowing" presupposes "willing." The shortcoming of the merely theoretical standpoint was that it did not recognize the practical dimension
of the activity of the "absolute I." The original "rupture" in the activity
of the "absolute I" turns out to be rather the necessary "opposition" of
"willing" and "knowing":

> It is claimed that the practical I is the I of original self-consciousness, that
> a rational being perceives itself immediately only in willing, and would
> not perceive itself, and consequently would not perceive the world, and
> hence would not even be an intelligence, if it were not a practical being.[26]

The "I" must posit itself as determining the "Not-I." But, as we shall see,
the "I" cannot posit itself as being freely efficacious on the "Not-I," unless
it is "called upon" to determine itself to a free efficacy by what it posits
as another "I" outside of itself, another rational being that, in issuing the

"call" or the *Aufforderung*, has already limited itself in its free efficacy in anticipation of the self-limitation of the first. And Fichte thinks that with this notion of *Aufforderung* he can deduce the individual.

But before we examine this idea, I want to make an observation that might cast some doubt on the validity of Fichte's procedure. The constraints that Fichte deduces in the course of the *Wissenschaftslehre*, and consequently also the "individual" he deduces, follow from a commitment to "freedom." This is the existential component of which I spoke earlier and which must be present in the deduction of limits from the beginning. Fichte's procedure is to say, "Take this commitment to freedom seriously and I will demonstrate what the world must be like that accommodates this commitment." But my point is that it is a *certain kind* of freedom that Fichte is committed to. The *Wissenschaftslehre* relies on the energy of actual individuals who are committed to regarding their determinations ultimately as the products of a pure *Agilität*. But in order to ascend to the standpoint where this *Agilität* can generate its first product, one has to abstract from all individuality. The point of this abstraction is to reenact that first moment when, according to the myth, humanity fell into conflict with itself. Now we know that we can never grasp this pure activity, this pure identity of the "Subject-Object" as such. Fichte calls it an *X*, an empty place. Philosophy begins with a scandal, a breakdown, or a fall. And this failure and the resulting limitation are supposed to be contained in the pure energy of the "I." But is it not perhaps the other way around, that instead of being the *driving* force that it is proclaimed to be, this "I" is rather *being driven*, that at this highest point of philosophical abstraction the "I" is being *haunted* by the very individual that it meant to leave behind? Perhaps the *Wissenschaftslehre* is only feeding off the energy of individuals who have a problem with themselves as individuals. In that case, the scandal or the embarrassment of the "I" that wants to be pure but finds that it cannot, would be the individual. And so the deductions of the *Wissenschaftslehre*, while accommodating *Fichte's* idea of "freedom," would at the same time hide the embarrassing demands of the *real* individual behind a veil of idealizations that substitute a *fake* "individual," custom-tailored to what the haunted "I" can live with. In other words, instead of accommodating a legitimate requirement of freedom, the results of the *Wissenschaftslehre* would merely accommodate a "self" that has burdened itself with problems that are not necessarily our own. They are not necessarily our own because, apart from *Fichte's* philosophical commitments, we might find nothing to recommend the idea of a fallen humanity.

It is with this question in mind that I want to look at what the doctrine of the *Aufforderung* can accomplish. The difficulty with this issue will be seen to lie in the fact that the transition from the standpoint of *Wissenschaftslehre* to the standpoint of ordinary life can only be made by practical means, through a coercive system of education. By invoking such a system, the *Wissenschaftslehre* would actually create the sort of humanity that would yearn for the salvation it promises. Education, with which Fichte increasingly occupied himself in later years, seals the magic circle that is the *Wissenschaftslehre*.

To get back then to the *Aufforderung:* As we know, in the theoretical part the *Anstoß* is presented as a kind of inner conflict within the "I" that the imagination finally mediates by supplying a sense-content which the "I" must apprehend as if it were simply given. But this is merely a "determination in general," and that in itself, as Fichte emphasizes, is nothing at all. If we remained confined to the theoretical standpoint, we would necessarily become skeptics. In order to have genuine "friction," the "I" must posit itself as "willing" or "doing." But the "I" cannot posit itself as "doing" without the "doing" being the "doing of something." But "doing" as such is in principle infinite. Thus the determination of the "something" cannot come from the "doing" itself. Rather, it must come from outside. Thus we have a natural belief in a real thing existing outside of us. But a problem remains, for whatever determinate thing we identify outside of us as the object of our efficacy, some other thing can always be found that determines it, so that we never reach a definite "something" to which our efficacy could be directed. On these assumptions, the efficacy still lacks a real resistance that, in other words, would make it a "doing of something." This leads Fichte to the conclusion that what must originally come from outside the "I" is not the determination as such, but a "determination to determine itself to a free efficacy." This determination is an *Aufforderung* or a "call." It is a constraint that takes the energy of the subject into account and is contained in that energy. A "call" or a "vocation" is a self-given limit that, however, implies the presence of an "other" and of a shared language. The *Aufforderung* is distinguished from the *Anstoß,* as engaging an "other" in discourse is distinguished from observing "something." Only in the former case is the "other" objectified as subject. But there must be at least two such subjects. Hence Fichte concludes that in recognizing and answering or heeding the "call" the "I" posits itself as "individual."

Fichte says that the human being only becomes human (fulfills its vocation) among human beings. His deductions lead to the conclusion that there must be, as he puts it, a point outside of the "I" at which the thread of consciousness can be attached.[27] The "I" must have a point of origin outside of itself. It must be *given* the concept of itself as a finite rational being by a finite rational being outside of itself which in treating it in terms of that concept displays its recognition that the original "I" is itself a potentially rational being. Another way of putting this idea of an *Aufforderung* is to say that the "I" must be "raised" or educated by another "I" outside of itself to actualize its freedom.[28]

In a novel the novelist invites or calls upon the reader to participate in the action through its characters. The novelist thus counts on the subjectivity of the reader. Albeit indirectly or at a remove, the reader must nonetheless actively engage the characters of the novel and to an extent, at least, respect their limits, as if they were actual persons. She or he must share their language. And this sharing of a language must be such that one encounters resistance in an "other." A character in a novel must be able to rub us the wrong way, for example.

Now the *Wissenschaftslehre* itself begins with an *Aufforderung*. Recall the opening line of the so-called "First Introduction": "Attend to yourself!" We should note Fichte's increasing emphasis that it is only through the *Tathandlung*, that is, only through a certain self-determination, that one gains entrance into this science. And finally, the popular book that arguably concludes the period of the Jena *Wissenschaftslehre* is entitled *Die Bestimmung des Menschen,* which has been aptly translated as *The Vocation of Man*. What Fichte is offering us is, in a sense, a call to determine ourselves as free beings. Now that we have advanced to the "deduction of the individual," we must ask whether we should accept this invitation. What I mean is, whether you and I in the ordinary sense of these words can seriously engage what Fichte offers as "individuals." Certainly Fichte has been using the language of subjectivity all along, and even though at the beginning, in the context of the *Anstoß*, this language sounded strange and abstract, now, in the context of the *Aufforderung*, it starts to sound more familiar. But, of course, with respect to the Fichtean problem, we should not be convinced by words alone, for they might be drawing illegitimately on ordinary usage.

Again, a novel can make us reflect on ourselves and cause us to "determine" ourselves *vis-à-vis* an "other." But then this relationship between the reader and the "other" through the novel is clearly derivative from relationships between real individuals. In Fichte's case, such a relationship is first to be established by means of the *Aufforderung*. We must bear in mind that in terms of Fichte's system it is only through this special impact of the "call" that a reference to *anything* outside of the "I" is first to be established. In accessing this point of reference outside of itself, the "I" itself likewise "goes outside" of itself, as it were. The "I" goes outside of itself *qua* "pure I" and establishes a reference to itself *qua* "empirical I" or individual person. Hence through the "call," according to Fichte, the original "I" establishes a dual reference: to itself, as a rational or potentially rational individual, and to an "other," as a rational individual or "I" with whom the original "I" is confronted. As Fichte had promised to Jacobi in the letter that I cited at the beginning:

> It can be shown through deduction that a finite being can only think itself as a sensible being in a sphere of sensible beings, on a part of which (those that cannot *begin*) it exercises causality, and with the other part of which (on which it confers the concept of a subject) it stands in interaction; and in so far it is called an individual. *(The conditions of individuality are called rights.)*[29]

The casual reader might wonder why in the deduction of the individual Fichte has recourse to "rights" as a way of determining "individuality." But given his position, Fichte has no choice but to try to determine the "individual" as a legally defined person. For as Fichte himself says, a priori, it can only be shown that there must be *one* individual and *one* "call" or "impact through freedom" that raises the "I" to freedom and to rationality.[30] But this really means that in Fichte's system the "individual" remains only a *possibility*, a legal entity.[31]

What we are looking for in Fichte's system, of course, is a determinate constraint, a definite limit to the freedom of the "I." Now Fichte claims that even on the presupposition that there is only *one* individual outside of me and that only *one* "impact through freedom" occurs on me, "the first state, the root of my individuality as it were, is not determined through my freedom, but through my connection with another rational being."[32] But I want to suggest that it is illegitimate to infer the existence of a genuine individual on the basis of only *one* actual "impact through freedom." This move would be illegitimate because such a singular impact is possibly deceptive. For what does it mean to speak of an individual in connection with *one* "encounter"? It seems that, as far as the original "I" is concerned (that is, the "I" that has not yet actualized its potential for rationality, that has not yet established a definite reference, and therefore has not yet been able to posit itself as self-conscious) the *one* "call" would be quite anonymous. And if the "I" establishes its self-identity as a rational individual on the basis of *that*, that is, if it responds to such an anonymous "call" and actually *does* what it is called to do, namely, limit itself, the "I" could be deceiving itself. Of course, if it could be established that the "I" were *intentionally* being deceived, that is, deceived by *someone* in particular, then the "I" would at least have encountered a definite limit, and to that extent would not have been deceived. But the identity of this "someone" is just what is in question. "Someone" as such does not make a definite or identifying reference. But in Fichte's system, the "I," if it is to become conscious of itself and hence conscious of anything at all, has no choice but to act on *one* "call" from *some* one, whose identity it cannot establish.

The "I" must act, for "the practical I is the I of original self-consciousness" and "a rational being perceives itself immediately only in willing,"[33] but it seems that it cannot be guaranteed that it is not acting merely on a blind impulse, taking as an invitation to establish its identity *vis-à-vis* that of an "other" what is perhaps merely a product of its imagination. What I mean to say is that the "friction" might be real, the "invitation" or *Aufforderung* might be there, but it might be one that is induced by the haunted identity of the "I."

I shall make my point with reference to the *Naturrecht.* The "call" is supposed to take us beyond the "I," now considered as "individual." That is to say, by means of the "call" Fichte seeks to account for our ordinary view of the world, according to which there are persons and material objects outside of us. He seeks to deduce such a world on the basis of the necessity of having to assume a legal relationship: "The finite rational being cannot assume other finite rational beings outside of itself without positing itself as standing in a certain relationship with these beings, which is called the legal relationship."[34] Just why Fichte thinks that we must assume such a relationship we shall see in a moment. First we must briefly sketch what this world would look like on Fichte's assumptions.

As a condition of the applicability of the concept of "right," Fichte deduces the human "body," as the sphere within which the "will" is immediately efficacious to the exclusion of any other "will." But the "body" is also needed as the medium through which rational beings interact with one another. For such interaction to be rational, that is, an exchange of concepts, there must be appropriate media through which rational beings can affect one another, while preserving each other's freedom. "Light" and "air" are deduced, and the "body" is further determined as necessarily divided into a "higher" and a "lower" organ, ordinarily known as "mind" and "body."[35]

In order to individuate this "body," such that in addition to being the body of "someone," it can be recognized as an identifiable rational individual, this "body" needs "property," by which Fichte understands "rights to free acts in the sensible world."[36] That is to say, the "body" or "person" individuates itself through the particular free efficacy it claims in the natural world. "Nature" is deduced as an outward sign of a "free efficacy." Significantly, "nature" is granted an existence *only* as an occasion for the human being to exercise its freedom. All natural objects must be marked off as someone's property. Nature that cannot be "tamed" or "domesticated," that is, nature that cannot be submitted to someone's purposes, and thus become property, is to be obliterated. That is to say, nature that does not lend itself to human purposes is something that on Fichtean grounds cannot be dealt with rationally at all, since as such it represents no definite limit. Of course, Fichte thinks that he has established a definite limit in the legally defined "person." But it is significant that the sanctity of this "person," that is, the sanctity of the "body," is in turn only guaranteed by the possession of "property."[37] Just as every "thing" must be the property of "someone," so every "person" must have "property." Every "person" must "declare" what they will do (must have an "occupation"), and this "property" must be "recognized" by every "person." And this mutual "declaration" and "recognition" must be guaranteed by a state power that can use coercive means to keep each person within their chosen sphere. Of course, the presupposition of this theory is that individuals have in fact freely chosen their occupation and have chosen to contract with one another in instituting the state power to guarantee that choice.[38]

Yet, for the original "I" this legally defined "individual" who has freely chosen represents only a possibility. The original "I" cannot directly encounter such an individual or posit itself as such an individual for the simple reason that, in order to be able to act as a legal person, it must first be "raised" or "educated." Yet Fichte claims that the "I" must posit itself as such a legal person. But what would make such a step necessary? I think that the answer to this question lies in the assumption that the "I" is "raised in fear."

Let us consider what, according to Fichte, necessitates the legally defined relationship in the first place. It is the uncertainty whether the "other," having originally treated the "I" as a rational being by means of the "call," will continue in the next moment to treat it in the same way, or whether it will rather treat it as a merely sensible being, as a mere "thing."[39] As Fichte points out, the rational being is only bound by "theoretical consistency" to continue the original treatment. And one cannot adduce an absolute ground why the rational being should be consistent and want the freedom of all rational beings outside of itself.[40] That is to say, the very "free choice" of the individual that gives the rule of law only conditional validity, since such rule is dependent on the free choice of every individual to contract with every other individual, is also what drives individuals into the state of law. The state *outside* the state of law, that is, the "state of nature," is for Fichte a Hobbesian state of a war of all against all.

Now, the significant point about this picture is that it leaves no room for any ordinary understanding of an *Aufforderung,* understood as a process of "raising" or "maturation" or "education." Whereas on any ordinary view of such a process, the potentially rational individual (the child) enters its first relation with innocent trust, the "innocence" of the Fichtean "I" must already be infected with suspicion. Fichte's *Aufforderung* reduces to a singular, anonymous event something that cannot substantiate the claim of an encounter between actual individuals. And so the "I" that seeks refuge in the Fichtean legal person is perhaps, as Jacobi suspected, only a philosopher's invention. It is an "I" that has been "raised" in fear of the "individual." But this "I" is a dangerous invention, for, as I suggested, this "I" is a *system* that can exploit and "rationalize" or "legitimate" the fears of actual individuals.

Notes

This paper was presented at the meeting of the North American Fichte Society, Milwaukee, March 1997.

1. Johann Gottlieb Fichte, quoted from the editorial introduction to the *Grundlage der gesammten Wissenschaftslehre* in *J. G. Fichte—Gesamtausgabe der Bayerischen Akademie der Wissenschaften,* ed. Reinhard Lauth and Hans Jacob (Stuttgart—Bad Cannstatt: Fromman-Holzboog, 1964ff.), I, 2, 231. All subsequent references to Fichte's writings are to this critical edition, hereafter abbreviated as *GA*.

2. Fichte, *GA* I, 2, 231f. See also Fichte's letter to Jacobi of 26 April 1796, where he makes a similar claim with regard to Jacobi's novel *Woldemar: GA* I, 2, pp. 233f.

3. Fichte, "Rükerinnerungen, Antworten, Fragen," *GA* II, 5, pp. 133f.

4. Fichte, "Fragment," *GA* III, 3, pp. 331f.

5. Ibid., p. 333.

6. The *Second Part or Applied Natural Right* appeared in 1797.

7. Fichte, "Rükerinnerungen, Antworten, Fragen," *GA* II, 5, p. 134.

8. In this analysis of our ordinary practice regarding the use of "I" I am following Strawson, "The First Person—and Others," in *Self-Knowledge,* ed. Quassim Cassam (Oxford: Oxford University Press, 1994), p. 210f.

9. Friedrich Heinrich Jacobi, *Allwill* (1792), xvi. Quoted from *F.H. Jacobi: The Main Philosophical Writings and the Novel Allwill,* trans. and ed. with a critico-historical study by George di Giovanni (Kingston and Montréal: McGill-Queen's University Press, 1994), p. 383. All subsequent references to Jacobi are to this edition.

10. Fichte, *Über den Begriff der Wissenschaftslehre, GA* I, 2, p. 147; *Grundlage der gesammten Wissenschaftslehre, GA* I, 2, p. 365.

11. Fichte, *GA* III, 3, p. 332: "What one is caught up in, what one is oneself [*was man selbst ist*], one cannot know. One must go outside of it and transpose oneself to a standpoint outside of it. This going outside of actual life, this standpoint outside of it, is speculation." A few paragraphs earlier Fichte had said that,

in his system, he would not think of going beyond our common thinking; rather, through it, he merely wants to comprehend common thinking and present it exhaustively.

12. Salomon Maimon, *Versuch einer neuen Logik oder Theorie des Denkens. Nebst angehängten Briefen des Philaletes an Aenesidemus,* in *Salomon Maimon: Gesammelte Werke,* ed. Valerio Verra (Hildesheim: Georg Olms Verlagsbuchhandlung, 1964), V, pp. 24, 377f. All subsequent references to Maimon are to this edition, hereafter abbreviated as *GW.*

13. Maimon, *Versuch über die Transcendentalphilosophie, GW* II, p. 202; *Versuch einer neuen Logik oder Theorie des Denkens, GW* V, pp. 24, 377f., 386.

14. Maimon, *Versuch über die Transcendentalphilosophie, GW* II, p. 29 f.

15. Ibid., p. 168.

16. Maimon, *Versuch einer neuen Logik oder Theorie des Denkens, GW* V, pp. 24, 386.

17. Fichte makes several references to a "circle," most prominently perhaps in the *Grundlage, GA* I, 2, 393. For the "magic" that Jacobi sees in Fichte's system, which at one moment threatens so to engulf him that he "almost feels ashamed of being of a different opinion" while at the next so repels him that his "whole inner self . . . shudders in horror and fright," see especially the published letter in *F.H. Jacobi: The Main Philosophical Writings and the Novel Allwill,* pp. 497–536. Appended to that letter we find a passage from *Woldemar,* an appendix which seems designed to show Fichte that he, Jacobi, saw the circle before Fichte made it his own:

> Or was this will perhaps only the immediate consequence of a *personal consciousness attached to universal concepts and images?* Only the *striving for self-preservation* essential to all natures but *in pure rational form?*—It then had no object except its own activity, and the prototype and origin of all virtues was the pure empty form of *being in thought—personality without person or distinction of persons.*
>
> So the whole magic lay in a *deception of concepts and words,* and as this deception is removed, the discomfiting mystery of a mere spinning out of being after being, *just for the sake of being there,* raised its head. (*F.H. Jacobi: The Main Philosophical Writings and the Novel Allwill,* p. 534)

18. Fichte discusses Maimon's skepticism, "imagination," and "deception" in *Grundlage, GA* I, 2, p. 368f., and in *Grundriß des Eigenthümlichen der Wissenschaft-slehre, GA* I, 3, 189ff.

19. For Fichte's characterization of the position of the "dogmatists" in contrast with his own, see especially the two "Introductions" of the *Versuch einer neuen Darstellung der Wissenschaftslehre, GA* I, 4, pp. 183–269.

20. Fichte, *GA* I, 4, p. 242f.

21. See ibid., 2, p. 281.

22. Ibid., 3, p. 253.

23. Fichte, *Grundlage des Naturrechts, GA* I, 3, p. 334.

24. Fichte, Letter to Jacobi, August 1795, *GA* I, 2, p. 232.

25. See especially *GA* I, 4, pp. 242f.

26. Fichte, *Grundlage des Naturrechts, GA* I, 3, p. 332.
27. Ibid., pp. 341f.
28. Ibid., p. 347.
29. Fichte, *GA* I, 2, p. 231.
30. Fichte, *System der Sittenlehre, GA* I, 5, p. 201.
31. See ibid., p. 203.
32. Ibid., p. 202.
33. Fichte, *Grundlage des Naturrechts, GA* I, 3, p. 332.
34. Ibid., p. 349.
35. See ibid., pp. 361–79.
36. Ibid., 4, p. 8.
37. Ibid., 3, p. 422.
38. Ibid., 4, p. 9.
39. Ibid., 3, p. 355f.
40. Ibid., pp. 385f.

The Displacement of Recognition by Coercion in Fichte's *Grundlage des Naturrechts*

Robert R. Williams

I n the following essay I begin with a brief summary account of Fichte's argument in *Grundlage des Naturrechts* (1796), in which right is grounded in intersubjective recognition. I shall then point out a contradiction in Fichte's argument concerning recognition as the foundation of right. I shall contend that, in the first part of the work, Fichte proceeds on the assumption that people recognize and relate to each other in rational-reciprocal ways. This is Fichte's positive account of intersubjectivity, in which reciprocal recognition grounds right and community, and community is both the condition and expression of freedom's actuality in the world. In the latter half of the work, however, Fichte introduces the problem of a loss of trust and confidence that appears to shatter not only his account of intersubjectivity, but also to undermine his claim that right is grounded in mutual recognition. Further, Fichte contends that trust and confidence, once lost, cannot be restored. This impossibility leads him to replace the community based on recognition of freedom with a concept of community as an instrument of coercion. I shall conclude with Hegel's critique of Fichte. Hegel rejects Fichte's subordination of rights and freedom to the question of security, while developing Fichte's positive account of recognition as the intersubjective mediation of freedom that is also the foundation of right.

ROBERT R. WILLIAMS

Beyond Natural Law Theory

Fichte was a student and exponent of both Kant and Rousseau. Like Kant, Fichte accepts Rousseau's concept of the social contract, but argues that social contract rests upon deeper intersubjective ontological conditions, namely, mutual recognition. Recognition is supposed to mediate and effect the transition from the lawless state of nature, where suspicion and mistrust prevail, to a civilized legal-constitutional community founded on co-equality and consent. The social contract theory thus breaks with nature and natural law theory. Rousseau begins the articulation of this break when he conceives freedom and consent as the basis of the state. But Rousseau conceives the state as a social contract derivative from antecedent, independent individuals. Fichte accepts social contract theory, but argues that social contract presupposes that people already recognize each other and have reciprocally-mutually agreed that contract is a proper way of settling disputes and making agreements. In short, social contract presupposes recognition.

Fichte would probably accept Kant's concept of right, namely, "Right is . . . the sum total of those conditions within which the will of one person can be reconciled with the will of another in accordance with a universal law of freedom."[1] Fichte believes that while Kant is correct, he fails to articulate the sum total of such conditions adequately, because he omits an account of intersubjectivity, including intersubjective agreement and reciprocity. Fichte seeks to supplement Kant's analysis of right by supplying the conditions Kant omits, or tacitly presupposes. The result is Fichte's introduction of the idea, not merely of intersubjectivity, but of an intersubjective grounding of both freedom and the concept of right in reciprocal recognition *(gegenseitige Anerkennung)*.

The starting point of Fichte's *Grundlage des Naturrechts* is the concept of right. He tells us that "[t]he concept of right is . . . an original concept of reason."[2] Since Kant had shown that pure reason can be practical, and since the concept of right belongs to practice, the concept of right is a mode of practical action. But what sort of practical action? Right is an action whereby two or more wills can be brought to agreement, or can be reconciled with one another. Right implies an intersubjective grounding of law. Kant never gives an account of such an intersubjective grounding, however. Fichte undertakes this task. He tells us that the significance and intention of the concept of right is that

> the rational being cannot posit itself as self-consciousness, without
> positing itself as an individual, as one among a plurality of rational
> beings, which it assumes outside of itself just as it assumes itself. . . . In

the same undivided action wherein I posit myself, I posit at the same time another free being. Through my power of imagination I describe a sphere for freedom which is shared by many other free beings. I do not ascribe to myself all the freedom that I have posited, because I still affirm other free beings and must ascribe to these a space for their freedom. I limit myself in my appropriation of freedom by the fact that I allow space for other freedom. The concept of right is therefore the concept of a necessary relation of free beings to each other.[3]

Fichte modifies and transforms Kant's transcendental philosophy. Kant had spoken of the moral law as a "fact of reason." This fact of reason shows that Kant modifies his transcendental program in the practical sphere by opening it to experience, namely, the experience of obligation. Fichte proposes to open transcendental philosophy to experience even more than Kant had done. Fichte opens the transcendental to intersubjectivity and introduces the idea of an intersubjective mediation of reason and freedom. His thesis is that right is an action whereby individuals are reconciled with one another; it is a mutual voluntary self-limitation that solicits, and permits another to exercise his freedom. Thus the concept of right intends "a community between free beings as such."[4] It is not necessary that everyone live in such a community. But if such a community is to be, then "every member of the society [must] allow his own external freedom to be limited by his internal freedom, so that all others next to him can also be free in the world. This is the concept of right."[5] For Fichte right involves a reciprocal self-limitation of freedom.

Right is closely linked to freedom in both accounts. Fichte supplies what Kant tacitly presupposes or implies, however, namely, an intersubjective conception of freedom. Fichte inherits Kant's problem of the consciousness of freedom, that is, the problem of access to oneself as an object. Unless there is a self-consciousness of freedom, freedom remains a mere possibility. But Fichte does not, like Kant, invoke the moral law as the *ratio cognoscendi* of freedom, or "fact of reason." Instead, he introduces the thesis that "[t]he finite rational being cannot ascribe to itself an efficacious freedom in the world without ascribing the same freedom to others, and therefore assuming other finite rational beings besides itself."[6]

What lies behind or justifies this assumption? It is the underivable, undeducible encounter with an other, whereby the self is objectified or made available to itself in a unique way that it cannot accomplish by itself. Objectification by the other is irreducible to a cognitive or intellectual act. Nor can the other be cognitively mastered. Where Kant had spoken of the fact of reason, Fichte speaks of the *Anstoß,* an initiative from elsewhere, he discussed in his *Wissenschaftslehre* of 1794. Two years later he moves from the *Anstoß* to the *Aufforderung,* which can be translated both as summons and as solicitation.[7] The other solicits/summons the self to responsible, free self-activity.[8] This solicitation is different from any natural causality that the *Anstoß* may reflect. The solicitation/summons *(Aufforderung)* is conditioned upon the willingness of the summoner to limit his possibilities of freedom in order to make room for the possible response and action of the summoned. This self-limitation creates a space for the exercise of freedom on the part of the summoned.

According to Fichte, the self-consciousness of freedom is not something that individuals can give to themselves. The solicitation/summons presupposes a concept of another freedom. The solicitation/summons requires the independence and irreducibility of the other. The other, who summons the subject to freedom, cannot be reduced to, or derived from, the subject, because the summons precedes and founds the subject's consciousness of her freedom. Fichte treats the *Aufforderung* as a "fact of consciousness" *(Tatsache des Bewusstseins).* A *Tatsache* is a *given;* it cannot be derived from anything other than the fact of its occurrence. It is not an inference or a deduction of something not already present. The sheer fact of being summoned constitutes a phenomenological proof of the existence of the other: "If such a summons to action actually occurs, a rational being besides and outside of the self must be assumed as its cause, and so it is absolutely necessary to posit a rational being outside the subject."[9]

The self discovers itself as free, only as already summoned and obligated by an other. Further, this other must be an intelligent rational being, for only such a being can, by limiting its freedom, summon me to responsible free action. The influence of the other is not a causal one, but an influence compatible with freedom and intelligence. The summons is an action directed toward and solicitous of the rational free agent as an end in itself. Fichte maintains that "The summons to free self-activity is usually called education."[10] But this is not education in any narrow professional sense; it is synonymous with upbringing, cultivation *(Bildung)* that has as its goal the development of independence and rightful freedom. Fichte points out that "the human being (and so all finite beings generally) becomes human only among others. . . . Consequently the concept of humanity is not at all that of a single individual, for the individual per se is inconceivable. Rather the concept of human being is that of a species."[11]

The *Aufforderung* is an asymmetrical relation between the summoner and the summoned. The summons is an action on the part of the summoner toward the summoned in which the former has the initiative and the latter is receptive. Further, she or he may ignore the summons or respond to it. The *Aufforderung* or summons is asymmetrical because the summoner takes priority over the summoned. This priority and apparent absence of reciprocity are not absolute, however, but relative. This relativity and reciprocity become evident in a second move, namely, recognition *(Anerkennung)*. Recognition, if it is to occur, must be two-sided, reciprocal. The response to the summons, as Fichte evidently envisages it, is not fundamentally different from the summoning act itself. Since the summoner limits his freedom out of respect for the other's freedom, so the summoned responds in a similar way; he thus learns to limit his freedom in response to the first's self-limitation. In this way the suspicion, mistrust, and violence of the state of nature are supposed to be overcome.

This second step to reciprocal relation is important because it reveals and discloses the rational concept of right. That is, through reciprocity, the self-limitation and "allowing to be" *(Freilassen)* constitutive of right are no longer essentially tied to or bound up with a single individual or single encounter. Through reciprocity, the self-limitation constitutive of right becomes generalized and extended to every possible future encounter with every rational being. With this extension the concept of right is socially and rationally constituted: "The finite rational being cannot assume other finite rational beings outside of him, without positing itself as standing in a determinate relation to these, which we call the relation of right [*Rechtsverhältniss*]."[12] Reciprocal recognition is thus the genesis of both community and of law. It is the genesis of community, because freedom for Fichte has a dual ground, partly in the self and partly in the other who summons to freedom.[13] Reciprocal recognition is the genesis of law that expresses the mutual equality and reciprocal conditions under which two or more wills are capable of reconciliation and agreement.

The transition from *Aufforderung* to *Anerkennung* is not for Fichte a dubious inference or logical-conceptual transition, but rather is inherent in the empirical moment of Fichte's expanded transcendental program, namely, the interactive experience of summoning and being summoned.[14] In spite of the apparent asymmetry, both summoner and summoned are equiprimordial; neither can be reduced to the other. Both are independent and co-equal; but this mutual independence and co-equality becomes explicit only in reciprocal recognition. *Aufforderung* presupposes a self-limitation of freedom on the part of the summoner, and the one summoned, if she or he responds in a rational manner, should respond in a way that also involves self-limitation, that is, respect for the freedom of the original summoner. This response constitutes mutual recognition of freedom, in which there is an essential logic of reciprocity at work:

> The relation of free beings to each other is a relation of interaction through intelligence and freedom. Neither can recognize the other if both do not reciprocally recognize each other. Neither can treat the other as a free being unless both mutually do so. *This concept* [of mutual reciprocal recognition] *is of the utmost importance for our purposes, because our entire theory of right depends on it.*[15]

The Issue of Coercion

Although Fichte first introduces and lays out the concept of mutual recognition as the foundation and condition of the concept of right, and even asserts that it is foundational for his entire theory of right, it is puzzling that as Fichte actually executes and carries out his *Rechtslehre*, reciprocal recognition is neither the principle nor the criterion, nor even a deep structure of Fichte's account of right.[16] In spite of his bold beginning with mutual recognition as the principle of communal life, it plays no affirmative, constitutive, or substantive role in Fichte's applications and determinate analyses. Instead, recognition is pushed to the margins, undermined by Fichte's procedure and above all by his treatment of the problems of mistrust and coercion.

Kant had noted that the concept of right is not only a question of respect for freedom, but also includes a consideration of the rightful use of coercion.[17] Kant's discussion of coercion is directly linked with the issue of violation of freedom and right. Fichte's discussion of the right of coercion is not so restricted, however. He discusses this right of coercion in three different contexts. The first is the issue of the ontological-social conditions of community, namely, the transition from the state of nature to the civilized community of law. Community comes about as an expression and condition of freedom's affirmative relation to another freedom. As Fichte observes, this goal is attainable only on the condition that the other person has given himself the law of respecting the freedom and fundamental rights *(Urrechte)* of others. But this goal and the means to it are not at all applicable, Fichte believes, to the situation of how to conduct oneself toward someone who has not agreed to or imposed the law of respect for freedom upon himself. Fichte maintains that

> Even though I have subjected myself to this law of respect for freedom
> in general, I am not bound by this law to respect the freedom of this
> particular person. . . . In the first case I act legally under the command
> of the law and thus I have rights. But in the second case, I may attack his
> freedom and personality, and my right is a right of compulsion.[18]

Note that this train of thought contains no reference to an explicit violation of law. It almost appears as if Fichte is arguing for a right of coercion
against those who are outsiders, who refuse to accept the conditions and
law of community, namely, respect for freedom, and so on, or those who
simply refuse to join the community. The community thus has the right to
judge and to exert coercion against "outsiders." Fichte does not explain
why this is so, but one possibility is that in this way the community of rights
secures its own existence. The right of compulsion thus becomes linked
with the problem of security, not of individuals, but of the state itself. To
be sure, once the outsider accepts the fundamental right of freedom to
respect, the right of others to compel him would cease.

A second situation in which Fichte discusses the right of coercion
is a case of criminal action, a criminal trespass. It should be recalled
that Kant had argued that a crime is a hindrance to freedom. Consequently, the punishment of the crime is a hindrance to a hindrance of
freedom. This is the core of Kant's retributive theory of punishment.
Fichte also takes up the issue of an unjust action, but analyzes it within
an intersubjective-social context. In other words, his analysis of crime
assumes that community and therefore the concept of lawfulness are
already established. This means that the criminal has already accepted
the law that he has broken. Consequently, the crime is more than a
hindrance or coercion of freedom. Fichte says that crime "proves that
for the criminal the rule of right is not an unbreakable law, and that
his prior abstention from illegality rests upon other grounds."[19] Perhaps
the criminal followed the law only to gain a tactical advantage for the
commission of his crime.

Third, the issue of criminal action not only raises the issue of punishment as a means of upholding the law, but also raises the issue of
security of the public realm. The security of the public sphere rests upon
respect for law, freedom, and personality. The criminal shows that he
does not respect these, and thus undermines the security of all. No one
can be secure until the attacker subjects himself to the law. This raises the
question whether those whose security is threatened can be assured that
the criminal really has changed his mind and now sincerely subjects himself to the law. Fichte thus raises the issue of trust, that is, the credibility
of conversions, confessions, and promises. The putative change of heart

and mind must be made manifest. But how can this be done if credibility itself is at stake? Fichte takes a very hard line; he *rejects* as evidence of good faith the following: repentance and regret, the promise of future improvement, or assurances of voluntary submission to the law. Fichte rejects all these as insufficient grounds to believe in or trust the person's honesty.[20]

This means that for Fichte, once trust and confidence have been lost, they cannot be restored. In section 8 of the *Naturrechct* Fichte points to the paradox and problem of promising: there is no way to effect or create credibility for the whole of future experience.[21] Assurances and guarantees are insufficient. The problem of promising appears insoluble; consequently another way to social order and security must be found.

Mistrust is an intersubjective impasse. The solicitor or summoner cannot be sure of the other, and thus no reciprocal recognition and no intersubjective grounding or preservation of right seems possible. Since there seems to be no way out of this impasse, that is, no way to reestablish trust, Fichte turns to coercion.[22] When laws are violated, order breaks down; against this background, the contracting parties can no longer trust each other. They must place the issue of security and the power to guarantee it in the hands of a third party, whom they both trust. Fichte does not explain how, if the parties cannot trust each other's guarantees of security for the whole of future experience, they nevertheless can trust a third party. But he is quite clear that this third party can bypass the intersubjective impasse and mistrust between the first two parties, because it has the power to coerce and compel both. The outlines of Fichte's proposed "solution" to the problem of security are becoming clear: coercion by an external third party displaces mutual recognition and trust.

Recognition Displaced by Coercion

In his *Naturrecht,* Fichte seems to have two views concerning recognition and community. The *first* view is that recognition effects the transition from the state of nature to a civilized condition by grounding social contract and rights in intersubjective freedom. The general will is constituted by reciprocal recognition. We can call this the "community of freedom argument from recognition." Here community is not a heteronomous subjection to an alien freedom or power, but an extension and condition of rational freedom. Thus the subjection of individual freedom to community is not a subjection to an alien will of an arbitrary individual, but to a universal rational will, which is the principle *(Begriff)*, of right and freedom. Moreover, what undergoes "subjection" is the wild, lawless freedom of the state of nature. Fichte remarks:

> Hence far from losing my rights by such subjection, I rather first obtain them through it, since only by this subjection [to universal rational will] have I fulfilled the condition under which alone the human being attains rights. Although I am subject, I am subject only to my own will. . . . All that has been taken from me is the concern to carry out my legal claims by my own physical might.[23]

Later he adds, "It is clear that the individual who enters such an agreement receives his freedom although he renounces it, and receives it *because* he renounces it. Through these concepts all contradictions are dissolved and through their realization the rule of right is also achieved."[24] Human beings are not repressed by community, but rather find themselves recognized in a just community. In this view, community is not inherently heteronomous or tyrannical; rather freedom cannot be actual save in community, and community is the expression and realization of rightful freedom.

Fichte's treatment of the question of fundamental human rights *(Urrechte)* is instructive in this regard. According to liberal political theory, fundamental human rights *(Urrechte)* are rights that supposedly somehow inhere in individuals as such, apart from community and its legislation. These rights are those that must be surrendered or limited to form a community. Fichte points out that such a conception of primordial right is a methodological fiction:

> There is no situation or state of primordial rights, and no original rights of man as such. The human being has actual rights only in community with others, just as he can be conceived—as previously indicated—only in community with others. An original right is therefore a mere fiction, but one that is necessary for the sake of scientific analysis.[25]

Methodological individualism is an abstraction from human existence as fundamentally interhuman. The right of individuals is not a given, but must be socially recognized and guaranteed.

Fichte's *second* view is that community is necessary to deal with the issue of mistrust and lack of security because only a community, and not the individual, has the power and resources to uphold and enforce rights. In this second view, community is primarily a condition and instrument of coercion. Consequently, in this second view, recognition seems to be displaced and replaced by coercion.

How are these two views related? I am not sure. Ludwig Siep suggests that in sections 1 through 7 of the *Naturrecht* Fichte proceeds on the assumption that human beings behave rationally, that is, reciprocally recognize each other. This reflects the first strand of Fichte's thought, the recognition argument for community and freedom.

In sections 8 through 16, however, Fichte raises the twin issues of egoism and mistrust, which require a third party, or a coercive community. This is the starting point of the second strand of Fichte's thought. The issue is in part the problem of an evil will that comes to expression in transgression, a breakdown of law and order. A transgression of the mutual recognition already present and expressed in law shows that the transgressor does not regard the rule of law as inviolable, and that his prior apparent respect for law was based on other, perhaps merely tactical grounds.[26] This break with the law and its underlying mutual recognition creates a new situation. Fichte observes that the rational beings that he originally described as reciprocally recognizing each other are, in fact, *uncertain* whether they can depend on their rights being secured against the attacks of others.[27] This posits a situation in which trust, confidence, and security have broken down.

If mutual confidence and trust between persons have been lost, mutual security and legal relations between them likewise become impossible.[28] However, while trust and confidence—in short, the good will—cannot be compelled, behavior and conduct that accords with them can be compelled. Fichte observes that "[e]ach wills and has the right to will that the other party's acts shall always be such as would result if he had a good will. Whether this good will really is the incentive of those acts or not, is a matter of indifference. Each has claim only to the *legality* of the other, not to his *morality*."[29] Fichte thus distinguishes between right and morality, between the legal community (state) and the moral community (church). The crux of the distinction is this: while morality cannot be publicly enforced, legality, that is, legal behavior, can be enforced against individuals who might act otherwise.

Several points deserve notice. First, Fichte's general procedure in the *Naturrecht* is to develop his position by formulating antinomies. Consequently, in pointing out an antinomy in his thought, one is never sure whether this is a criticism or rather an illustration of Fichte's point. To be clear, I intend the following explication of a particular contradiction concerning recognition as a criticism.[30] The antinomy is this: on the one hand, Fichte argues that reciprocal recognition is supposed to remove the uncertainty, mistrust, and loss of confidence that make coercion necessary as, for example, in the state of nature. The *telos* of mutual recognition is a reciprocal *Freilassen,* or liberation. On the other hand, he argues that trust and confidence can break down and have broken down; when this happens, legal relations become impossible without coercive enforcement.

Even more important, Fichte maintains that "once trust and confidence have been lost, they cannot be restored . . ."[31] It is as if the transgression of law returns us to the Hobbesian state of nature. Given the destruction of trust and confidence, the security of both parties is open to chance and contingency.[32] Such contingent security is insufficient for Fichte; the security Fichte wants requires a quasi-mechanical necessity from which no exception is possible.[33] Here the state becomes a mechanism of surveillance to detect and punish crime. Only such a mechanism can provide an ironclad guarantee of security. If I am sure that my misdeeds will be detected and punished, I will be deterred from such actions as irrational, counterproductive. Note that recognition has become superfluous, displaced by surveillance, deterrence, and coercion.

Second, when Fichte asserts that mutual confidence and trust have been lost, he undermines the concept of recognition and turns it into something wholly external. As if mutual trust and confidence did not presuppose or involve mutual recognition! Fichte here betrays how superficial and external his concept of recognition is. Consider the following text:

> The free being by its mere presence in the sensible world, compels every other free being to recognize it as a person. . . . In this way there arises a communal knowledge [*gemeinschaftliche Erkenntniss*] and nothing more. *Each internally recognizes the other, but they remain isolated as before.*[34]

That is, *after* a joint action of mutual recognition—in which there is supposed to be an "internal" mediation of the self to itself by the other— each person remains as isolated as she or he was *before* that act. It is as if the mutual mediation of freedom in reciprocal recognition has no impact and makes no difference to self-identity or the self in relation to itself. This seems to contradict Fichte's original thesis, that recognition is the deep structure of social contract and effects the transition from the state of nature. In the above cited text, however, Fichte does not indicate any changes or transformations that recognition effects in the recognizing selves, no breaking down of barriers, no breaking through limits, no ethical transformation. Yet it was precisely such intersubjective mediation and transformation of freedom and self-identity that mutual recognition was supposed to provide and thereby take care, at least in principle, of such issues as mutual trust and confidence. In Fichte's account of recognition, there is no intersubjective-social universal, no We or community of selves. Despite Fichte's argument that social contract presupposes and is grounded in mutual recognition, community does not arise immanently out of the mutual mediation of freedoms. Rather community remains external, and if it is external then it requires a forcible union. This contradicts Fichte's earlier claim concerning recognition. If the persons who recognize each other remain as isolated after recognition as before, then any intersubjective "mediation" of freedom is merely formal, superficial, and external. If that is so, recognition not only cannot mediate the self's freedom to the self, it cannot ground the social contract either. Mutual recognition constitutes merely an external relation and grounds only an externally related aggregate, what Hegel calls civil society.

The potential threat of negation inherent in otherness that becomes explicit in transgression remains for Fichte an external negation. External negations are supposed to leave subjects unaffected. Fichte's "subjects," however, are affected in spite of their "external" relations. Crime is a betrayal that leads to a loss of public trust and confidence; hence Fichte's subjects are no longer certain of one another. For Fichte, there is no way out of this impasse. Since Fichte believes that the loss of faith and confidence cannot be restored by mutual recognition, he abandons recognition and instead turns to coercion as the means of maintaining social order and security.

Third, it is one thing to argue that faith and confidence have been lost as a result of a criminal action. It is quite another to argue, as Fichte does, that they cannot be restored. How does Fichte know this? His assertion seems to be a priori. If so, he would be claiming to know all possible future experience, which, by his own admission, is impossible. The claim that trust and confidence cannot be restored seems to be a dogmatic one, that rests upon metaphysical premises. Fichte seems to be arguing that mistrust undermines and renders impossible the reconciliation of one will with another, which is central to the idea of right. No reconciliation is possible; but if that is so, then right itself is impossible.

Fourth, to counter the loss of trust, Fichte embraces coercive mechanisms of punishment to enforce conduct and action in conformity to law. He thereby reveals the irrelevance of recognition to his system of rights. Mutual recognition, which was supposed to be the foundation of right, becomes displaced by coercion. Fichte introduces coercion as a permanent feature of the quasi-mechanical community of coercion. To be sure, this occurs in Fichte's discussion of punishment. Punishment is a quasi-mechanical contrivance that is supposed to make the lawless will annihilate or cancel itself. This bears certain similarities to Kant's conception of retributive punishment. Fichte shows that punishment is supposed to be a contrivance that coerces coercion and thus nullifies it. Since punishment is supposed to be a hindrance of a hindrance of freedom, the threat of punishment is supposed to keep the lawless will within limits. Fichte draws the conclusion that the mechanism of punishment, rendered universal and certain, would make ethics and the good will superfluous: "The good will would be rendered superfluous for the external realization of right, since the bad will would be forced by its very badness to effect the same end."[35] The good will has become superfluous, at least as far as right is concerned. Ethics and politics thus become separated.

From this consideration of community as a means and condition of justice, it is but a short step to Fichte's subsequent elaboration on the supervisory, policing function of public authority that carries the coercion strand of his thought to its extreme conclusion. Fichte haplessly confirms Foucault's thesis concerning the militaristic model of the modern state and its disciplinary apparatus.[36] Fichte is explicit about the surveillance of the population that compels persons to become visible, and this gives a sinister twist to the concept of recognition:

> The chief principle of a well-regulated police is necessarily the following: that each citizen shall be recognized as this or that person at all times and places when it may be necessary. No one must remain unknown to the police [public authority]. This can be attained only in the following manner: each one must always carry a pass with him, signed by his immediate government official, in which his person is accurately described. There must be no exceptions to this rule.[37]

Fichte embraces surveillance as a deterrent to crime:

> The source of all evil in our states as presently constituted is disorder. . . . In a state such as we have described, each citizen has a definite position, and the police know pretty well where each citizen is, and what he does at every hour of the day. . . . By means of his pass each citizen can be identified at a glance. Crime is something very unusual in such a state.[38]

Conclusion: Hegel's Criticism of Fichte

To conclude, I should like to review briefly Hegel's criticisms of Fichte, because I believe that Hegel was both significantly influenced by Fichte

ROBERT R. WILLIAMS

and that his criticisms are on target. Hegel's *Philosophy of Right* carries out a debate with Fichte's *Grundlage des Naturrechts*. I contend that Hegel develops Fichte's argument for recognition as the intersubjective grounding of community and law in his own *Philosophy of Spirit* and *Rechtsphilosophie*, while rejecting Fichte's embrace of coercion and his version of a police state.[39] Hegel advances a metaphysical critique and a phenomenological-political critique of Fichte. The metaphysical critique is found in the *Differenzschrift;* and the phenomenological-political critique is found in his essay on *Natural Law*.

In the *Differenzschrift,* he points out the basic dualisms in Fichte's system: the ego and nonego have no positive relation, but merely the negative character of being other.[40] Because otherness is seen primarily as negative by Fichte, freedom is also understood as negative; it is not the suspension of opposition, but rather fixed in opposition to its other, the *Anstoß*, etc. Because the nonego is understood only negatively as being-other than ego, freedom is likewise fixed and understood in primarily negative terms.[41] On Fichte's premises, Hegel asks, "What union is possible, though, once absolute opposites are presupposed? Strictly speaking, none at all, obviously."[42] Given such premises, community can only be a limit to freedom. On the other hand, since Fichte sets for himself the task of uniting opposites, what sort of union is possible when, as Fichte contends, individuals remain external to each other in their relationships? Hegel believes that on Fichte's assumptions any "union is forcible. The one subjugates the other. The one rules, the other is subservient."[43] Thus ego and nonego are supposed to be related reciprocally, but in fact they never constitute a whole or community; instead, the one dominates and the other is dominated and goes into servitude.[44] Since Fichte conceives recognition in terms of such fundamental oppositions, it is no surprise that he sanctions coercion. Forcible union and coercion are built into his fundamental metaphysical outlook.

Fichte's account of mutual recognition subverts itself because individuals remain external to each other in spite of their relationship. Thus community is either impossible, or not genuine, exhibiting a system of forcible unions that both conceal and sanction coercion and oppression. Once separation has been made basic, there is no longer any possibility of mutual relation and connection. "Rather, every connection is one of dominating and being dominated."[45]

In his essay on *Natural Law*, Hegel diagnoses Fichte's declaration that once mutual trust and confidence are lost they cannot be restored as a popular expression and symptom of the fundamental metaphysical dualism at the heart of his system.[46] On this assumption only a formal and external union is possible; moreover, relation as such is identified negatively as inherent compulsion.

> In this way the external character of oneness is utterly fixed and posited as something absolute and inherently necessary; and *thereby the inner life, the rebuilding of lost confidence and trust, the union of universal and individual freedom, and ethical life itself, are made impossible. . . .* It really is an attempt at a consistent system that would have no need of the religion and ethics that are foreign to it.[47]

Here Hegel diagnoses the fundamental contradiction in Fichte's account: The recognition argument is supposed to lead to ethical life and community; but the coercion argument and its underlying premises of metaphysical dualism render irrelevant or impossible the rebuilding of lost confidence and trust. The coercion argument undermines recognition and the ethical life that recognition is supposed to generate. While coercion is undoubtedly important to uphold right and community, so that these may prevail over potential usurpations, it does not exhaust what community is, much less clarify why community is more than an instrument or tool. Hegel complains that Fichte considers community not as an end in itself, or as something good in itself, but merely as a condition of law and justice.[48] For Hegel, community (that is, the state) is necessary for the realization of freedom in the world. In contrast to Fichte's assertion that once faith and confidence have been lost they cannot be restored, Hegel believes that the wounds of spirit can heal. This somewhat poetic way of putting the issue means that the future is not fated to be coercion all the way down, but that reconciliation and liberation remain possible. Hegel believes that trust and confidence might be restored. Hegel's analyses of forgiveness are important here.[49]

From the above fundamental considerations, Hegel points out further problems in Fichte's account. First, Fichte's concepts of recognition and state are superficial. They represent and are constituted by external relations. Fichte's state is what Hegel calls civil society, the external state or *Notstaat.*

Hegel dismisses Fichte's "mania" for security. Although Hegel does not deny the importance of public security or public authority or of punishing crime, he parts company with Fichte over the latter's approval of surveillance and other measures of population control:

> Fichte's state is centered on the police, to whom it seeks to accord a particularly wide scope, but it is also a state based on need. According

to Fichte, no persons can go out without having their identity papers on them, and he deems this very important to prevent crimes. But such a state becomes a world of galley slaves, where each is supposed to keep his fellow under constant supervision.[50]

This world of galley slaves is precisely what Hegel wants to avoid in his conception of ethical life. While Hegel reluctantly sanctions some supervision by public authority, he is clear about its meaning and purpose: "This police supervision must go no further than is necessary. . . . *The purpose of what is hidden is that public life should be free.*"[51]

Nevertheless, in spite of his criticisms, Hegel does not simply reject Fichte. Rather he appropriates and develops Fichte's concept of recognition and claim that mutual recognition is the foundation of right. The irony is that Hegel upholds Fichte against Fichte! That is, Hegel upholds and defends Fichte's recognition argument for community against Fichte's coercion argument for community that displaces recognition. Hegel's *Philosophy of Right* is in part a further, more consistent and complete development of Fichte's argument that recognition is the basis of community and right. In this strand of his thought, Fichte does not think of community as inherently a tyranny, much less simply an instrument of coercion. Rather, his point is exactly the opposite, namely, that a community of mutual recognition, in which arbitrary lawless freedom is renounced and exchanged for recognized, civil, lawful freedom, is the condition under which genuine freedom and right are realized. Hegel agrees; right is recognition of freedom's existence. Thus recognition for Hegel becomes important to his attempt to renew and reformulate the public sphere of life; recognition underlies not only the institution of ownership *(Eigentum)*, but also Hegel's account of abstract right, morality, ethical life, and politics.[52] Hegel's concept of ethical life transforms and surpasses Fichte's unsatisfactory concept of intersubjectivity and community.

Notes

1. Kant, *Metaphysics of Morals,* in *Kant: Political Writings,* trans. H. Nisbet (Cambridge: Cambridge University Press, 1970), p. 133. *Metaphysics of Morals* appeared in 1798, two years *after* Fichte's *Grundlage des Naturrecht* (1796). Thus, if there is any influence, it could be argued that Fichte influenced Kant. I cite Kant not to suggest any influence of Kant on Fichte in this case, but because his position is better known than Fichte's.

2. Fichte, *Grundlage des Naturrecht, Fichtes Werke,* ed. I. H. Fichte (Berlin: Walter de Gruyter, 1971), vol. III, p. 8. The de Gruyter edition is a reprint of Johann Gottlieb Fichte's *Sämmtliche Werke,* edited by von I. H. Fichte and published in eight volumes by Viet and Co., Berlin, between 1845 and 1846. *Grundlage des Naturrecht* is hereafter abbreviated as *GNR.* All translations are my own.

3. *GNR,* p. 8.

4. Ibid., p. 9.

5. Ibid.

6. Ibid., p. 30.

7. Ibid., pp. 33–36.

8. Ibid., p. 36.

9. Ibid., p. 39.

10. Ibid.

11. Ibid.

12. Ibid., p. 41.

13. See also my fuller treatment of this issue in *Hegel's Ethics of Recognition* (Berkeley: University of California Press, 1998), chapters 2 and 3.

14. I follow Ludwig Siep in this interpretation. (Cf. L. Siep, *Praktische Philosophie im deutschen Idealismus* [Frankfurt: Suhrkamp, 1992], pp. 41–64.) Fichte's account of recognition, in other words, is an incipient phenomenology of intersubjectivity and freedom. Jean Hyppolite also interprets Fichte in this way, and as an important precursor of Hegel's *Phenomenology.* (See Jean Hyppolite, *Genesis and Structure of Hegel's Phenomenology of Spirit,* trans. Samuel Chernick and John Heckman [Evanston, Ill.: Northwestern University Press, 1974].)

15. *GNR,* p. 44. My italics.

16. See Ludwig Siep, *Anerkennung als Prinzip der praktische Philosophie* (Freiburg: Alber Verlag, 1979).

17. Kant, *Metaphysics of Morals,* p. 134.

18. *GNR,* p. 95.

19. Ibid., p. 97.

20. Ibid., p. 98.

21. Ibid.

22. Ibid., p. 100.

23. Ibid., p. 104; J. R. Fichte, *The Science of Rights,* trans. A. E. Kroeger (London: Trübner, 1889), p. 152 (hereafter *SR*).

24. *GNR,* pp. 109–10; *SR,* p. 159.

25. *GNR,* section 9, p. 112.

26. Ibid., p. 97. See also Siep, *Praktische Philosophie,* p. 58.

27. *GNR,* p. 137; *SR,* p. 189.

28. *GNR,* p. 139; *SR,* p. 192.

29. *GNR,* p. 139; *SR,* p. 192.

30. The antinomy occurs in the context of Fichte's discussion of punishment and legal coercion *(Zwangsrecht).* In section 13, Fichte introduces the principle of coercion; in general, his view is like that of Kant and Hegel, namely, that coercion is justified not as an end itself, but only as a response to a prior illegitimate coercion.

31. *GNR,* pp. 139–40.
32. *GNR,* p. 137; *SR,* p. 189.
33. *GNR,* pp. 137–38; *SR,* pp. 189–90.
34. *GNR,* pp. 85–86; *SR,* p. 126. My italics.
35. *GNR,* p. 142; *SR,* p. 195. Elsewhere he explains the point thus:

[T]o the extent that the state is related to the evil will, to the extent that it is a
compulsory power, then its final aim is undoubtedly to make itself superfluous,
i.e., to make all compulsion unnecessary. This is an aim which can be achieved
even if good will and the confidence in it do not become universal. For if everyone
knows on the basis of long experience that every act of injustice will surely bring
misfortune and that every crime will surely be discovered and punished, then one
may expect that from prudence alone they will not exert themselves in vain, that
they will not willfully and knowingly bring harm upon themselves. (Fichte, *Lectures
on the Vocation of the Scholar,* in *EPW,* p. 157 n.)

36. Michel Foucault, *Discipline and Punish,* trans. Alan Sheridan (New York:
Random House Vintage, 1979).
37. *GNR,* p. 295; *SR,* p. 378.
38. *GNR,* p. 302; *SR,* p. 386.
39. See my *Hegel's Ethics of Recognition,* chapters 12 and 13.
40. *The Difference between Fichte's and Schelling's System of Philosophy,* trans. H. S.
Harris and W. Cerf (Albany: SUNY Press, 1977), p. 128.
41. Ibid., p. 133.
42. Ibid., p. 126.
43. Ibid., p. 115.
44. Ibid., p. 138.
45. Ibid., p. 144.
46. *G. W. F. Hegel: Natural Law,* trans. T. M. Knox (Philadelphia: University
of Pennsylvania Press, 1975). My italics.
47. Ibid., p. 85. My italics.
48. Ibid., p. 83ff.
49. See my *Recognition: Fichte and Hegel on the Other* (Albany: SUNY Press,
1992).
50. Hegel, *Lectures on Natural Right and Political Science,* trans. J. M. Stewart
and P. C. Hodgson (Berkeley: University of California Press, 1995), p. 212. My
italics.
51. Ibid. My italics.
52. In my work *Hegel's Ethics of Recognition,* I offer a development of this
claim.

The "Subtle Matter" of Intersubjectivity in the *Grundlage des Naturrechts*

F. Scott Scribner

W hy would anyone pay heed to Fichte's references to the out-moded quasi-science of "subtle matter" in the context of a work that otherwise represents Fichte's most important contribution to social and political theory—his transcendental deduction of the social in the *Grundlage des Naturrechts* (1796)?[1] Yet what if during Fichte's day the idea of "subtle matter" was itself a significant and perhaps rival account of social interaction, an account ultimately so important to Fichte that Xavier Léon would later describe it as essential to his conception of the self in the later *Wissenschaftslehre*?[2] If what broadly distinguishes Fichte's philosophy in the later *Wissenschaftslehre* from earlier descriptions is its questioning of the limits of transcendental philosophy, and if, according to Léon, the essence of this later work was gleaned from the dynamics of subtle matter, then what I am suggesting is that the term "subtle matter" cannot be written off easily as a mere anomaly in the *GNR*, but in fact signaled Fichte's own early awareness of the limit of a transcendental account of the social. Specifically, it is my contention that Fichte's turn to the idea of "subtle matter" was the effect of a deeper explanatory crisis within the developing argument for a transcendentally grounded intersubjectivity within the *GNR*.

To my knowledge this essay represents the first attempt to explain the use and significance of the term "subtle matter" for Fichte's account of intersubjectivity with the *GNR*.[3] It centers on articulating Fichte's particular use of the term "subtle matter" through a detailed exposition of a rather short section in the *GNR:* "The Deduction of the Applicability of the Concept of Right" *(Deduktion der Anwendbarkeit des Rechtsbegriffs)*. Our explanation of Fichte's use of the term, however, cannot be divorced from the historical horizon from which Fichte appropriates it. An articulation of the meaning of subtle matter for Fichte's account of social interaction within the *GNR*, then, would require a brief overview of the eighteenth- and nineteenth-century description of subtle matter as a potential rival theory to Fichte's own account of the social (which, I argue, Fichte ultimately incorporates into his own work).

This essay is divided into five sections. The first section attempts to outline the scientific and social meaning of "subtle matter" that was contemporary with Fichte's own work. This historical overview functions as a prolegomena to the second section, which shows how the notion of subtle matter functions as the cornerstone and support to Fichte's concept of intersubjective recognition. In the third and fourth sections, it is suggested that the role of subtle matter in recognition inaugurates a communicative paradigm that not only seems to lend support to the transcendental account, but might also represent a rival explanatory paradigm. Finally, in the fifth section, by reference to Fichte's later work in the *Tagebuch über den animalischen Magentismus* (1813), the new communicative paradigm of subtle matter is shown to be a dynamic of imitation that profoundly threatens not only Fichte's transcendental account in the *GNR*, but perhaps also his entire later metaphysics of the image *(das Bild)*.

1

The notion of "subtle matter" arose as a key term in the long history of the search for a material imponderable. During the eighteenth century, this term, laden with the universality of an *ur*-matter, ultimately provoked a historical development in which the fundamental impetus in the quest for subtle matter changed from an implicitly scientific to an openly political concern.[4] The postulation of an invisible medium for explaining observable phenomena, for instance, also known as subtle or ethereal fluid, was extremely widespread among natural philosophers throughout the 1770s.[5] Even Kant, in the *Opus Postumum*, writes (only later to delete it) that in regard to what he calls "original fluid," "physics must adopt hypothetical concepts whose reality is uncertain and which, with regard to their possibility, require a deduction from a priori principles."[6] In short, for Kant, one could justly infer invisible, subtle fluids. The postulation of a universal invisible fluid, however, soon exceeded its explanatory role as *ur-element* of obscure causal phenomena (like electricity, heat, and magnetism), and further evolved through certain theorists to explain the social phenomena of human interaction and illness.

A genealogy of psychoanalysis or dynamic psychiatry typically finds its modern scientific origin in the figure of Anton Mesmer, because although the notion of a universal or subtle matter clearly predates him, it was Mesmer who first theorized the power of subtle matter as a social medium. It was in the year 1774 that Mesmer first came to the realization that *if* the entire world were imbued with a magnetic fluid that could go out of balance and cause illness within individuals, then a redirection and harmonization of this subtle matter would certainly effect a cure. With this theory, magnetic or dynamic psychology was born. While Mesmer's essentially physiological explanation of subtle fluid demanded a material redirection of this fluid with magnets and so on, his insistence on the primacy for cure of rapport, or an affective harmony, between doctor and patient clearly led his followers to more psychological hypotheses, as we will see momentarily with Puysegur. Nonetheless, whether individuals were physically linked to enhance the flow of fluid, or simply bound by the gaze of the doctor-patient relation, the idea of a rapport, or an affective tie between individuals, was at least of enough political significance to be perceived as a potential social threat. In France, a secret report from a commission appointed by Louis XVI concluded that "magnetic rapport cannot but be a threat to morality."[7] Further, during the French Revolution, Mesmer's notion of subtle matter helped spawn several radical political sects that embraced the ubiquity of subtle matter as their fundamental tenet.[8] While initially mesmerism had a vast public audience only in France, the theory began to make its way into Germany in 1786 through Mesmer's disciple Puysegur. In brief, Puysegur acknowledged the existence of Mesmer's subtle fluid, but began to emphasize a more psychological approach in which the actual agent of cure was not rooted in a material magnetism but in the magnetizer's will, and thus in the "rapport" itself.[9] Besides Puysegur's articulation of magnetism, the open embrace of mesmerism by the German university, Romanticists, and philosophers of nature led to a particular German appropriation of this theory. Fichte was no exception.

While Fichte in the *Tagebuch über den animalischen Magnetismus* describes his personal witness to magnetic rapport in 1813, his detailed mastery of the literature in this work suggests that he was concerned with the phenomenon at a much earlier date. In fact, Fichte's deep concern in the 1790s with the French Revolution and French affairs, I believe, would have made it virtually impossible for him to have remained ignorant of the social mania of mesmerism that gripped France. Although Fichte was no doubt aware of the interpretations of ethereal fluid by natural philosophers (like Kant), even if Fichte was unaware of Mesmer's theory of subtle fluid or matter at the time he composed the *GNR*—which seems unlikely—two questions nonetheless remain: What did Fichte mean to articulate through this term "subtle matter"? And why did he include it in what is perhaps his most important work on social and political theory?

2

While Fichte's references to "subtle matter" (and the theory of "affection" it entails) in the fifth theorem in "The Deduction of the Applicability of the Concept of Right" would seem to function as an explanatory support for his transcendental deduction of the social, one nevertheless wonders if the "support" subtle matter offers doesn't in fact signal certain fundamental limitations of the transcendental method itself. If, as we suggested in the first section, "subtle matter" stood as a rival account of social interaction, we must ask what motivation first led Fichte to incorporate this notion within his transcendental deduction of the social. Would the description of subtle matter function to buttress his transcendental account? Or, looking ahead to his work in the *Tagebuch über den animalischen Magnetismus* (1813), might not Fichte's references foreshadow an implicit capitulation to another explanatory paradigm?

Such questions must begin with the perennial problem that haunts not only Fichte's transcendental deduction of intersubjectively constituted right, but the entire project of transcendental philosophy from Descartes to Husserl—namely, the problem of solipsism.[10] Thus, when Fichte asserts that the relation of right *(Rechtsverhaltnis)* is deduced by acknowledging that "each limits his own freedom through the possibility of the freedom of the other,"[11] one's relation to the other nonetheless still exists as a difficult problem. In *Über die Bestimmung des Gelehrten*, Fichte clearly articulates the problem. He writes, "[H]ow does the human being come to assume or recognize that there are rational beings similar to it outside of it, since such beings are not at all immediately or directly given or present in its pure self-consciousness . . . how do we come to such a presupposition?"[12] According to Fichte, of course, we should be able to arrive at such a presupposition through a transcendental deduction. Admittedly, Fichte's method would seem to avoid many of the glaring problems of solipsism that, for example, Descartes would encounter, insofar as "the other" for Fichte is posited as a transcendental condition of the very possibility of consciousness. Nevertheless, the fact that the other is transcendentally deduced as a necessary condition for the possibility of consciousness does not in itself alleviate the specter of solipsism. To begin with, it is not enough to explain *that* the other must exist as a condition of self-consciousness; one must further attempt to explain *how* this relation is constituted. Fichte recognizes this. He will attempt to avoid the problem of solipsism by buttressing the transcendental account of a merely posited other through an articulation of our dynamic relation to the other via the terminology of *Aufforderung* (summons) and *Anerkennung* (recognition).

This terminology, however, which was intended to further the aims of the transcendental project, will, I suggest, factually produce rather unintended results. As we will see, since Fichte is ultimately only able to give a satisfactory explanation of the dynamic of *Aufforderung* and *Anerkennung* through reference to the dynamic of subtle matter, this terminology, which at the outset was to fortify the transcendental project against the charges of solipsism, appears, in fact, to be grounded in a rival paradigm of social interaction. Thus, I will argue that the ideas of *Aufforderung* and *Anerkennung* do not in fact fortify the transcendental claims, but, by reference to subtle matter, actually function to undermine the transcendental spirit of Fichte's project.

We begin to offer support for this claim through an analysis of this terminology. According to Fichte, there is an anonymous call. The call that summons me to freedom and responsibility I nonetheless recognize as emanating from another rational being, and as such it comes to the consciousness of both the summoner and myself, as summoned. But what, then, is the nature of this call or summons, and how does one come to recognition? This is a question of utmost importance for Fichte, which, however, I will argue, he is not altogether successful in answering. On the one hand, the summons is a given, like the transcendental fact of the *Anstoß* in the WL of 1794; self-consciousness would be unthinkable without it.[13] Simply, there is a call. On the other hand, the question of recognition complicates the simplicity of the appeal to the "givenness" of this transcendental fact.

If the summons is to be a summons at all, it must at least have the capacity to be recognized: to be recognized as a form of communication emanating from another rational being. Of course, one may either respond, that is, recognize, it as an intelligible communication or refuse, that is, fail that recognition.[14] While the reciprocal communicative influence described through the terminology of the "summons" and "recognition" suggests that the transcendental deduction of the other is not enough, a further difficulty arises in this new discourse. Namely, how is recognition possible? How does one, prior to one's own self-consciousness, come to recognize a call or summons as issuing from another rational being in distinction from, say, some other noise, like the barking of a dog? Fichte's response is extremely complex. What he begins to develop through the notion of subtle matter is a theory of intellectual influence by which intelligible beings can influence one another by virtue of their own higher meaning *(hohere Sinn)*.

3

With the idea of subtle matter Fichte will offer a theory of intellectual influence that appears to operate outside the paradigm of rational communication. Subtle matter will function as the key medium in the communicative exchange known as recognition. Recognition is possible for Fichte because the human figure *(Gestalt)*, or perhaps even the human face or look *(Gesicht)* compels one to recognition by virtue of its very being. Fichte explains:

> A human body must, in its quietude, without any act, produce an influence: subtle matter must here in this influence be posited, that subtle matter becomes modified through the purely quiet figure [*bloss ruhende Gestalt*], and consequently this contained modification modifies the higher meaning/sense [*Sinn*] of a possible other rational being.[15]

The human body or figure, through its very existence, then, has the power of conveying a higher meaning or influence to another rational being. Yet Fichte will not stop with the explanation that recognition takes place by virtue of the human form. He further details how the human figure or face produces an intellectual influence through the medium of subtle matter that would compel us to recognition.

As Fichte's description of influence, however, relies more and more on a material and quasi-material paradigm exemplified in the notion of "subtle matter," so too must the communicative form come to take part in the more bodily conditioned communication of affection that distances itself from the ideals of a strict transcendental inquiry. Thus while the summons that made recognition possible is said *not* to operate like the principle of material causality (cause/effect),[16] it is nonetheless curiously described not simply as an influence, but as a material with the capacity of influence. The notion of influence would seem to require some sort of material cause, some matter, no matter how subtle. Fichte writes: "The summons is the *material of influence* [*die Materie der Wirkungs*] and a free influence [*freie Wirksamkeit*] of rational beings."[17] It is my contention, then, that read in the context of the problem of "subtle matter," Fichte's description of the summons in terms of a "material influence" is no mere turn of phrase, but the result of his extreme difficulty of trying to describe a form of intersubjective influence that exhibits the conflicting properties of something at the limits of ideal and material worlds. Fichte needs to describe an idea of influence that is free from the necessities of causality, and thus preserves a spiritual and rational autonomy, despite its emergence from a material paradigm.

It is not a surprise then that Fichte begins to develop the idea of subtle matter in sections four, five, and six in "The Deduction of the Applicability of the Concept of Right," in which he makes the transition from an intellectual to a bodily account of intersubjective influence. Here, in his explanation of the role of the body in intersubjectivity, he intends to further develop this idea of a noncausal, or quasi-material influence. Like the first *Theorem,* which posited the self as free, followed by the second, which insisted on the role of the other,[18] the fourth and fifth *Theorems* will mirror this same movement, except in the material register of the body.[19] In this section Fichte is making the broader claim that the body itself is a necessary condition for the consciousness of right *(Rechtsbewusstsein)*. In brief, he is arguing that the intuition of one's own freedom by the pure will is possible only through the body, and that the inference of this freedom within another is the fundamental moment of the consciousness of right. Yet if, as Fichte argues in the *WL nova methodo,* the body is the representation of freedom in the sensible world,[20] is the other's freedom merely transcendentally deduced, or does intersubjective recognition not also involve something on the order of a quasi-material influence, or affection? After all, why speak of bodies at all?

Fichte states in the fourth *Theorem,* a "rational being cannot posit itself as an effective individual without ascribing to itself a material body through which it determines itself."[21] In other words, the body, as a material manifestation of the pure will, has causal force in the world. The body is the will as act.[22] Here, Fichte seems to affirm a double-aspect monism in which body and will are different manifestations of the same obscure power. Yet even Fichte's insistence that "my body and I—my mind and I . . . mean the same thing"[23] does not seem to move us beyond the solipsism in which, like Descartes, and even the Cartesianism of Husserl, we simply infer or project our own properties upon another.[24] Unless, of course, as any double-aspect monism would require, intellectual communication can also be described in the register of bodily communication—that is, as affection.

The problem facing Fichte, like Kant before him, was how an individual, subject to material influence, could be conceived at the same time as free. While Kant was able to posit a noumenal realm to resolve this difficulty, Fichte's inclination toward a dual-aspect monism makes his response more complex. Such a problem forces Fichte to reconfigure the traditional psyche/soma problem through a new vocabulary of higher *(hohere)* and lower *(niedere)* organs, which (as we will see) find efficacy in subtle and gross matter, respectively. In one sense Fichte has already solved this dilemma, insofar as the subject understands that self limitation is the transcendental condition of freedom, and therefore freely chooses to limit himself; thus although determined, as self determined, he remains free. Yet in another sense the intimacy of "body" and "will" allow the problem of material determination to remain a threat to Fichte. Like Descartes's rather improbable solution to the mind/body problem in the pineal gland, Fichte needs to address how nonverbal or noncognitive communication would be possible between two beings across the divide of the material world. While we have already begun to outline this schism, Fichte's articulation of a subtle and gross matter, I believe, is the culmination of his attempt to work out this rather complex problem within the *GNR*.

4

The theory of subtle matter will offer Fichte a means of explaining communication between material and intellectual worlds, and will thus allow the dynamic of intersubjective recognition to escape the problem of solipsism, by conceiving recognition on the order of an "affective" rapport. Yet while we have noted that this communicative rapport between rational beings is not one of rational discourse, we have yet to explain just how this communication takes place. In this section we will begin to articulate Fichte's description of this unique form of communication. As we will see, Fichte will describe this communication across the spiritual/material divide through a process of imitation or copying *(Nachbildung, Nachahmung)*, made possible by the medium of subtle matter.

We begin explaining Fichte's account of this obscure form of communication, in the fifth *Theorem*, by distinguishing subtle matter from its gross counterpart. Since Fichte conceives gross matter—quite like the traditional philosophical notion of substance—to operate and influence through a material causality, his description is rather clear and to the point. He writes: "As the very same condition I must posit outside of myself a viscous durable material capable of resisting the free movement of my body, and so the sense world [*Sinnenwelt*] is further determined through the further determination of my body."[25] At the level of material casualty, body and world reciprocally determine and influence one another. What remains at issue, however, is the rather difficult and obscure term of subtle matter. The ground of influence in the deduction of right is the inference of another rational being. The mere material impact of another body, we suggested, is not enough: there must be a higher meaning or sense *(Sinn)*—like that conveyed in the *Aufforderung*. And it is with this assumption of a higher meaning that the body of the subject is truly modified by the other.[26] This is the moment of recognition in which a higher meaning is conveyed from one human being to another; it is a communicative encounter, the higher meaning of which constitutes recognition as such, and therefore allows us to differentiate it, for instance, from an encounter with anther form of plant, animal, or mineral. Without this higher meaning a person could not be grasped as human, and in turn, as free. Fichte affirms:

> In the described influence the subject's organ [the body] becomes actually modified through the person outside of him. Now this happened neither through an immediate bodily touch of this person, nor as conveyed by viscous (gross) matter; since then . . . the subject would not then perceive itself as free.[27]

It is clear then that freedom can be neither assumed nor inferred through a material influence conveyed by what we have been calling gross matter. Communication does not take place at the level of material causality. What Fichte has prepared us for is a type of influence that is not merely part of the substantial causal chain, but a peculiar type of matter that arises from the meaningful body in its totality—a subtle matter.

This influence by which the material passivity of one being conveys a higher, that is, intellectual, meaning to another, proceeds through the dynamic of imitation. And subtle matter will form the key medium for this fundamental moment of recognition. For Fichte, recognition between spiritual beings is possible through an essential mode of relating between the higher and lower organs by means of a process of copying or imitating *(Nachbildung)* in which the higher organ copies the determined movement *(bestimmte Bewegung)* of the lower.[28] It is this mirroring between spiritual and material worlds that makes communication possible. It is a communication, or order of affection, that takes place through the pure will.[29] This structure of influence, however, applies not only to higher and lower organs in the self same being; it also begins to explain, as we will see, how intersubjective recognition would function on the order of subtle matter, in other words, how the image of the other produces a recognition of right.

As we noted earlier, certainly other rational beings can be deduced, but how does one know when she or he has encountered one? The answer lies here, in the notion of imitating, in which one rational being is able to able to communicate a recognition of the other through a mimetically grounded rapport, or in Fichte's abstract language: the subtle matter of the higher organ expresses its capacity to imitate the determined movement of the lower. Fichte explains:

> [I]n that case the higher organ is modified through a determined form of the more subtle matter, and held; and so if the person is to perceive, he must suppress the movement of the lower organ, insofar as it relates itself to that part of the higher. But nonetheless even though innerly it must imitate, in the same organ the determined movement which it would have to make if it itself were to generate the determined given modification of the higher organ.[30]

The higher organ, the intellectual aspect, makes a copy of the lower, the material aspect; and this copying is made possible through the medium of subtle matter. And it is by restraining the lower organs that subtle matter receives an impression and makes an inner copying of the higher organs possible. It is worth noting that there is a striking affinity between this description of restraint and that present in the dynamic of the *Aufforderung*. Communication in each instance is the effect of restraint. Here there is a restraint of the lower organs *vis-à-vis* the higher, which makes copying, and thus communication, possible; while in the *Aufforderung* the summoner restricts his or her bodily freedom, thereby communicating, and in effect, summoning the other.

This rather abstract account of how the material realm is able to communicate with the spiritual world through the medium, or middle term, of subtle matter, however, has yet to settle the problem of intersubjective recognition. Fichte will address the problem of human reciprocity and explain recognition through the dynamic of perception and the singularity of the face *(Gesicht)*.[31] It is the face that produces the impression in the aesthetic act of copying. And it is subtle matter that is the medium of this imitative *aesthesis*. Fichte writes:

> [I]f a figure [*Gestalt*] in space becomes perceived through sight [*Gesicht*], and becomes innerly, and very quickly . . . the feeling of the object [*Gefuhl des Gegenstandes*], that is, the pressure . . . which is imitated, it

produces the figure through an aesthetic [*plastik*] art, but the impression
in the eye is held as the schema of this imitation [*Nachahmung*].[32]

Fichte is explaining the capacity for a rational being to be "affected"
by another. Our perception of another produces an impression within
us, through a subtle matter that, according to Fichte, conveys a higher
meaning.[33] The perception of a human body by another rational being
is totally unlike the perception of a mere object, because since it conveys
a higher meaning in and of itself—or at least we unavoidably infer that
meaning—it has the capacity to affect us through a subtle matter by virtue
of its mere existence. Any form of copying, as an aesthetic act, seems to
give our own body a higher meaning. But one would wonder whether the
copying of one being by another, as a recognition of its rational capacity,
is a privileged sort of imitation, or aesthetic. After all, Fichte's central
example in this section is the imitation of one individual by another in
the dynamic of listening and speaking.[34] Fichte intends that this imitation
expressed when one innerly copies and speaks what one hears be not a
mere mime, but an active production. In the final section of this essay,
however, through an exploration of Fichte's analogy in his later work
linking the dynamic of pedagogy, pedagogical rapport, and the magnetic
rapport of subtle matter, we will question the true ground of Fichte's
communicative paradigm. In other words, although Fichte will insist that
the copying present in his theory of communication be a productive, not
reproductive, imitation, the analogy between pedagogical and magnetic
rapport perhaps suggests otherwise.[35] If Fichte's theory of communication proves to be imitative and reproductive, despite his assertions to the
contrary, it will have profound repercussions for our understanding of
intersubjectivity and the communication that grounds such recognition.

5

Through a brief look forward to Fichte's more extended engagement
with the notion of subtle matter in his later work, the *Tagebuch über den
animalischen Magnetismus* (1813), this section shows that Fichte, in fact,
will later conceive "subtle matter" as a dangerous imitative power of re-
production. If subtle matter, however, is not productive, but as Fichte
later concedes, reproductive, in what way then could one come to understand a dynamic of intersubjectivity that was grounded in a communicative recognition, whose medium in subtle matter showed the dynamic of
social relations to be fundamentally mimetic? In other words, if—as we

have been arguing—the communicative exchange known as recognition is made possible by the medium of subtle matter, and if the character of this exchange is a copying that is wholly imitative, then Fichte's entire transcendental deduction of right is put in jeopardy by the more "affective" account of the social represented by "subtle matter."

In the *TAM*, Fichte is quite concerned to distance himself, and his conception of pedagogy, from subtle matter and the dynamic of this universal fluid present in magnetic rapport. He thus characterizes the phenomenon of magnetic rapport and its subtle fluid as an imitative phenomenon that must be sharply distinguished from any similarities one might come to recognize in the dynamic of pedagogy and the paradigm of truth it represents for Fichte. He writes:

> The first discoverer becomes led to animal magnetism through a completely unknown law and power to which he conducts himself, like the student to the teacher. But still there appears to be a difference, the universal psychical property [*allgemeine Geistige*] appears to conduct itself differently with the discoverer, than the student to the teacher. Thus: the discoverer appears himself as the absolute last principle for the construction: in the immediate intuition.[36]

Two things need to be noted. First, that magnetic rapport is clearly conceived as an imitative, inferior phenomenon, which is a mere copy of the truth of pedagogic rapport. Yet if in the *GNR*, as we have been arguing, *Aufforderung* and *Anerkennung* become embroiled in the imitative structure of subtle matter, one might understand Fichte's attempt in the *TAM* to separate pedagogical rapport from magnetic rapport—to the extent that Fichte has long associated *Aufforderung* and *Erziehung*[37]—as one last attempt to free this terminology from subtle matter.

Fichte wants to argue that, with the student/teacher relation, imitation operates in the greater service of the truth, whereby the student should eventually have thoughts and ideas of his or her own; while on the other hand, with the magnetist, imitation is the final principle. Yet if one reads this section closely, it is clear that Fichte is rather desperately trying to make distinctions where none exist between types of rapport. But he must. The entire project of his later metaphysics will depend on it.

This distinction is central to the later concept, in *WL*, of the truth as a mode of the appearance of the Absolute. Fichte is adamant that his metaphysics of appearance is not imitative or reproductive, but the *Erscheinung* of absolute Being. The imitative structure of subtle matter, as I have argued elsewhere, is a model that threatens the entire project of his later metaphysics.[38] Thus, *if* Fichte cannot adequately make this distinction, *if* he cannot successfully free the mimesis of the appearance of the absolute from the concept of imitation embodied in magnetic rapport, then magnetic rapport returns to the heart of pedagogy, and the *affective* valence of subtle matter rears its head not only at the heart of his later metaphysics, but at the heart of a description of intersubjectivity that is at pains to keep the description of reciprocal influence within the purview and power of the transcendental subject and his discourse of rationality.[39]

Fichte's attempt to explain intersubjective recognition in the *GNR* through reference to subtle matter, then, does not, as he intends, support his transcendental account of the social. Rather, as we have argued, Fichte's need to ground the communicative exchange of intersubjective recognition in subtle matter only seems to have embroiled him in the complexities of subtle matter's rival paradigm of social interaction. In a sense, however, it is perhaps not so surprising that a transcendental justification of right would seek its ultimate conditions of possibility in a phenomenon that would anticipate the psychoanalytic science of the unconscious.

Notes

1. References to Fichte's work are to the 11-volume *Fichtes Sämmtliche Werke*, ed. I. H. Fichte (Berlin: W. de Gruyter and Co., 1971), hereafter abbreviated *SW* and cited according to volume and page number. All translations are mine, with the exception of citations from the *Wissenschaftslehre nova methodo*. Here I follow Breazeale's translation, published as J. G. Fichte, *Foundations of Transcendental Philosophy (Wissenschaftslehre) nova methodo (1796–99)*, trans. and ed. Daniel Breazeale (Ithaca: Cornell University Press, 1992), hereafter abbreviated *FTP*. The *Grundlage des Naturrechts* (1796) is hereafter abbreviated *GNR*.

2. Fichte's lengthy discussion in the *Tagebuch über den animalischen Magnetismus* (1813, *SW* XI) of the significance of "subtle matter" and "magnetic rapport" for the later *Wissenschaftslehre* would seem to confirm Léon's intuition. The *Tagebuch über den animalischen Magnetismus* is hereafter abbreviated as *TAM*. Among other things, Leon writes of Fichte that "he would remark that the phenomena of somnambulism would carry with it a key to one of the essential theses of the *WL*: this of the non-existence, or at least, of the essential relativity of the individual." Xavier Léon, *Fichte et son Temps,* vol. 2, pt. 2 (Paris: Libraire Armand Colin, 1927), p. 282.

3. Since the time this essay was first presented, Günter Zöller has also become interested in the role subtle matter plays in the *GNR*. Our work differs, however, to the extent that Zöller's work has concentrated upon a straight exposition of the section in which "subtle matter" occurs within the *GNR*, whereas I

F. SCOTT SCRIBNER

have been concerned to situate both the *GNR* references to subtle matter and those appearing in the *TAM* within the context of the concern in eighteenth- and nineteenth-century Germany with the phenomena of magnetic psychology. Nevertheless, for excellent textual exposition of sections 5 through 7 of the *GNR*, see Zöller's paper "Leib, Materie, und gemeinsames Wollen als Anwendungs- bedingungen des Rechts," forthcoming in *Fichtes Grundlage des Naturrechts*, ed. J. Ch. Merle, Reihe Klassiker auslegen (Berlin: Akademie Verlag).

4. The turn from conceiving ethereal fluids as objects of purely scientific inquiry to more social and psychological interpretations of such fluids can be attributed, for the most part, to the work of Anton Mesmer (1735–1815). See Henri Ellenberger, *The Discovery of the Unconscious* (New York: Basic Books Inc., 1970).

5. See Larry Lauden, "The Medium and Its Message: A Study of Some of the Philosophical Controversies about Ether," in *Conceptions of Ether*, ed. G. N. Cantor and M. J. S. Hodge (Cambridge: Cambridge University Press, 1981), p. 158.

6. See Immanuel Kant, *Opus postumum*, trans. E. Forster and M. Rosen (Cambridge: Cambridge University Press, 1993), p. 37.

7. See L. Chertok and R. De Saussure, *The Therapeutic Revolution: From Mesmer to Freud*, trans. R. H. Ahrenfeldt (New York: Brunner/Mazel, Publishers, 1979), p. 11.

8. See Robert Darton, *Mesmerism and the End of the Enlightenment in France* (New York: Schocken Books, 1970).

9. Ellenberger, *Discovery of the Unconscious*, p. 72.

10. In the *Meditations of First Philosophy*, in the "Second Meditation," Des- cartes vividly exemplifies how the certainty gained through the assertion "I think, therefore I am" leads to solipsism. While he is sure of his own thinking, and thus his own existence, his relations to others, and thus his social existence, still remain in doubt. Descartes concedes that in his relation to others he cannot be sure that he sees "any more than hats and coats which could conceal automatons" (*The Philosophical Writings of Descartes*, vol. 1, trans. J. Cottingham, R. Stoothoff, and D. Murdoch [Cambridge: Cambridge University Press, 1984], p. 21). One should note that Husserl's discussion of "empathy" in the fifth meditation of the *Carte- sian Meditations* continues to grapple with the problem of solipsism that haunts transcendental philosophy. See Edmund Husserl, *The Cartesian Meditations*, trans. Dorian Cairns (The Hague: Martinus Nijhoff Inc., 1970).

11. *SW* III, pp. 120–21.

12. Ibid., IV, p. 302.

13. While it is my view that Fichte makes no significant distinction between the *Anstoß* of the *WL* of 1794 and the *GNR*'s *Aufforderung*, this point is widely disputed. For a concise view of the positions, see Robert R. Williams, *Recognition: Fichte and Hegel on the Other* (New York: SUNY Press, 1992).

14. *SW* III, p. 8.

15. Ibid., p. 75.

16. Ibid., p. 36.

17. Ibid.; my italics.

18. Ibid., pp. 17–24.

19. Ibid., pp. 57–62.

20. *FTP,* p. 320.

21. *SW* III, p. 56.

22. *FTP,* p. 327.

23. Ibid., p. 321.

24. See note 10 above.

25. *SW* III, pp. 68–69.

26. Ibid., p. 69.

27. Ibid., pp. 69–70.

28. Or perhaps it is the reverse. Fichte's footnote shows that he himself is unclear about this dynamic. See *SW* III, pp. 70–71.

29. Ibid., p. 70.

30. Ibid., pp. 70–71.

31. Hans-Jakob Wilhelm has pointed out to me the manner in which the German word *Gesicht* is able to present both the subjective and objective aspects of perception simultaneously through its polyvalent meaning of both "sight" and the "face."

32. *SW* III, pp. 71–72.

33. Ibid.

34. Ibid.

35. If Fichte intends this use of copying to be productive, not reproductive, his use of the term *Nachbildung,* for copying, is perplexing to say the least. He goes to great lengths in works such as *WL* 1794 and "Concerning the Difference between the Spirit and the Letter within Philosophy" to distinguish between the productive and reproductive imagination in order to clarify the manner in which *Nachbildung* is an inferior and derivative form of the productive spirit of the imagination.

36. *SW* XI, p. 301.

37. Ibid., III, p. 39.

38. In a paper given in Germany at the *Internationalen-Fichte-Gesellschaft* (1997), I have argued that Fichte's search for a physical proof for the last *WL* of the phenomena of magnetic rapport ultimately threatens to cast his entire later metaphysics of appearance into the abyss of imitation. See "Die 'Physicirung des Idealismus' im *Tagebuch uber den animalischen Magnetismus:* Beweis der letzten Wissenschaftslehre oder Das Ende des Idealismus?" *Fichte-Strelien* 17 (2000): pp. 319–28.

39. Lacoue-Labarthe articulates the notion of freeing "mimesis from imitation" in *Typography: Mimesis, Philosophy, Politics,* ed. Christopher Fynsk (Cambridge: Harvard University Press, 1989), p. 119.

PART   II

ESSAYS ON THE
*WISSENSCHAFTSLEHRE
NOVA METHODO,*
1796–1799

Toward a Completion of German Idealism: Fichte's Transition from his *Grundlage der gesammten Wissenschaftslehre* to the *Wissenschaftslehre nova methodo*

Johannes Brachtendorf

From its beginnings, German idealist thinking was dominated by the idea of making philosophy more rational. Love of wisdom was to be transformed into secure knowledge.[1] Fichte was among the first of the philosophers who realized the methodological implications of this idea, implications concerning mainly the beginning of the system, its second step, and its end. In the first part of this essay, I will give a brief exposition of these issues. In the second part, I will analyze how Fichte treats these methodological problems in the *Grundlage*. The third part contains a similar analysis pertaining to the *Wissenschaftslehre nova methodo* (hereafter *WLnm*). By comparing the earlier and the later solution, I will argue that the second *Wissenschaftslehre* differs essentially from the first one. Although Fichte's later answer is not completely without preparation in the *Grundlage*, the *WLnm* is far from being merely a new presentation of earlier ideas. In particular, with regard to the problem of the second step, the *WLnm* contains significant changes in the very foundation of Fichte's project.

A Theory of Principles and Its Methodological Requirements

Freedom from Presuppositions

According to Fichte, a truly foundational philosophy must not make any presuppositions. The first principle cannot rest on any reason other than itself. This axiom has an epistemological and a metaphysical meaning. In epistemological terms, the first principle needs to be secure by itself.[2] Metaphysically, it has to be an indeterminate totality. Determinacy is based on negation. Everything determinate is what it is because it is *not* something else. Thus, it presupposes what it is not to be able to be what it is. Hence, a first principle that does not rest on any presupposition needs to be free from negation and, therefore, indeterminate. Since neither a real nor a possible being can be external to it, the principle is a totality. Indeterminacy and totality imply each other. There is only one first principle.[3]

The Second Step

At this point, the problem arises that such a principle by itself does not provide any further development of a theory. Nothing can be derived or concluded from an indeterminate totality. If the beginning of the theory shall not be its immediate end, a second element must be introduced that accounts for a first negation and thereby for determinacy. In a first step, we may have found the ground of everything. However, if the theory shall not only maintain that everything can be *re*duced to this principle, but also claims that some things can be *de*duced from it, a second step is needed that sets the theory in motion. In a conception like Fichte's, the principle and the second element interact in a specific manner, so that a first negation produces a series of further negations and determinations.[4] Developing ever more concrete results, the theory unfolds in a way that can be called linear. Naturally, the character of the second element is the crucial problem of this kind of philosophy, because it cannot be external to the principle and yet allows the theory go beyond indeterminacy.

Completeness

Not only is a rational philosophy supposed to be secure in all its parts, it also has to contain all possible results. Hence, a criterion of completeness is needed. One must be able clearly to discern when the development reaches its end. Fichte argues for circularity as a criterion of completeness. We know that a discourse is finished when it returns to its beginning, that is, when its last result matches its starting point.[5]

In the following section of this essay, I will try to show that the early *Wissenschaftslehre* offers not one but three competing interpretations of the second step and its relation to the principle. The first one, employing the linear method, is based on a limitation of the negative element; it is largely dismissed in the *WLnm*. The second interpretation, connected with the notion of circularity, postulates a gradual dissolution of this element; it is completely dispensed with in the second *Wissenschaftslehre*. The third interpretation, claiming a unity of indeterminacy and determinacy under the title "power of imagination," will be part of Fichte's new *Wissenschaftslehre*.

Methodological Problems of the *Grundlage*

Quantifiability

As an introductory argument, Fichte reflects on a secure logical proposition, namely, the *principium identitatis* (A = A), to show that it presupposes an even securer principle, the self-positing I. By definition, the first principle cannot be derived from higher premises,[6] but it can be approached from below, so to speak, by reference to a logical axiom whose truth is universally recognized.[7] If it can be shown that this axiom depends on a higher ground, we know that this ground is secure, since it is the source of a secure logical axiom.[8] To gain a second element, Fichte picks up another logical proposition in a similar procedure, the *principium contradictionis:*—A not = A, to reveal its principle: "a Not-I is absolutely posited in opposition to the I."[9] Apparently, the second *Grundsatz* is not derived from the first one but takes its own beginning. Thus the question: Is the not-I a second principle beside the self-positing I?

Fichte, of course, has another solution in mind that rests on two premises. (1) The not-I does not stand beside the I, but *in* it, so that the I can still be considered the all-comprising totality. (2) I and not-I are not simply opposites but contradict each other. A contradiction is a most valuable methodological device for a theory like Fichte's. Nothing follows from a simple opposition, but a contradiction demands a solution, and this solution will be the first real result of the deduction. Why, then, does the not-I contradict the I? Fichte interprets the identity of the I expressed in the term "I = I" as "I being posited *in* the I." "I = I" means the I is *in* the I. But if the not-I is posited *in* the I, as the first premise says, the I cannot be *in* the I. Opposites can coexist if they are separated from each other, but they cannot both exist at the same time in the same spot, so to speak. By demanding that I and not-I are both posited *in* the I, Fichte sets up a situation that turns coexistence into mutual exclusion. If the not-I is posited in the I, as the second *Grundsatz* states, the I cannot be posited there. Since it is the very essence of the I to be posited in the I, the positing of the not-I denies the possibility of an I. The second *Grundsatz* falsifies the first one. On the other hand, the not-I has to be posited in the I, and if there is no I, there can be no not-I either. The second *Grundsatz* is self-destructive because the not-I abolishes the condition of its own existence.[10] But neither the first nor the second *Grundsatz* can be dropped since both were proven to be secure. Hence, one is entitled to look for a different solution to the contradiction between I and not-I. In virtue of the validity of the first and second *Grundsatz*, a synthesis can be postulated.[11] The title of this synthesis is quantifiability: The totality of the all-comprising I is divided up among the limited I and the limited not-I both posited *in* the I.[12]

By now the methodological foundations of the *Grundlage* should be clear. A general synthesis has been discovered and its validity secured. All that is left to be done in order to gain more results is simply to exhaust the contents of this synthesis. The execution of this program as given in the fourth paragraph of the *Grundlage* is complicated in detail, but simple in principle. The third *Grundsatz* is split up into two contradicting sentences that are—as we now know—synthesized by the principle of quantifiability. Each of these sentences can be broken down into two even simpler sentences whose synthesis is contained in the general synthesis and has to be understood as a specification of quantifiability. This procedure could be continued until elementary sentences are found that cannot be further broken down. According to this method, a general synthesis unfolds to two more concrete syntheses, which on their part contain four even more concrete syntheses, and so forth. The theory takes on a pyramidal form that fulfills the requirement of a linear progress from indeterminacy toward determinacy and from a secure principle to equally secure results.[13]

The Power of Imagination

Unfortunately, Fichte himself does not honor this method. As he points out at the end of section 4, the exhaustion of the general synthesis leads to contradictory elements, namely, the infinity and the finitude of the I, which cannot be reconciled by an appeal to quantifiability and therefore require another synthesis afforded by the marvelous[14] faculty of the power of imagination.[15] Against Fichte, one has to say that this is impossible within a procedure that rests on a valid synthesis and simply specifies what has already been proven. Seemingly, Fichte has already abandoned his first solution; for if quantifiability could really account for determinacy, the power of imagination would not be needed. If it is needed, something must be wrong with quantifiability.

The problem that is supposed to be solved by the power of imagination can be traced back to the third paragraph. Quantifiability was already postulated on behalf of the identity of the I, but it afforded only the coexistence of I and not-I in the I. The limitation of the I brought about by the positing of a not-I *in* the I destroyed the unity of the I rather than preserved it, since it causes an opposition of the unlimited and the limited I.[16] Quantifiability was introduced to demonstrate that there *can* be a not-I for the I,[17] namely, by being posited in the I in coexistence with the quantifiable I that is also posited in the I. But quantifiability cannot avoid the destruction of the identity of the I, for even a limited not-I abolishes this identity by putting the I that it is opposed to in a contradiction to the I in which it is contained. Thus, the power of imagination does not unfold a synthesis that is already afforded by quantifiability, but is supposed to heal the contradiction between the infinite and the finite I, a contradiction brought about by quantifiability.

Practical Idealism and Check

Even more problems are posed by the practical part of the first *Wissenschaftslehre*. At the beginning of the third part of his *Grundlage*, Fichte still finds a "contradiction between the intelligent I that as such is limited, and the absolutely posited, unlimited I."[18] Fichte does not analyze the *Grundsatz* of the practical part in order to find more concrete syntheses. Instead of applying the linear method analogously to the theoretical part, he asserts that there is still an unreconciled conflict between the infinite and the finite I, and that the practical part has the task of settling this issue.[19] Although the limitation of I and not-I should have preserved the unity of the I, and although the power of imagination was designed in order truly to safeguard this unity, Fichte sets out to solve the problem of determinacy a third time.

In contrast with the power of imagination, the idea of circularity is brought to bear on the solution of the practical part. The *Wissenschaftslehre* starts with the pure I; the influence of the not-I brings the limited, intelligent I into existence; the practical part, finally, shall remove any limitation and let the limited I merge into the absolute I. Thus, the pure I stands at the beginning and at the end of the theory; the circle closes. But Fichte points out that a complete removal of any limitation presupposes an abolishment of the not-I, which is impossible because, according to the second *Grundsatz*, the not-I is posited *schlechthin*. There is no practical solution to the contradiction between the infinite and the finite I. What can be done is to aspire to such a solution, that is, to strive for a gradual resolution of the not-I and, thereby, to widen the range of the limited I step by step in a process guided by a projected but unattainable goal.[20]

In his *Grundlage,* Fichte calls a philosophy that can prove that only the I is real, "idealism," whereas a doctrine that attributes reality to a second element beside the I is named "realism." According to the early Fichte, the *Wissenschaftslehre* is a "practical idealism."[21] It is not a true idealism because it allows for two real principles, the I and the not-I, but it includes the demand that only the I should be real. "Practical idealism" establishes a complete idealism as a principle that regulates the practice of an intelligent being whose existence depends not on one, but on two principles.

The reality of the not-I becomes clear in the infamous doctrine of the check (*Anstoß*),[22] which is a metaphor taken from mechanics, first introduced in connection with the theory of imagination, and then extensively used in the practical part. In the theoretical part, Fichte distinguishes two different explanations of representation, namely, the realistic idea of a transcendent not-I that has an effect on the I, and the idealistic conception of a self-related I that creates all its determinations autonomously by itself.[23] Both conceptions fail, the first one because it cannot give any account of the fact that all determinations of an I have to be *for* the I, the second because its idea of self-reflection is without any real determinacy and thus empty. Nevertheless, each of these conceptions emphasizes an element that has to be included in a sound theory of representation in particular and in an explanation of the relationship between I and not-I in general. These elements are the I's pure activity and an influence on the I that is not posited by the I itself. In the course of his early *Wissenschaftslehre,* Fichte specifies these conceptions and makes the idealistic approach as strong as possible, for instance by pointing out that the real problem does not concern the relationship between I and not-I, but only the reconcilability of two activities of the I, namely, its positing itself infinitely and finitely.[24] But the finitude of the I's activity can still not be explained by reference to the I alone.

The concept of a check represents the most refined form of the realistic idea of an external influence on the I. Indeed, Fichte emphasizes that the check has no qualities other than those ascribed to it by the I,[25] and that it cannot have any effect on the I unless the I concurs with it.[26] But ultimately the check is not posited by the positing I and therefore brings an element of realism into the *Wissenschaftslehre.* Fichte sees clearly that he is at a loss here. He tries to save the idealism of the *Grundlage,* asserting that it is indeed realistic but not A "transcendent," that is, not going beyond the I. Consciousness cannot be explained without the assumption of an element independent from the I, but Fichte asserts that this explanation of consciousness on its part follows the I's rules of thinking. This means to Fichte that the check is not truly independent of the I, because the idea of a check is a product of a thinking, that is, philosophizing, I. He admits, however, that there would be no thinking I at all without a prior effect of the check on it, but this is again an idea of a thinking I, and so forth *ad infinitum*.[27] According to Fichte, the *Wissenschaftslehre* is a *Real-Idealismus* or a *Ideal-Realismus*.[28] He also calls it a "critical idealism," meaning by "critical" that it is based on an infinite regress that makes the problem of an idealist or a realist interpretation of the check insoluble.[29]

Fichte's attempt at avoiding transcendence does not convince me. His assertion that the check cannot be external to the I because the theory of the check is made up by a thinking I is simply not true. Theories are always set up by thinking beings, but this does not mean that the objects of these theories exist only in thought. The early *Wissenschaftslehre* is not only ambivalent in that it offers three competing treatments of the problem of determinacy, it also poses the problem in a way that makes the assumption of an external influence on the I unavoidable.

The *Wissenschaftslehre nova methodo*

Determination and Self-Reflection

In his second *Wissenschaftslehre*, Fichte sets up a new introductory argument for the first principle. Instead of starting with a reflection on the *principium identitatis,* he now tries to show that consciousness of any object presupposes an immediate subject-object unity, which he calls *unmittelbares Bewusstsein.* This unity, again, is an indeterminate totality. Furthermore, Fichte does not again pick up a second logical axiom to introduce a negative element required for the second step, but instead refers to self-reflection as an essential feature of the I. According to Fichte, the immediate self-consciousness is only a potential consciousness. Real consciousness rests on self-reflection, in which the I grasps itself, so that it knows about itself. Knowing itself means the real I apprehends itself *as* itself, that is, it recognizes itself as something particular and thereby discerns itself as being not something else. The word "as" indicates the determinacy that comes with self-reflection. In his second *Wissenschaftslehre,* Fichte gains determinacy without reference to the not-I, simply by introducing self-reflection.

Indeed, Fichte has to make an assumption here. He needs to postu-late that the indeterminate totality is able to step out of itself, as it were, to confront and reflect on itself. Fichte claims that the indeterminate princi-ple has the capacity for self-mediation and self-determination. The *reality* of self-determination cannot be derived from higher reasons. Therefore, Fichte concludes, it is an act of absolute freedom.

> No grounds can here be adduced for this action, for we have reached the limit of all reasons. . . . [N]othing mediates. The I undertakes this movement of transition because it undertakes this movement of transi-tion; it determines itself because it determines itself. It accomplishes this transition by means of a self-grounding act of absolute freedom, and this is a creation out of nothing, an act of producing something that did not exist before, an absolute beginning.[30]

This idea of freedom is significantly different from what Fichte says in his *Grundlage*. According to the first *Wissenschaftslehre*, freedom is the power of the already limited I for widening its boundaries.[31] In the second *Wissenschaftslehre*, freedom is the capacity for self-limitation.

As I said above, the concept of self-determination is not without preparation in the *Grundlage*, where Fichte says: "The I shall not only posit itself for another intelligence, but it ought to posit itself *for itself;* it shall posit itself *as* posited by itself. As an I, it shall have the principle of life and consciousness in itself. Without further reason, the I as such must have in itself the principle of reflecting upon itself."[32] This sounds very much like self-limitation, but in his early *Wissenschaftslehre* Fichte holds the view that self-reflection presupposes the check. In his mechanistic metaphors he says that the I's centrifugal activity needs to be bent back, so that the I can reflect on itself. This bending back is accomplished by the check. Indeed, Fichte knows already that a real I posits itself *as* positing itself, but in his *Grundlage* he asserts that the I can only do so because of an external influence on it. If the check did not reverse the direction of the I's activity, there would be no self-consciousness.

In detail, Fichte argues along the following lines: The I has in itself the principle of self-reflection. This means it exerts two activities, a cen-trifugal one going to infinity and representing the I's unlimited reality, and a centripetal one accounting for the I's self-reflection.[33] But the interaction of these two activities does not constitute any real conscious-ness, because both of them are infinite and thus cannot be distinguished from each other.[34] For this reason, self-consciousness of an infinite being like God is incomprehensible. Human self-consciousness rests on the discernibility of these two activities by their directions, which is made possible through the inversion of the centrifugal activity and through the limitation that lies therein, both caused by the check.[35] Since the I has the principle of reflection in itself, it interacts with itself even before any check occurs, and by this interaction an external influence on the I becomes possible,[36] but it is only through the check that limitation and thus self-consciousness becomes real.[37] According to the *WLnm*, the I does not only account for the possibility of self-consciousness, but also affords the transition from this possibility to real self-consciousness. This is the I's "creation out of nothing." In Fichte's first *Wissenschaftslehre*, the I is externally and, so to speak, unwillingly restricted to a finite sphere. Therefore, it strives for a widening of its sphere and ultimately for a removal of all its boundaries. According to the second *Wissenschaftslehre*, the I restricts itself by an autonomous act of absolute freedom.

The Deduction of Being

Whereas the *Grundlage* explains self-reflection as a consequence of a check by the not-I, the *WLnm* conversely describes the not-I as a result of the I's self-determination.[38] The subject-object unity is a totality. Reflecting upon itself and grasping itself *as* something determinate, it necessarily picks up some elements of the totality and neglects others. Fichte says, the I cannot find itself without finding more than itself at the same time. He calls this surplus *das Gegebene,* that which is given,[39] indicating thereby that the I, when it apprehends itself, necessarily experiences something different in addition to what it finds itself to be. This givenness is, of course, a mere appearance resulting from the fact that reflection causes determinacy. What seems to be given is truly that part of the totality which did not become the contents of the self-determination. According to Fichte, it is the law of reflection that the indeterminate totality, once it reflects upon itself, determines itself *as* being itself, that is, *as* being something particular, and thereby distinguishes itself from a sphere of what it is not. But this sphere is only part of the active I, and it is constituted *as* a sphere by the same I through the process of self-determination. In contrast with the *Grundlage,* this explanation makes clear, right from the beginning, that the not-I is nothing else than a part of the total I.[40] Transcendence is no longer a threat to the *Wissenschaftslehre.*

Fichte gives a detailed argument to characterize the features of the determined I and the "given" not-I. In summary, he says that the I, when it reflects upon itself, finds itself as an activity. At the same time it experiences a seemingly external element that is in a state of repose. "The Not-I is nothing other than another way of looking at the I. When we consider the I as an activity, we obtain the I; when we consider it in a state of repose, we obtain the Not-I. One cannot view the I as active without also viewing it in a state of repose, i.e., as Not-I."[41] Fichte still names this element "not-I," but more often and more significantly he calls it "being" *(Sein),*[42] because "being" indicates passiveness and stability and thereby brings its opposition to activity to attention. Fichte takes some pride in pointing out that he accomplishes what had seemed to be impossible for all metaphysicians thus far, namely, a deduction of being. Whereas traditional metaphysics said that "being" is the most general concept which needs to be presupposed in whatever we want to speak about, Fichte claims that "being" rests on a higher ground from which it can be derived, namely, on the I and its free act of self-determination.[43] The idea of a spontaneous and completely autonomous self-determination of the I is most important for Fichte's project of a truly idealist philosophy. This idea permits him to dispense with a not-I, which, to be able to generate determinacy, had to be ultimately independent from the I. The not-I is no longer a cause but a consequence of self-determination. This is the reason why concepts like *Real-Idealismus, Ideal-Realismus,* and *praktischer Idealismus* do not occur anymore in the second *WL.*[44]

The Method of the *WLnm*

Since the second step of the *WLnm* is designed differently from the *Grundlage,* the entire theory takes a new course. The circular method in the previous sense of a return to the first *Grundsatz* is dropped. Some similarity with the method of the theoretical part of the *Grundlage* is preserved. There, Fichte thought that, after having proved the synthesis of quantifiability to be secure, the contents of this synthesis need to be detected and developed. In his second *Wissenschaftslehre,* he no longer employs *Grund- und Lehrsaetze,* but he keeps the idea that, once the act of self-determination is secured, one simply has to reveal all the conditions that have to be fulfilled so that this act becomes possible. Since self-determination is real, the fulfillment of these conditions can be taken for granted. All the *Wissenschaftslehre* needs to do is give a list of these conditions and show how they are related to one another. This may be called a circular procedure; however, not in the former meaning of a reestablishment of the indeterminate totality by means of human practice, but in the sense of a complete understanding of the second step. With the second step, the act of self-determination was introduced just as a matter of fact, and it is not until the end of the *WLnm* that this act with all its implications is completely comprehended.[45]

In the course of his *WLnm,* Fichte rearranges many materials of the *Grundlage,* in particular the results of sections 6 through 11. I cannot go into the details of Fichte's arguments, but I want to point to what Fichte says is the most fundamental condition of self-determination, namely, the power of imagination. In paragraph 17, which to my mind is the center of the *WLnm,* Fichte asks how it is possible that the reflecting I selects some of the contents of the subject-object-unity, if this unity is an indeterminate totality in which nothing can be discerned. Selection *(Wahl)* presupposes the discernibility of particular features to be selected. But how is this possible in a realm of "intermediating"? Similar to the *Grundlage,* Fichte ascribes the capacity of intermediating between indeterminacy and determinacy to the power of imagination. In virtue of this power, the I can apprehend its own infinity in the mode of "quasi-determination," which Fichte also calls "determinability." After having made itself determinable, the I can achieve real self-determination. "The power of imagination is the basis of all consciousness."[46] The most distinctive feature of this power is its nondiscursiveness. Conceptual thinking is subject to the law of reflection, that is, it determines its objects, isolates them, and thereby causes the separation that characterizes the sensible world. But this law does not obtain at the very beginning of consciousness where categories do not yet apply and where imagination allows for apprehending infinity without transforming it into finitude. This is the realm of genuine reality, a realm that is free of mere appearance and deception. Fichte calls it the "intelligible world."

To summarize: Between 1795 and 1796, Fichte altered his *Wissenschaftslehre* significantly to make it methodologically homogeneous. This process goes along with an abandoning of the early hybrid position for the sake of a complete idealism. Thereby Fichte sets the stage for all his later versions of the *WL.* Whether one appreciates this completion depends on whether or not one considers Fichte's ontological monism together with the affiliated idea of a deduction of being to be a promising project.

Notes

1. Cf. *Über den Begriff der Wissenschaftslehre oder der sogenannten Philosophie,* Vorrede zur ersten Ausgabe (*SW* I, 29; *GA* I, 2, 109). (Fichte's writings are cited here according to the edition by his son I. H. Fichte, *Johann Gottlieb Fichtes sämmtliche Werke* [Berlin: Viet and Co., 1845–46], hereafter abbreviated *SW,* and according to *Gesamtausgabe der Bayerischen Akademie der Wissenschaften,* ed. R. Lauth, H. Gliwitzky, and E. Fuchs [Stuttgart-Bad Cannstatt: Frommann-Holzboog, 1964 ff.], hereafter abbreviated *GA.* The *Wissenschaftslehre nova methodo,*

hereafter abbreviated *WLnm,* is cited according to the edition by E. Fuchs [Hamburg: Meiner, 1982].) See also complaints by the early Kant about a lack of progress in metaphysics; *De mundi sensibilis atque intelligibilis forma,* Werkausgabe, ed. W. Weischedel, Bd. V, A p. 11, section 8. According to Kant's own words, the *Critique of Pure Reason* is to be understood as a "Traktat von der Methode" (B XXII) that leads metaphysics "in den sicheren Gang einer Wissenschaft" (B XXIII). Kant praises Chr. Wolff for his attempts at making metaphysics more rational (B XXXVI f). In his answer to the question "Welches sind die wirklichen Fortschritte, die die Metaphysik seit Leibnitzens und Wolf's Zeiten in Deutschland gemacht hat?" Kant calls transcendental philosophy a *Wissenschaftslehre* because of the secure progress that it can make (Bd VI, A p. 44).

2. In his *Über den Begriff der Wissenschaftslehre,* Fichte says: "Dieser Grundsatz—der Wissenschaftslehre, und vermittelst ihrer aller Wissenschaften und alles Wissens—ist daher schlechterdings keines Beweises fähig, d.h. er ist auf keinen höheren Satz zurück zu führen, aus dessen Verhältnisse zu ihm seine Gewissheit erhelle. Dennoch soll er die Grundlage aller Gewissheit abgeben; er muss daher doch gewiß und zwar in sich selbst, und um sein selbst willen, und durch sich selbst gewiss seyn" (*SW* I, 47; *GA* I, 2, p. 120).

3. "Das absolute Ich des ersten Grundsatzes ist nicht *etwas* (es hat kein Prädikat, und kann keins haben); es ist schlechthin, *was* es ist, und dies lässt sich nicht weiter erklären. Jetzt vermittelst dieses Begriffes (sc. der Teilbarkeit, J.B.) ist im Bewusstseyn *alle* Realität; und von dieser kommt dem Nicht-Ich diejenige zu, die dem Ich nicht zukommt, und umgekehrt. Beide sind etwas; das Nicht-Ich dasjenige, was das Ich nicht ist, und umgekehrt" (*SW* I, p. 109 f.; *GA* I, 2, p. 271).

In scholastic treatises on ontology, such as Chr. Wolff's (cf. his *Philosophia prima sive Ontologia,* in *Gesammelte Werke,* ed. Jean Ecole [Hildesheim: Olms, 1983], II. Abt. Bd. 3), the distinction between the indeterminate and the determinate was considered one of the principles of being as such (cf. the chapter "De Essentia et Existentia Entis agnatisque nonnullis Notionibus," in which the section "De Determinato et Indeterminato" immediately precedes the definition of *ens*. This principle became controversial because of the use Leibniz made of it when he linked it to the principle of sufficient reason and, ultimately, to his ontological proof of God's existence (cf. Leibniz, *Theodizee* I, section 44, and Wolff's interpretation in *Ontologia,* section 75). According to Kant's critique, Leibniz argued that every determinate being is "zum Teil real, zum Teil negativ" (cf. *Preisschrift,* A 126 f.). Since negation is a restriction of reality, the concept of a determinate being implies the idea of an *ens realissimum* that is prior to any restriction. In his *Preisschrift,* Kant says: "Wahr ist es, daß, wenn wir uns a priori von einem Dinge überhaupt, also ontologisch, einen Begriff machen wollen, wir immer, zum Urbegriff, den Begriff von einem allerrealsten Wesen in Gedanken zum Grunde legen, denn eine Negation, als Bestimmung eines Dinges, ist immer nur abgeleitete Vorstellung, weil man sie als Aufhebung (remotio) nicht denken kann, ohne vorher die ihr entgegengesetzte Realität als etwas, das gesetzt wird (positio s. reale) gedacht zu haben" (A p. 125).

This God of metaphysics "enthält den Stoff zur Erzeugung aller anderen möglichen Dinge, wie das Marmorlager zu Bildsäulen von unendlicher Man-nigfaltigkeit, welche insgesamt nur durch Einschränkung (Absonderung des übrigen von einem gewissen Teil des Ganzen, also nur durch Negation) möglich sind" (A 126). According to Kant, however, this is only a logical principle pertain-ing to our subjective thinking, not a transcendental principle that determines reality. In the post-Kantian context, Fichte as well as Hegel (cf. the beginning of his *Wissenschaft der Logik*) reclaimed the idea of the indeterminate in its method-ological meaning to gain a starting point that is free from presuppositions.

4. Cf. also the configuration of *Sein, Nichts,* and *Werden* in Hegel's *Wis-senschaft der Logik.*

5. "Wir bedürfen eines positiven Merkmals zum Beweise, dass schlechthin und unbedingt nichts weiter gefolgert werden könne; und das könnte kein an-deres seyn, als das, dass der Grundsatz selbst, von welchem wir ausgegangen wären, zugleich auch das letzte Resultat sey" (*SW* I, p. 59; *GA* I, 2, p. 131).

"Die Wissenschaftslehre hat also absolute Totalität. In ihr führt Eins zu Allem,und Alles zu Einem. Sie ist aber die einzige Wissenschaft, welche vollen-det werden kann; Vollendung ist demnach ihr auszeichnender Charakter. Alle andere Wissenschaften sind unendlich, und können nie vollendet werden; denn sie laufen nicht wieder in ihren Grundsatz zurück" (*SW* I, p. 59; *GA* I, 2, p. 131).

6. "Wir haben den absolut-ersten, schlechthin unbedingten Grundsatz alles menschlichen Wissens *aufzusuchen. Beweisen* oder *bestimmen* lässt er sich nicht, wenn er absolut-erster Grundsatz sein soll" (*SW* I, p. 91; *GA* I, 2, p. 255).

7. "Wir müssen auf dem Wege der anzustellenden Reflexion von irgend einem Satze ausgehen, den uns Jeder ohne Widerrede zugiebt" (*SW* I, p. 92; *GA* I, 2, p. 256).

8. "So wie dieser Satz (sc. den uns jeder ohne Widerrede zugibt) zuge-standen wird, muss zugleich dasjenige, was wir der ganzen Wissenschaftslehre zum Grunde legen wollen . . . zugestanden seyn" (*SW* I, p. 92; *GA* I, 2, p. 256).

9. Cf. *SW* I, p. 104 (*GA* I, 2, p. 266). "Aus dem gleichen Grunde, aus welchem der erste Grundsatz nicht bewiesen, noch abgeleitet werden konnte, kann es auch der zweite nicht. Wir gehen daher auch hier, gerade wie oben, von einer Thatsache des empirischen Bewusstseyns aus, und verfahren mit derselben aus der gleichen Befugniss auf die gleiche Art" (*SW* I, p. 101; *GA* I, 2, p. 263).

10. "Insofern das Nicht-Ich gesetzt ist, ist das Ich nicht gesetzt; denn durch das Nicht-Ich wird das Ich völlig aufgehoben. Nun ist das Nicht-Ich *im Ich* gesetzt: denn es ist entgegengesetzt; aber alles Entgegensetzen setzt die Identität des Ich, in welchem gesetzt, und dem gesetzten entgegengesetzt wird, voraus. Mithin ist das Ich im Ich nicht gesetzt, insofern das Ich darin gesetzt ist. 2) Aber das Nicht-Ich kann nur insofern gesetzt werden, inwiefern im Ich (in dem identischen Bewusstseyn) ein Ich gesetzt ist, dem es entgegen gesetzt werden kann. Nun soll das Nicht-Ich im identischen Bewusstseyn gesetzt werden. Mithin muss in demselben, insofern das Nicht-Ich gesetzt seyn soll, auch das Ich gesetzt seyn. 3) Beide Schlußfolgen sind sich entgegengesetzt" (*SW* I, p. 106; *GA* I, 2, p. 268).

11. "Hierdurch wird nun unsere Aufgabe bestimmt. Es soll nemlich irgend ein X gefunden werden, vermittelst dessen alle jene Folgerungen richtig sein

können, ohne dass die Identität des Bewusstseyns aufgehoben werde" (*SW* I, p. 107; *GA* I, 2, p. 269).

12. "Das Ich sowohl als das Nicht-Ich sind, beide durch das Ich und im Ich, gesetzt als durcheinander gegenseitig beschränkbar, d.i. so, dass die Realität des Einen die Realität des Anderen aufhebe, und umgekehrt (§ 3)" (*SW* I, p. 125; *GA* I, 2, p. 285).

13. "Alle übrigen Synthesen, welche gültig seyn sollen, müssen in dieser (sc. der Synthesis des dritten Grundsatzes, J.B.) liegen; sie müssen zugleich in und mit ihr vorgenommen worden seyn: und so, wie dies bewiesen wird, wird der überzeugendste Beweis geliefert, dass sie gültig sind wie jene" (*SW* I, p. 114; *GA* I, 2, p. 275).

"Wir haben demnach in den durch sie (sc. die höchste Synthesis, J.B.) verbundenen Ich und Nicht-Ich, insofern sie durch dieselbe verbunden sind, übriggebliebene entgegengesetzte Merkmale aufzusuchen, und sie durch einen neuen Beziehungsgrund, der wieder in dem höchsten aller Beziehungsgründe enthalten seyn muss, zu verbinden" (*SW* I, p. 144 f.; *GA* I, 2, p. 275). Cf. also *SW* I, p. 124 (*GA* I, 2, p. 284).

14. Cf. *SW* I, p. 208; *GA* I, 2, p. 353.

15. "Wir sehen, dass gerade derjenige Umstand, welcher die Möglichkeit einer Theorie des menschlichen Wissens zu vernichten drohte, hier die einzige Bedingung wird, unter der wir eine solche Theorie aufstellen können. Wir sahen nicht ab, wie wir jemals absolut entgegengesetzte sollten vereinigen können; hier sehen wir, dass eine Erklärung der Begebenheiten in unserem Geiste überhaupt gar nicht möglich seyn würde, ohne absolut entgegengesetzte; da dasjenige Vermögen, auf welchem alle jene Begebenheiten beruhen, die productive Einbildungskraft, gar nicht möglich seyn würde, wenn nicht absolut entgegengesetzte, nicht zu vereinigende, dem Auffassungsvermögen des Ich völlig unangemessene vorkämen" (*SW* I, p. 226; *GA* I, 2, p. 367).

16. "Mithin ist das Ich, insofern ihm ein Nicht-Ich entgegengesetzt wird, selbst entgegengesetzt dem absoluten Ich" (*SW* I, p. 110; *GA* I, 2, p. 272).

17. Cf. Fichte's own interpretation of the theoretical part at the very beginning of the practical part.

18. Cf. *SW* I, p. 247 (*GA* I, 2, p. 386). "Es liegt nemlich in diesem Satze (sc. im Grundsatz des praktischen Teils, J.B.) eine Haupt-Antithese, die den ganzen Widerstreit zwischen dem Ich, als Intelligenz, und insofern beschränktem, und zwischen ebendemselben, als schlechthin gesetztem, mithin unbeschränktem Wesen umfasst, und uns nöthiget, als Vereinigungsmittel ein praktisches Vermögen des Ich anzunehmen" (*SW* I, p. 247; *GA* I, 2, p. 386).

19. "In Erörterung des aufgestellten Satzes: das Ich setzt sich, als bestimmend das Nicht-Ich, könnten wir gerade so verfahren, wie wir in Erörterung des obigen Satzes: das Ich setzt sich als bestimmt durch das Nicht-Ich verfuhren. Es liegen in diesem ebensowohl als in jenem mehrere Gegensätze; wir könnten dieselben aufsuchen, sie synthetisch vereinigen, die durch diese Synthesis entstandenen Begriffe, wenn sie etwa wieder entgegengesetzt seyn sollten, abermals synthetisch vereinigen, u.s.f. und wir wären sicher nach einer einfachen

und gründlichen Methode unseren Satz völlig zu erschöpfen. Aber es giebt eine kürzere, und darum nicht weniger erschöpfende Art, ihn zu erörtern" (*SW* I, p. 247; *GA* I, 2, p. 386).

20. "Der Mensch soll sich der an sich unerreichbaren Freiheit ins Unendliche immer mehr nähern" (*SW* I, p. 117; *GA* I, 2, p. 277). "Es ist vielmehr eine Aufgabe meines Geistes . . . welche aber nur nach einer vollendeten Annäherung zum Unendlichen gelöset werden könnte" (*SW* I, p. 117; *GA* I, 2, p. 278). "[B]is die absolute Einheit hervorgebracht sey; welche freilich, wie sich zu seiner Zeit zeigen wird, nur durch eine geendete Annäherung zum Unendlichen hervorgebracht werden könnte, welche an sich unmöglich ist" (*SW* I, p. 115; *GA* I, 2, p. 276). "Die reine in sich selbst zurückgehende Thätigkeit des Ich ist in Beziehung auf ein mögliches Object ein Streben; und zwar, laut obigem Beweiss ein unendliches Streben" (*SW* I, p. 261; *GA* I, 2, p. 397).

21. "Jener Widerstreit der Vernunft mit sich selbst (sc. bezüglich einer dogmatisch realistischen und einer dogmatisch idealistischen Erklärung der Vorstellung) muss gelöst werden, wenn es auch nicht eben in der theoretischen Wissenschaftslehre möglich wäre: und da das absolute Seyn des Ich nicht aufgegeben werden kann, so muss der Streit zum Vortheile der letzten Folgerungsart entschieden werden, ebenso wie im dogmatischen Idealismus (nur mit dem Unterschiede, dass unser Idealismus nicht dogmatisch, sondern praktisch ist; nicht bestimmt, was *ist,* sondern was seyn *solle*)" (*SW* I, p. 156; *GA* I, 2, p. 311).

22. A helpful analysis of this doctrine can be found in Daniel Breazeale, "Check or Checkmate? On the Finitude of the Fichtean Self," in *The Modern Subject: Conceptions of the Self in Classical German Philosophy,* ed. K. Ameriks and D. Sturma (New York: SUNY Press 1995), pp. 87–114.

23. "Setzet, als den ersten Fall nach dem blossen Begriffe der Wirksamkeit, dass die Einschränkung des Ich einzig und allein von der Thätigkeit des Nicht-Ich herkomme. . . . Das Ich wäre im angenommenen Falle allerdings eingeschränkt, aber es wäre seiner Einschränkung sich nicht bewusst. Das Ich wäre . . . allerdings *bestimmt;* aber *es setzte sich nicht* als bestimmt, sondern irgend ein Wesen ausser ihm könnte es als bestimmt setzen" (*SW* I, pp. 146 f.; *GA* I, 2, p. 303).

"Oder setzet als den zweiten Fall nach dem blossen Begriffe der Substantialität, dass das Ich schlechthin und unabhängig von aller Einwirkung des Nicht-Ich ein Vermögen habe, willkürlich ein vermindertes Quantum der Realität in sich zu setzen (. . .). Das Ich setzte denn allerdings sich als bestimmt, aber nicht als bestimmt *durch das Nicht-Ich*" (*SW* I, p. 147; *GA* I, 2, p. 303).

24. "Insofern das Ich absolut ist, ist es *unendlich* und *unbeschränkt.* Alles, was ist, setzt es; und was es nicht setzt, ist nicht (*für* dasselbe; und *ausser* demselben ist nichts). Alles aber, was es setzt, setzt es als Ich; und das Ich setzt es, als alles, was es setzt. Mithin fasst in dieser Rücksicht das Ich in sich alle, d.i. eine unendliche, unbeschränkte Realität. Insofern das Ich sich ein Nicht-Ich entgegensetzt, setzt es nothwendig *Schranken* (' 3), und sich selbst in diese Schranken. Es vertheilt die Totalität des gesetzten Seyns überhaupt an das Ich und an das Nicht-Ich, und setzt demnach insofern sich nothwendig als *endlich.* Diese zwei sehr verschiedenen Handlungen lassen sich durch folgenden Sätze ausdrücken. Der erste: das Ich

setzt schlechthin sich als *unendlich* und *unbeschränkt*. Der zweite: das Ich setzt schlechthin sich als *endlich* und *beschränkt*" (*SW* I, p. 255).

25. "Der letzte Grund aller Wirklichkeit für das Ich ist demnach nach der Wissenschaftslehre eine ursprüngliche Wechselwirkung zwischen dem Ich und irgend einem Etwas ausser demselben, von welchem sich weiter nichts sagen lässt, als dass es dem Ich völlig entgegengesetzt seyn muss . . . ; das Ich wird durch jenes Entgegengesetzte bloss in Bewegung gesetzt, um zu handeln . . . Jenem bewegenden kommt aber auch nichts weiter zu, als dass es ein bewegendes sey, eine entgegengesetzte Kraft, die als solche auch nur gefühlt wird" (*SW* I, p. 279; *GA* I, 2, p. 411).

"Sie (sc. die WL) behauptet aber auch nichts weiter, als eine solche entgegengesetzte Kraft, die von dem endlichen Wesen bloss *gefühlt*, aber nicht *erkannt* wird. Alle mögliche Bestimmungen dieser Kraft, oder dieses Nicht-Ich, die in die Unendlichkeit hinaus in unserem Bewusstseyn vorkommen können, macht sie sich anheischig, aus dem bestimmenden Vermögen des Ich abzuleiten, und muss dieselbe, so gewiss sie Wissenschaftslehre ist, wirklich ableiten können" (*SW* I, p. 280; *GA* I, 2, p. 411).

26. "Der (durch das setzende Ich nicht gesetzte) Anstoss geschieht auf das Ich, insofern es thätig ist, und er ist demnach nur insofern ein Anstoss, als es thätig ist; seine Möglichkeit wird durch die Thätigkeit des Ich bedingt: keine Thätigkeit des Ich, kein Anstoss. Hinwiederum wäre die Thätigkeit des Bestimmens des Ich durch sich selbst, bedingt durch den Anstoss: kein Anstoss, keine Selbstbestimmung.—Ferner keine Selbstbestimmung, kein objectives, u.s.w." (*SW* I. p. 212; *GA* I, 2, p. 356).

27. "Ohnerachtet ihres Realismus aber ist diese Wissenschaft nicht transcendent, sondern bleibt in ihren innersten Tiefen *transcendental*. Sie erklärt allerdings alles Bewusstseyn aus einem unabhängig von allem Bewusstseyn vorhandenen; aber sie vergisst nicht, dass sie auch in dieser Erklärung sich nach ihren eigenen Gesetzen richte, und so wie sie hierauf reflectirt, wird jenes Unabhängige abermals ein Product ihrer eigenen Denkkraft, mithin etwas vom Ich abhängiges, insofern es für das Ich (im Begriff davon) da seyn soll. Aber für die Möglichkeit dieser neuen Erklärung jener ersten Erklärung wird ja abermals schon das wirkliche Bewusstseyn, und für dessen Möglichkeit abermals jenes Etwas, von welchem das Ich abhängt, vorausgesetzt: und wenn jetzt gleich dasjenige, was fürs erste als ein Unabhängiges gesetzt wurde, vom Denken des Ich abhängig geworden, so ist doch dadurch das Unabhängige nicht gehoben, sondern nur weiter hinausgesetzt, und so könnte man in das unbegrenzte hinaus verfahren, ohne dass dasselbe je aufgehoben würde" (*SW* I, p. 280; *GA* I, 2, p. 411).

28. *SW* I, p. 281; *GA* I, 2, p. 412.

29. "Dies, dass der endliche Geist nothwendig etwas absolutes ausser sich setzen muss (ein Ding an sich) und dennoch von der anderen Seite anerkennen muss, dass dasselbe nur *für ihn* da sey (ein nothwendiges Noumen sey), ist derjenige Cirkel, den er in das unendliche erweitern, aus welchem er aber nie herausgehen kann. Ein, System, das auf diesen Cirkel gar nicht Rücksicht nimmt, ist ein dogmatischer Idealismus; denn eigentlich ist es nur der angezeigte

Cirkel, der uns begrenzt und zu endlichen Wesen macht: ein System, das aus demselben herausgegangen zu seyn wähnt, ist ein transcendenter realistischer Dogmatismus. Die Wissenschaftslehre hält zwischen beiden Systemen bestimmt die Mitte, und ist ein kritischer Idealismus, den man auch einen Real-Idealismus, oder einen Ideal-Realismus nennen könnte" (*SW* I, p. 281; *GA* I, 2, p. 412).

    30. *WLnm* 47; see also *Fichte: Foundations of Transcendental Philosophy (Wissenschaftslehre) nova methodo,* ed. and trans. Daniel Breazeale (Ithaca, N.Y.: Cornell University Press, 1992), p. 139.

    31. Cf. *SW* I, p. 279; *GA* I, 2, p. 411.

    32. Section 5, *SW* I, p. 274; *GA* I, 2, p. 406.

    33. "[U]nd so haben wir ursprünglich das Ich in zweierlei Rücksicht, theils, inwiefern es reflectirend ist, und insofern ist die Richtung seiner Thätigkeit centripetal; theils, inwiefern es dasjenige ist, worauf reflectirt wird, und insofern ist die Richtung seiner Thätigkeit centrifugal, und zwar centrifugal in die Unendlichkeit hinaus" (*SW* I, p. 274; *GA* I, 2, p. 406).

    34. "[B]eide Richtungen der Tätigkeit des Ich, die centripetale und die centrifugale, fallen zusammen, und sind nur Eine und ebendieselbe Richtung. . . . So ist demnach aus dem oben vorausgesetzten kein Bewusstseyn abzuleiten: denn beide angenommenen Richtungen lassen sich nicht unterscheiden" (*SW* I, p. 275).

    35. "Nun aber soll die ins unendliche hinausgehende Thätigkeit des Ich in irgend einem Puncte angestossen und in sich selbst zurückgetrieben werden; und das Ich soll demnach die Unendlichkeit nicht ausfüllen." (*SW* I, p. 275) "Nemlich nach der Forderung des absoluten Ich sollte seine (insofern centrifugale) Thätigkeit hinausgehen in die Unendlichkeit; aber sie wird in C reflectirt, wird mithin centripetal, und nun ist durch Beziehung auf jene ursprüngliche Forderung einer ins unendliche hinausgehenden centrifugalen Richtung . . . die Unterscheidung möglich" (*SW* I, p. 275 f.).

    36. "So steht das Ich, als Ich, ursprünglich in Wechselwirkung mit sich selbst; und dadurch erst wird ein Einfluss von aussen in dasselbe möglich" (*SW* I p. 276; *GA* I, 2, p. 409).

    37. "Hinwiederum, ist das Ich nicht Intelligenz, so ist kein Bewusstseyn seines praktischen Vermögens, und überhaupt kein Selbstbewusstseyn möglich, weil erst durch die fremdartige, durch den Anstoss entstandene Richtung die Unterscheidung verschiedener Richtungen möglich wird" (*SW* I, p. 278).

    "Nach der soeben vorgenommenen Erörterung ist das Princip des Lebens und Bewusstseyns, der Grund seiner Möglichkeit,—allerdings im Ich enthalten, aber dadurch entsteht noch kein wirkliches Leben, kein empirisches Leben in der Zeit; und ein anderes ist für uns schlechterdings undenkbar. Soll ein solches wirkliches Leben möglich seyn, so bedarf es dazu noch eines besonderen Anstosses auf das Ich durch ein Nicht-Ich" (*SW* I, p. 279; *GA* I, 2, p. 411).

    38. Fichte himself compares the procedures of his first and second WL: "In diesem Stücke nun (sc. *WLnm* § 2, J.B.) ist der in dem compendio (sc. WL 1794, J.B.) beobachtete Gang völlig umgekehrt. Es wird da (sc. WL 1794, J.B.) ausgegangen vom Entgegengesezten des NichtIch, und es wird postulirt

als absolut (§ 2). Aus dem Entgegensezen wird das Bestimmen abgeleitet (§ 3)" (*WLnm*, p. 44).

"Der 3te § würde jezt der 2te sein, und umgekehrt. Mit dem NichtIch ist abermal ein anderer Weg eingeschlagen worden, das NichtIch ist nicht unmittelbar, sondern mittelbar postulirt worden" (*Wlnm*, p. 44).

"[A]ber wir folgern hier nicht die Schranken aus dem Nicht-Ich, sondern aus der Beschränktheit des Ich wird das NichtIch gefolgert" (*Wlnm*, p. 73).

Fichte understates the differences when he says "Beide Wege sind richtig; denn die nothwendige Bestimmtheit des Ich und das nothwendige Sein des NichtIch stehen im Wechsel. Man kann von Einem zum andern übergehen. Beide Wege sind möglich." (*Wlnm*, p. 44) As a matter of fact, it is only the new conception of the I that enables Fichte not to repeat what he had said in his early Wissenschaftslehre about the check and the not-I.

39. *Wlnm*, p. 39.

40. "Das Ich, welches in dem beabsichtigten liegt, und das Nicht-Ich, welches in dem Gegebenen liegt, sind 1 und daßelbe. Es sind nur zwei unzertrennliche Ansichten, darum weil das Ich Subject = Object sein muß" (*Wlnm*, p. 42).

41. *WLnm*, ed. Fuchs, pp. 42 f.; *WLnm*, ed. Breazeale, p. 133.

42. "Sein ist Charakter des NichtIch, der Charakter des Ich ist Thätigkeit, der Dogmatismus geht vom Sein aus, und erklärt dieß fürs erste, unmittelbare" (*Wlnm*, p. 42).

43. For a proper evaluation of this claim, one has to be aware that most metaphysicians would not have shared the presupposition underlying Fichte's deduction, namely, that being is to be understood as passivity. According to the Aristotelian and Thomist tradition, being is an act, not a state of repose.

44. The term *kritischer Idealismus* occurs several times, as the index to Fuchs's edition shows, but it takes on a meaning that has nothing to do with the idea of an infinite regress in explaining the not-I. It may be called an oddity of the historiography of philosophy that some of the notions that still stick to Fichte's name, such as *unendliches Streben* or *absolute Forderung*, were abandoned by Fichte himself as early as 1796. The famous fifth paragraph of the *Grundlage* was one of the most short-lived parts of Fichte's project.

45. "Es ist zu erweisen, daß das Ich sich nicht sezen könne, ohne noch manches andere zu sezen" (*Wlnm*, p. 21).

"Von nun an haben wir die Möglichkeit des bisher aufgestellten anzugeben; und die Bedingungen dieser Möglichkeit vollständig aufzuzählen. Wir haben jetzt unser bestimmtes Ziel, bei dem wir ankommen müßen, wir haben schon die Vollendung imAuge. Wenn wir dahin kommen, wo wir begreifen, daß das Ich sich selbst seze, als durch sich selbst gesezt, so ist unser System geschloßen" (*Wlnm*, p. 63 f.).

46. *WLnm* section 17; *WLnm*, ed. Fuchs, p. 209; *WLnm*, ed. Breazeale, p. 415.

First Steps: Lessons on Becoming a Philosopher from the Early Chapters of the *Wissenschaftslehre nova methodo*

Janet Roccanova

The following study is an interpretative explication of the first steps of the *Wissenschaftslehre* as it was presented in Fichte's lectures in Jena between 1796 and 1799. The interpretation offered herein is additionally influenced by Fichte's published writings about the *Wissenschaftslehre*, especially the two introductions and first chapter comprising "An Attempt at a New Presentation" published in the *Philosophisches Journal* between 1797 and 1798. The present study is, to a lesser extent, also informed by the earlier "Concerning the Concept of the *Wissenschaftslehre*," published originally in 1794 and republished in 1798, and the later "A Crystal Clear Report to the General Public Concerning the Essence of the Newest Philosophy: An Attempt to Force the Reader to Understand," from 1801.

This study will stay as close as possible to the text of the *nova methodo* lectures, along with the introductions (both published and unpublished). The reason for this close textual analysis is the working assumption that there is indeed an interpretation that can incorporate all that Fichte says in these texts without concluding that Fichte was anywhere grossly inconsistent. Ultimately, this study is the result of an attempt to force myself to understand exactly what the philosopher was doing and not doing in those crucial steps leading up to the first principle and in the steps taken immediately afterward. The larger aim, then, is to provide the necessary context in which to comprehend correctly the remainder of the argument of the *Wissenschaftslehre nova methodo*.

1

Prior to illuminating the first steps taken by the philosopher of the *Wissenschaftslehre* it is necessary to discuss a few philosophical concepts and how Fichte employs these concepts.

Consciousness (Bewußtsein) is a broad category for Fichte signifying any form of awareness that we as conscious subjects are capable of. There are several types of consciousness, but what all consciousness has in common is that it is always consciousness *of* something. Although Fichte never explicitly presents this observation in the form of a thesis, for the purposes of this essay I will nevertheless borrow a term from Husserl's phenomenology and call this the "intentionality thesis."

In the first introduction to the *Wissenschaftslehre*, we see Fichte distinguishing three types of consciousness according to the relation between the object of consciousness and the conscious subject.[1] What we could call "imagination" is a type of consciousness in which the object "appears to be something first produced by means of the intellect's representation of it."[2] In what could be called "objective experience," the object of consciousness "appears to be something present without any help from the intellect," such that the properties of the object "appear to be determined along with the object itself."[3] And finally, in what Fichte calls "immediate self-consciousness," the mere existence of the object (in this case the I) is present without any help from the intellect, "while its properties are determinable by the free intellect."[4]

Fichte also distinguishes the "philosopher's consciousness" from "ordinary consciousness," but we must save a discussion of this distinction until after we have examined what the philosopher does. We can say preliminarily though that intellectual intuition, or at least what Alain Perrinjaquet calls "pure intellectual intuition,"[5] is a type of philosophical consciousness, and that Fichte characterizes ordinary consciousness as a complete or "completely determined" consciousness, by which Fichte emphasizes that there is no consciousness apart from a thing ("intentionality thesis") and no thing apart from consciousness.[6] Another version of the "intentionality thesis" can be seen in the relation between intuition and concept. The above notion of a "complete consciousness" entails that such a consciousness is composed of the activity of consciousness and the "thing" or object of consciousness.[7] In phenomenological terms, this is referred to as *noesis* (or noetic activity) and *noema* (or noematic object). Similarly, an intuition for Fichte is composed of the activity of intuiting and that which is intuited. The intuiting activity is the means by which we gain access to the intuited object, but we only become fully aware of this object by representing it to ourselves. For the object of a sensible intuition to become part of our experience of the world, for it to increase our experiential knowledge base, we must become explicitly aware of this object, which means that we must *think* it. But all thinking occurs by means of concepts; so all intuitions require concepts.

In ordinary consciousness, at least, the activity of intuiting and the concept arise together in a single act called an intuition. An intuition, though, is still a form of consciousness, as consciousness is the broader category.

Positing (setzen) is yet another characterization of a form of consciousness. It, too, is a broad category, and one that is closely related to conceptualizing, insofar as to posit something is to represent it to ourselves. We cannot posit something without being aware of it (which is why this is such a choice term for Fichte to use). Positing is an act; it is something the conscious subject does; and it thus simultaneously affirms both the active nature of the conscious subject and, thereby, also the essential "intentionality" of experience. From the philosophical or transcendental standpoint, we understand that all experience is a result of the activity of consciousness, and in this sense everything that is in consciousness is posited, that is, it is placed there by the intellect.

There is a sense in which positing, representing, and intuiting are all the same sort of activity, and that is insofar as they are all instances of ideal activity. Fichte describes ideal activity as an act of copying or mirroring.[8] (As it turns out, at least in the act in which the I posits itself, what is copied by ideal activity is real activity, which is free or willed activity, the act of freely initiating a movement of consciousness.)

2

The task Fichte gives his students in the *nova methodo* lectures is to "construct the concept of the I and observe how you do this."[9] To begin this task Fichte suggests that the students think or intuit something—the wall, for instance.[10] This seemingly simple request is actually an ingenious tactic on Fichte's part that assures that the students will have acted freely, by freely choosing to determine or focus their consciousness at Fichte's request. (Because the dogmatist would deny the possibility of freely acting, this move of Fichte's thus either bars the consistent dogmatist's entry into the *Wissenschaftslehre*, or trips up the inconsistent dogmatist who thereby actively falsifies his own claims against freedom.) Once the students or philosophers-to-be have performed this free focusing of conscious attention (or free determining of their representation), Fichte points out the necessary distinction between the object of their conscious attention and themselves as the conscious subject. Fichte also points out the determinateness of their representation, that is, that it is not a representation in general, but is necessarily a particular representation.[11] These two points set the stage for what I am calling the "intentionality thesis."

Then Fichte requests that the students freely focus their consciousness once more; but this time they are to "abstract" from the object of the current representation and focus instead on the conscious subject, or what is the same thing, on the activity of consciousness in that representation. *This* act of freely focusing their consciousness, whereby the subject and object of consciousness converge, or whereby the I itself becomes the object of a determinate representation, the act that one observer of Fichte's lectures said "caused obvious confusion and embarrassment" for many students,[12] is what Fichte calls "intellectual intuition."[13] And if the students were able to accomplish this act, they had thereby arrived at the common border of ordinary and philosophical consciousness.

Now the students could step over (or up) into the philosophical standpoint and become philosophers by beginning to observe carefully and reflectively the activity of consciousness they were now intellectually intuiting. These newly hatched philosophers are to watch what happens as this I in itself, this conscious activity, generates a world out of itself before their very "eyes."[14] What the philosopher observes is the activity of consciousness, the acting of the I, and even more precisely, what the philosopher observes are the necessary ways of acting of this I,[15] as necessary, which then become for the philosopher the "laws of reason."

All that I have described thus far actually occurs in consciousness, in the philosopher-to-be's consciousness. Fichte is absolutely clear on this point. This is one of the advantages idealism has over dogmatism, that is, that its first principle is able to occur actually in consciousness.[16] But Fichte is also clear that the first principle of the *Wissenschaftslehre* does not occur in consciousness *as* a first principle, *as* the explanatory ground of experience.[17] That the I in itself, the I as subject-object, which is posited by the philosopher as a result of this intellectual intuition, that this I is the explanatory ground of experience—this is a *postulate*. The philosopher, whose task and only whose task it is to provide an accounting of experience, to ground experience, *postulates* that the I as subject-object is the explanatory ground, is the first principle of a system of idealism. And it is only at the end of the philosopher's derivation, at the end of a *successful* derivation of experience from this first principle, that the provisional or hypothetical nature of the philosopher's claim will be removed.

Before we examine more specifically the role of the new philosopher, who is looking for the necessary ways of acting or for how he is required to act in constructing the concept of the I, I would like to make a brief aside into something that has not been adequately addressed with respect to transcendental idealism. Given that Kant's metaphysical deduction of the categories is generally conceded to have been unsuccessful, or at least insufficient, how is it that the transcendental deduction can claim any validity without a prior deduction or other justification of reason? Kant is, after all, deducing the *rationally* necessary conditions of our experience of an object as a synthetic whole—or is he? This question, I believe, is the essence of Fichte's question to Kant, and it points to how Fichte could claim that Kant's entire philosophy is itself a product of intellectual intuition.[18]

Let me fill this out a bit: One of Fichte's main advantages over Kant in his presentation of transcendental idealism, not to mention over the philosophy of Descartes along with most, if not all, philosophers of the modern period, is that he does not simply assume the validity of reason as a methodological handmaiden of philosophy, but instead *discovers* reason within or along with the intellectual intuition of the activity of consciousness. This is to say that simultaneous with the beginning of the *Wissenschaftslehre* as a system of idealism, Fichte discovers a "single basic law of reason."[19] This basic law of reason is, Fichte says, "immediately establishe[d] within consciousness."[20] The philosopher then *postulates* that this discovered law of reason is the "necessary and fundamental law of reason as a whole."[21] Again, the truth of this postulate can only be proven by the success of the philosopher's derivation, by the success of the *Wissenschaftslehre* in using its postulated fundamental law of reason to derive the entire system of necessary representations, or experience as a whole, as (rational) conditions for the possibility of the self-positing of the I, which is a fact/act *(Tathandlung)* that has already been performed by each of the student philosophers.[22] This is the sense in which the *Wissenschaftslehre* is a gigantic transcendental argument, which derives the whole of experience as a series of necessary conditions for the possibility of this just performed fact/act of the I's self-positing, an act which brought the I into "existence" and resulted in the concept of the I as a subject-object.

So what is this basic law of reason discovered by the philosopher in intellectual intuition? In observing his own free self-positing of his I, the philosopher "discover[s] that he is obliged to proceed in a certain way."[23] In other words, this free act of constructing the concept of the I must be performed in a certain way, in a necessary manner, if it is to be performed at all.[24] Even *free* acting must follow the rules.

The rule that the philosopher discovers goes by various names in the *Wissenschaftslehre nova methodo* (such as the "principle of determinability" or "principle of reflective opposition"), but, for the purposes of this paper, it is what I will refer to in general as the "principle of opposition."[25] In chapter one of the *Wissenschaftslehre nova methodo,* the philosopher realizes that the way the concept of the I, or rather, since we have not yet actually constructed the concept of the I, the way the intellectual intuition of the activity of consciousness, of the activity of intuition, came to be was by willfully "wrenching" himself away from a state of repose and transporting himself into the activity of self-positing.[26] The state of repose Fichte is referring to here is the concept that was part of the original intuition, the concept of the wall, for example. In intuiting or focusing their attention on the wall, or what is the same thing, in making the wall the object of a determinate representation, the students formed the concept of the wall. And in this sensible intuition of the wall the conscious subject, or activity of consciousness, was absorbed into the object or concept.[27] Fichte's subsequent request to his students, to intuit or focus on the I as the conscious subject, was achieved only by wrenching themselves away from the concept or object, by opposing the activity of consciousness (the *noesis*) to the passivity of the object (the *noema*). The conscious subject, the activity of consciousness, is that in the sensible intuition that is *not* the object. Whatever is left over after abstracting from the object, *that* is the I, *that* is the conscious activity.[28]

This opposing, which is the necessary way of achieving the free act of focusing on the actively conscious subject, is discovered by the philosopher in the intellectual intuition as part of this activity. Here again an act of abstraction on the part of the philosopher was required to enable the philosopher's intuition of this necessary law of acting. This abstraction must be freely and intentionally performed by the philosopher to gain access to the intuition of this "law" of acting.

By this point, then, the philosopher has performed two separate acts of abstraction and has thereby gained access to two distinct intellectual intuitions. First the philosopher-to-be abstracted from the object of a sensible intuition (the intuition of the wall), which enabled the intellectual intuition of the activity of consciousness. Next, since the philosopher by this point is able to intuit his conscious activity as such, he then abstracts from this activity in order to intuit the necessary laws of this activity. Abstraction was required in both instances because, first of all, the conscious activity does not occur separately from the object of consciousness. Remember, all consciousness is consciousness of something. And second, the laws of acting are not separable from the acting. The laws are laws *of* acting, and acting must occur according to these laws.

Talking of "laws" here is perhaps a bit misleading. The fact is that the laws of reason, the necessary laws of acting, as "laws," are in a sense *inventions* of the philosopher. All that really exists is activity, activity that occurs in a certain way. Fichte's position, at least in the "Crystal Clear Report," is that the philosopher immediately intuits that the way the activity occurs is the only way it can occur and that this is the same for all I's.[29] But it is the philosopher who, in reflecting on the necessary ways of acting, isolates these ways of acting by way of abstraction and considers them as "laws."[30]

3

Next we must consider the *concept of the I,* which is generated by the intellectual intuition of the activity of consciousness. The philosopher, whose task it is to observe *how* the concept of the I comes to be, realizes that the concept of the I comes about by an application of the principle of opposition. The philosopher who has been observing or reflecting on this entire process of conscious activity, and who is also the conscious subject of the activity, immediately intuits the freedom of his activity. First the conscious subject freely focused on the wall, and then this subject acted freely again in making itself the focus of its own intuiting activity.[31] It is simply impossible to perform the actions freely without at the same time immediately intuiting them to be *free* actions (and also therefore without believing in one's own freedom before even attempting to perform these acts). The freedom and the belief in freedom are inherent in the actions, one could say.

But because of the necessary ways of conscious activity the conscious subject cannot intuit this free activity, cannot understand or comprehend it as free, unless it understands it as a movement of transition of consciousness and, moreover, as a movement of transition to a particular determination of consciousness, to a particular object of consciousness, or as Fichte says, to a state of determinacy. But a movement of transition is always (by definition) to one state from another state. Thus the conscious subject necessarily opposes a prior state of indeterminacy or determinability to the freely determined state of its current representation, and it must do this if it is to think the I, if it is to think free conscious activity.

All of this is right there in the accomplished fact/act of the self-intuition of the conscious subject. To become aware of the free activity of consciousness is at the same time to posit this activity. But posited activity is precisely not activity as active, but is rather activity in repose. Anything posit*ed* is in repose, only the act of posit*ing* is active.[32] Activity in repose is merely the power of activity, it is the possibility of becoming actively conscious, actively focused, of generating a determinate representation. It is, in Fichte's words, *determinability*. And this is the concept of the I that is produced by the intellectual intuition of conscious activity. The I is the *power* of consciousness.[33] And the philosopher observes that this process of generating the concept of the I occurs in conformity with the principle of opposition intuited previously (which comes as no surprise to the philosopher who already postulated that this principle was the fundamental principle of reason).[34]

The concept of the I as determinability, as the power or capacity of consciousness, is also what Fichte calls "immediate consciousness." Immediate consciousness is what is presupposed by and grounds all possible consciousness[35] and so can never itself be captured in consciousness. We are never conscious of immediate consciousness itself.[36]

As determinability, immediate consciousness is activity in repose, inactive activity. But what is this? It is nothing more than an *Idea*,[37] "something posited in accordance with the laws of reflection,"[38] that is, in accordance with the principle of opposition. Determinability is the *capacity* of consciousness, a capacity as such.[39] But we can never experience a capacity unless it is actualized, unless it is in activity, in agility. But an actualized capacity is no longer a capacity as such. Thus it is simply impossible to be directly conscious of capacity, of determinability, of immediate consciousness.[40]

Also, because all consciousness is consciousness *of* something, all consciousness is therefore determinate consciousness (it is determined by its object). But the I is not any particular consciousness (a consciousness of a particular object). The I as the conscious subject, as the "subjective factor in all consciousness,"[41] is consciousness as such, whether as an activity or as an ability. But because of the "intentionality thesis," there really is no pure consciousness as such, except as a philosophical Idea.

Now the philosopher really does intuit intellectually his own activity of consciousness. But a *completed* act of self-positing requires more than this. It requires also constructing the concept of the I, which is truly an act of *construction* on the part of the philosopher, a construction that is performed in accord with the principle of reflective opposition. It is the philosopher as philosopher who, in reflecting on this activity of self-positing, as it is underway, realizes that there is a co-incidence of subject and object in this act.[42] The philosopher then posits the I, his own I, as a subject-object, and he does this on the basis of the intellectual intuition of his activity of consciousness. Accordingly, this posited pure I, this I in itself, this I as subject-object, is the first principle of the system of idealism known as the *Wissenschaftslehre*.

4

At this point I would like to consider the chart from chapter two (in the Krause and Halle editions) of the *Wissenschaftslehre nova methodo* (see figure 1). This chart and Fichte's exposition of it serve his purposes as a summary of the elements of the *Wissenschaftslehre* brought into the deduction thus far (that is, through chapter two). For my purposes, I would like to use this chart and Fichte's exposition of it as a way of simultaneously confirming my interpretation and further explicating that interpretation.

First it should be noticed that Fichte divides these elements of the deduction into two spheres. The sphere of the *intended* is the sphere of what the philosopher willfully brings to consciousness (Fichte also calls this what is "subjective"), while the sphere of the *given* is the sphere of what is necessarily conjoined with what is intended, which is not so purely willed but is rather in a certain sense "found" by the philosopher (and Fichte calls this what is "objective"). In the intended sphere, Fichte locates the "real determinate activity," labeled *A,* as well as what he says comes into being by means of this activity, which is the concept of the I, labeled as *B.* Situated in the sphere of the given is *C,* the determinable activity, and what is brought about by means of *C,* which is the not-I, labeled *D.*

As I interpret this chart, *A* is the intellectual intuition of conscious activity that the philosopher willfully initiates by intentionally wrenching himself away from the object of the sensible intuition (from the wall). This is the "real determinate activity." It is real because real activity is willful, free, acting, which is precisely the character of this intellectual activity achieved by the philosopher. It is determinate because, as all intuition and all consciousness must have a concept or object, that is, something intuited or conscious-ed, so too does even intellectual intuition have its object. But the object of intellectual intuition, as opposed to that of sensible intuition, is unique insofar as intellectual intuition is an intuition of the activity of consciousness itself, rather than an intuition of some object distinguishable (even if not separable) from the conscious activity. This lack of any "sensible content" is why Fichte calls it *intellectual* intuition. It is a "pure intuition," an "intuition of acting," an "intuition of intuition."[43]

The object or concept connected with *A* as the intellectual intuition of the activity of consciousness is thus *C. C* is the intuition, the intuiting activity, the conscious activity, which is freely determinable or focusable, and it is what the intellectual intuition *(A)* is *of.* It is important not to

FIGURE 1. Summary of Elements in the *Wissenschaftslehre* per Krause and Halle

A. The real determinate activity B. The concept of the I.	Both as intended.
C. The determinable activity D. The Not-I.	Both as given.[1]

To the sphere of *what is intended* (subjective) pertain:	To the sphere of *what is given* (objective) pertain:
Activity; determinate activity; the concept of the I.	Repose; what is determinable; the concept of the Not-I.
Let us call the real, determinate activity that lies within this sphere, i.e., the activity in agility, *A,* and let us call what comes into being thereby, i.e., *the concept of the I, B.*	Let us call the determinable activity in a state of repose that lies within this sphere *C,* and let us call the Not-I that is produced thereby *D.*[2]

The first sphere thus includes the following:	The sphere of the given likewise includes the following:
1. real, self-reverting activity = *A,* and	1. determinable activity (i.e., activity that is determinable, in the sense that it can turn into actual acting, although it may itself be determined in other respects) = *C,* and
2. that which has come into being by means of activity = *B.*	2. the Not-I that is produced by means of this determinable activity = *D.*[3]

For clarity and emphasis, material that in the original sources appeared as regular text I have here reconfigured into a table format.
1. *WLnm[H],* p. 2 (*GA* IV, 2, p. 37; *FTP,* p. 128).
2. *WLnm[H],* p. 2 (*GA* IV, 2, p. 36; *FTP,* p. 128).
3. *WLnm[K],* p. 2 (*FM,* p. 37; *FTP,* p. 128).

confuse C as determinable activity with determinability, for determinability is more properly B, that is, the concept of the I that is intentionally produced by the philosopher by means of, or on the basis of, A. B is the concept of what is active, what is acting, what is intuiting itself. Fichte does remark that, in fact, B and C are equivalent, and this is true, except that B, as the capacity of consciousness, is what is actively conscious, consciousness itself, a mere concept or Idea, while C, as the activity of consciousness, is the activity that B does. But since the I is really nothing over and above its activity, B and C are in that sense equivalent.

Of course, as the *concept* connected with intellectual intuition A, C is itself in repose; all concepts are in repose. But considered in a different light, C is an active intuition, the intuition of the wall, for example. This is why Fichte says C is both a concept and an intuition. C is a concept in relation to intuition A, while in relation to D (the wall, for example) it is an intuition.[44]

D, then, is the object, or concept, of the first intuition that Fichte requested of his students (for example, the concept of the wall), the object away from which the students had to wrench themselves in order to perform the second requested intuition of the intuition itself, the intuition of intuiting activity.

In this sense, then, we can say that A is an intuition of an intuition (A is the intellectual intuition of C as a sensible intuition) while, because C is also a concept in relation to intellectual intuition A, and further because D is the concept or object connected to intuition C, D then is, as Fichte says, "a state of repose in a state of repose,"[45] or what is the same thing, a concept of a concept.

C thus turns out to be crucial for Fichte's deduction. As both a concept in relation to A and an intuition in relation to D, C is what bridges the gap between the two spheres (the intended and the given, or the subjective and the objective). C is also, as both a concept and an intuition, the essence of the self-positing I, which is conscious activity focused upon itself, both the intuiting and the intuited (*noesis* and *noema*, in unity). It is C that provides the required link between the innermost (self-consciousness) and the outermost (not-I) of consciousness.

Thus Fichte says that the fact that in the *Wissenschaftslehre* the I is both a concept and an intuition is what distinguishes the *Wissenschaftslehre* from all other systems, including Kant's.[46] And it is ultimately this, the fact that the I can intuit or be conscious of itself, that allows Fichte to derive the experiential world from this subject-object I.

5

Now I would like to return to the previously mentioned distinction between ordinary consciousness and philosophical consciousness. Although intimately related to it, this distinction is not strictly equivalent
to the distinction between the standpoint of life and the standpoint of
philosophy. The standpoint distinction is based upon the relevant tasks or
roles that one takes on at each standpoint. The standpoint of philosophy,
for instance, is *not* the standpoint of living our daily lives and interacting
with our world directly in a practical way, but rather the task of the
philosopher is to explain the possibility of our everyday experience, to
explain how the same subject who is able to be self-conscious, who is able
to say "I am I," is also able to be conscious of a world external to it, is also
able to say "I am not that" and "I am not you."

The consciousness distinction, though, is not about the different
tasks of the philosopher and the nonphilosopher, but is more properly
about the different *abilities* of the philosopher and the nonphilosopher,
and more important, it is about the different experiences the philosopher and the nonphilosopher have on the basis of these abilities. Even
more precisely, the distinction is about an ability that the philosopher
has that the common man does not have, or rather that the common
man has but does not exercise, and consequently, an experience that the
philosopher has that the common man does not have.

In the above chart Fichte himself calls the sphere of the intended
(which includes intellectual intuition and the concept of the I) "subjective" and the sphere of the given (which includes sensible intuition
and the not-I) "objective." Partly on the basis of this description, then, I
suggest that philosophical consciousness is what we could call "subjective
experience," while the only experience accessible to the common man
is "objective experience."[47] This results in "experience" being a broader
category, within which there are two general types of experience, parallel-
ing the two general types of consciousness. This also means that the task
of the philosopher is more properly to account for *objective* experience,
which he does on the basis of subjective experience. Subjective experience is not the *ground* of objective experience; the explanatory ground
of experience and the first principle of the *Wissenschaftslehre* is still the
pure I (I as subject-object), the concept of which is constructed by the
philosopher. But subjective experience is the *method* of the transcendental philosopher's deduction of objective experience; it is the mode of
access to the object of idealism.

My goal in this paper has been primarily to open the door to subjective experience, and I interpret Fichte's task as a professor as having

been that of taking his students through that door, which is the door that leads to the standpoint of philosophy.

The question that begs to be asked here is whether this means that we might now need a deduction of subjective experience, and whether I might have opened the door as well to an infinite regress, similar to that of the reflection theory of self-consciousness, the likes of which Fichte worked hard to avoid.[48] The answer to this question is "No," and the reason it is "No" has to do with the nature of this subjective experience. Not only is there nothing to explain with respect to subjective experience (in particular, there is no epistemological need to explain how the "outside" gets "inside" since there is no "outside"), but even more important, there is nothing that *can* be explained. This innermost experience, this awareness of the activity of consciousness (as opposed to the awareness of a mere fact of consciousness) is verifiable only from the inside (and in this sense is related to conscience), which is one reason why each philosopher must do the *Wissenschaftslehre* for him- or herself.[49]

We could, though, learn more about this subjective experience, and more about the transcendental subject, by asking after the possibility of transcendental philosophizing. In particular, we need to ask about what inter-relations there may be, or may need to be, between subjective and objective experience, or between philosophical and ordinary consciousness, in the person of the philosopher. For after all, there is a unity here, in the sense that the philosopher is the same subject of both experiences, of both consciousness, just as there is, I would emphasize, a single memory connected with all the philosopher's experiences, including both types of consciousness. And in fact, if that were not the case, the *Wissenschaftslehre* would be impossible. Although the pure I is a construction of the philosopher, and does not "exist" prior to the act of pure intellectual intuition,[50] which is the basis for the philosopher's concept of the I, there must be a prior I; the philosopher must be aware of his own I in some sense, *before* he can even begin to philosophize. An "I" must already be there that then wills to become explicitly conscious of itself in response to Fichte's request that it do so.

To solve this dilemma of the prior I, we must remember that the I as subject-object, which is the self-positing I that the philosopher postulates as the explanatory ground of consciousness, is a philosophical construction. This is the pure I of which we can never become conscious and that the philosopher can represent only as an Idea. But this should not be taken to mean that the philosopher's construction of this concept of the I is arbitrary. On the contrary, it is directly grounded in the pure intellectual intuition and is *rationally* generated out of this intellectual intuition ("rationally" meaning "on the basis of the principle of opposition"). But this pure I, which arises only in philosophical consciousness, cannot be the only meaningful sense of I.

If we return to our question of how the philosopher becomes a philosopher, with how the philosopher is able to transform himself from a common man to a philosopher, or, in other words, with how it is possible for someone to achieve a pure intellectual intuition of their activity of consciousness, we find another sense of "I" operative. As it happens, the answer to this question is also what guarantees the primacy of the practical in Fichte's philosophy, and that is the following: it is only possible to achieve a pure intellectual intuition of the activity of consciousness if, as a common man, the philosopher-to-be already has a lively sense of his own freedom,[51] and is already aware of his I as freedom. This awareness is what Fichte calls "real intellectual intuition,"[52] which he describes as "moral consciousness."[53]

In reflecting on ordinary consciousness, the philosopher must be sure to distinguish therein the I of real intellectual intuition, as the implicit self-awareness of freedom, and the I as personal individual, which perhaps might include both an objectively experienced self and this implicit self-awareness of freedom. More investigation is required concerning the relation between these two senses of "I" in ordinary consciousness.

Our point here is that only on the basis of real intellectual intuition, only if the philosopher-to-be is already to a certain degree self-aware, and more specifically, is aware of her- or himself as freely active, as free, will she or he be able to understand and carry out Fichte's instructions to construct the concept of the I.[54] (Which is precisely why Fichte argues that you can never teach an old dogmatist new tricks.)

Only on the condition of a real intellectual intuition of freedom in ordinary consciousness will the philosopher be able to achieve a pure intellectual intuition in philosophical consciousness, which is an act that merely brings to clarity in philosophical consciousness what was always already there obscurely in ordinary consciousness.

The next step, then, would be to determine what sort of awareness is real intellectual intuition, and especially to see if it might be characterizable as a *feeling*. Feeling plays many and varied roles in Fichte's philosophy, particularly in the *nova methodo* lectures, and undoubtedly an investigation into these roles of feeling would prove quite beneficial to a thorough understanding of Fichte's transcendental philosophy.

Notes

1. "Erste Einleitung in die Wissenschaftslehre" (1797), p. 4. Hereafter abbreviated as 1.Ein, this work appears in *J. G. Fichte: Gesämtausgabe der Bayerischen*

Akademie der Wissenschaften (hereafter abbreviated as *GA*), ed. Reinhard Lauth, Hans Jacobs, and Hans Gliwitzky (Stuttgart-Bad Cannstatt: Friedrich Frommann, 1964 ff.), at *GA* I, 4, pp. 183–208; and in *Johann Gottlieb Fichtes sämmtliche Werke* (hereafter abbreviated as *SW*), ed. I. H. Fichte, 8 vols. (Berlin: Veit, 1845–46), reprinted as *Fichtes Werke*, 11 vols. (Berlin: de Gruyter, 1971), at *SW* I, pp. 417–49. An English translation ("Preface" and "First Introduction" to *An Attempt at a New Presentation of the Wissenschaftslehre*) appears in *Introductions to the Wissenschaftslehre and Other Writings*, ed. and trans. Daniel Breazeale (Indianapolis: Hackett, 1994), pp. 1–35, hereafter abbreviated as *IWL*. For 1.Ein, p. 4, see *GA* I, 4, pp. 189–91; *SW* I, pp. 427–9; and *IWL*, pp. 12–15.

2. 1.Ein, p. 4 (*GA* I, 4, p. 189; *SW* I, p. 427; *IWL*, p. 12).

3. Ibid.

4. For these quotes, see 1.Ein, p. 4. The corresponding references are, for the first, *GA* I, 4, p. 191; *SW* I, p. 429; and *IWL*, p. 14; and, for the second, *GA* I, 4, p. 189; *SW* I, p. 427; *IWL*, p. 12.

5. See Alain Perrinjaquet, "Some Remarks Concerning the Circularity of Philosophy and the Evidence of its First Principle in the Jena *Wissenschaftslehre,*" in *Fichte: Historical Contexts—Contemporary Controversies*, ed. Daniel Breazeale and Tom Rockmore (New Jersey: Humanities Press, 1994), pp. 71–95 (esp. pp. 84–88).

6. *Sonnenklarer Bericht an das grössere Publikum, über das eigentliche Wesen der neuesten Philosophie* (1801), Lesson Five. This work appears in *GA* I, 7, pp. 185–268, and in *SW* II, pp. 323–420; the English translation, "A Crystal-Clear Report to the General Public Concerning the Actual Essence of the Newest Philosophy: An Attempt to Force the Reader to Understand," by John Botterman and William Raush, appears in *Philosophy of German Idealism*, ed. Ernst Behler (New York: Continuum, 1987), pp. 39–115. For *Sonnenklarer Bericht*, Lesson Five, see the following: *GA* I, 7, p. 250; *SW* II, p. 400; and Botterman, Raush, p. 100. See also *Sonnenklarer Bericht*, Lesson Three (*GA* I, 7, p. 219; *SW* II, p. 362; and Botterman, Raush, pp. 69–70).

7. *Sonnenklarer Bericht*, Lesson Five.

8. *Wissenschaftslehre nova methodo*, the "Halle transcript," p. 3. Hereafter abbreviated as *WLnm[H]*, this transcript of the lectures of 1796–99 appears in *GA* IV, 2, pp. 17–267; an English translation of part of the lectures appears in *Foundations of Transcendental Philosophy (Wissenschaftslehre) nova methodo*, trans. and ed. Daniel Breazeale (Ithaca, N.Y.: Cornell University Press, 1992), hereafter cited as *FTP*. For *WLnm[H]*, p. 3, see *GA* IV, 2, p. 44, and *FTP*, p. 141.

9. *Wissenschaftslehre nova methodo*, the "Krause transcript," p. 1. Hereafter abbreviated as *WLnm[K]*, this transcript of the lectures of 1798–99, not included in either *GA* or *SW*, appears in *Wissenschaftslehre nova methodo*, ed. Erich Fuchs (Hamburg: Felix Meiner, 1982), hereafter abbreviated as *FM;* an English translation appears in *FTP*. For *WLnm[K]*, p. 1, see *FM*, p. 34, and *FTP*, p. 119.

10. *WLnm[K]*, p. 1 (*FM*, p. 29; *FTP*, pp. 110–1).

11. Ibid.

12. See *FTP*, p. 111n11. The observer was Henrick Steffens, who attended some of Fichte's lectures in 1798 to 1799.

13. *WLnm[K]*, p. 1 (FM, p. 31; *FTP*, p. 115).

14. See 1.Ein, p. 7 (*GA* I, 4, pp. 201–2, *SW* I, pp. 442–3, and *IWL*, pp. 27–29); also *Sonnenklarer Bericht*, p. 3 (*GA* I, 7, p. 218; *SW* II, p. 361; and Botterman, Raush, p. 69). See also Fichte's statement that "the *Wissenschaftslehre* allows this I to act in accordance with its own laws and thereby to construct a world." *WLnm[K]*, p. 1 (*FM*, p. 28, and *FTP*, p. 109).

15. "The intellect acts; but, as a consequence of its very nature, it can only act in a certain, specific manner." 1.Ein, p. 7 (*GA* I, 4, p. 200; *SW* I, p. 441; and *IWL*, p. 26). See also Fichte's comment that "the laws of thinking must then be derived from these premises before our very eyes." 1.Ein, p. 7 (*GA* I, 7, p. 202; *SW* I, p. 443; *IWL*, p. 28).

16. 1.Ein, p. 5 (*GA* I, 4, p. 192; *SW* I, p. 430; *IWL*, p. 15).

17. "The object of idealism has an advantage, therefore, over that of dogmatism, for the former can be shown to be present within consciousness—not, to be sure, as the explanatory ground of experience, for this would be contradictory, and would transform this system itself into a portion of experience; yet it can still be shown to be present, as such, within consciousness. In contrast, the object of dogmatism cannot be considered to be anything but a pure invention, which can be made into something real only by the success of this system." 1.Ein, p. 4 (*GA* I, 4, p. 190; *SW* I, p. 428; *IWL*, p. 14).

18. *WLnm[K]*, p. 1 (FM, p. 32; *FTP*, p. 115).

19. 1.Ein, p. 7 (*GA* I, 4, p. 204; *SW* I, p. 445; *IWL*, p. 30).

20. Ibid.

21. 1.Ein, p. 7 (*GA* I, 4, p. 205; *SW* I, p. 445; *IWL*, p. 31).

22. "A complete transcendental idealism has to demonstrate the truth of this presupposition by actually providing a derivation of this system of representations, and precisely this constitutes its proper task." 1.Ein, p. 7 (*GA* I, 4, p. 205; *SW* I, pp. 445–46; *IWL*, p. 31).

23. 1.Ein, p. 7 (*GA* I, 4, p. 204; *SW* I, p. 445; *IWL*, p. 31).

24. Ibid.

25. "We saw above how the entire mechanism of the human mind is based upon the necessity of positing one thing in opposition to another." *WLnm[K]*, p. 2 (*FM*, p. 42; *FTP*, p. 132). "We reached this conclusion by means of the law of reflective opposition [*das Reflexionsgesez des Entgegensezens*], and we established this law within intuition." *WLnm[K]*, p. 2 (*FM*, p. 38; *FTP*, p. 125). "One does not and cannot think clearly of anything at all without also thinking at the same time of its opposite." *WLnm[K]*, p. 2 (*FM*, p. 36; *FTP*, p. 123). "Before I can intuit or think anything, I must posit something in opposition to it." *WLnm[K]*, p. 2 (FM, p. 37; *FTP*, pp. 124–5). See also, *WLnm[K]*, p. 1 (FM, p. 32; *FTP*, p. 116); "principle of determinability," *WLnm[K]*, p. 2 (FM, p. 51; *FTP*, p. 146); "law of reflection," *WLnm[K]*, p. 2 (FM, p. 44; *FTP*, p. 134; and "general laws of intuition," *WLnm[K]*, p. 8 (FM, p. 98; *FTP*, p. 219).

26. "In order to be able to perceive myself as positing myself, I must presuppose that I have already been posited. I transport myself from a state of repose and inactivity to the activity of self-positing, and I oppose this activity to my previous state of repose and inactivity. Otherwise, one would be unable to notice the

representation of activity, which is a wrenching away from a state of repose and a movement of transition to activity. {It is only by wrenching ourselves away from a state of repose and transporting ourselves into the opposite state that we are able to obtain any consciousness [i.e., any intuition] of our activity. Only through this opposite state do we obtain a clear awareness of what 'acting' is [for this is something we are quite unable to define].} Consequently, it was only by means of opposition that I was able to become clearly conscious of my activity and to obtain an intuition of it." *WLnm[H]*, p. 1 (*GA* IV, 2, p. 31; *FTP*, p. 116).

27. *WLnm[K]*, p. 1 (*FM*, p. 29; *FTP*, pp. 110–1).

28. "If I now abstract from whatever it is I am thinking of and attend only to myself, then I myself become, in this object, the object of a determinate representation." 1.Ein, p. 4 (*GA* I, 4, p. 189; *SW* I, p. 427; *IWL*, p. 12).

29. "Accordingly, it is clear to it [the *Wissenschaftslehre*] in immediate intuition that for every rational being it must attach itself in just this way." *Sonnenklarer Bericht*, 3rd Lesson (*GA* I, 7, p. 233; *SW* II, p. 380; Botterman, Raush, p. 84); and "However, insofar as [the philosopher] thinks and construes what he intended, something else arises for him that he did not at all intend, which is simply necessary and accompanied by the apparent conviction that it must arise in just this way for all rational beings. . . . Hence, in this linking of one manifold to another the laws of consciousness . . . manifest themselves." *Sonnenklarer Bericht*, Lesson Three (*GA* I, 7, p. 224; *SW* II, p. 368; Botterman, Rash, pp. 74–75).

30. "If one considers the intellect's necessary modes of acting in isolation from any [actual] acting, then it is quite appropriate to call these the 'laws of acting.' Hence there are necessary laws of the intellect." 1.Ein, p. 7 (*GA* I, 4, p. 200; *SW* I, p. 441; *IWL*, p. 26).

31. "Such self-consciousness does not impose itself upon anyone, and it does not simply occur without any assistance from us. One must actually act in a free manner, and then one must abstract from the object and attend only to oneself. No one can be forced to do this." 1.Ein, 4 (*GA* I, 4, p. 191; *SW* I, p. 429; *IWL*, p. 14).

32. *WLnm[K]*, p. 1 (FM, p. 34; *FTP*, p. 119).

33. "One could call this state of repose or this determinability an 'ability' or 'power' [*Vermögen*]." *WLnm[K]*, p. 1 (FM, p. 38; *FTP*, p. 126).

34. "Thus the procedure by means of which we accomplished the transition from one term to another was the same in both inquiries." *WLnm[K]*, p. 2 (FM, p. 39; *FTP*, p. 126).

35. "Immediate consciousness is itself the ultimate reason or foundation upon which everything else is based and to which everything else has to be traced back, if our knowledge is to have any foundation." *WLnm[K]*, p. 1 (FM, p. 31; *FTP*, p. 114).

36. "Immediate consciousness is the foundation of all consciousness. We have postulated this, since immediate consciousness never appears as an object of consciousness. Instead it is the subjective factor in all consciousness, the factor that constitutes the conscious subject. . . . Nothing that we can be conscious of is immediate consciousness itself; instead, it is present within all consciousness

and lies at its foundation, but only as the subjective factor, the Idea, something posited in accordance with the laws of reflection." *WLnm[H]*, p. 2 (GA IV, 2, p. 37; *FTP*, pp. 128–29); see also *WLnm[K]*, p. 1 (FM, p. 40; *FTP*, p. 128).

37. "The I in a state of repose is the same thing as (activity considered as) determinability, for a passive state of repose has the same character as a determinable activity. If one removes what is determinate from an activity, then it remains merely determinable; in other words, it is a power—that is to say, that which makes an action possible—or an activity in a state of repose that cannot be further explained but can only be grasped conceptually. This is how activity becomes a *state of repose* or a *power* or *determinability*" (*WLnm[H]*, p. 2 [GA IV, 2, p. 36; *FTP*, p. 127]).

38. *WLnm[H]*, p. 1 (GA IV, 2, p. 37; *FTP*, p. 129).

39. "Nor is a power the same as an activity. A power is not an action; it is that by means of which an action first becomes possible. When an activity is grasped by means of concepts, it is transformed into a state of repose. Power, repose, and determinability are one and the same." *WLnm[K]*, p. 2 (FM, p. 39; *FTP*, p. 127).

40. In chapter 3 we discover that "immediate consciousness," "determinability," "pure I," is really freedom. But here again, freedom is an Idea. We can never experience freedom itself, but only free acts. We experience freedom only indirectly, through its products.

41. *WLnm[H]*, p. 2 (*GA* IV, 2, p. 37; *FTP*, p. 128).

42. *WLnm[K]*, p. 2 (*FM*, p. 42; *FTP*, p. 132).

43. *WLnm[K]*, p. 1 (*FM*, p. 31; *FTP*, pp. 114–15).

44. "[T]his concept [of a determinable activity] is a concept only in relation to the intuition of the I; in relation to the Not-I, it is itself an intuition. In the intuition the activity is in action, whereas in the concept it is not in action; there it is a mere power." *WLnm[K]*, p. 2 (FM, p. 39; *FTP*, p. 127).

45. *WLnm[K]*, p. 2 (FM, p. 41; *FTP*, p. 130).

46. *WLnm[H]*, p. 2 (GA IV, 2, p. 38; *FTP*, p. 130).

47. Kantian "inner sense" would also belong to the realm of "objective experience." What I am calling "subjective experience" is something Kant never explicitly discusses, although hints of it can be found in his occasional references to "transcendental" or "a priori" consciousness; Kant, *Critique of Pure Reason*, A 117 note and B 135, respectively. See also, B 133 and B 153.

48. On Fichte's aversion to a reflection theory of consciousness and its infinite regress, see the excellent article by Dieter Henrich, "Fichtes Ursprüngliche Einsicht," in *Subjectivität und Metaphysik, Festschrift für Wolfgang Cramer*, ed. Dieter Henrich and Hans Wagner (Frankfort am Main: Vittorio Klostermann, 1966), pp. 188–232; an English translation by David R. Lachterman, "Fichte's Original Insight," appears in *Contemporary German Philosophy 1* (1982): pp. 15–52. See especially pp. 35–6.

49. "No one can be forced to do this [i.e., generate an immediate self-consciousness]. And if someone pretends to act in this manner, no one else can ever know whether he is proceeding correctly and in the manner requested. In a word: this type of consciousness cannot be proven to anyone." 1.Ein, p. 4 (*GA* I, 4, p. 191; *SW* I, p. 429; *IWL*, p. 14).

50. And even after the act of pure intellectual intuition, the Pure I "exists" only as an object of subjective experience, which is, needless to say, a very distinctive mode of existence.

51. See, for example, 1.Ein, p. 5 (*GA* I, 4, p. 194; *SW* I, p. 433; *IWL,* p. 18), and "Zweite Einleitung in die Wissenschaftslehre" (1797), p. 10 (*GA* I, 4, p. 259; *SW* I, p. 507; *IWL,* p. 92). ("Zweite Einleitung in die Wissenschaftslehre" [1797], appears in *GA* I, 4, pp. 209–69; *SW* I, pp. 453–518; and in English translation as a "Second Introduction" to *An Attempt at a New Presentation of the Wissenschaftslehre* in *IWL,* pp. 36–105.)

52. *Das System der Sittenlehre nach den Principien der Wissenschaftslehre* (1798), 3 (*GA* I, 5, p. 60; *SW* IV, p. 47; see also the English translation, *The Science of Ethics as Based on the Science of Knowledge,* trans. A. E. Kroeger, ed. W. T. Harris [London: Kegan Paul, Trench, Trübner, 1897; 2d ed., 1907], p. 52). Kroeger translates "wirklichen intellectuellen Anschauung" as "actual intellectual contemplation."

53. See Alain Perrinjaquet's discussion of this in "Some Remarks," esp. pp. 84–88.

54. "[The philosopher] comprehends his act as an instance of *acting as such* or *acting in general,* of which, as a result of his previous experience, he already possesses a concept." "Zweite Einleitung," p. 4 (*GA* I, 4, p. 215; *SW* I, p. 461; *IWL,* p. 44).

The Individuality of the I in Fichte's Second Jena *Wissenschaftslehre,* 1796–1799

Günter Zöller

> ... *das Individuum muß aus dem absoluten Ich deducirt werden.*
> [T]he individual must be deduced from the absolute I.
> —*J. G. Fichte, letter to Fr. H. Jacobi, 30 August 1795*

There has been a remarkable upsurge of interest in the "new presentation" of the *Wissenschaftslehre* that Fichte offered in lecture courses and fragmentary journal publications between 1796 and 1799.[1] To be sure, one of the lecture transcripts of the *Wissenschaftslehre nova methodo,* the *Hallesche Nachschrift,* had been accessible to scholars since its discovery at the beginning of the twentieth century[2] and available in published form since 1937.[3] But it seems that only the re-edition of that lecture transcript in the Academy edition of Fichte's Collected Works[4] in 1978 together with the recent discovery and subsequent publication of a second lecture transcript of the *Wissenschaftslehre nova methodo,* the Krause Nachschrift,[5] in 1980 and 1982, respectively, as well as its virtually immediate translation into French and English,[6] has moved Fichte's second presentation of the *Wissenschaftslehre* from his Jena years to the forefront of scholarly and philosophical attention.[7]

Chiefly among the reasons for the remarkable growth of interest in a body of work that for the most part was neither authored nor authorized by Fichte himself is the central role that the *Wissenschaftslehre nova methodo* accords to the doctrine of interpersonality[8] in the development of transcendental philosophy.[9] By contrast, the topic of interpersonal relations seems to be altogether missing from Fichte's first, and only, published detailed presentation of the *Wissenschaftslehre,* the *Foundation of the Entire Wissenschaftslehre* of 1794 to 1795.[10] In Fichte's published works, the theory of interpersonality first emerges in rigorous form in his two-part system of practical philosophy, the *Foundation of Natural Law* (1796 to 1797) and *The System of Ethics* (1798),[11] which are more closely related to the emerging new presentation of the *Wissenschaftslehre* than to its published predecessor,[12] and therefore may be grouped together with the *Wissenschaftslehre nova methodo* as forming the second phase of the Jena *Wissenschaftslehre* (1796 to 1799).

It is a matter of continuing dispute and conjecture whether the introduction of interpersonality into the second Jena presentation of the *Wissenschaftslehre* represents a substantial, doctrinal change in Fichte's transcendental philosophy or a more complete restatement of the first Jena presentation in a different methodological guise.[13] That issue may well have to remain essentially unsettled given the incompleteness of the *Foundation of the Entire Wissenschaftslehre* according to that work's own conception[14] and hence the lack of conclusive evidence about the possible extent of the foundations of transcendental philosophy in the period 1794 to 1795 beyond the material that Fichte worked out in the lectures of his first two semesters of teaching at Jena.

In addition to the central topic of interpersonality, there is a second, closely related doctrinal feature that emerges at the very core of the writings from the phase of the new presentation of the *Wissenschaftslehre*. It is Fichte's doctrine of the individuation of transcendental subjectivity.[15] Now it might seem that the individuality of the I is a feature strictly correlated to the I's interpersonal relation to one or several other finite rational beings, or even that individuality is subordinated to interpersonality. But it can be shown that in important systematic regards individuality is a more basic concept of Fichte's theory of transcendental subjectivity than interpersonality. Moreover, a closer examination of Fichte's thinking about the individuality of the I in the years from 1796 through 1799 can point to the very limitations of an interpersonalist grounding of subjectivity that seem to have compelled Fichte himself to move beyond the *Wissenschaftslehre nova methodo* at the turn of the century and to abandon the project of its publication.[16]

Recent discussions of individuality and interpersonality in Fichte are typically oriented against the influential twin caricatures of Fichte's philosophy as individualistic to the point of solipsism or anti-individualistic to the point of "totalism". In response to those standard charges, the sympathetic interpretations portray Fichte either as striking a delicate balance between individual and community[17] or as moving from such an initial balanced view to a more "totalist" conception in his later works.[18] It seems indicated to supplement the focus on the social relation between individual and community with an account of the foundational, proto-social relation between individuality and transcendental subjectivity in Fichte.

The following discussion of the individuation of subjectivity in Fichte's second Jena presentation of the *Wissenschaftslehre* draws, in section one, on the *Foundation of Natural Law;* in section two, on *The System of Ethics;* in section three, on the "Second Introduction" of the *Attempt At a New Presentation of the Wissenschaftslehre;* and, in section four, on the Krause transcript of the *Wissenschaftslehre nova methodo.*[19] The essay concludes, in section five, with a brief general assessment of individuality in Fichte.

1

The first part of the *Foundation of Natural Law* (1796) takes its point of departure from the notion of a finite rational being *(endliches Vernunftwesen)* and seeks to determine the necessary conditions for self-consciousness on the part of such a being. In particular, Fichte seeks to show that a being relevantly like us humans can only come to an awareness of itself and its states if it ascribes to itself ("posits") free efficacy (section 1) and thereby determines a world of sense *(Sinnenwelt)* outside of itself (section 2). Moreover, the possible self-consciousness of a finite rational being requires the assumption *(annehmen)* of other finite rational beings outside of itself, at least one of which has to address a solicitation *(Aufforderung)*[20] to the emerging rational being to realize its potential for rational self-determination (section 3). The precise relation between a finite rational being and the other finite rational beings assumed to be outside of it is the relation of right *(Rechtsverhältnis)*, according to which each finite rational being freely limits the exercise of its freedom through the concept of the possible freedom of everyone else (section 4).

In limiting its exercise of free efficacy in the world of sense under the conception of the law of right *(Rechtsgesetz)*, the finite rational being ascribes to itself a "sphere for its freedom" *(Sphäre seiner Freiheit)*, over which it and it only exercises choice *(wählen)* (section 5).[21] Other beings are not to choose in that sphere, and the being in question is not to choose in another rational being's sphere. The sphere makes up the "individual character" *(individueller Charakter)* of the finite rational being in question.[22] The latter is the one it is, and not someone else, by virtue of the particular, determined sphere of freedom in which it exercises choice. Fichte further explains the determinacy thus introduced into the I by contrasting the I *qua* subject *(Subject)* with the sphere for freedom as the former's predicate *(Prädikat)*. Through the self- ascription of the sphere, the formal I ("subject") is said to become material or determined. Fichte's term for the I in this capacity as materially determined individual is "person" *(Person)*.[23]

Fichte further stresses the perceived independence of the sphere from the I *qua* subject. To the finite rational being itself the sphere appears as something over which it has exclusive control but which is not brought about by the I's own activity. The sphere appears to the I as a "part of the world" *(Theil der Welt)*, albeit one to which it is linked differently than to any other of the world's parts. More specifically, the individual sphere appears to the individual rational being as its "articulated body" *(artikulierter Leib)*, the movements of which are under its immediate and exclusive control.[24] Yet, behind such appearances, and unbeknownst to the individual *finding* itself willing, freely effective in the world of sense, interacting with other finite rational beings and embodied, lies the reality of the positing and counterpositing transcendental activity of the I. Fichte explains the discrepancy in insight by resorting to the distinction between the standpoint of the individual, which is immersed in its life of thinking and willing, and the standpoint of the philosopher, who speculates on the "clandestine" *(heimlich)*, prerepresentational activity of the subject that first makes possible and in that sense brings about the manifest picture of self and world.

Fichte's account of the person and its "individual character" is built on the distinction between the universal, *formal* character of "mere I-hood" *(blosse Ichheit)*,[25] which the person shares with all other finite rational beings, and its particular, *material* character, which constitutes the person's identity as this particular being. An important feature of this conception of individuality is its origin in the I's practical nature as freely acting and efficacious being. Moreover, the individual character of a person is not defined by thingly limits to its exercise of freedom but with reference to the legal project of mutual respect for the exclusive nature of every person's sphere of freedom. The materiality of the I under conditions of individuality is therefore not, at least not originally, the materiality of matter. The latter only comes into view as part of the subject's "clandestine" self-interpretation of its practical limits as reflective of a world in which bodies made of matter influence each other.

2

The original nature of the rational individual as material but not matterly is further developed in Fichte's account of individuality in *The System of*

Ethics.[26] The additional insights into the foundation of subjectivity in general and the role of individuality in particular to be found in *The System of Ethics* are due to the peculiar status of an ethics *(Sittenlehre)* which lies much closer to the core concerns of the *Wissenschaftslehre* than any other special or applied philosophical discipline, including the transcendental theory of right in the *Foundation of Natural Law.*[27]

The validity and applicability of the law of right as such remains conditional upon each person's freely continued recognition of the other person's freedom. Subjecting oneself to the law of right is not an unconditional practical necessity but a conditional theoretical necessity, contingent upon the person's decision to continue the recognition of the other rational individual and not to forego the protection of its own freedom afforded by the law of right. By contrast, the validity and applicability of the "principle of morality" *(Princip der Sittlichkeit)*[28] is unconditional and based on the practical nature of the free but finite human being, which is forever striving toward total spontaneity *(Selbstthätigkeit)* and independence *(Selbstständigkeit)*[29] in relation to everything and everyone else. On Fichte's transcendental account of human action in general and moral agency in particular, the world encountered by the agent who sets out to change it is but a reflection of the agent's own finite nature, projected into space and time as an outside world. Accordingly, to change the world is to change oneself, and vice versa:

> *My world* is changed means *I* am being changed; *my world* is further determined means *I* am being further determined.[30]

The integration of self and world in a unified theory of self-objectifying subjectivity, as carried out in the extensive proto- and meta-ethics of *The System of Ethics,* also encompasses a radical integration of the natural self and the supernatural or moral self. Rather than viewing the natural side of human existence as distinct from or even opposed to the moral life, Fichte argues that the driving force behind the moral life, the moral drive *(sittlicher Trieb),* is a mixed drive *(gemischter Trieb)* resulting from the coalition of the absolute, pure drive *(reiner Trieb),* which provides the striving impetus, and the natural drive *(Naturtrieb),* which provides content to the striving. Moreover, the two basic drives that enter into the constitution of the mixed moral drive (pure and natural drive) are to be regarded as so many differentiations of the prerepresentational archdrive *(Urtrieb).* The duplication of the original drive occurs necessarily given the conditions of finite reflection. The reconstitution of the original predisjunctive unity ("subject-objectivity") is the infinite goal of the reintegration of reason and nature under the principle of morality.[31]

In Fichte's portrayal of human agency as a unified dynamic field of disjoining and rejoining drives, the body of the individual human being, and indeed the entire sensuous, empirically determined human being, assumes the role of a "tool and vehicle" *(Werkzeug und Vehicul)* for the, always only partial and imperfect, realization of radical autonomy. The infinite goal of moral perfection or of perfect morality is the independence and spontaneity of reason "in general" *(überhaupt)* and "not the independence of a single reason [*Einer*], insofar as the latter is individual reason."[32] For Fichte, the individual is not the end but the means of moral activity.

While the point of Fichte's conception of law *(Recht)* in the *Foundation of Natural Law* is the possibility of the coexistence of free individuals in the sensible world, and hence the mutual preservation of rational individuals as such, his conception of the moral law *(Sittengesetz)* in *The System of Ethics* involves the subordination of everyone's individuality under the supra-individual universal end of reason's radical independence. Fichte's theoretical as well as practical advocacy of radical individualism in the legal-political sphere thus goes hand in hand with a defense of individualism in the moral sphere. To be sure, Fichte does not envision the actual submergence of individuality in some undifferentiated, mystical union of everyone with everyone else.[33] The point is rather that, in the pursuit of morality, the concern is not with what is individual about a human being but with the individual's universal, rational nature.

On Fichte's account of free but finite existence, it is a matter of necessity that each (finite) I be an individual, but it is not necessary that a given individual be the particular individual it is. The contingency of particular individuality is due to two factors that stem from the individual's freedom and finitude, respectively. As a *free* being, each individual is able to freely determine itself and thereby determine the particulars of its individuality. However, there is a principal limit to the radical freedom of individual self-determination. For as a *finite* being, each individual finds itself originally in a particular situation from which the exercise of its free self-determination has to take its starting point. And while any or all subsequent choices and decisions of the individual may be made in free self-determination, the range of choices to be made is still predetermined by the preceding path of choices, which ultimately reaches back to that primal scene that the individual was not in a position to choose.[34]

Fichte terms the original limitation of freedom, which takes a different form in each individual, the "root of all individuality" *(Wurzel aller Individualität)*,[35] thereby indicating that there is an original and unchangeable core to an individual's particular identity and suggesting the derivative status of subsequent, self-given determinations of individuality.

But no matter how different the original and derivative strata of individuality might be, they are all contingent upon something other than reason in general and hence extraneous to the cultivation of reason through morality. What matters from the moral point of view is not who in particular wills the act promoting the universalization of reason but that the act be willed:

> I will morality in general; whether in me or without me is entirely indifferent to me.[36]

Under the principle of morality, every finite rational being is to will not as the particular individual that it happens to be but as an individual *in general;* the given individual is to act *as* everyone else:

> We are all supposed to act identically.[37]

To be sure, the conception of morality as promoting generic individuality at the expense of particular differences in human beings has the status of an idea that orients human practice toward an unobtainable but infinitesimally approachable end *(finis)*. The ideal state of perfect harmony in and between human beings would indeed be the end *(terminus)* of humanity as we know it. Fichte specifically mentions the falling away of social classification, of church and state.[38] But for the time being, that is, as long as human beings are human beings, the moral regard for everyone else still has to take into account that different individuals will different things and that no one ought to will for the other one.

3

A key feature of Fichte's second or "new presentation" of the *Wissenschaftslehre* is the incorporation of extensive introductory writings addressing methodological and metaphilosophical issues into the body of transcendental philosophy.[39] To a large extent, Fichte's increased efforts at self-interpretation and self-commentary may have been occasioned by the grave misunderstandings encountered by the *Wissenschaftslehre* upon its first publication in 1794 to 1795.[40] Among the chief obstacles to an adequate reception of Fichte's speculative philosophy was his choice of the nominalized pronoun of the first person singular *(das Ich)* to designate the ground or principle of subjectivity, a choice that exposed the *Wissenschaftslehre* to psychological, individualist misunderstandings.

In the "Second Introduction" of the *New Presentation,* Fichte addresses several objections raised against the first writings on the *Wissenschaftslehre* by insisting on the distinction between the "pure I," which he identifies with pure apperception or pure self-consciousness in Kant, on the one hand, and the "empirical I" with its "consciousness of our individuality" *(Bewußtsein unserer Individualität),* on the other hand.[41] Particularly illuminating for Fichte's understanding of the nature and status of individuality is his response to an objection raised by a colleague at Jena, Friedrich Karl Forberg, who had argued that what is left over after the requisite complete abstraction from all individual personality is no longer anything that could justifiably be called an "I" *(Ich)* and might just as well be labelled an "It" *(Es).*[42]

Fichte's response to Forberg turns on the introduction of a twofold opposition involving four different terms: the opposition between I *qua* pure I and It, and the opposition between I *qua* individual I and You *(Du).* The first opposition involves the absolute and unconditional acts through which the "I-hood" *(Ichheit)* posits itself and op-posites or counterposits *(entgegengesetzen)* to itself the It or "mere objectivity" *(bloße Objectivität).*[43] The absolute positing of I and It corresponds to the absolute positing of I and Not-I in the first and second principles of the *Foundation of the Entire Wissenschaftslehre.*[44]

The second opposition, between I and You, proceeds from the first, between I and It. The I-hood of the first opposition is transferred onto the It of the first opposition, and the two are united in a "conditioned synthesis" *(bedingte Synthesis)*[45] to form the You, to which is opposed the I positing itself *as such* in a "synthesis of the I with itself" *(Synthesis des Ich mit sich selbst):*[46]

> That which in the act described posits itself, not in general but *as I,* am I; and that which in the same act is posited as I *by me,* and not *by itself,* is you.[47]

Thus the terms of the two oppositions are defined through the thetic, antithetic, and synthetic acts in which they originate: the pure I originating in the absolute thesis; the mere It in the absolute antithesis; the individual I in the synthesis of the I with itself; and the individual you in the synthesis of the I with the It.

The individual I and the you are therefore of the same, synthetic status and, moreover, come about in an original opposition such that one cannot be without the other. Yet the co-originality of individual I and You includes positing activity only for the I and not for the you. Rather than positing itself or anything else, the You is posited by the I; more precisely, it is posited as an It that is an I. It is not the you itself but the "*consciousness of a You*"[48] that must accompany all my determined thinking.

The "Second Introduction" also contains a further elucidation of the middle position that the individual I occupies between the preindividual "I as intellectual intuition" (the mere form of I-hood), on the one side, and the post-individual "I as idea" (the complete matter of I-hood), on the other side. Again Fichte stresses that the latter idea will never be realized but is to be approximated into infinity.[49]

4

In his lecture course on the foundations of transcendental philosophy preserved in Krause's lecture transcript of the *Wissenschaftslehre nova methodo,* Fichte follows the manner of presentation employed in the foundational sections of the *Foundation of Natural Law* and *The System of Ethics.* The method of elucidating the conditions of the possibility of self-consciousness on the part of a finite rational being is now carried farther in two directions, however. It is used to cover a wider range of phenomena of consciousness, and it serves to go deeper yet into the foundational structure of transcendental subjectivity. In particular, Fichte seeks to reconstruct the ultimate point of origin of all conscious life, in an effort to determine the precise relation between what is self-made, or a matter of freedom, and what is given, or a matter of facticity in all finite consciousness and its objects.

At the center of Fichte's advanced transcendental account of the origin and development of subjectivity in the *Wissenschaftslehre nova methodo* stands the specter of a circle in the relation between the theoretical or cognitive and the practical or volitional activity of finite rational consciousness and the postulated solution of that circle in some original, *pure fact* of finite reason.[50] The circle consists in the mutual requirement of cognition and volition for the original coming about of consciousness. According to Fichte's practicist theory of cognition, knowledge is always the knowledge of some possible end. Yet all willing of an end requires the cognitive grasp of the end to be pursued.

While the mutual requirement of willing and knowing is unproblematic in all those cases where some prior instance or instances of knowing or willing are available, a problem arises for the origin of all cognition and volition. There can be no first cognition without a preceding volition, and there can be no first volition without a prior cognition:

Real efficacy is possible only in accordance with a concept of a goal; a concept of a goal is possible only on the condition of a cognition; and such a cognition is possible only on the condition of a real efficacy; consequently, consciousness would be explained by a circle and hence would not be explained at all.[51]

Now Fichte argues that since consciousness is indeed possible (because it is actual), the radical origin of subjectivity must be such that it combines the overtly separate features of cognition and volition in some unitary yet originally complex state of affairs. Fichte's postulatory inference goes from what is possible to what makes it possible, namely, some originary state of affairs in and about the I that is proto-cognitive as well as proto-volitional.[52] He identifies the postulated nonempirical, predisjunctive arch-condition of subjectivity as "pure willing" or "pure will" (*reines Wollen* or *reiner Wille*).[53]

Fichte's fundamental but exceedingly obscure conception of pure willing is to be understood in the context of the theory of discursive thinking that informs the *Wissenschaftslehre nova methodo*. According to Fichte's transcendental theory of thinking, everything that is to be *for* the I, has to be brought under the form of thinking. This intellectual formatting of information consists in the exercise of determination *(Bestimmung)* by which something undetermined but determinable *(Bestimmbares)* is being determined *(bestimmt)*.[54] On Fichte's account, the thinking in a free but finite being is the production or bringing forth of some determination on the basis of some determinable which itself is not given as such but introduced as a by-product of the thought activity.[55]

Now the postulated pure willing at the root of all subjectivity, and hence of all objectivity, is to be distinguished from all empirical willing. The latter always involves deliberating *(deliberiren)*, which in turn requires the prior cognition of possible ends among which to choose. Yet *ex hypothesi* no such prior cognition and therefore no deliberation is possible in the case of pure willing.[56] Lacking any empirical content, predeliberative pure willing is also not determined by, or determinative of, something which it wills. Rather the only determination involved in pure willing as such is that of being the sum-total of determinability.

Moreover, any transition from the pregiven sum total of determinability (pure willing) to some willing that is specific in terms of content or end (determined willing), is supposed to be brought about freely by the subject in the activity of self-determination. Accordingly, pure willing has to be thought as determination to (free) self-determination:

> This determinacy, which constitutes my main character, consists in the
> fact that I am determined to determine myself in a certain way.[57]

Fichte's conception of pure willing combines the *"original* limitation"
(ursprüngliche Beschränkung) or "determinacy" *(Bestimmtheit)* of finite existence with the radical freedom of the subject in all subsequent determinations that are to be self-determinations.[58]

But the subject is not only finite in the original limitation imposed
by its other-given rather than self-made, "absolute being" *(absolutes Sein)*.
The subject is also finite in the grasp of its finite being through discursive
thinking:

> But all this comes from [our own] absolute being and from the absolute
> limitation of our ability to grasp this absolute being. With respect to
> reality, I am not everything; with respect to ideality, I am unable to grasp
> what I am all at once.[59]

Under conditions of real and ideal finitude, the pure willing takes on the
form of an ought *(Sollen)*. The addressee of the pure, absolute ought is
the *individual* to whom it specifies the pure will that the individual ought
to have in time and over time.[60]

Fichte distinguishes between the conception of pure willing as the
"supreme determinable" *(das höchste bestimmbare)* and the two levels of its
determination. The first level of determination is individuality as such or
generic individuality, which manifests itself sensibly as the I's body *(Leib)*
and intelligibly as the I's (moral) character. That first level of determination of pure willing functions in turn as the determinable for further
determination at the second level. Here the determination consists in
the single instances of willing or in specific, specifically determined individuality.[61]

For Fichte, generically determined pure willing is the absolute,
nonempirical, atemporal "main character" of the individual whose temporal existence consists in the discursive unfolding of that character in
a series of free acts, each building freely on the preceding one.[62] Yet
all individuation *qua* determination requires something undetermined
but determinable. In the case of a finite rational individual, the determinable is "all reason" *(alle Vernunft)* or the "realm of rational beings"
(Reich vernünftiger Wesen) in relation to which the individual defines itself:

> Self-consciousness originates with seizing myself out of a mass of rational
> beings in general.[63]

In tracing the necessary presupposition of other rational beings to the deep structure of discursive thinking, Fichte provides a deduction of solicitation *(Aufforderung)*. The latter is the way in which the determination to self-determination *appears* to the individual *in a worldly guise,* as embodied minds influencing the embodied individual.[64] Strictly speaking, however, everything the individual experiences originates in the subject's own individuality as the latter's original determination is unfolded in time and space. The solicitation to free acting is a "phenomenon" *(Phänomen).*[65]

To be sure, for the individual itself the solicitation and the rational agent or agents behind it assume independent status. The realm of reason in general, along with the other rational individuals in it, appears to the individual as prior to itself and as a necessary condition of its own individuation. But upon deeper analysis, it becomes clear that the necessary dependence of a given individual on the solicitation through another individual does not really explain how rational individuality comes about in the first place. If no individual is self-sufficient in the realization of its rationality, then there remains the problem of accounting for the first, unsolicited solicitor. It is at this point that Fichte suggests that the ultimate foundation of individuality is located not in some other individual but in something altogether different from finite individuals and perhaps incomprehensible to them, in some solicitor general: No individual is able to account for itself on the basis of itself alone.

> Consequently, when one arrives—as one must—at a first individual, one
> must also assume the existence of an even higher, incomprehensible
> being.[66]

In the framework of the *Wissenschaftslehre nova methodo,* the necessary presupposition of a supra-individual ground of individuality refers back to the necessary thought of the highest determinable to all possible determination. In his continuing attempts to elucidate this ultimate ground, Fichte seeks to reconcile two insights: that the presupposition of the absolute ground is still a thought produced by the individual in accounting for its own original determination, and that it is nevertheless the thought of something radically different from and independent of all finite thinking, something on which all finite thinking is supposed to depend. Fichte's first effort at thinking the thought-independent absolute ground of subjectivity is to be found in the popular, overtly theistic presentation of *The Vocation of Man,* where the "pure will" is identified with the infinite, divine will.[67] The sustained speculative treatment of this task is at the core of the later presentations of the *Wissenschaftslehre.*

5

Fichte's account of individuality in the key writings of the second Jena presentation of the *Wissenschaftslehre* provides a challenging extension of previous philosophical conceptions of individual being.[68] In Fichte's usage, the term "individual" denotes a singular finite rational being in contradistinction to the latter's species concept. The individuality of finite rational beings is moreover part of a comprehensive dynamical structure and functions as the infinitely extended intermediary stage of a process of reason's materialization, which stretches from the most generic and formal notion of reason (pure I) through its individual imperfect realization (empirical I) toward its unobtainable complete realization (ideal I). Individuality in Fichte is defined as the stage of reason's division among many beings. As the indivisible individual or atomic endpoint of division,[69] individuality is also the starting point for the reintegration of reason.

As a basic concept of Fichte's transcendental theory of subjectivity, individuality partakes in the double nature of free but finite beings. It indicates the original limitation of human existence, as expressed in the uncircumventable givenness or facticity of an individual's main character or basic being. But it also indicates the individual's freedom of self-determination in the cultivation of its character. In both cases, the emphasis is on the practical nature of individuality as the constraint or lack of constraint involved in human activity. Moreover, the cultivation of individuality can take two basic forms: the *working out* of individuality under the law of right and the *working off* of individuality under the moral law. In both cases, the cultivation of individuality involves the assumption of other individuals and the mutual interaction among individuals. And while the introduction of interpersonal relations may seem to leave behind the confines of individual consciousness, the presuppositions, assumptions, and inferences regarding interpersonal relations still have their point of origin in subjectivity structure of individual consciousness. For Fichte, *interpersonality* remains *intrasubjectivity*.

Notes

Research on this essay was carried out during my affiliation with the Obermann Center for Advanced Studies at the University of Iowa during the spring semester of 1997. I gratefully acknowledge the material and immaterial support provided by Jay Semel and his staff.

1. Fichte himself published only two introductions and the first chapter of his *Attempt at a New Presentation of the Wissenschaftslehre* [*Versuch einer neuen Darstellung der Wissenschaftslehre*] in 1797–98; cf. *J. G. Fichte-Gesamtausgabe der Bayerischen Akademie der Wissenschaften*, ed. Reinhard Lauth, Hans Gliwitzky, and Erich Fuchs (Stuttgart-Bad Cannstatt: Frommann-Holzboog: 1962 ff.), henceforth abbreviated *GA*, at *GA* I, 4, pp. 183–281. An English translation appears in *Introductions to the Wissenschaftslehre and Other Writings*, ed. and trans. Daniel Breazeale (Indianapolis: Hackett, 1994), henceforth abbreviated *IWL*, at *IWL* pp. 1–118. The continuation of the publication of the *New Presentation* was first interrupted by the outbreak of the atheism controversy in 1799 and then rendered obsolete by Fichte's further development of the *Wissenschaftslehre* after 1800.

2. Cf., e.g., the reliance on the original manuscript of the Halle transcript of the *Wissenschaftslehre nova methodo* in Heinz Heimsoeth, *Fichte* (Munich: Ernst Reinhardt, 1923), pp. 72 ff. and 219–21 n. 39.

3. Johann Gottlieb Fichte, *Nachgelassene Schriften*, Bd. II, ed. Hans Jacob (Berlin: Junker und Dünnhaupt, 1937), pp. 341–612. Italian translation under the title, *Teoria della scienza 1798 "nova methodo,"* trans. A. Cantoni (Milan: Biblioteca "Il pensiero," 1959); Spanish translation under the title, *Doctrina de la Ciencia nova methodo*, trans. Manuel Ramos and José Luis Villacañas (Valencia: Universidad de Valencia, 1987).

4. *GA* IV, 2, pp. 17–267.

5. Johann Gottlieb Fichte, *Wissenschaftslehre nova methodo. Kollegnachschrift K. Chr. Fr. Krause 1798–99*, ed. Erich Fuchs (1982); 2nd, improved ed. (Hamburg: Felix Meiner, 1994). The revised edition is henceforth abbreviated as *WLnm[K]*.

6. Johann Gottlieb Fichte, *La Doctrine de la Science Nova Methodo. Suivi de Essai d'une nouvelle présentation de la Doctrine de laScience*, trans. Ives Radrizzani (Lausanne: L'Age d'homme, 1989); and Fichte, *Foundations of Transcendental Philosophy (Wissenschaftslehre) Nova Methodo (1796–99)*, trans. Daniel Breazeale (Ithaca and London: Cornell University Press, 1992), henceforth abbreviated as *FTP*. Cf. also my review of the English translation in *The Philosophical Review* 103 (1994): pp. 585–8.

7. Cf. the bibliographies on work on the *Wissenschaftslehre nova methodo*, in *WLnm[K]*, p. XXXV f., and *FTP*, pp. 477–9. The first monograph on the *Wissenschaftslehre nova methodo* is by Ives Radrizzani, *Vers la fondation de l'intersubjectivité chez Fichte. Des Principes à la Nova Methodo* (Paris: Vrin, 1993). Cf. also my review in *Philosophischer Literaturanzeiger* 47 (1994): pp. 366–8. The *Wissenschaftslehre nova methodo* also plays a central role in Peter Rohs, *Fichte* (Munich: Beck, 1991), pp. 65–85, and in my *Fichte's Transcendental Philosophy: The Original Duplicity of Intelligence and Will* (Cambridge: Cambridge University Press, 1998), especially chapters 5 through 8.

8. The pioneering piece on interpersonality in Fichte is Reinhard Lauth, "Le problème de l'interpersonalité chez J. G. Fichte," *Archives de philosophie* 35 (1962): pp. 325–44; translated into German as "Das Problem der Interpersonalität bei J. G. Fichte," the article appeared in Reinhard Lauth, *Transzendentale Entwicklungslinien von Descartes bis zu Marx und Dostojewski* (Hamburg: Meiner, 1989),

GÜNTER ZÖLLER

pp. 180–95. Cf. also Edith Düsing, *Intersubjektivität und Selbstbewußtsein. Behavioristische, phänomenologische und idealistische Begründungstheorien bei Mead, Schütz, Fichte und Hegel* (Cologne: Dinter, 1986), pp. 179–289; and Claudio Cesa, "Zur Interpretation von Fichtes Theorie der Intersubjektivität," in *Fichtes Lehre vom Rechtsverhältnis. Die Deduktion der §§ 1–4 der "Grundlage des Naturrechts" und ihre Stellunmg in der Rechtsphilosophie,* ed. Michael Kahlo, Ernst A. Wolff, and Rainer Zaczyk (Frankfurt/Main: Vittorio Klostermann, 1992), pp. 53–70.

9. Fichte himself indicates the close relation between Kantian transcendental philosophy and Fichtean *Wissenschaftslehre* in the Latin announcement of his lectures on the *Wissenschaftslehre nova methodo* as "*fundamenta philosophiae transcendentalis* (vulgo, *die Wissenschaftslehre*) nova methodo, libera et perpetua oratione, adhibitis tamen meis libris," *WLnm[K]*, p.XII.

10. For an attempt to attribute a theory of interpersonality to the *Foundation of the Entire Wissenschaftslehre,* cf. Alexis Philonenko, *La liberté humaine dans la philosophie de Fichte* (Paris: Vrin, 1966). Fichte himself addressed the social existence of human beings in the second lecture of the popular, "open" lecture course he gave during his first semester at Jena (1794) and immediately brought to publication under the title *Some Lectures Concerning the Scholar's Vocation [Einige Vorlesungen über die Bestimmung des Gelehrten]*; cf. *GA* I, 3, pp. 33–41; *Early Philosophical Writings,* trans. and ed. Daniel Breazeale (Ithaca and London: Cornell University Press, 1988), pp. 153–61.

11. *Grundlage des Naturrechts (GA* I, 3, pp. 311–460, and *GA* I, 4, pp. 5–165); *Das System der Sittenlehre (GA* I, 5, pp. 21–317). In the present essay all translations from these works are my own.

12. As instances of applied, object-specific *Wissenschaftslehre,* the *Foundation of Natural Law* and *The System of Ethics* present themselves in their subtitles as developed "according to principles of the *Wissenschaftslehre*" and "according to the principles of the *Wissenschaftslehre,*" respectively. While this might be taken to indicate the grounding of those works in the *Foundation of the Entire Wissenschaftslehre,* the phrases can also be read as more generic references to the *project* of a transcendental system of philosophy, as announced in *On the Concept of Wissenschaftslehre* (1794) and subsequently reformulated in the lectures on the *Wissenschaftslehre nova methodo.* Cf. *WLnm[K],* pp. 240–4; *FTP,* pp. 467–74 (Deduction of the Subdivisions of the *Wissenschaftslehre*). From a methodological point of view, the *Foundation of Natural Law* and *The System of Ethics* are closer to the second than to the first Jena presentation of the *Wissenschaftslehre:* like the *Wissenschaftslehre nova methodo,* and unlike the *Foundation of the Entire Wissenschaftslehre,* the two object-specific works start from the postulate of actual self-consciousness and elucidate the latter's transcendental conditions. The point at which the new presentation emerges from the old presentation of the *Wissenschaftslehre* is the conception of transcendental philosophy as "a pragmatic history of the human mind," which informs the latter half of the *Foundation of the Entire Wissenschaftslehre;* cf. *GA* I, 2, p. 364 ff.; J. G. Fichte, *Science of Knowledge with the First and Second Introductions,* ed. and trans. P. Heath and J. Lachs (Cambridge: Cambridge University Press, 1982), p. 198 ff. On Fichte's overall conception of philosophy,

cf. Reinhard Lauth, "J. G. Fichtes Gesamtidee der Philosophie," in *Zur Idee der Transzendentalphilosophie* (Munich and Salzburg: Pustet, 1965), pp. 73–123.

13. For a recent defense of the continuity thesis on the relation between the first and the second Jena presentations of the *Wissenschaftslehre*, cf. Ives Radrizzani, *Vers la fondation de l'intersubjectivité chez Fichte,* p. 51 ff. For a recent defense of the discontinuity thesis, cf. Christian Klotz, "Reines Selbstbewußtsein und Reflexion in Fichtes Grundlegung der Wissenschaftslehre (1794–1800)," *Fichte-Studien* 7 (1995): pp. 27–48.

14. Cf. Reinhard Lauth, "Die Frage der Vollständigkeit der Wissenschaftslehre im Zeitraum 1793–96," in *Vernünftige Durchdringung der Wirklichkeit. Fichte und sein Umkreis* (Neuried: Ars Una, 1994), pp. 57–120.

15. The individuality of the I is also a central feature of Schelling's *New Deduction of Natural Law* [*Neue Deduction des Naturrechts*], which, while published in the *Philosophisches Journal einer Gesellschaft Teutscher Gelehrten,* in April 1796 and April 1797, was written and submitted in late 1795. Schelling's deduction of natural law turns on the distinction between individual and universal will *(individueller Wille, allgemeiner Wille)* and stays much closer to the methodological outlook of the *Foundation of the Entire Wissenschaftslehre* than does Fichte's *Foundation of Natural Law.* Fichte was one of the two editors of the *Journal* at the time, so it is very likely that he was familiar with Schelling's brief aphoristic treatise while preparing the publication of the first part of the *Foundation of Natural Law,* which appeared in March 1796.

16. While not advancing the *Wissenschaftslehre nova methodo* to publication, Fichte prepared a "second, improved edition" of the *Foundation of the Entire Wissenschaftslehre* in 1801 (Tübingen: Cotta, 1802).

17. Cf. Alain Perrinjaquet, "Individuum und Gemeinschaft in der WL zwischen 1796 and 1800," in *Fichte-Studien* 3 (1991): pp. 7–28, and Alain Renaut, *Le Système du droit. Philosophie et droit dans la pensée de Fichte* (Paris: Presses Universitaires de France, 1986).

18. Cf. Edith Düsing, "Das Problem der Inidividualität in Fichtes früher Ethik und Rechtslehre," in *Fichte-Studien* 3 (1991): pp. 29–50, and Edith Düsing, "Sittliche Aufforderung. Fichtes Theorie der Interpersonalität in der *WL nova methodo* und in der *Bestimmung des Menschen,*" in *Transzendentalphilosophie als System. Die Auseinandersetzung zwischen 1794 und 1806,* ed. Albert Mues (Hamburg: Felix Meiner, 1989), pp. 174–97.

19. The *Krause Nachschrift* is somewhat superior to the *Hallesche Nachschrift* in terms of detail and presumed accuracy on some of the points addressed in this essay. The marginal page references in Fuchs's edition of the *Krause Nachschrift* to the corresponding pages in the *Hallesche Nachschrift,* as reprinted in the academy edition, make it easy to carry out a specific comparison of passages.

20. Breazeale translates *Aufforderung* as "summons." The fact that the appeal is addressed to the called-upon individual insofar as it is free to heed or not heed the call suggests a reading of *Aufforderung* closer to "invitation" and its social connotations. Cf. also the title of Carl Maria von Weber's piano piece *Aufforderung zum Tanz* (op. 65), now mostly heard in the orchestration by Hector Berlioz, whose title is customarily rendered in English as "Invitation to the Dance."

21. *GA* I, 3, p. 361.
22. Cf. ibid.
23. Cf. ibid.
24. Cf. *GA* I, 3, p. 364 f. On Fichte's transcendental theory of the body, cf. my essay, "Leib, Materie und gemeinsames Wollen als Anwendungsbedingungen des Rechts," in *J. G. Fichte, Grundlage des Naturrechts,* ed. Jean Christophe Merle, Klassiker auslegen (Berlin: Akademie Verlag, forthcoming).
25. *GA* I, 3, p. 361.
26. In addition to the work published in 1798, there is a second text by Fichte entitled *The System of Ethics,* published posthumously by Fichte's son and based on a set of lectures that Fichte held at the newly established University of Berlin in 1812. Cf. *Fichtes Werke,* ed. I. H. Fichte, 11 vols. (Berlin: de Gruyter, 1971), 11, pp. 1–118 (reprint of *Johann Gottlieb Fichte's nachgelassene Schriften,* ed. I. H. Fichte, 3 vols. [Bonn: Adolph-Marcus, 1834–35], 3, pp. 1–118). On *The System of Ethics* of 1812 in the context of Fichte's late work, cf. my essay "Denken und Wollen beim späten Fichte," forthcoming in *Fichte-Studien.* For a comparison of the two presentations of *The System of Ethics,* cf. my essay "Fichtes Wollen," forthcoming in *Philosophisches Jahrbuch.*
27. *GA* I, 5, p. 199.
28. Ibid., p. 69.
29. Ibid., p. 27 and p. 63, respectively.
30. Ibid., p. 80: "Meine Welt wird verändert, heißt, Ich werde verändert; meine Welt wird weiter bestimmt, heißt, Ich werde weiter bestimmt."
31. On Fichte's transcendental theory of action in *The System of Ethics,* cf. my *Fichte's Transcendental Philosophy,* chapter 4.
32. *GA* I, 5, p. 209 f.
33. Cf. ibid., p. 142.
34. Cf. ibid., p. 204 f.
35. Ibid., pp. 222, 231.
36. Ibid., p. 232: "Ich will Sittlichkeit überhaupt; in oder ausser mir, dies ist mir ganz gleichgültig."
37. *GA* I, 5, p. 233: "Wir sollen alle gleich handeln."
38. Cf. *GA* I, 5, p. 253.
39. In addition to the two published introductions that form part of the aborted *Attempt at a New Presentation of the Wissenschaftslehre* (*GA* I, 4, pp. 186–208 and 209–70; *IWL,* pp. 7–35 and 36–105), there are the two introductions in the Krause transcript of the *Wissenschaftslehre nova methodo* (*WLnm[K],* pp. 3–11 and 11–25; *FTP,* pp. 77–86 and 87–107). There is only one introduction to the Halle transcript of the *Wissenschaftslehre nova methodo* (*GA* II, 2, pp. 17–27).
40. Cf. the reviews of the first edition collected in *J. G. Fichte in zeitgenössischen Rezensionen,* ed. Erich Fuchs, Wilhelm G. Jacobs, and Walter Schieche, 4 vols. (Stuttgart-Bad Canstatt: Frommann-Holzboog, 1995), vol. 1, nos. 29, 32, and 33 through 36.
41. *GA* I, 4, p. 229; *IWL,* p. 61 (translation modified).
42. Cf. Friedrich Karl Forberg, "Briefe über die neueste Philosophie," in

Philosophisches Journal einer Gesellschaft teutschen Gelehrten 6, pp. 44–88, and 7, pp. 259–72. The argument for the neutral status of Fichte's pure I is made in volume 6, p. 60 f. A parallel criticism of a nonempirical conception of the I, this one addressed to Kant himself rather than Fichte, can be found in several of Georg Christoph Lichtenberg's posthumously published aphorisms, including the famous one in which he suggests to emend Kant's "I think" into "it thinks" *(es denkt)* in analogy to the phrase "it lightens" *(es blitzt)*. Cf. my essay, "Lichtenberg and Kant on the Subject of Thinking," *Journal of the History of Philosophy* 30 (1992): pp. 417–41.

43. *GA* I, 4, p. 255; *IWL*, p. 87.

44. *GA* I, 4, p. 255; *IWL*, p. 87.

45. *GA* I, 4, p. 255; *IWL*, p. 87.

46. *GA* I, 4, p. 255; *IWL*, p. 87.

47. *GA* I, 4, p. 255; *IWL*, p. 87 (translation modified).

48. *GA* I, 4, p. 229; *IWL*, p. 61 (my emphasis; translation modified).

49. Cf. *GA* I, 4, p. 265 f.; *IWL*, p. 100 f.

50. There are interesting affinities, which cannot be explored here, between Fichte's presentation and solution of the circle of consciousness and Kant's discussion of the "hidden circle" between freedom and the moral law in the *Foundations of the Metaphysics of Morals* and the closely related doctrine of the "fact of pure reason" in the *Critique of Practical Reason*. Cf. *Kant's gesammelte Schriften*, ed. Royal Prussian Academy and its successors (Berlin, later Berlin and New York: Reimer, later de Gruyter, 1900 ff.), vol. 4, pp. 450, 453, and vol. 5, p. 31 f. There is also a precursor to the circle of consciousness in the *Wissenschaftslehre nova methodo* in Fichte's own discussion of a possible circle between end-setting and object-cognition in the *Foundation of Natural Law* (cf. *GA* I, 3, p. 340). There the solution is provided by the doctrine of solicitation *(Aufforderung)*. Elsewhere in the *Wissenschaftslehre nova methodo*, Fichte employs the term "circle" not to designate a (fallacious) inference but to provide an image for the construction of the I from a center (pure willing) and the periphery attached to the latter according to the laws of discursive thinking. Cf. *WLnm[K]*, pp. 207 and 227; *FTP*, pp. 412 and 446. In a dynamical form, the circle also appears as an image for the periodic internal circulation of the main elements of consciousness ("synthetic periodus": *WLnm[K]*, pp. 188 ff.; *FTP*, 371 ff.); cf. my *Fichte's Transcendental Philosophy*, chapter 8. Finally, the circle in question is not to be confused with the circle in a "reflection theory of consciousness," as diagnosed by Henrich. Cf. his "Fichte's Original Insight," *Contemporary German Philosophy* 1 (1982): pp. 15–53 (previously published in German as *Fichtes ursprüngliche Einsicht* [Frankfurt/M.: Klostermann, 1967]); and, more recently, "Noch einmal in Zirkeln: Eine Kritik von Ernst Tugendhats semantischer Erklärung von Selbstbewußtsein," in *Mensch und Moderne: Beiträge zur philosophischen Anthropologie und Gesellschaftskritik*, ed. C. Bellut and U. Müller-Scholl (Würzburg: Königshausen und Neumann, 1989), pp. 93–132.

51. *WLnm[K]*, p. 152; *FTP*, 306 f.: "Reelle Würksamkeit ist nur möglich nach einem Zweckbegriffe, und ein Zweckbegriff nur unter der Bedingung einer

Erkenntniß, und diese unter der Bedingung einer reellen Wirksamkeit möglich; und das Bewußtsein würde durch einen Zirkel, und sonach gar nicht erklärt." (Translation modified.)

52. For a sustained examination of Fichte's key doctrine of the I's originary dual structure, cf. my *Fichte's Transcendental Philosophy.*

53. Cf. *WLnm[K],* p. 152 pass.; *FTP,* pp. 73, 308 pass.

54. Cf. *Wissenschaftslehre nova methodo,* 35 ff.; *FTP,* p. 121 ff.

55. For a detailed account of Fichte's account of determination in the *Foundation of the Entire Wissenschaftslehre* and the *Wissenschaftslehre nova methodo,* cf. my *Fichte's Transcendental Philosophy,* chapters 3, 5, and 6.

56. *WLnm[K],* p. 175f.; *FTP,* p. 347f.

57. *WLnm[K],* p. 148; *FTP,* p. 300: "Diese Bestimmtheit, die meinen Hauptcharakter ausmacht, besteht darin, daß ich bestimmt bin, mich auf eine gewisse Weise zu bestimmen." (Translation modified.)

58. *WLnm[K],* p. 150; *FTP,* p. 303.

59. *WLnm[K],* p. 156; *FTP,* p. 314: "Alles aber kommt her aus dem absoluten Sein, und aus dem absoluten Beschränktsein im Auffaßen dieses Seins. In realer Rücksicht bin ich nicht alles, in idealer kann ich was ich bin nicht auf einmal auffassen."

60. *WLnm[K],* p. 169; *FTP,* p. 337. Cf. also *WLnm[K],* p. 139 f.; *FTP,* p. 287 f.

61. Cf. *WLnm[K],* p. 176; *FTP,* p. 349 f.

62. For a more detailed treatment of Fichte's noumenalism in the second presentation of the *Wissenschaftslehre,* cf. my essay "Geist oder Gespenst? Fichte's Noumenalism in der *Wissenschaftslehre nova methodo,"* *Fichte-Studien* 12 (1997): pp. 297–306.

63. *WLnm[K],* p. 177; *FTP,* p. 351: "Das Selbstbewußtsein hebt an von meinem herausgreifen aus einer Maße vernünftiger Wesen überhaupt." (Translation modified.) Cf. also *WLnm[K],* p. 149; *FTP,* p. 301 f.

64. Cf. *WLnm[K],* p. 233; *FTP,* p. 456 f.

65. *WLnm[K],* p. 231; *FTP,* p. 454. On the inclusion of interpersonal relations in the sphere of consciousness and their subordination under the principle of self-consciousness, cf. also Ives Radrizzani, "Existe-t-il une déduction de l'intersubjectivité chez Fichte?" forthcoming in *Fichte-Studien.*

66. *WLnm[K],* p. 178; *FTP,* p. 352: "Kein Individuum kann sich aus sich selbst erklären; wenn man also auf ein erstes Individuum kommt, worauf man kommen muß, so muß man auch noch ein höheres unbegreifliches Wesen annehmen." In the corresponding passage of the Halle transcript of the *Wissenschaftslehre nova methodo* (*GA* IV, 2, p. 176), Fichte refers to the corollaries to section 3 of the *Foundation of Natural Law,* where the same thought is already expressed. Cf. *GA* I, 3, p. 347 f.

67. Cf. *GA* I, 6, p. 292; *The Vocation of Man,* ed. Roderick M. Chisholm (New York: Macmillan, 1986), p. 134.

68. On the conceptual history of "individual" and "individuality" in general and on the varying identifications of the principle of individuation in particular (matter, negation, space and time, etc.), cf. the entries "Individuation, Individ-

uationsprinzip" (author, J. Hüllen) and "Individuum, Individualität" (author, T. Borsche) in *Historisches Wörterbuch der Philosophie*, ed. Joachim Ritter and Karlfriedrich Gründer (Basel/Stuttgart: Schwabe and Co., 1976), vol. 4, pp. 295–9 and pp. 300–23, respectively.

69. The English word "individual," like its equivalents in many other modern European languages, is a loan word from the Greek *atomon.*

Reflection and Feeling and the Primacy of Practical Reason in the Jena *Wissenschaftslehre*

C. Jeffery Kinlaw

F ichte confronts the problem of the unity of reason, inherited from Kant, by demonstrating that reason is basically and essentially practical. Theoretical reason, whereby we posit and determine the objects of our experience, presupposes a more basic, practical function of the I. Our representation of an object—that is, any object (actual or ideal)— presupposes as the condition of its possibility a limitation and determination of what Fichte calls our inherent "practical power" *(praktische Vermögen)*. In this sense, the activity of theoretical reason is a specific limitation or determination of the I's practical activity. Our representation of the world in experience arises, according to Fichte's reconstruction in the *Wissenschaftslehre,* from a series of reflective acts, which attempt to interpret or explain "feelings." These feelings are simple subjective states, which arise from the restriction or limitation of the I's self-expressive activity and are the expression of the I's restriction. The argument for the priority of practical reason coincides with the presentation of the *Wissenschaftslehre* itself; namely, by reference to the striving doctrine in the *Grundlage* and the function of the will in the *Wissenschaftslehre nova methodo.* But what does it mean to affirm that reason and the I itself are *essentially* practical? Fichte answers this question in part by arguing that representation itself has a practical foundation, and he supports his argument by demonstrating that a free act of self-determination is a necessary condition for representing any object at all. I intend to argue, however, that Fichte's claim is stronger than this. In short, I contend that, for Fichte, the representation of objects serves—or, perhaps, more accurately, *ought* to serve—the more fundamentally practical concern of self-determination. This is an admittedly strong claim, but one that I think can be defended. Equally important, it is a claim whose defense will provide an additional payoff, namely, a clear conception of Fichte's view of the nature *and* function of practical rationality and the philosophical anthropology that underlies practical reason.

An initial glance might advise that my claim is misleading if not false. Even though the I to some extent is self-determining when representing objects, Fichte himself maintains that in representing those objects one feels constrained (in one's activity) to present something as present and to do so precisely *as* that something presents itself. The resulting representations are those Fichte describes in the *Second Introduction* as being accompanied by a feeling of necessity. But Fichte also stresses that absolute activity determines objective or representational activity and that this absolute activity, the foundation for freedom and self-determination, is the basis for the spontaneous reflection intrinsic to theoretical reason and for willing in practical reason.[1] The issue I intend to confront is precisely the practical nature of the I's absolute activity *in its relation to the activity of representing objects,* that is, the nature and scope of the I's self-determination and the manner in which its self-configuration affects the entire range of its activity.

This essay will proceed initially with an analytic reconstruction of the dynamic interplay of reflection and feeling with the aim of showing that the standard picture of this interplay—representation of objects—is guided by one of several possible drives *(Triebe)* or dispositions (in this case, the disposition to represent objects). More important, I hope to show that the disposition to representation is guided by a more basic, comprehensive, and practical disposition to reflection. That the drive to reflection *(berhaupt)* underlies the reflective activity of representation is not a controversial claim, the latter being a more concrete or determinate application of the former. Yet Fichte maintains that representation presupposes a more basic, and, for his anthropology, more important, type of thinking. Accordingly, the disposition to represent objects is subordinate precisely because it serves—at least in the best of all practical worlds—a particular conceptual aim that has been projected as an image by the I's reflection upon and thereby concretizing of its self-determination.[2] The concept of a goal or aim is self-generated by the I as a guide for its purely self-determined action. It is what we freely will to bring about. If thinking that projects an image of what willing and, thereby, free activity is to produce is to determine thinking as representation of objects, this would mean that thinking as willing is to determine thinking as representation of objects. That would be a controversial claim but one to which I will argue Fichte is committed.

The absolute activity (what Fichte calls pure willing in the *Wissenschaftslehre nova methodo*), presupposed by objective activity (the activity whereby we represent objects), is the I's own inherent practical power to develop itself as a free being. This power or capacity functions within the I as what Peter Baumanns has called a "foundational disposition" *(Triebunterlage)* to which all other dispositions are subjected.[3] As I will argue, theoretical reason is subordinate precisely because theoretical knowledge of the world is simply one way—and not the primary way—of relating to the world.[4] For Fichte, our relation to the world in its most fundamental sense is practical, that is, we relate to the world by means of our practical concerns. The world itself, first and foremost, is the theater of our self-development. It is the arena within which our practical capacity *(praktische Vermögen)* or our ability to be *(Seinkönnen)* is actualized. As such, however, the world's malleability has its limits. Our aims are often challenged and frustrated. Even though, as Fichte explains in the *Wissenschaftslehre nova methodo,* feelings (the material with which the world is represented by the imagination) determine the sphere of our action, the formation of practical goals for our actions places our reflective activity well beyond the restriction on our activity expressed in any determinate set of feelings. The I finds itself within opposition between its free capacity and the inescapable limitations it confronts. Transcending these limitations by appropriating (as effectively as possible) what the I confronts within the world as a means to its various ends is the manner in which the I properly transforms its practical power (its absoluteness as a transcendental foundation) into its ideal destiny: complete self-determination or a fulfilled freedom.

1

The task of the *Wissenschaftslehre* is to show how the structure and content of experience can be derived from specific acts of the I. The I, however, finds itself disposed to act in various ways. It is so disposed precisely because, in a certain sense, it cannot act. Simply stated, its activity is not efficacious. Although the I's activity may follow directly from its self-expressive freedom, that activity (the activity that is merely dispositional) does not lead to genuine action. That is, it does not produce something out of itself or of its own making. This is exactly the case with the activity of representing objects. Representation of objects is an act of the I, but one in which the I is determined to act in a specific manner. What results from the action—the representation of an object—is not generated purely from the I, nor does the motive force for the act of representation lie solely within the I. The I simply represents what is given to it to represent, and these representations are accompanied by a feeling of necessity.[5] The I's activity (and the determining power or efficacy of that activity) has been checked and redirected inward. By being arrested and directed inward, the I's determining power is refocused on the I itself. Determining becomes thereby a self-determining. Accordingly, a disposition to act is a self-determination that arises within the confrontation between striving and limitation or from the clash of opposing directions of activity. Fichte calls this stalemate between striving to action and restriction on action a drive or disposition *(Trieb).* A disposition to act is a determinate or concretized striving. Associated with it is an expression of compulsion *(Zwang)* or, more precisely, a *"Nicht-Können,"* which involves a continuation of striving (the inability is mine) and a limitation of the I's real activity.[6] One is thus disposed to do what one cannot do immediately and automatically.[7] The restriction upon the I's activity in conjunction with the endeavor to overcome the restriction is the basis for all representation of objects. Since representation of objects is an *act* of representation, unless my activity is checked and then focused in a particular way, I could not explain why I represent a specific object rather than another—or any object at all—and why I feel compelled to do so.

The basic inability that characterizes a disposition to act and that results from a restriction on the I's activity expresses itself in the I as feeling *(Gefühl).* Feeling is the way in which the stalemate between striving to act and determine the other and being affected and determined by the other registers in the I. In the words of one commentator, feeling characterizes the conflict and interconnection between the I's real activity being arrested *(Angehaltsein)* and its will to go forward *(Weiterwollen).*[8] As such, feeling is a mere affection. It is a purely subjective state that is both elementary and nonanalyzable. Feelings are the ultimate limits and units of consciousness that come to consciousness initially as what Locke called a simple idea (for example, as the perception red, cold, or sweet).[9] Feelings are subjective, atomistic states, which have no intrinsic connection to any other feelings. The feeling of "sweet" bears within itself no connection to "red" or any other feeling. Any connection among feelings results from an act of the productive imagination, which synthesizes feelings into a concrete unity and posits them as qualities of an object (for example, "That apple is red and sweet").[10] Feeling is thus a specific limitation of the I, as well as the manner in which a determinate limitation of the I is "immediately perceived" or practically felt.[11]

While feeling arises from restriction on real activity, it is interconnected with ideal or reflective activity. In this sense, feeling mirrors the stalemate within the I that it expresses: I *feel* and thus am limited (a compulsion is present), but *I* feel, and the activity by which I feel is reflective activity. For feelings to enter consciousness, the I must separate itself from its immersion in feeling and assume the relation of feeling subject. I feel, but at the same moment, Fichte explains, I "wrench myself away" from feeling; I reflect upon it, intuit or see it.[12] I not only feel myself affected, but become aware by this act of reflection of the specific, concrete affection: I taste sweet, feel cold, or see red. The reflective act, whereby I separate myself from the content of feeling and adopt a subject-object relation to it, is an utterly spontaneous act that has its foundation in the tendency to self-reflection intrinsic to the I.[13] Within the context of striving, this reflection is more precisely characterized as a disposition to reflection. Directed to feeling, the disposition to reflect becomes a disposition to represent, which determines feeling by projecting an interpretation or explanation outside feeling for what is felt. To reflect is thus to direct ideal activity toward something and thus to determine that something's specific character.[14] This reflective activity is actually a series of acts involving the intuiting act of ideal activity and the synthetic act of the productive imagination. The former initially brings feelings to consciousness; the latter synthesizes the manifold of feelings and posits the manifold as an object with distinctive qualities.

The ideal activity by which the I reflects is determined in two respects. First, this activity is determined by that to which it is directed. Accordingly, it is an activity that simply depicts but does not determine its object. Since ideal activity is directed inwardly, it is efficacious only upon the I itself. As a result, ideal activity simply mirrors within the I the content of the I's affection in feeling. Ideal activity simply projects an image or copy *(Nachbild)* of what is already present within feeling.[15] Ideal activity is merely an observing activity. To this extent, it is passive, since it projects an image of the affect of real activity on the I. The I is affected or determined by the not-I, and the affect or precipitate of the determination is a feeling. Ideal activity takes the first step toward bringing a manifold of feelings to consciousness as the awareness of an object by fashioning an image or copy of what lies before ideal activity in feeling. It is important to emphasize that this imaging or intuiting activity is only an initial step (though a necessary one for a feeling to be *für mich*) in the representation of an object. Since ideal activity only copies what it encounters in feeling, the object appears to it as something indeterminate and incomprehensible that simply "hovers" before the I. At this point, the "object" is simply the original material out of which the imagination will represent an object once a manifold of feelings has arisen within the I.[16]

Second, viewed from the perspective of disposition rather than the perspective of feeling, ideal activity is determined by a disposition to act in a certain manner. From this perspective, ideal activity is pointed outwardly and directed to posit something that fulfills the disposition. Directed to feeling, reflection becomes a more concrete form of reflection, namely, the ideal activity that is guided by the drive to represent objects. Ideal activity is driven to bring forth what the disposition to representation would produce on its own and from itself if it were able to do so.[17] Since it is determined by feeling, the act of representing objects is thus an interpretative activity, which provides an objective interpretation or explanation for what it finds subjectively in feeling.

In this initial act in the complex activity of representation with which we have been concerned, intuiting and feeling are interconnected and can thus be separated only by philosophical analysis. In fact, the content of intuition and feeling is the same. In the transition from feeling to intuition, what was first merely felt simply as the experience of being affected becomes something vaguely recognizable as an impression of "sweet." That I experience the world is determined by a specific reflective activity and thus particular self-determination. What I experience is grounded in feeling.[18] The simple impression of "sweet" is thus a synthetic association *(Zusammenhang)*—necessarily effected by the productive imagination—of feeling and intuition. For Fichte, intuition and feeling are related biconditionally. Without feeling intuition is merely an act of imaging without anything to copy, and without intuition feeling is the manifestation of an affection without the I being aware of the content of that affection.[19]

The reflective activity of intuition projects an image of what it encounters in feeling and thereby makes feeling *visible* as a discrete impression. Since, as noted earlier, any feeling possesses no intrinsic relation to other feelings, the connection among a manifold of feelings is the work of imagination. It synthesizes a manifold of feelings and posits the synthetic unity as an object. As Fichte describes the imagination in the *Grundlage* and the *Wissenschaftslehre nova methodo,* it attempts to reconcile the opposition being activity and restriction. More specifically, the imagination reconciles the conflict between opposed feelings: the feeling of limitation and the feeling of longing for a fulfillment of our disposition to represent.[20] As a result, we perceive an object with particular characteristics corresponding to our specific feelings or impressions.

Although I intuit something just as I feel it, I am not compelled to determine the object in the same way that I intuit it. Whereas I normally see a tree with orange leaves in my backyard during autumn, I can choose to attribute the color purple to the leaves on the tree. This is what I do, for instance, when I fantasize, and when I do so, feeling and intuition disconnect. The feeling subject and the intuiting subject separate, and for this reason what I project in fantasy does not correspond to the truth. When I fantasize, I represent the world not as it is but as I might wish it to be. Truth indicates the necessary connection between feeling and intuition and the way in which the content of a particular intuition follows necessarily from the content of a specific feeling. Fichte writes:

> Truth, objectivity, reality: these apply to those of my representations which necessarily follow from a feeling, when the feeling is capable of activating the representing subject, when it exercises causality upon the ideal activity of the representing subject, when the I reflects upon the feeling. This or that determinate intuition follows from this state of the feeling subject: this is truth.[21]

Truth, and thus objective representation, requires that I represent objects as guided by the material content that I encounter in feeling. But I am neither compelled to pursue, nor to remain preoccupied with, empirical truth. In this sense, as Fichte indicates, my "intellectual compulsion" is conditional.[22] At the same time, fantasy presupposes truth, since my capacity to imagine the world differently presupposes a previous encounter with the world as it is (setting aside, of course, standard objections of skepticism). My capacity to represent the leaves on my tree as purple is thus parasitic on a previous encounter with the tree as having orange autumn leaves. While my observation about our capacity to fantasize about the world might appear as trivial, it calls attention to the *inherently* conditional nature of representation that enables us to uncover the more important practical foundation for thinking that Fichte defends. Fantasy seems trivial precisely because it is idle speculation; that is, it does not serve a significant purpose or attempt to represent the world in any practically or theoretically useful manner. Yet, as Kant had argued in the *Critique of Pure Reason,* our knowledge of the world extends well beyond the mere representation of objects and involves more than what can be provided solely by the understanding. If we are to extend our knowledge of the world—indeed, if we are to engage in scientific investigation of the world—we must be able to envision the world differently than we have comprehended it before. Thinking the world as being different from its representation by the understanding is the work of reason. Fichte appropriates this function of reason from Kant, yet configures it not only as purely practical but also as serving a practical end. In short,

Fichte attempts to disclose the intrinsically practical nature of reason by executing a reconstructive analysis of the nature of representation. His argument takes the form of an analysis that uncovers a practical mode of representation, one in which thinking and willing are interconnected. As I will argue, this connection between thinking and willing effects a reversal of the relation between determination and ideal activity and, more important, shows that the representation of physical objects is not the primary way in which we relate to the world.

Susan Neiman[23] has argued that reason for Kant not only plays a more extensive role in our "knowledge" of the world than has been recognized traditionally but also that the theoretical use of reason has a practical dimension. As Neiman points out, the application of the categories by the understanding occurs automatically, whereas the principles of reason are freely applied to experience represented by the understanding. Her crucial point is to emphasize the limited scope and function of the understanding and the essential role of the function of reason for any scientific pursuit. The understanding only represents what is *presently given* and thus does not possess the perspective by which to put questions to the world, as would a scientist. For that purpose, one would have to be able to look beyond experience, to propose models that envision the world other than it has been previously comprehended, and to test whether experience can confirm the new models. Not only can reason alone perform that function, but only reason can provide the *motive* for doing so.[24] In sum, reason's capacity to think the world other than what is simply given in experience provides the necessary framework for genuine scientific knowledge of the world.[25] Reason—and this point is crucial—must then be dynamic and free to project models and guide scientific pursuits. Herein lies its practical dimension: reason projects ideas of the world's structure or its basic systematic unity and thereby insists that experience *ought* to conform to that systematic order.[26] Fichte appropriates and further develops this conception of reason inherited from Kant. Yet he demonstrates that this practical dimension of reason, one which enables us to demand that experience fulfill the aims of reason, lies at the foundation of an analysis of representation itself. He attempts to show, furthermore, that the practical dimension of reason is reason's essential nature.

Throughout the Jena *Wissenschaftslehre*, Fichte argues that positing X as something determinate presupposes what X is not. Therefore, X as something determinate stands in opposition to what X is not, namely, that which is not determinate but determinable. The sphere of the determinable, in relation to X, indicates what X could be if it were not the specific thing that it is. This claim that actuality involves a negation—X

C. JEFFERY KINLAW

is something determinate only in relation to what is excluded from the sphere of X—Fichte applies to intuition and representation of an object. Herein lies the possibility of positing not an actual object but an ideal object, one that provides the concept of a goal for the I's activity. When we intuit a manifold of feelings and then represent them as a particular object, we represent something that is actual or something that exists. As something actual, the object is what it is only as a limitation of the range of possibility. The actual object that is represented thus excludes another object, which is a possible object. The possible object does not exist, because it stands opposed to the actual object. Yet, as something possible, the possible object opens up the prospect for the I to posit and determine it as an ideal.[27] There are thus two possible objects of an intuition: (1) an object that explains the limitation of the I's real activity and constrains the I's reflective activity to represent it in a particular way; and (2) the determinable object that becomes the object of striving and that does not compel reflective activity to posit the object in any determinate fashion.[28] As we will see, the object of striving becomes for Fichte the concept of a goal that guides the I's genuine self-determining and productive activity. Fichte, however, views the capacity of reason to view the world as it could be rather than as it simply presents itself not primarily as a basis for scientific pursuits but as the basis for developing the pure, practical capacity of the I. The projection of an end to guide the I's determination of objects serves first and foremost the development of the I's own inherently practical power or its capacity for self-determination. As we will see, this is the sense in which our most basic encounter with the world, and the one that is the most significant for philosophical anthropology, is practical and the sense in which Fichte tries to show what it means to contend that the world *ought* to conform to the laws of the I's self-determination. As one commentator has written: "The most original encounter of the world is not a neutral intuition but a projection of the world as a means for the ends of humanity."[29] When we therefore develop our capacity for true self-determination, representation in part is guided by a more basic and essential disposition, namely, our striving to actualize the absoluteness that lies within us initially as an unfinished practical capacity.

2

Fichte maintains that we have the sheer freedom to abstract and reflect, that is, the freedom to direct ourselves toward something or to divert our attention from it. This freedom, Fichte writes, distinguishes his view from fatalism:

Fatalism and the basis on which it rests, that our activity and will are
dependent upon the system of our representations, is destroyed at its
foundation, in that, as is shown here, our representations are dependent
on our dispositions and will. And this is also the one way to oppose
fatalism at its foundation.[30]

This freedom of reflection is surely not trivial, since it refers to the will's
ability to direct our ideal or representational activity to posit and determine objects in a particular manner. But the will is also restricted
by feeling, since the I is constrained to posit objects whose content is
determined by the way in which the I has been affected in feeling. The
object of the will, however, is not an empirical object but an ideal object,
one that serves as a concept of a goal for a possible action. In this case,
feeling may set the range for objects of the will—that is, feeling fills out
the sphere of what is determinable—but the will is able to choose how
it determines its object. The ideal object is thus not a representation of
what is but of what ought to be. It is a projection of a possible action
within the empirical world that then demands that the world answer to
the concept of that action.

The ideal object or the concept of a goal is freely generated by the
I's inherent, practical capacity, the I's only restriction being, as noted
above, that it must construct the concept of a possible action from the
sphere of determinability. The concept of a goal is an image of what
ought to result from I's self-determined action. In this sense, it represents the way in which we can *think* free activity in a determinate way,
and that involves projecting a rule for the synthesis of possible feelings
into the representation of an object that designates the result of the
I's activity were that activity fully efficacious. In constructing the concept of a goal, thinking and willing are therefore interconnected. Acting
must be guided by the concept of what is to be produced by the action.
Accordingly, willing something requires the thinking of what one is to
will. And, to think the concept of a goal for an action involves willing
that action. Willing then becomes a determinate way of thinking and
a thinking that, unlike the representation of empirical objects, has "inner efficacy."[31] Thinking that is willing produces its object spontaneously
(that is, *von selbst*) from the sphere of possible actions available to the
I. In this sense, the concept of a goal is not a copy of the affect of real
activity on the I as manifested in feeling, but the projected image of a
purely self-determined action. Rather than being a mere *Nachbild,* the
concept of a goal is a *Vorbild* that provides a rule of procedure for the
imagination in its projection of an object.[32]

The construction of the concept of a goal is the concretizing of the
activity of pure willing whereby the absoluteness of willing can manifest

itself in the empirical world by providing guidance for the I's self-determination. In the language of the *Grundlage,* ideal objects are intended by the way in which absolute, self-reverting activity determines objective or representational activity. And this, Fichte argues in the *Grundlage,* provides the basis for dislodging the dependence of the I as an intelligence that is required for a resolution of *Hauptantithesis* 5. As Fichte argues, the not-I represented by the check on the I's activity must be determined by the I's absolute activity. Put differently, the I itself selects the place where its indeterminate activity is to be checked and thereby made determinate. This is what takes place when the I constructs the concept of a goal. And in so doing—again in the language of the *Grundlage*—the I's absolute activity determines the objective activity or the way in which the I is to represent the object.[33] In the language of the *Wissenschaftslehre nova methodo,* the ideal activity, which is simply an intuiting activity in the representation of empirical objects, becomes a real, efficacious activity by actually generating the concept of a goal for action. Real, self-determined activity is in that way transformed into an activity that *thinks* something that is ideal or something that ought to be, namely, something that ought to result from the I's own freely determined action.[34]

The resolution of *Hauptantithesis* 5 requires that the I's absolute and self-reverting activity provide the determining ground for its representation of objects. The final fulfillment of this requirement is an idea of practical reason that represents the ultimate achievement of the I's capacity for self-determination. Realizing that ideal would thus demand that all representation of objects come forth as a pure self-determination of the I. In short, the resolution of *Hauptantithesis* 5 solves a contradiction within the nature of the I itself between its being determined and its capacity for free, self-determination that is a necessary condition for the I to act at all. By constructing and acting on the concept of a goal, the I is actualizing within the empirical world its inherent capacity for self-determination. Fichte writes:

> My I, considered as the subject of my practical power (that is, as forming an image of itself and developing itself accordingly, as self-intuiting and as consciously acting), must therefore always construct for itself in advance the concept of this goal. It requires, as it were, a model, the realization of which is the goal of real action.[35]

The projection of the concept of a goal is a determinate thinking *of the I itself,* the genitive in this phase being an objective genitive. In other words, the ideal object is a prescription for a possible way of being for the I, which sets forth one step in the I's incremental advance toward fulfilled self-determination. And the I's self-determination requires that it propose aims and strategies for action that it imposes upon the empirical world and demands at least that the world provide an arena for the fulfillment of the I's aims. For Fichte, reason is essentially practical, precisely because reason, which is free and self-determining, is first and foremost the thinking of the concept of goals for action along with the demand that the empirical world conform to reason's demands.

3

The I's projection of aims is grounded in its absoluteness or capacity for self-determination. As the I attains its goals, it develops its capacity for self-determination and actualizes within the finite, temporal world the absoluteness which constitutes its nature. To develop my self-sufficiency is precisely what it means for me to be a rational being. Fichte writes in the *Sittenlehre:* "The rational being, considered as such, is absolute, self-sufficient, and utterly the ground of itself. Originally, that is, without its own assistance, it is utterly nothing; what it is to become, it must make itself into that something through its own deed."[36] The I posits itself initially as a simple capacity for self-determination. The I's power of acting is thus a pure capacity *(Vermögen)*, which initially, though thinkable as actual, contains no specific marker identifying the manner in which the I's self-determination is to be developed and realized. What I am to become, I must fashion myself by actualizing my goals. And if I am self-determining, what I become will be what I have made of myself.[37]

The I finds itself always within opposition, and in constructing its aims it must confront the world it represents in experience. To this extent, feeling determines the I's most basic disposition, namely, the disposition to self-determination that indicates the core of what it means to be an I. Although the disposition to self-activity and thereby self-determination provides a "real, inner explanatory ground of actual self-sufficiency,"[38] feelings provide the field for the I's self-activity. Again, the I is characterized by opposition; it is unfinished or "a being on the way,"[39] in the words of one commentator. It is self-extended between the absoluteness of its nature and the absoluteness of its destiny as fully self-determining. As so self-extended, the I is suspended between its basic *Sein-Können* and the *Nicht-Können* that it confronts in feeling. With the goals it projects, the I not only determines the "real world" considered in a practical sense but also the empirical world as it demands conformity to its projects and strategies.

The ultimate goal of striving, however, is the I itself, namely, the I as a completely self-sufficient and self-determining being. By constructing goals for its activity, the I therefore configures itself and presents possible ways of working out and fulfilling its practical power within the finite and temporal world. With the ultimate aim of full and accomplished self-determination, the I aspires to what it cannot become. This goal, however, determines the projection of intermediate and concrete goals, that is, if an individual I has the fortitude to aspire to moral genius. The I does not respond to every possible satisfaction of striving, of course, nor would it satisfy any disposition were the conditions conducive for transforming disposition into action. When functioning properly, the I manages its dispositions and thus subordinates all dispositions to the comprehensive disposition to self-determination that expresses itself "in the entire I."[40]

I hope to have demonstrated that the disposition to represent objects presupposes a more basic disposition to project aims, and finally, that the projection of individual aims presupposes a fundamental disposition to self-determination. Reflection and feeling are interwoven functionally in the representation of any object, empirical or ideal. Reflection embraces feelings and represents objects, by means of the imagination, on the basis of what it finds in feeling. Feeling thus determines the range of reflection and thereby the scope of our aims. When representing objects, the imagination attempts to resolve an opposition that it finds within feeling, an opposition between being determined and determining (or it attempts to reconcile conflicting feeling). Yet the reconciliation of opposition that leads to representation of objects serves the attempt to reconcile an opposition within the I itself. The projection and realization of goals attempts to reconcile the I's basic *Sein-Können* with its *Nicht-Können*. The task is to overcome the *Nicht* and actualize the *Können*. Even to consider how this might be accomplished places the I beyond its determinations, that is, already beyond the *Nicht* that it confronts in its very being.

There remains, unsurprisingly in a project as global as Fichte's, an unresolved tension in his view of self-determination and in the way in which the real objects of the empirical world are to conform to the ideal objects of practical reason. Fichte has adopted Kant's view of theoretical reason as the projection of ideas or models onto the sensible world for his project of practical self-determination. The concept of a goal is an image or model for the I's action, but also an image or model of the way in which the world ought to be. How are we to understand the way in which the empirical world is to conform to the intelligible world of practical goals? In short, how close is the conformity to be? One possible explanation would be something like this: Objective experience is to be harnessed for the realization of practical ends. We are constrained, of course, in our representation of empirical objects and must represent the content of those objects according to the way in which those objects affect us. That the I determines the not-I means that the empirical objects that we are constrained to represent provide no obstacle for the realization of our goals (and thus no impediment to self-determination and self-actualization) but rather are transformed into means for the realization of our self-determination. For instance, I am constrained to represent the dogwood tree in my backyard according to the way in which my senses are affected when I encounter the dogwood. However, my representation of the dogwood can be determined by my practical goal of selecting the proper time to plant my spring garden. In this instance, I am attentive to certain features of the dogwood—that it is blooming, for instance—as a sign that the proper time has arrived for spring planting. And yet, there might be some serious questions as to whether this interpretation provides for a strong enough idealism. There are plenty of passages in the Jena writings, as well as in the post-1800 versions of the *Wissenschaftslehre*, that indicate that Fichte means that the representation of the world is to conform precisely to the laws of the I's own self-positing. Accordingly, the representation of objects would conform directly with the content of the I's proposed goals for action and would not simply be the means for realizing those goals. The projection of goals certainly places demands on the world and requires some conformity between the intelligible world and the empirical world. But it is difficult to comprehend what strict conformity between the empirical world and the I's goals would be like; that is, it is difficult to describe such a world in an intelligible way. At any rate, if the fulfillment of the I's self-determination requires the strict conformity between the two worlds, then the ultimate actualization and accomplishment of free self-determination would entail the destruction of consciousness, since consciousness presupposes opposition between thinking and what is thought.

Notes

1. Fichte, *Grundlage der gesammten Wissenslehre,* in vol. 1 of *Fichtes Werke,* ed. I. H. Fichte (Berlin: De Gruyter, 1971), a reprint in 11 vols. of *Johann Gottlieb Fichtes sämmtliche Werke* (Berlin: Viet and Co., 1845–46), 8 vols., and *Johann Gottlieb Fichtes nachgelassene Werke* (Bonn: Adolphus-Marcu, 1834–35), 3 vols. *Fichtes Werke* is hereafter cited as *SW*. All translations from the *Grundlage* are mine.

C . J E F F E R Y   K I N L A W

2. How thinking as willing, the mechanism by which we project a conceptual aim *(Zweckbegriff)*, is served by thinking that represents objects, is never fully resolved in Fichte's thought, as we shall see. It is clear that Fichte seems committed to the view that the aims or concepts of goals projected by thinking as willing are more "real," at least in a practical sense, than the empirical world represented in experience. How these two "worlds" ultimately are related or conjoined, while preserving the integrity of both, is not resolved.

3. Peter Baumanns, *Fichtes ursprüngliche System: sein Standort zwischen Kant und Hegel* (Stuttgart-Bad Cannstatt: Fromann-Holzboog, 1972), p. 139.

4. This commits Fichte to the view that the practical or "moral world" is more "real" than the natural world.

5. Although the representation of objects cannot be explained without presupposing certain free acts on the part of the I, acts that Fichte brings to light in his reconstruction of necessary conditions for representation, the I is not free in *what* it represents, that is, not with representations that are felt to be necessary.

6. By "real" activity, Fichte means activity that is self-generating and that produces something solely on its own.

7. *SW* I, p. 289.

8. Ulrich Claesges, *Geschichte des Selbstbewusstseins: Der Ursprung des spekulativen Problems in Fichtes WL von 1794–1795* (The Hague: Martinus Nijhoff, 1974), p. 115.

9. There is, of course, an important difference between what Fichte calls feelings and Lockean simple ideas. Whereas Fichte maintains that feelings are not felt without being related to an object, feelings themselves do not have any intrinsic intentional or representation quality. Relating feelings to objects and thereby predicating some quality of an object (that is, the inference from the feeling of "sweet" to the proposition "That is sweet") involves a separate act of the I. Therefore, feelings become representative only by being posited as such. All objects, along with their specific determinations, are posited; they are not felt. The I feels only itself or, more precisely, its own determinate states. Here is one indication of Fichte's rejection of Kant's separation of thought and intuition. For Fichte, an object of intuition, insofar as it is an object (however indeterminate, that is, apart from the application of any categories), presupposes an act of determination by the I. So, there is some act of thinking already embedded in intuition itself. "I prefer [feeling] to Kant's sensation, for sensation comes to be only through relation to an object by means of thinking." (*Zweite Einleitung in der Wissenschaftslehre*, in *SW* I, p. 490. Translation mine.)

10. See *Foundations of Transcendental Philosophy (Wissenschaftslehre) nova methodo*, trans. Daniel Breazeale (Ithaca: Cornell University Press, 1992), pp. 170–7. All citations of the *nova methodo* are from the Breazeale translation. Hereafter cited as *WLnm*.

11. "[U]nmittlebare Wahrnehumung." *SW* I, p. 490.

12. *WLnm*, p. 195.

13. "I cannot intuit any feeling outside of me, but only within myself, and indeed in such a manner that the act of feeling itself acquires complete reality or

becomes a concept. Intuition arises only after this, insofar as an act of reflection simply occurs—that is, occurs with absolute freedom." *WLnm*, pp. 180–81.

14. *WLnm*, p. 86.

15. "It [ideal activity] is to bring forth in the I a determination, as it exists in the not-I." *SW* I, p. 310. Ideal activity, however, is not a blind mechanism. Fichte's interpretation of transcendental apperception maintains that the I is also an eye, meaning that an awareness of its own activity coincides with the I's acts.

16. See *WLnm*, pp. 193–97.

17. *WLnm*, p. 296.

18. "All our knowledge proceeds from such an ultimately subjective relation to feeling, for without feeling no representation of a thing outside us is possible." *SW* I, p. 314.

19. Fichte applies Kant's famous statement about the relation between intuition and concepts to the connection between feeling and intuition. "Thus intuition sees but is blind; feeling is related to reality but is empty." *SW* I, p. 319. The difference, as noted earlier, is important and indicates the more complete conception of transcendental idealism that Fichte defends. He refuses to accept the intuition-concept distinction because, as he tries to show, intuition itself involves the determination of thinking.

20. *SW* I, p. 290.

21. *WLnm*, p. 230.

22. *WLnm*, p. 218.

23. Susan Neiman, *The Unity of Reason: Rereading Kant* (Oxford: Oxford University Press, 1994).

24. Ibid., pp. 59–60.

25. "The laws of the understanding are not derived from a source external to the understanding, but they are restricted to experience and applied automatically, leaving no room for the exercise of choice and judgment involved in the application of a regulative principle. This makes the principles of the understanding second-rate. The capacity to act freely according to chosen ends confers value not only upon all human activity, but, Kant suggests, upon the world as a whole. A science that dispenses with reason's use, substituting constitutive for regulative principles, would be the work of automata, bereft of the value that belongs to our pursuit of natural science." Ibid., p. 91.

26. Ibid., p. 113.

27. *WLnm*, p. 199.

28. *WLnm*, p. 200.

29. Wilhelm Weischedel, *Der frühe Fichte: Aufbruch der Freiheit zur Gemeinschaft* (Stuttgart-Bad Cannstatt: Fromann-Holzboog, 1973), p. 71.

30. *SW* I, p. 295.

31. *WLnm*, p. 264.

32. "By constraining my own imagination in this way, I become immediately conscious of this act, of this constraining; and this is how the intelligible world is connected with the world of appearances." *WLnm*, pp. 254–65.

33. See *SW* I, pp. 250–69, for a more detailed presentation.

34. For a detailed and helpful discussion, see Günter Zöller, *Fichte's Transcendental Philosophy: The Original Duplicity of Intelligence and Will* (Cambridge: Cambridge University Press, 1998), especially chapters 5 and 6 (pp. 71–93).

35. *WLnm*, p. 150.

36. Fichte, *System der Sittenlehre nach den Principien der Wissenschaftslehre, 1798,* in *SW* IV, p. 50.

37. *SW* IV, p. 38.

38. *SW* IV, p. 40.

39. Weischedel, *Der fruhe Fichte,* p. 74.

40. *SW* IV, p. 40.

The Unity of Philosophy in Fichte's *Wissenschaftslehre nova methodo*, 1798–1799

Angelica Nuzzo

Philosophy as System

In the *Transcendental Doctrine of Method* of the *Critique of Pure Reason*, the post-Kantian philosophers could find the most important suggestion for their own work—namely, the idea of philosophy as "system" or the idea of the "systematic unity" of philosophy. The form of the "system" is, according to Kant, that which first raises ordinary knowledge to the level of *science*. The structure of the system is proper to philosophy because it is proper to reason in the first place—and this holds true because reason itself *is* ultimately a system.[1] The systematic method is therefore "natural" to reason as it reflects reason's own nature or constitution. Even if Kant did not develop this last suggestion himself, he certainly opened up a new perspective to Fichte, who follows it through in his *Wissenschaftslehre nova methodo*. In Kant's view, a system is the "unity of the manifold modes of knowledge under one idea."[2] The idea of the system carries within itself an essential ambiguity, since it refers both to the *objective* character of the form of an object and to the *subjective* character of an ideal structure—namely, to the way in which we think of an object. In other words, "system" is both an *ontological* and an *epistemological* concept. "System" is a concept of reason *(Vernunftbegriff)*—or an "idea" *(Idee)* in the proper sense of the term—that prescribes a peculiar logic to the totality which is to be organized according to it. (a) "System" is, first of all, a *totality* of elements that are its *parts*—a *totum* and not a *compositum,* a *whole* and not an *aggregate.* System is not the result of a sum of previously given elements but is rather the *form* of a whole that first posits its elements as parts and determines a priori the structure, the relations, and the topological position of those parts in the totality as well as relatively to each other. In the system the parts are always homogeneous to the whole to which they belong. (b) System is, second, the *teleological* organization of a totality. The idea that unifies the manifold of the parts is the concept of an *end* to which all the parts relate and in the idea of which they stand in relation to one another. (c) Since the whole determines its parts and, in so doing, first determines itself as a system, "system" becomes the principle of a reflexive *self-determination.* (d) An immediate corollary of this assumption is that the system provides the necessity of its own inner division *(Einteilung)* that appears as the *self-division* of the totality.[3] I have already mentioned that the parts of the whole are not *given* before the totality to which they belong because they first arise as the result of the internal "limitation" *(Beschränkung)* or "particularization" *(Besonderung)* of its extension. Through "limitation" the system reaches its immanent internal division. This division must contain the *complete determination* of the whole. Consequently, *all the possible* parts of the systematic totality must be parts in which the whole is *actually* divided; and this means that the whole cannot be further determined nor can other parts be successively added to it. (e) From this it follows that the development of the system can only be described in terms of an organic growth from within, and never as the external addition of new elements. (f) Given all these formal characteristics, a system can be described as the original, synthetical *unity* of its constitutive elements or parts. The "idea" of the system is thus the principle of the unification of all its possible elements in an actual whole.[4]

From the very beginning, Fichte accepts Kant's thesis that philosophy, in order to be—or become—science, must acquire the form of a system. He shares with many contemporaries the belief that Kant's transcendental philosophy represents the critical "foundation" of the system, or the "propaedeutic" to it, but has not yet given the developed and complete system itself. Fichte's program aims therefore at developing Kant's principles in order to bring philosophy to its final completion in the form of an ultimate system. In this system, philosophy should finally reach its most proper and profound unity. An immediate implication of the well known statement about the inadequacy of Kant's doctrine to its own premises is that Kant's philosophy is not able to overcome the stage of an inconclusive dualism. This dualism presents a twofold character and requires, accordingly, to be overcome on two different levels. I will try to follow through the realization of Fichte's systematic program concentrating on these two different issues. These issues will allow Fichte to go beyond the structure and method of the *Foundations of the Entire Wissenschaftslehre* (1794) and to reach the new perspective of the *Wissenschaftslehre nova methodo* (1798 to 1799). They are, first, the issue of the systematic unity of philosophy and the necessity of overcoming the distinction between the theoretical and the practical parts of philosophy; and, second, the issue of a new definition of the "practical" *(das Praktische)*[5] that should be able to range over different meanings such as the "morality" of Kant's pure practical reason, the "sensible" and pathological texture of inclinations and instincts, and the sphere of right and the realm of intersubjectivity. Only in this enlarged sense is the "practical" able to finally establish its "primacy" over and in the theoretical sphere of philosophy. First in this sense can a "science of the practical" become the true foundation and the accomplished realization of the system of philosophy.

Kant's dualism was expressed, first of all, by the distinction of two radically separate parts of philosophy corresponding to two distinct functions of reason: the theoretical and the practical. Pointing out Kant's failure in tracing those functions back to their—yet to be announced—common root or source,[6] Fichte attempts to restore the unity of reason as the unity of its theoretical and practical functions. The fact that the *Foundations,* against this programmatic intention, was still maintaining the formal organization or division into a theoretical and a practical part, is what Fichte found unsatisfactory with it. The purpose of revising this insufficiency leads Fichte to the necessary formulation of a "new method." As Fichte states in a letter to Reinhold of 1795, with his principle of the self-positing I he was trying to overcome Kant's distinction, and thus to unify in a single presentation speculative reason, practical reason, and judgment, thereby displaying "the unity underlying all three Critiques." To see the unity of reason limited to Reinhold's *Principle of Consciousness* and therefore to the "unity of speculative reason" alone—or even only to its mere "announcement"—appeared to Fichte as an insufficient task.[7] Fichte's intention in presenting the first principle of the *Wissenschaftslehre* was to discover that proposition from which "*all philosophy,* i.e. the entire operation of the human mind, must be developed." Reinhold's principle, on the contrary, appeared to Fichte not as the principle of "*all* philosophy," but only of "*theoretical* philosophy."[8] For the purpose of this more radical unification, however, a systematical unity was needed stronger than the one established by the *Foundations.* The *Wissenschaftslehre* of 1794, according to its author, was giving off "sparks of spirit," but it was not yet "a single flame."[9] Yet that "single flame" was necessary to grasp—or more precisely to "intuit"—the unity of philosophy in the series of its propositions.[10] The problem that Fichte is able to address at this point shows two distinct aspects. He feels the necessity, on the one hand, to bring philosophy to its highest systematical unity; but he is well aware, on the other hand, that this entails a further demand, namely a correspondingly adequate "presentation" *(Darstellung)* of science. It is not enough to show *that* philosophy should be constructed as a unified whole; it is necessary to address the further question of how the system can ever be apprehended from a finite consciousness. It is only in the *Wissenschaftslehre nova methodo* that Fichte attempts, for the very first time, to present "philosophy as a whole"[11]—namely, both as a unity and as a system—and tries to unify in this task the problem of the *Darstellung* and that of the *subjective comprehension* of science.

Kant's split in the foundation of the system was grounded in the necessary distinction between appearance and thing-in-itself. According to Kant's premises, only if theoretical knowledge is recognized as limited to the sphere of appearance does "transcendental freedom"—and with it "practical freedom" and the primacy of practical reason—become possible.[12] The consequence is, however, a conception of human nature that remains necessarily divided between the sphere of its physical existence as phenomenon and the realm of its intelligible causality and free agency as *noumenon*.[13] Kant's very idea of practical philosophy accordingly shows a fundamental dualism that opposes pure practical reason to the sensible and pathological motivation of the will. Fichte's reaction to this Kantian doctrine is a new idea of the primacy of practical reason reached by means of a different meaning attributed to the "practical."[14] Moreover, the distinction between the theoretical and the practical intersects with another distinction that is deeply grounded in Fichte's thought—namely, the relation between "philosophy" and "life."[15] As a result of his assessment of the systematic unity of philosophy, Fichte ascribes to the "practical" part the whole content of philosophy itself. What he needs to demonstrate is not simply "the practical primacy of practical reason, but its primacy within the theoretical sphere as well."[16] This amounts to showing that practical reason is actually able to construct the whole system of philosophy itself, and, at the same time, to present the means for its subjective apprehension. The issue of an active systematical project in which not just philosophy, but the very activity of philosophizing should engage is the new perspective that Fichte opens up in the *Wissenschaftslehre nova methodo*.

In his letter to Kant of 24 June 1797, J. S. Beck was communicating to the old philosopher the outrageous news that in his "new" *Wissenschaftslehre* Fichte was professing *"only one* philosophy without assuming any distinction between *theoretical* and *moral* philosophy." Beck's statement entails two different but related points that I want to address in the following reflections. On the one hand, Beck correctly points out that Fichte's idea of the unity of philosophy is precisely that which characterizes the "new" exposition of the *Wissenschaftslehre;* but on the other hand, since that *reductio ad unum* takes place in the name of "practical" philosophy,

Beck fails to notice that Fichte's "practical" is not exactly the equivalent to Kant's "moral" philosophy. Beck envisages the ground of Fichte's move toward the unity of the science in his strong belief that "*everywhere* [that is, not only in the sphere of moral philosophy] the understanding posits the things through its absolute freedom."[17] Beck's remark can be viewed as a further interpretation, from the Kantian side, of Fichte's presentation of his own philosophy as a radicalization of Kant's "transcendental idealism." Then, whereas Kant clings to the view that the manifold of experience is something given, Fichte maintains that "even this manifold is produced by us through our creative faculty."[18] On the ground of Beck's completely justified conclusion, Fichte here follows through an idea that he could find at the basis of Kant's transcendental philosophy and that he had already developed in the *Foundations*. The fundamental character of all activity of the mind is a *practical* one: knowledge is praxis, and *knowing* is essentially *doing*.[19] In 1794, discussing the distinction between a theoretical and a practical part of the *Wissenschaftslehre*, Fichte was pointing out that the theoretical question "What is the nature of things in themselves?" can only receive its answer in the practical part of the science. And the only possible answer here is that things are constituted "as we *must* make them."[20] The primacy of the "practical" over the theoretical dimension of reason is clearly stated by Fichte in a twofold way: first of all, it is a primacy both as *ratio essendi* and as *ratio cognoscendi* of the constitution of things; second, that "doing" *(Machen)* through which reason relates to its objects is a *normative* one—that is, it entails a fundamental *Sollen*. Since for Fichte reason is "everywhere" productive of its objects, the step to the more straightforward method of the *Wissenschaftslehre nova methodo* is immediately evident. In this "new" exposition, "the realm of the practical is the immediate object, and the theoretical is derived therefrom."[21]

The *Wissenschaftslehre nova methodo* and the Idea of the Systematic Unity of Philosophy

In the *Wissenschaftslehre nova methodo*, Fichte's claim that philosophy should be "system" rests on his very "Idea of philosophy." Against Kant, who wrote "only *Critiques*, i.e. preliminary inquiries concerning philosophy"[22] and its possibility, Fichte's program is to engage in the actual deduction of the idea of philosophy. This deduction is nothing but the enterprise of "actually constructing a system of philosophy."[23] Fichte's conception of that system seems to follow immediately from Kant's. The "system" requires both a metaphysical and a transcendental deduction through which, on the one hand, (a) the precise limits of the whole, (b) its completeness, and (c) the principle of its unity should be attained, while on the other hand the objective validity of all our representations should be granted.[24] Yet, the particular perspective that Fichte assumes both in specifying the content of that system and in constructing his "idea" of philosophy as a whole introduces a radical difference from Kant.

In his earlier *Concerning the Concept of the Wissenschaftslehre* (1794), Fichte was clear in assuming that philosophy should present the *form* of a "system of all the human sciences in general,"[25] or the form of a system of the fundamental *propositions* that were able to ground those sciences. Correspondingly, in the *Foundations*, he was structuring the first part of the *Wissenschaftslehre* as a doctrine of *principles*. Yet, if the aim is to deduce the whole science from a first principle that should represent the original foundation of the whole, the system is nothing but the instrument or the form that allows the *Darstellung* of science. In this perspective, the system does not represent the essential *goal* of the construction, but rather the simple *means* of its exposition. If Fichte claims that the *Wissenschaftslehre* should be the "system" of all human sciences or of all *Wissen*, as such, "system" is here only the "form" of the science, and is not yet able to produce the necessary content of the science itself. Kant's inability to go beyond the foundation or the propaedeutic to the system seems to apply also to Fichte's work of 1794. At the time, Fichte's use of the idea of "system" agrees with Reinhold's interpretation of Kant.[26]

In his programmatic work of 1794, however, Fichte was already aware that the idea of system was more deeply grounded in human reason as being a simple means for the presentation of science than one might suspect. This further assumption led him to reverse the previous judgment by stating that philosophy is nothing but the "adequate exposition of the *original system* present in the human mind."[27] (Thus Fichte's argument runs now as follows: the system is not the means to present philosophy; but, rather, philosophy is the way to express the original system of reason.) In the work of 1794, however, Fichte abandons this last conception of the system in favor of the first, merely formal one. At the time, the idea of a system of human reason was in evident contradiction to the program of a foundation of philosophical science from a first principle.[28] If "system" designates the original structure of rationality as such, then the system of all human *Wissen* is totally independent from the system of science that is actually derived—or is to be derived—from the first principle. What is needed, in this case, is not a *first principle*, but rather the *ultimate aim* of the whole. The teleological and circular structure of a self-grounding foundation takes the place of the deductive and linear procedure of the presentation from a first principle.[29]

The *Wissenschaftslehre nova methodo* develops along the perspective opened by the suggestion presented—and yet abandoned—in *Concerning the Concept of the Wissenschaftslehre*. According to the lectures of 1798 to 1799, "philosophy is not a collection of propositions; . . . it is a certain way of looking at things [*Denkart*], a particular way of thinking that one must generate within oneself."[30] Correspondingly, the system is not just a formal means through which we can unify the propositions of the science; it is rather an internal "vocation of mankind" *(Bestimmung der Menschheit);* it is something that both corresponds to an original "need" of the human mind and that expresses the true "interest of reason"[31] already mentioned by Kant.[32] "System" is now a *telos* proper of the constitution of reason itself: "We are destined for complete and systematic knowledge."[33] Only systematic knowledge yields to science; and only the *Wissenschaftslehre* opens the secure path to science. Its goal is not just to ground a formal structure that is able to reunify the theoretical and the practical parts of philosophy; its aim is to further reconcile theory and praxis in the *life* of man. The unity that this system is going to produce is nothing but the unity of the original *act* of philosophizing. The systematic unity that in the *Foundations* was still guaranteed by a first *principle* is now traced back to the unique *action* that philosophy itself is and that the philosopher has to perform. This action represents the "single point to which everything else is connected"[34] and from which everything else can be derived—being, as such, the true principle of the "system." In this way, Fichte links the idea of an original system of reason to its fundamentally practical activity. "System" is neither just an "idea" of reason—as for Kant—nor an epistemological means for scientific knowledge—as in the works of 1794. "System" is now, at the same time, the name for the original, free activity of the mind and the name for the teleological constitution (and destination) of reason itself.

The consequences of this new perspective are essential in the construction of the system of philosophy proper to the *Wissenschaftslehre nova methodo*. First, as far as the *content* of the system is concerned, Fichte assumes that the philosophical science is neither a system of propositions or principles nor a collection of given objects or determinations of those objects, but is rather the system of the "actions of rationality itself": "philosophy encompasses a system of those actions by means of which objects come into being for us."[35] Second, this characterization of the systematic form of philosophy leads Fichte both to a new insight into the question of how philosophy should *begin,* and to a particular comprehension of the *"new method"* of the *Wissenschaftslehre*. I have already mentioned Fichte's claim that in order to really demonstrate the systematic character of philosophy, removing all possible skeptical objections against its possibility, what is required is the willingness to "actually construct a system."[36] This task, as well known, starts with an "Act" (*Thathandlung*) as opposed to a *fact* (*Tatsache*). Fichte argued against Reinhold in this way from the very beginning of his philosophical career. In order to start philosophizing, we must perform in ourselves that original act. "So too must the reader or the student of philosophy *begin by doing something.*"[37] Therewith Fichte reaches the new beginning of the *Wissenschaftslehre:* "Think the concept 'I' and think yourself as you do this." And further: "Think of any object at all—the wall, for example, or the stove" and observe what you do when you think of this.[38] Thus the *postulate* represented by that "act," together with the actual performance of it, takes the place of the principles of the first part of the *Foundations.* The problem of the *construction* of the system of reason coincides with the question of its *Darstellung,* and ultimately with the attempt to a *subjective appropriation* of it. Fichte needs, however, to specify further the way in which the original act develops in the whole of the science. It is at this point that a new beginning in the form of the "intellectual intuition" is required. Only such an intuition, then, is able to grasp the immediate synthesis of the theoretical and practical in one undivided act.

> The essence of reason consists in my positing myself; but I cannot do this without positing a world in opposition to myself, and indeed a quite specific world: a world in space, within which appearances follow one another sequentially in time. *This all occurs in one single undivided act.* When this first act occurs, all the others occur *simultaneously.*[39]

This is the beginning of science. Philosophy, and especially the *Wissenschaftslehre,* wishes to become acquainted with this single act. In order to do so, philosophy must proceed by "dissembling and dissecting" this first original and unique act. In that way, philosophy proceeds beyond that beginning: "We thereby obtain *a series of interconnected actions* of the I; for we are unable to grasp this single action all at once, since a philosopher is a being who must do this thinking within time."[40]

The "new method" of philosophy develops according to these premises. It is the *genetic* method through which the original activity of human reason is led to the actual realization of its system. This method produces the unity of "philosophy *as a whole.*" In so doing, it overcomes the traditional distinction between theoretical and practical philosophy and allows reason to follow its "*natural*"—namely systematic—path. At the end of the *First Introduction* to his course *nova methodo,* Fichte discusses the main differences between the two presentations of his *Wissenschaftslehre.* (a) The "first presentation" was structured into two parts, a theoretical and a practical one. (b) The objection that Fichte now raises against this division is that it did not follow the "natural order" in which the conditions for the possibility of consciousness present themselves in consciousness. (c) Methodologically, he notices that the first version proceeded from the theoretical to the practical part. The implicit conclusion of Fichte's argument is that the distinction between theoretical and practical (not the sequence theoretical-practical, in the first instance, but their very separation) is not a "natural" distinction. What does "natural" mean in this case? And more specifically: does it refer to the way in which the distinction itself is drawn, or rather to the very existence as well as to the legitimacy of that distinction? According to Fichte, the "present version" of the *Wissenschaftslehre* follows a method that is not only different, but "just the *opposite*" of the one assumed in 1794.

(a) Opposing the former duality of theoretical and practical, the *nova methodo* professes the unity of philosophy itself and presents "philosophy as a whole" in which "theoretical and practical philosophy are *united.*" (b) Correspondingly, the method that accomplishes that unification "follows a much more natural path"—then it responds to the natural tendency of reason toward the unifying movement of the system as well as its natural "need" for it. (c) Interestingly enough, however, Fichte does not claim the necessity of a total elimination of that distinction, but a radically new foundation of it—namely, its systematic deduction.[41] Fichte's argument can be summarized in the following way: according to the natural constitution of human reason, the method of philosophy must be a systematic one; this requires that philosophy be one and a single whole; the distinction between theoretical and practical philosophy cannot therefore be an original or given distinction; it can only be systematically deduced from the totality itself. Theory and praxis are thereby two "parts" of the whole in the strong, systematic sense of the term. The new presentation does not just reverse the former one. It begins indeed with the practical sphere, but it also proceeds by "inserting the practical into the theoretical, in order to explain the latter in terms of the former."[42]

The Meaning of the "Practical" According to Fichte

Kant's distinction between theoretical and practical philosophy results directly from his distinction of two "faculties" proper of the mind.[43] Kant recognizes two different types of knowledge as derived from those *Vermögen*: "theoretical knowledge" as "knowledge of what *is,*" and "practical knowledge" as "the representation of what *ought to be.*"[44] In the *First*

Introduction to the Critique of Judgment, Kant addresses the fundamental question of the division of the *"system* of rational knowledge through concepts."* The main division is the one between the "formal" (logic) and the "material" (real) parts of philosophy. The "real system of science," in its turn, comprehends two parts: *theoretical* philosophy or *Naturphilosophie* and *practical* philosophy or *Moralphilosophie.*[45] The fundamental question becomes, however, to understand what exactly is "practical philosophy"—or what is the precise meaning of "practical" *(praktisch)*?[46] The difficulty arises as there are practical propositions that belong to theoretical philosophy. Then all propositions that regard the possibility of an object through our faculty of choice *(Willkür)* belong to our knowledge of nature. Only those propositions that "give the law to freedom"[47] are claimed by practical philosophy. These—and only these—practical propositions are specifically *moral (sittlich).* They determine an action simply through the necessary representation of its form. The "principle" of "moral-practical" *(moralisch-praktisch)* propositions is the "idea of freedom."[48] On the other hand, the concept that determines the form of causality proper to the first type of practical propositions is a concept of nature. Their principle is accordingly a "technical-practical" *(technisch-praktisch)*[49] one.

   Fichte's idea of practical philosophy has its origin in the project of overcoming these Kantian distinctions and in the attempt to formulate a new concept of "practical" that could embrace the whole content of philosophy. Directly linked to this project is Fichte's attempt to reformulate Kant's notion of transcendental freedom in order, first, to eliminate its dependency upon the form of "causality," and second, to allow in it the whole sphere of sensibility. If the *Foundations* still maintains the distinction of a theoretical and a practical part, it shows already the quest for replacing the theoretical and practical *faculties* with an "ideal" and a "real" *activity* inherent to one and the same subject. This is the standpoint that Fichte is going to assume in the *Wissenschaftslehre nova methodo.* The problem here is to show that the idea of the systematic unity of reason generates not only the *form* of the science but its very *content* as well. Now, since the unity of reason is assessed in the name of its practical primacy, it must be possible to derive from the practical functions or activities of reason the whole content of science—even the theoretical part of it. In his work *Concerning the Concept of the Wissenschaftslehre,* the "science of the practical" is assumed as the necessary foundation and justification of the theoretical part of the *Wissenschaftslehre.* More specifically, the "practical" gives the foundation of all particular sciences that should constitute the system of philosophy. The content of the practical part comprehends all those philosophical disciplines that Kant developed both in the third *Critique* and in his moral writings (a theory of the "pleasant, the beautiful, the sublime, the free obedience of nature to its own laws, God, the so-called common sense or the natural sense of truth," and finally a theory of "natural law and morality"). Among all the specific questions that a "science of the practical" is supposed to address, however, none shows a direct reference to a sphere that could be named "moral" in the Kantian sense *(moralisch-praktisch)*. Fichte stresses, on the contrary, that the principles of his practical philosophy are "not merely formal but material."[50]

This result is unavoidable once Kant's conception of transcendental freedom is abandoned in favor of Fichte's idea of the original activity through which the absolute I determines itself as an I. Moreover, Fichte's concept of freedom implies a radical revision of Kant's idea of "causality through freedom."[51] What is here at stake is the conceptual relation between the notions of "causality" and "freedom"—and more precisely the crucial question: can freedom ever be described in terms of a causal process? The practical part of the *Wissenschaftslehre* deals with an absolute I that is not taken as "representing" but rather as an "I that possesses absolute causality." The not-I should be determined precisely by that absolute causality. But what kind of "causality" is this? It is a causality that contradicts itself as it would cancel the not-I by the same act in which it posits it. It is therefore "a causality that is not a causality." This is the concept of *Streben*,[52] which provides the foundation for the practical part of the *Wissenschaftslehre*. Ultimately, the notion of *striving* represents Fichte's final effort to eliminate Kant's link between freedom and causality, showing its inevitable and necessary contradiction. The content of the practical part of the *Wissenschaftslehre* is, according to the program of 1794, the deduction of the laws according to which the I strives. This *Streben* is conditioned by the efficacy of the not-I upon feeling. Thus, far from being an "epiphany of freedom,"[53] the practical part of the *Wissenschaftslehre* is the sphere in which the necessary limitations of the I are represented. Consequently, Fichte's "practical" science entails that sphere of feelings, passions, and sensible instincts that Kant excluded from the "pure moral" philosophy. If Fichte accepts Kant's assumption that the ultimate vocation of man is indeed a moral one, he sees that the fulfillment of this vocation is possible only through the accordance between the thinking and the appetitive powers of man. In this regard, Fichte does not share Kant's suggestion that between the sensible and the intelligible character of man lies a gap that only the supreme form of the moral command is able to overcome. His problem is, therefore, to explain the transition or the accordance between the two sides of man's "practical" nature.[54]

Despite his project of an overcoming of Kant's conceptual distinctions, Fichte needs, in his turn, to acknowledge that the concept of the "practical" bears two very different meanings. According to an early formulation, "practical philosophy" entails the two distinct elements of a "sensible-practical" *(sinnlich-praktisch)* and a "moral-practical" *(moral-praktisch).*[55] Only after a deduction—or a genetic exposition—of the sensible functions of the mind (*Streben,* desire, feeling, sensation) does a moral philosophy become possible that bears no contradiction with the results of theoretical philosophy. This view describes Fichte's systematic purpose since 1793. In the *Foundations,* Fichte uses the "sensible-practical" element in order to create the transition from the theoretical to the practical part. The practical part of the *Foundations* is an exposition of the structures of the mind. Its task is to demonstrate how from a metaphysical premise, that is, the absolute I, a transition to life—to the I's life—can be gained. Therefore, the relation between theoretical and practical intersects with the necessary transition from the absolute I to the finite I. The first stage of this development is represented by the unconscious functions of the mind. Far from being an alternative to reason, those functions are, on the one side, its very realization, and, on the other, its conditions. The hindering-function that sensibility presents in relation to reason's absolute character becomes a constitutive moment of the structure of the finite I. Since the practical part of the *Foundations* is an exposition of the structures of the mind, it is easy to understand why it could not entail a "theory of morals, a theory of right, a theology."[56] The theory of the "sensible-practical" as what first constitutes the practical part of the science gives a description of all that which lies between thinking and willing. It is, in Fichte's words, a "pragmatical history of human spirit."[57] This means, however, that a doctrine of morals and a theory of rights must find another foundation in the system of philosophy.

As becomes evident in the later discussion between Fichte and Jacobi,[58] the crucial problem of the *Foundations* was the way in which the transition from the absolute to the finite I was attained. If this transition were not sufficiently grounded the menace of "practical *Egoismus*"—a modification of "Spinozismus" in its subjective appearance—seemed to make a *theory of intersubjectivity,* and consequently a scientific deduction of natural rights, impossible. This is the problem on which Fichte is working in 1795. In his letter to Jacobi of 30 August 1795 Fichte declares:

> My *absolute* I is obviously not the *individual* though this is how . . . irate philosophers have interpreted me, in order that they may falsely attribute to me the disgraceful *theory of practical egoism.* Instead, *the individual must be deduced from the absolute I,* and the *Wissenschaftslehre* will *immediately* proceed to such a deduction in conjunction to its treatment of natural rights.

In the *Foundations,* the transition between the absolute and the individual I was possible only in a mediate way—namely, only through the deduction of the sensible faculties of the mind that led to the "practical part of the science." In contrast, the immediate character of the transition sketched out in this letter is due to the intervention of the new concept of intersubjectivity. Whereas the absolute I acts according to its absolute freedom, the finite I is described by the causality of the *Streben.* It is precisely this causality that first defines it as a physical being in the realm of other physical beings. The causality of the finite I becomes now a reciprocal "interaction." From now on, as a consequence of this shift from the concept of *Streben* to that of *intersubjectivity,* the genesis of the finite, empirical I takes place in the "*Sittenlehre.*" Fichte rejects Kant's definition of transcendental—and consequently of practical—freedom as a particular form of causality, modifying those Kantian concepts in a twofold way: on the one hand, absolute freedom is not causality anymore, but is rather self-determination as the free *Tathandlung* of the absolute I; on the other hand, the idea of causality is transformed, first, in the self-contradictory causality of the *Streben* proper of the finite I, and second, in the *Wechselwirkung* in which the finite I finds itself in the structure of intersubjectivity.

As we have seen, in the *Wissenschaftslehre nova methodo* Fichte not only abandons the division of philosophy into a theoretical and a practical part, but also eliminates the doctrine of the "sensible-practical"—namely, the doctrine of the faculties of the mind that he previously used in constructing the transition between the theoretical and the practical part. The turning point is now represented by the concept of *intersubjectivity.* Fichte's suggestion is that the condition for the positing of the I is the "summons" *(Aufforderung)* to free activity of another rational being.[59] Once again, according to Fichte, the concept of the "summons" is "not supposed to exercise any causality,"[60] for if it did, the I would be determined in a purely mechanical way, and this would contradict its freedom. Given this new position, the former deduction of the functions of the mind is no longer required in order to attain the finite subject—and precisely its sensibility and life. The different moments that constituted the "practical" are not eliminated, however. Yet, they are placed in different contexts, following a new organization of philosophy as a whole. The "practical part" of science is now understood as "ethics."[61]

The consequences of this reorganization for the system of philosophy are reflected in the Appendix to the last paragraph of the *Wissenschaftslehre nova methodo,* entitled: *Deduction of the Division of the Wissenschaftslehre.* Here Fichte faces, once again, the problem of the transition from the theoretical to the practical part of philosophy within a "complete" system of science.[62] (1) Following Kant, Fichte states that the object of theoretical philosophy is nature, and that this part of the science explains "how the world is and must be, how the world is given to us."[63] (2) Practical philosophy starts instead with the "summons" or the "ethical command" that brings every particular individual to a free acting in the world. The practical part of the *Wissenschaftslehre* is now *allgemeine Sittenlehre* or *Ethik*. "Ethics explains how the world ought to be constructed by rational beings."[64] Whereas the result of theoretical philosophy is "pure empirical experience," ethics leads to an "ideal" outcome. Fichte has now a twofold solution to the problem of the relation between theoretical and practical philosophy. He needs a double mediation between the "real" viewpoint in which the finite human being is located and the "ideal" viewpoint proper to the philosopher. Therefore he constructs a double transition with the help of two "middle ground" disciplines. (3) The first transition is granted by the "*theory of right or natural law*," which is "theoretical and practical philosophy at the same time."[65] Closely related to the theory of right is philosophy of religion. Together, these disciplines constitute a third part of philosophy—the "real" mediation between theoretical and practical—"the philosophy of the postulates."[66] This third part develops its theoretical-practical disciplines considering the human being from the "real" viewpoint.[67] (4) The second transition is made possible by another middle term—"*aesthetics*" which represents "the middle-ground between theoretical and practical philosophy" from the "ideal" viewpoint. To aesthetics, the world—which is a theoretical concept—appears as it "ought to be made"—namely, in a practical perspective. "From the aesthetic point of view, the world appears to be given to us just as if we had produced it and to be just the sort of world we would have produced."[68]

The *Deduction of the Division of the Wissenschaftslehre* provides a conclusive demonstration of what Fichte meant by the "new method" of organizing the complete system of philosophy. The more natural path of mediating between its two fundamental components was announced as the procedure of "*inserting* the practical into the theoretical."[69] Now it is clear how this "insertion" develops into a dialectical mediation between the theoretical and the practical activity, the real and the ideal standpoint.

Notes

1. *Kritik der reinen Vernunft* (hereafter abbreviated as *KrV*) B 765–66: "Die Methode [kann] immer *systematisch* sein. Denn unsere Vernunft (subjektiv) *ist selbst ein System*" (my emphasis).

2. *KrV* B 860.

3. Kant, *Prolegomena zu einer jeden künftigen Metaphysik, die als Wissenschaft wird auftreten können,* section 39 A 118; this is a crucial passage for the post-Kantian reflection on the idea of system.

4. For a further discussion of the formal structure of the "system," see T. Rockmore, *Hegel's Circular Epistemology* (Bloomington: Indiana University Press, 1986), especially chapter II, and A. Nuzzo, *Logica e sistema: Sull'idea hegeliana di filosofia* (Genova: Pantograf, 1992). Very useful, with particular relation to Kant, is A. J. Dietrich, *Kants Begriff des Ganzen in seiner Raum-Zeitlehre und das Verhältnis zu Leibniz* (Halle: Max Niemeyer, 1916).

5. See the important contribution of C. Cesa, "Sul concetto di 'pratico' in Fichte" in C. Cesa, *J. G. Fichte e l'idealismo trascendentale* (Bologna: Il Mulino, 1992), pp. 101–19.

6. *KrV* B 29: *Sinnlichkeit* and *Verstand* are presented here as the "zwei Stämme der menschlichen Erkenntnis . . . *die vielleicht aus einer gemeinschaftlichen, aber uns unbekannten Wurzel entspringen*" (my emphasis). Kant's later *Critique of Judgment* entails precisely the search for that "common" even if "to us unknown" source. The quoted proposition of the first *Critique* was very influential in the development of post-Kantian idealism.

7. Fichte's letter to Reinhold of 2 July 1795.

8. Ibid.

9. Fichte's letter to Reinhold of 21 March 1797.

10. See the quoted letter to Reinhold of 2 July 1795.

11. *Wissenschaftslehre Nova Methodo, Kollegschrift K. Ch. Fr. Krause 1798/99* (hereafter abbreviated as *WLnm*), ed. E. Fuchs (Hamburg: Meiner, 1982). An English translation has been published as *Foundations of Transcendental Philosophy (Wissenschaftslehre Nova Methodo)* (hereafter abbreviated as *FTP*), trans. and ed. D. Breazeale (Ithaca: Cornell University Press, 1992). *WLnm*, p. 10 (*FTP*, p. 85).

12. *KrV* B 562: "Es ist überaus merkwürdig, daß auf diese transzendentale Idee der Freiheit sich der praktische Begriff derselben gründe"; and "Die Aufhebung der transzendentalen Freiheit [würde] zugleich alle praktische Freiheit vertilgen."

13. See on this topic H. Heimsoeth, "Zum kosmologischen Ursprung der Kantischen Freiheitsantinomie," in *Kant Studien* 57 (1966): 206–29; and his "Freiheit und Charakter nach den Kant-Reflexionen, Nr. 5611 bis 5620," *Tradition und Kritik,* Festschrift für R. Zocher, ed. W. Arnold and H. Zeltner (Stuttgart, 1967), pp. 123–44. On the implications of this doctrine, see A. Nuzzo, "Metamorphosen der Freiheit in der Jenenser Kant-Rezeption (1785–1794)," *Evolution des Geistes: Jena um 1800,* ed. Fr. Strack (Stuttgart: Klett-Cotta, 1994), pp. 484–518.

14. It is historically interesting to observe how in Thomasius' and Crusius' "voluntarism" (or, in Kant's words, in their theory of the primacy of practical over theoretical reason) we can find a first example of the tendency, later followed by Fichte and Hegel against Kant, to integrate in a unity the moral law and the multiplicity of sensible tendencies, desires, and passions. According to Crusius, instincts and passions should not be repressed or fought, but should rather be *versittlicht*—"made ethical." This historical connection is particularly important if

we think of the influence that Crusius had not only on Kant, but also on the young Fichte. (For the influence of Crusius on Kant see J. Schmucker, *Die Ursprünge der Ethik Kants in seinen vorkritischen Schriften und Reflexionen* (Meisenheim a. Glan, 1961); G. Tonelli, Preface to Ch. A. Crusius, *Anweisung, vernünftig zu leben* (1744), repr. Nachdr. (Hildesheim: Olms, 1969), VII–CII. For the relation of Crusius to Fichte see the letter of C. G. Fiedler to Fichte of 28 January 1785 (*Gesamtausgabe der Bayerischen Akademie der Wissenschaften,* hereafter abbreviated as *GA,* ed. R. Lauth, H. Gliwitzky, and E. Fuchs [Stuttgart: Frommann-Holzboog, 1962 ff.], III, 1, 9 s.), where Fiedler draws Fichte's attention to Crusius' antideterminism; J. G. Fichte, *Aphorismen über Religion und Deismus* (1790), GA II, 1; C. Cesa, "Fichte critico di Reimarus? A proposito di uno scritto giovanile di J. G. Fichte," in *Studi di storia medievale e moderna per Ernesto Sestan* (Firenze: Olschki, 1980), pp. 865–83.

15. See D. Breazeale, "The 'Standpoint of Life' and the 'Standpoint of Philosophy' in the Context of the Jena Wissenschaftslehre (1794–1801)," in *Transzendentalphilosophie als System: Die Auseinandersetzung zwischen 1794 und 1806,* Schriften zur Tranzendentalphilosophie, ed. A. Mues (Hamburg: Meiner, 1989), pp. 81–104.

16. D. Breazeale, Editor's Introduction in *FTP,* p. 12; see also D. Breazeale, "The Theory of Practice and the Practice of Theory: Fichte and the 'Primacy of Practical Reason,' " in *International Philosophical Quarterly* 36, no. 1 (1996): 47–64; M. Casula, "Der Mythos des Primats der praktischen Vernunft," in *Akten des 4. internationalen Kant- Kongresses* Mainz 1974 (Berlin: DeGruyter, 1974), Teil 2.1., pp. 362–71.

17. Beck's letter to Kant of 24 June 1797 (my emphasis).

18. Fichte's letter to Jacobi of 30 August 1795.

19. In relation to Kant see M. Baum, "Erkennen und Machen in der Kritik der reinen Vernunft," in *Probleme der Kritik der reinen Vernunft,* Kant-Tagung in Marburg 1981, ed. B. Tuschling, (Berlin: DeGruyter, 1984), pp. 161–77.

20. *Grundlage der gesammten Wissenschaftslehre* [Foundations of the Entire *Wissenschaftslehre*], hereafter abbreviated as *GWL,* section 6; *GA* vol. I, 2, p. 416: "Wie sind denn nun die Dinge an sich beschaffen? . . . So wie wir sie machen *sollen*" (my emphasis).

21. *WLnm,* p. 72 (*FTP,* p. 182).

22. *WLnm,* p. 5 (*FTP,* p. 80).

23. *WLnm,* p. 4 (*FTP,* p. 79).

24. *WLnm,* pp. 5–6 (*FTP,* p. 80).

25. *Über den Begriff der Wissenschaftslehre* [Concerning the Concept of the Wissenschaftslehre] (1794), section 3: "System des menschlichen Wissenschaften überhaupt" and "System des Wissens überhaupt."

26. K. L. Reinhold, *Über das Fundamet des philosophischen Wissens; nebst einigen Erläuterungen über die Theorie des Vorstellungsvermögens* (Jena: Mauke, 1791), pp. 110, 116.

27. *GA* I, 2, p. 87: philosophy is the "getroffene Darstellung des *ursprünglichen System im Menschen*" (my emphasis).

28. See W. Schrader, "Philosophie als System—Reinhold und Fichte," in *Erneuerung der Transzendentalphilosophie im Anschluß an Kant und Fichte,* R. Lauth

zum 60, Geburtstag, ed. K. Hammacher and A. Mues (Stuttgart: Frommann-Holzboog, 1979), pp. 331–44.

29. This point is further developed in A. Nuzzo, *Logica e sistema*, cap. 2, I; more generally on circularity and foundation see T. Rockmore, "Fichtean Epistemology and the Idea of Philosophy," in *Der transzendentale Gedanke: Die gegenwärtige Darstellung der Philosophie Fichtes*, ed. K. Hammacher (Hamburg: Meiner, 1981), pp. 485–97; and Rockmore's "Antifoundationalism, Circularity, and the Spirit of Fichte," in *Fichte: Historical Contexts, Contemporary Controversies*, ed. D. Breazeale and T. Rockmore (Atlantic Highlands, New Jersey: Humanities Press, 1994), pp. 96–113; D. Breazeale, "Circles and Grounds in the Jena Wissenschaftslehre," *Historical Contexts*, pp. 43–71; A. Perrinjaquet, "Some Remarks Concerning the Circularity of Philosophy and the Evidence of its First Principle in the Jena Wissenschaftslehre," *Historical Contexts*, pp. 71–96.

30. *WLnm*, p. 11 (*FTP*, p. 87).

31. *WLnm*, p. 17 (*FTP*, p. 95).

32. See, for example, *KrV* B 832.

33. *WLnm*, p. 7 (*FTP*, p. 81).

34. *WLnm*, p. 9 (*FTP*, p. 84).

35. *WLnm*, p. 22 (*FTP*, p. 102).

36. *WLnm*, p. 27 (*FTP*, p. 108).

37. *WLnm*, p. 28 (*FTP*, p. 110).

38. *WLnm*, pp. 28–29 (*FTP*, pp. 110–11); my emphasis.

39. *WLnm*, p. 9 (*FTP*, pp. 83–84); my emphasis.

40. Ibid.; my emphasis.

41. The two parts are "unified" as parts of the system. Fichte never denies the existence of these parts. His point regards the methodological use and status of them.

42. *WLnm*, p. 10 (*FTP*, p. 86).

43. In this theory Kant follows an analogous use made by Ch. Wolff. Wolff referred to "theoretical" and "practical" in two fundamental meanings: namely, according to the *faculties* to which they belong and according to their *content*. In the first sense, to the *anima* belong two *facultates*—respectively, the cognitive and the appetitive power. The science that studies the "use of the cognitive power in the knowledge of truth" is *logic,* while the science of the "use of the appetitive power in choosing the good and avoiding the evil" is *practical philosophy*. See Ch. Wolff, *Discursus praeliminaris de philosophia in genere* (Franofurti and Lipsiae: Libraria Rengerina, 1728), sections 60–62: logic deals with the "usus facultatis cognoscitivae in cognoscenda veritate," and practical philosophy is the part "quae usum facultatis appetitivae in eligendo bono ed fugiendo malo inculcat." See C. Cesa, "Sul concetto di 'pratico,' " p. 104.

44. *KrV* B 661.

45. See, for example, *Kritik der Urteilskraft*, Introduction XII.

46. Kant, *Erste Einleitung in die Kritik der Urteilskraft*, in Kant, *Gesammelte Schriften*, Hrsg. v. der (König) Preußischen (später Deutschen) Akademie der Wissenschaften (Berlin: DeGruyter, 1910 f.), Bd. 20, pp. 195–96.

47. Ibid., p. 197.

48. Ibid., p. 199.
49. *Kritik der Urteilskraft,* Introduction XIII.
50. *GA* I, 2, p. 151 (for an English translation see *EPW,* p. 135).
51. See A. Nuzzo, "Metamorphosen der Freiheit."
52. *GA* I, 2, p. 151.
53. For this and the following analysis, see C. Cesa, "Sul concetto di 'pratico,' " p. 106.
54. See H. Heimsoeth, "Freiheit und Charakter nach den Kant-Reflexionen Nr. 5611 bis 5620," in *Tradition und Kritik.*
55. *GA* II, 3, 247; for this distinction, see C. Cesa, "Sul concetto di 'pratico' " and D. Breazeale, "Theory of Practice," pp. 53–54.
56. *GA* II, 3, p. 185.
57. *GA* I , 2, p. 365.
58. See Fr. H. Jacobi, "Brief an Fichte," of 1799, in *Werke,* ed. F. Roth, F. Köppen, 6 vols. (Leipzig, 1812–25), reprinted by Nachdruck Darmstadt, Wissenschaftliche Buchgesellschaft, 1968, vol. III. See A. Nuzzo, *Nachklänge der Fichte-Rezeption Jacobis in der Schrift über die Göttlichen Dingen und ihre Offenbarung* (München: Fichte-Tagung, 1996).
59. *WLnm,* p. 177 (*FTP,* p. 350–51).
60. *WLnm,* p. 180 (*FTP,* p. 355–56); and furthermore, "what is posited in opposition [to my determinable self] . . . is something free, and, *to this extent, the concept of causality does not apply here*" (my emphasis).
61. See C. Cesa, "Sul concetto di 'pratico,' " p. 118, and D. Breazeale, "Theory of Practice," p. 53.
62. *WLnm,* p. 240 (*FTP,* p. 468).
63. *WLnm,* pp. 240–41 (*FTP,* p. 468).
64. *WLnm,* p. 241 (*FTP,* p. 469).
65. *WLnm,* p. 242 (*FTP,* p. 470).
66. *WLnm,* p. 243 (*FTP,* p. 471).
67. *WLnm,* p. 243 (*FTP,* p. 472).
68. *WLnm,* p. 244 (*FTP,* p. 473); see also *Das System der Sittenlehre,* section 31.
69. *WLnm,* p. 10 (*FTP,* p. 86).

Fichte's Philosophical Fictions

Daniel Breazeale

A Thought Experiment

The following remarks are a contribution to an ongoing inquiry into the distinctive *tasks, character,* and *method* of transcendental philosophy—more specifically, of the early *Wissenschaftslehre.*[1] As I have long since discovered, this turns out to be an extraordinarily difficult and complex topic. Among the many issues that must be addressed are the character of "construction" in transcendental philosophy; the methodological role of "intellectual" (and/or "inner") intuition in (various versions of) the Jena *Wissenschaftslehre;* the character and strategy of a transcendental "deduction"; the unavoidably circular character of all transcendental/foundationalist arguments; the respective roles of reflection, imagination, and intuition in philosophical proofs; the evidential force, within philosophical theory, of purely "practical" considerations; and the epistemic/ontological status of philosophical "first principles" and "explanations."

My working hypothesis is that there are deep and unresolved ambiguities or tensions in Fichte's conception of his own philosophical project and method, tensions evident both in the many "critical" or metaphilosophical treatises and comments he published during the period from 1793 to 1801 and in his actual practice as a transcendental philosopher during this period. Though the tensions in question can and should be described in various ways, for my present purpose it will suffice to point to the underlying tension between a broadly "constructivist" and a broadly "phenomenological" conception of the method of the *Wissenschaftslehre.*

Some interpreters have associated the former with the earlier Jena *Wissenschaftslehre* and the latter with the later version,[2] and it is certainly true that the "phenomenological" method is most evident in the *Wissenschaftslehre nova methodo*. On the other hand, there is also evidence of a similarly "phenomenological" approach in Part III of the *Grundlage der gesammten Wissenschaftslehre;* moreover, some of Fichte's most explicit endorsements of a "constructivist" methodology occur in the *Sonneklärer Bericht* and the unpublished "Neue Bearbeitung der Wissenschaftslehre," both of which were written in 1800, that is, *after* the lectures on "The Foundations of Transcendental Philosophy (*Wissenschaftslehre*) *nova methodo*." In my view, therefore, the methodological tension between "constructivism" and "phenomenology" permeates virtually all of Fichte's systematic and metaphilosophical writings of the Jena period and is not a reflection of an abrupt change of methodology that allegedly occurred in 1795 or 1796.

   This question concerning the basic "methodology" of the Jena *Wissenschaftslehre* is directly related to what are, for me anyway, the central questions about Fichte's entire project: namely, *what is going on here?* What, if anything, is really "explained" by transcendental philosophy? What *kind* of explanation is supposed to be provided by the *Wissenschaftslehre?* Assuming that what is to "explained" by Fichte's philosophy is, as he repeatedly claimed, nothing more nor less than "experience" itself, and especially our experience of "representations accompanied by a feeling of necessity," then two obvious, alternative answers to the second question suggest themselves: either the *Wissenschaftslehre* is a species of "philosophical anthropology," which "explains" experience by grounding it in certain psychological or anthropological (and perhaps social and historical) structures and facts about human beings, or else it is yet another in the long series of dogmatic metaphysical systems and, as such, "explains" experience (that is, the world of "appearances") by grounding it in and deriving it from a "higher," metaphysical reality ("the absolute I" or "pure willing"). Though each of these ways of interpreting the *Wissenschaftslehre* has had its advocates over the years, and though there is some internal evidence within Fichte's own writings to support each, the evidence *against* either of these interpretations (at least of the Jena *Wissenschaftslehre*, if not of the later versions of the same) is, I think, overwhelming.

   Virtually all contemporary scholars would agree that Fichte was constantly attempting to "perform a delicate balancing act," trying to "steer a middle course" between the two "equally unacceptable extremes" of "supernaturalist metaphysics" and "naturalist psychology," and that he understood his own "transcendental science" as just such a third path.[3] The question is, of course, *is there such a third way?* And if so, then *what is it?* Is it really distinct from the two others? Is it *viable* as such; that is, does it actually "explain experience"? And if, so what kind of "explanation" does it provide, and what is supposed to confirm the correctness of this explanation?

The remarks that follow do not answer these fundamental questions. Instead, my purpose is to invite the reader to join with me in performing a *hermeneutic experiment:* What happens if one takes with the utmost seriousness certain published and unpublished remarks by Fichte concerning the purely "fictional" status of his own first principles? What are the implications of interpreting the Jena *Wissenschaftslehre* as a foray into neither metaphysics nor psychology, but into the realm of philosophical *fiction?*

The word "fiction" occurs no more than a dozen or so times in Fichte's surviving writings, and more than half of these occurrences occur in unpublished manuscripts, lecture notes, and letters. The first occurrence is in the 1793 to 1794 manuscript "Eigne Meditationen über ElementarPhilosophie/Practische Philosophie," an important document that might almost be described as the "Ur-Wissenschaftslehre." The first (and one of the only two) public appearance of the term "fiction" is in Part One of the *Grundlage des Naturrechts.* The term is also employed on several occasions in Fichte's lectures "Logic and Metaphysics," as well as in his correspondence with I. A. Fessler and Schelling. Finally, it appears again in the *Sonnenklärer Bericht an das größerte Publikum über das eigentliche Wesen der neuesten Philosophie.*[4]

In order to launch our experiment, let us now turn to an extended consideration of each of these passages and to a discussion of the contemporary context within which they are to be understood. Only at the end of this examination will we attempt to ascertain the tentative results of this experiment.

Examining the Evidence

Salomon Maimon on the Use of Fictions in Philosophy

There can be no doubt that Fichte's remarks concerning the "fictional" character of philosophical explanations were originally inspired by his close reading of Maimon's *Philosophisches Wörterbuch* (1791) and *Streifereien im Gebiet der Philosophie* (1793), and, very probably, of his *Versuch einer neuen Logik* (1794).[5] All three of these works contain extended discussions of what Maimon calls *Fikzionen oder Erdichtungen* ("fictions or fabrications") and explicit proposals concerning the use of the same within philosophy. Though this is not the appropriate occasion for a full analysis of Maimon's "fictionalism,"[6] some familiarity with Maimon's position is nevertheless essential for understanding Fichte's later use of the term "fiction."

Many of Maimon's remarks on this topic, especially in his *Philosophisches Wörterbuch,* are simply corollaries of his skepticism concerning the legitimate application of the Kantian categories of the understanding to the sensory manifold and hence reflect his doubts about the *reality* of what Kant called "judgments of experience."[7] "Fiction" or "fabrication," "in the broadest sense," is thus defined as "an operation of the power of imagination, by means of which a nonobjective, necessary unity is produced in the manifold of an object."[8] Ironically enough, as many commentators have observed, Maimon's use of the term "fiction" in this broad, skeptical sense seems to have been directly inspired by Kant's own account, in the dialectic of the first *Kritik,* of "transcendental illusion" and of the "regulative" or "problematic" employment of the "ideas of reason" as "heuristic fictions."[9]

Fichte, of course, did not share Maimon's skepticism regarding the applicability of the categories, a skepticism he attributed to Maimon's own vestigial dogmatism concerning the relationship between "objective knowledge" and "things in themselves,"[10] and he thus saw no need to embrace Maimon's "fictionalist" interpretation of judgments of experience. What *did* attract Fichte's attention was a more limited feature of Maimon's discussion of this topic: namely, his account of what he called "the *method* of fictions" and his proposals concerning the *employment* of this method within philosophy.

Almost all of Maimon's discussions of the "method of fictions" begin with a discussion of *mathematics,* a discipline notable for its employment of such "fictional" concepts as those of a "limit" or of the square root of an irrational number. Such concepts, according to Maimon,[11] reflect the importance within mathematics of "the method of fictions," a method he describes as follows:

> An object which is alterable in a certain respect in accordance with a rule can be considered as if it had reached the highest level of the alteration in question, i.e., as if it were at the same time the same and not the same object. This is a *fiction,* and one that can be used in order to determine something about a real object.[12]

By applying this "method of fictions," the mathematician successfully employs self-contradictory concepts or principles (for example, that a continuous magnitude is composed of an infinite number of discreet parts) in order to discover new truths—truths that might never have been discovered otherwise, though, once discovered, they become susceptible of independent confirmation. Objectively speaking, such contradictory concepts are neither true nor false, since they explicitly extend beyond the domain within which truth and falsity are determinable. The employment of such a method of fictions in mathematics is justified solely by its *utility* and *fruitfulness,* that is, by the fact that it produces correct and independently verifiable results.

The utility of this method of fictions is not, however, limited to the mathematics; for it is also employed, at least on occasion, within physics and the other natural sciences. As illustrations of this point, Maimon appeals to the Cartesian explanation of gravity in terms of "vortices,"[13] as well as to such basic concepts of Newtonian mechanics as "absolute (empty) space," "absolute time," and the (vector) analysis of a single movement as the "combined product" of several others.[14] The "method of interpolation," which is employed by astronomers when, on the basis of several observations of a celestial body, they posit its position during the period when it was not (and perhaps could not be) observed is also cited as an application of the method of fictions within science.[15]

From such examples, however, it by no means follows that this "method of fictions" has any appropriate application within *philosophy.* Maimon, however, argued it does have such an application, and he invariably cited Leibniz's system as the clearest illustration of the use of fictions within philosophy. He thereby disposes of the celebrated question concerning how we are to understand the claim that infinitely divisible physical bodies are somehow "composed" of indivisible and extensionless monads by treating the entire theory of monads as no more than "a *mere fiction.* "[16] So too, Leibniz's controversial claims concerning the necessary occurrence of "obscure representations" during periods of sleep and so on are interpreted as legitimate applications of the "method of interpolation,"[17] and the "unconscious perceptions" posited thereby are explained by Maimon as "mere fictions."[18]

Nor does Maimon limit himself to the claim that Leibniz's philosophy is *compatible* with a "fictionalist" interpretation of its fundamental principles; he further maintains that this is precisely how Leibniz himself (in his esoteric, as opposed to his exoteric, teaching)[19] understood the basic concepts and principles of his own metaphysics: not as a descriptions of ultimate reality, but simply as so many "useful fictions."[20] When one grasps the "spirit" of Leibniz's philosophy in this manner,[21] then it no longer appears to fall prey to Kant's well-grounded objections against dogmatic metaphysics. Indeed, Maimon believed that one of the great virtues of viewing philosophical systems as applications of the "method of fictions" is that this facilitates a *reconciliation* not just between Leibniz and Kant, but between dogmatism and skepticism more generally.[22]

Despite this external advantage, the use of fictions within philosophy obviously requires some additional, internal justification in terms of the task and character of philosophy itself. Occasionally, Maimon seems to defend the use of fictions within philosophy in precisely the same terms he defends it elsewhere: viz., as essentially *heuristic* devices, "which are of great importance within *mathematics* as *means of discovery,* and which *could serve the same purpose within philosophy.* "[23] In fact, however, he recognized that there is a crucial difference between the method of fictions as employed in philosophy and the employment of the same in mathematics and physics: for whereas the latter may lead to the discovery of new objective *truths* (even though the fictional concepts that permit such discoveries are themselves neither true nor false), the use of fictions in philosophy does not produce or lead to the discovery of any new truths whatsoever—whether about things in themselves or about our own subjective constitution. This is why, according to Maimon, fictions such as those encountered in Leibniz's system,

> have within *philosophy* by no means the same utility that they have in *mathematics.* Within *mathematics,* differential calculus serves for *discovering new truths;* the *monadology,* in contrast, can, at most, be presupposed merely as an *explanatory basis* for *natural appearances,* without itself being used for this purpose [that is, for discovering new truths about nature].[24]

Precisely *what* are "explanatory fictions" supposed to contribute to philosophy, and what sort of "discovery" are they supposed to facilitate? The short answer to this question is "systematic unity": more precisely, systematic unity among our various knowledge claims *(Erkenntnisse)* and among the various sciences with which we possess an extra-philosophical acquaintance. This, moreover, is precisely what Maimon, in *Ueber die Progressen der Philosophie* and elsewhere, praises most highly about Leibniz's philosophy: that it manages to impose or to discover a greater *systematic unity* within our knowledge than is otherwise available to us. The task of philosophy is not to produce new cognitions or to establish new, material truths about objects; instead, its task is to unify the cognitions we already possess. This is why philosophy, by its very nature, is and must be *systematic:* its fundamental task is precisely "to obtain the most complete systematic form of any science whatsoever," that is, to subsume "the greatest possible multiplicity under the highest unity of principles in the most complete systematic order."[25] Maimon's defense of the use of fictions within philosophy is thus intimately connected with his conception of philosophy itself as a purely *formal* science, a strictly second-order science of science itself, the proper object of which is nothing other than "the form of science as such."[26]

If this is what philosophy is, then philosophical "knowledge" is not "real cognition" *(Reelerkentniss)* at all, and neither the first principles nor the conclusions (the system itself) of philosophy need make any claim to the kind of objective truth claimed (legitimately) by mathematics and (illegitimately) by empirical science. Hence the special character and importance of "fictions" in philosophy. What better word to characterize "principles" whose sole purpose is to find—or rather, to invent (for there is no real difference between "invention" and "discovery" within philosophy)—systematic links between the various things we already "know," thereby unifying our (putative) cognitions? Philosophical principles thus turn out, in Maimon's estimation, to be not unlike regulative ideas in the Kantian sense of the term. The only criterion for evaluating a proposed philosophical principle is what Maimon calls its "suitability" *(Tauglichkeit)* for producing the kind of systematic unity discussed above. A successful or warranted principle is simply one that produces a certain amount of unity. No degree of success, however, can transform such a "methodological fiction" into a metaphysical "truth." Nor is there any reason to think that there is one and only one "best" principle of philosophy or set of such principles.

One last feature of Maimon's account of philosophical principles remains to be mentioned: namely, his claim that such "fictions" are useful "for extending or grounding our knowledge."[27] We have already considered the various senses in which the method of fictions might be employed to "extend" our knowledge in mathematics and physics and have also noted a certain ambiguity present in Maimon's account of the same: namely, to the extent that the "truths" discovered by the use of this method can—and must?—be independently confirmed, one must be skeptical of any claims concerning the "grounding" provided by mere fictions in such cases. In the case of *philosophical* "knowledge," however, it might be appropriate to speak of a proposed (fictional) first principle as the *indispensable ground* of any such "knowledge," inasmuch as it is *only* by means of such a fiction that philosophy can make any progress at all toward its purely formal, systematic goal. In order to "expand" our knowledge in the only way in which it can be expanded by mere philosophy—that is, in order to extend the sphere of the systematic unity of the same—one has no recourse but to begin with a freely posited and frankly *fictional* "first principle," which one then tries to connect systematically with the various realms of actual knowledge and experience. Only then can one assess the success or "suitability" of the fiction in question for the purpose at hand. The greater the unity, the better the principle. To be sure, purely fictional principles can never really *explain* any natural appearances (in the only way that can be done: viz., by connecting them to others according to the immanent laws of nature itself),[28] even though one continues to proceed under the *fiction* that the latter are somehow "determined" by the former. From this it follows that the "method of fictions" is not simply *useful* within philosophy, but is absolutely *indispensable* to the same. No fictions, no systematic unity of knowledge; no systematic unity, no philosophy.

Maimon's general theory of fictions, and especially his proposal concerning the employment of the "method of fictions" within philosophy—and more specifically still, his "fictionalist" interpretation of Leibniz's system—did not go unnoticed by his contemporaries. On the contrary, his "fictionalist" conception of philosophy was singled out for explicit criticism by two anonymous reviewers of "Ueber den Progressen der Philosophie" and *Streifereien im Gebiete der Philosophie* in early 1794[29] and was systematically attacked a few months later by K. L. Reinhard in an essay "Ueber den Gebrauch der Fikzionen in der Philosophie."[30]

Undeterred by these public attacks, Maimon responded with a last-minute footnote to his *Versuch einer neuen Logik* (published in August 1794),[31] in which he not only reiterated his earlier conception of the purely "formal" character of philosophy and his previous proposal concerning the "use of fictions within philosophy," but also provided his most sustained and clearest account of that proposal itself:

> I reiterate my claim that *philosophy* is nothing else but the science
> of the mere *form of science* as such. It is concerned neither with the
> (metaphysical) truth of the *principles* with which it begins nor with
> the *results* at which it finally arrives (considered for their own sake).
> Instead, it is concerned simply with the suitability of these *principles,*
> considered simply as *principles,* for producing the highest *possible degree of
> rational unity.* Fictions are precisely such principles: they are not true in
> themselves, but are assumed for the sake of scientific form. . . . A genuine
> philosopher cannot be expected to determine whether our cognition
> possesses a *real ground* outside of our *faculty of cognition,* a ground that can
> be derived from this faculty (as the *Critical* philosophers maintain); and
> if he nevertheless adopts such a position, he does so only because this will
> produce the highest possible degree of *systematic unity* in our cognition,
> by means of which everything therein will be explicable in the most exact
> interconnection.[32]

In a second note to this same text, Maimon affirms that the only requirement that can be placed upon proposed "fictional principles" in philosophy is that they be free of internal contradiction,[33] and he thereby demonstrates a new and clearer awareness of one of the key differences between philosophical and mathematical fictions. According to his earlier discussion, certain mathematical concepts do indeed harbor contradictions,[34] but philosophical fictions, he now contends, must not violate the principle of contradiction (presumably since the results of their employment are not susceptible to the same kinds of independent and "intuitive" confirmation as are the results of employing fictions in mathematics).[35] Beyond that, however, anything goes, and the proof is in the pudding.

In passing, Maimon also repeats his claim that philosophical fictions are useful not simply for "producing unity" among our cognitions, but also for *grounding* the latter. Presumably, what this means is *not* that any real knowledge claims are actually grounded in philosophical fictions, but rather that the second order "knowledge claim" involved in the imposition—and subsequent recognition—of a certain unity among our first-order cognitions is itself grounded in the principles through which such unity is secured. These higher-order, philosophical claims, however, must always remain purely "hypothetical": what one "knows" in such a case is that, *if* we posit certain fictional principles, *then* we can impose upon our experience a certain degree of systematic unity.

Fichte's Reception of Maimon's Proposal Concerning the Employment within Philosophy of the "Method of Fictions"

Although the influence of Maimon upon Fichte has not gone unnoticed, almost no attention has been paid to the topic that here concerns us: Fichte's decade-long flirtation with Maimon's conception of the "fictional" character of philosophical first principles and the use, within philosophy, of "the method of fictions."[36] The earliest surviving evidence of Fichte's awareness of Maimon's ideas on this topic is to be found in the unpublished "Eigne Meditationen über ElementarPhilosophie/Practische Philosophie," which contains several direct and indirect references to the fictional character of philosophical principles, in one of which Maimon is even mentioned by name. After introducing the all-important explanatory concept of the "original striving of the I," Fichte adds that "we are not conscious of this *original* striving, because it is not represented. Just as an original I has to be assumed as subject, so too must an *original* striving be assumed. This can surely be assumed for the purposes of explanation, as a 'fiction," as Maimon says."[37] At the risk of belaboring the obvious, let me emphasize that what Fichte here endorses is the very significant claim that the "absolute I" with which the *Grundlage der gesamten Wissenschaftslehre* will later begin, and which reappears in one guise or another in all of Fichte's presentations of his philosophy during the Jena period—and beyond—is, qua philosophical first principle, neither more nor less that "a fiction."

Fichte's first *published* use of the term "fiction" came two years later, in Part One of the *Grundlage des Naturrechts,* where, immediately after the "deduction" of the concept of *Urrecht* or "primordial right," he candidly confesses that such a concept is nothing more than "a mere *fiction,* albeit one that necessarily must be fabricated for the sake of science."[38] This use of the term "fiction" is, of course, entirely consistent with Maimon's "method of fictions," as well as with the remarks in the "Eigne Meditationen."

Though the term "fiction" does not recur in Fichte's published writings for another five years, the underlying idea is—or so I shall maintain—implicit in many of his published and unpublished writings of the later Jena period and is—at least arguably—central for understanding his conception of the *Wissenschaftslehre* as a "pragmatic" or "genetic" history of the human mind. This becomes clearer when we consider his use of this term in his unpublished "introductory" lectures on "Logic and Metaphysics" (the so-called "Platner Lectures"), as well as in his correspondence. Consider, for example, a passage from the Platner lectures for the winter semester of 1796 to 1797, in which Fichte discusses Platner's conception of philosophy as a "pragmatic"—that is, "genetic"—"history of the human mind." (Platner's use of this expression, by the way, is unquestionably the source of Fichte's own use of it.)[39] A philosophical— which is to say, pragmatic or "genetic"—"history," remarks Fichte, can never be more than a sheer *fiction.* Though he then proceeds to criticize Platner's own proposed "pragmatic history" of the mind, he does so, not because it is a *fiction,* but because it is a *dogmatic* fiction, one which, Fichte suggests, should be replaced by a properly *Critical* history of the mind.[40] Note, however, that even the best and most "Critical" "history" of the mind—a history of the sort, for example, provided in the *Grundlage der gesamten Wissenschaftslehre* and *Wissenschaftslehre nova methodo*—will still be no more than a "fiction."

In a later lecture from the same semester, Fichte returns to this point and calls his students' attention to the unavoidably "fictional" character of any transcendental explanation of the possibility of experience. In order to "explain" and to account for the possibility of actual, conscious representations, the transcendental philosopher must isolate the various constituent moments or elements of the same. Accordingly, he explains those "representations" of which we are actually conscious by positing the necessary occurrence of various "unconscious representations," such as, for example, mere "intuitions" or "concepts." An "obscure representation" of this sort, however, is merely "inferred" by the philosopher for the purposes of his explanatory project. "But," as Fichte reminds his students, this means that "the concept of intuition itself is, to this extent, a fiction: something we have to presuppose in order to explain representation."[41] Neither "intuitions" nor "concepts" actually *exist* as such. The only reality they possess is their reality within the context of the philosopher's (fictional) account of the origin of actual representations.

This last point is reiterated in the Platner lectures from the summer of 1797, where Fichte defends his characterization of the "fictional" character of the basic concepts of transcendental philosophy with the remark that nothing does more harm within philosophy than the habit of viewing strictly philosophical concepts and distinctions as if they were actual things, when in fact such concepts are nothing more than "fictions," posited by the philosopher simply "in order to make something [else] comprehensible."[42]

Before concluding our brief survey of Fichte's uses of the term "fiction," let us pause to consider something he did *not* say on the subject: namely, his failure to reject Friedrich Karl Forberg's forceful public advocacy of a version of Maimon's thesis regarding the "fictional" character of philosophical explanations. In 1797, Forberg, at the time still a colleague of Fichte's at Jena, personally presented Fichte, who was by then the co-editor of the *Philosophisches Journal,* with a manuscript entitled "Briefe über die neueste Philosophie," in which, without mentioning either of them by name, he subjected the philosophy of Fichte and Schelling[43] to a series of sharp and specific criticisms. Fichte not only promised to publish Forberg's attack (and to pay a generous honorarium for the privilege of doing so), but to respond to it publicly and in detail.[44] In fact, he began replying to Forberg's attack even before publishing it, namely, in the first installment of the Second Introduction to his *Versuch einer neuen Darstellung der Wissenschaftslehre,* and he continued his detailed reply to each of Forberg's criticisms in the concluding installment of the Second Introduction, which appeared in the same issue of the *Philosophisches Journal* as the first installment of Forberg's "Letters."

Among Forberg's many objections to the *Wissenschaftslehre* is the following: Though it may be legitimate to employ the absolute I as the "first principle" of philosophy, it is not legitimate to pretend (as, Forberg implies, both Fichte and Schelling are guilty of pretending) that one has actually *discovered*—rather than merely invented or posited—this explanatory principle. In a passage that unmistakably echoes Maimon's position,[45] Forberg insists that one must not forget that no first principle was really discovered, and one must remember that one simply proceeded *as if* one had been discovered, and that one proceeded in this way simply in order to bring the system into being. In such a case, the absolute I would be nothing more than a *systematic fiction,* and it would have been necessary only while one was constructing that system.

Philosophical principles are thus not really "cognitions" at all, for they do not refer to anything real—in this world or any other. Instead, insists Forberg, they are simply *methodological devices* "for ordering the cognitions we have discovered" for the sole purpose of obtaining "the highest systematic unity of knowledge." The only sort of "proof" of which such principles are capable is the "confirmation" conferred by successfully employing them for this purpose.[46]

What is noteworthy about this passage is not so much Forberg's (unacknowledged) appropriation of Maimon's fictionalist interpretation of philosophy (for almost all of Forberg's ideas were adopted from someone else), but rather, Fichte's striking *silence* about this point in his detailed reply to Forberg's "Letters." Indeed, this appears to be the *only* suggestion or objection made by Forberg to which Fichte does *not* explicitly reply in his "Second Introduction." What, if anything, should one conclude from this remarkable silence?

In the absence of any other evidence, it would surely be unwise to conclude anything at all from Fichte's failure to address Forberg's thesis concerning the purely systematic function and fictional character of all philosophical first principles. As we have seen, however, there *is* additional evidence available, evidence which at least suggests that the reason Fichte did not explicitly and unequivocally reject Forberg's philosophical "fictionalism" is because he himself—to some qualified degree—*may have shared* this view with Forberg and Maimon.

Reinhold Lauth, who remains, so far as I have been able to discover, the only scholar to address this issue, argues that Fichte does reject Forberg's fictionalism in section 11 of the Second Introduction, albeit indirectly, in his characterization of the "absolute I" as an "intellectual intuition."[47] Lauth's contention, however, is unconvincing: first of all, because the relationship between the I as an intellectual intuition and the I as an idea of reason really does seem to be an issue quite distinct from Forberg's (and Maimon's) proposal concerning the use of fictions in philosophy; second, because the epistemic status of an "intellectual intuition" within the context of the later Jena *Wissenschaftslehre* is by no means clear (indeed, one might argue that the concept of an "intellectual intuition" is, on many occasions, best understood as a "fiction" in its own right); and finally, because of the independent, direct evidence that Fichte himself shared, at least to a certain extent and on some occasions, the view of Forberg and Maimon on this issue.

Nor is all the evidence in question to be found in works written *prior* to the "Second Introduction." On the contrary, two of Fichte's most interesting and relevant remarks on the subject of fictions in philosophy were not written until 1800. The first occurs in a letter to Schelling, dated 15 November 1800, in which Fichte, after gently criticizing Schelling's treatment of the "opposition" between transcendental philosophy and *Naturphilosophie*, adds that

> any science which, through a fine abstraction, makes nature itself into
> its object must, to be sure (and precisely because it abstracts from the
> intellect), posit nature as something *absolute* and must, by means of a
> *fiction,* allow nature *to construct itself*—just as transcendental philosophy,
> by means of a *similar fiction,* allows consciousness to construct itself.[48]

(Schelling, by the way, despite his differences with Fichte concerning the central point at issue between them, enthusiastically accepted the "fictionalist" interpretation of philosophical first principles proposed in Fichte's letter.)[49]

The second passage is from the *Sonnenklarer Bericht,* a work written during the fall of 1800, that is to say, at the same time as the above letter to Schelling, which was also—significantly, I believe—a period when Fichte was deeply involved in his last (and, as it turned out) unsuccessful effort to revise for publication his lectures on "The Foundation of Transcendental Philosophy *(Wissenschaftslehre) nova methodo.*"[50] In fact, I would argue that the *Sonnenklarer Bericht,* even though written in Berlin and not published until 1801, should be considered the final work of Fichte's "Jena period." In any case, in the fifth section of this text one finds the following passage:

> Actual consciousness exists. It is a whole and is completely finished,
> just as we ourselves are finished and self-conscious—which is the final
> step, with which the *Wissenschaftslehre* concludes. . . . According to
> our philosophy, this absolutely present reality can, in turn, be *treated
> and judged* within actual life *just as if* it had arisen through an original
> construction, such as is accomplished in the *Wissenschaftslehre.* . . . It is a
> crude misunderstanding to take this "just as if" for a categorical "that," to
> take this *fiction* [emphasis added] to be a narration of a true event that
> is supposed to have occurred at some time or another. Do you actually
> suppose that our construction of fundamental consciousness in the

> *Wissenschaftslehre* is intended as a history of the Acts [*Tathandlungen*]
> of consciousness before there was any consciousness, the life-history
> of a man prior to his birth? How could this be our intention, since we
> ourselves explain that consciousness exists simultaneously with all of its
> determinations?[51]

Here, at the very end of the period of the Jena *Wissenschaftslehre*,
we find Fichte returning to a point first broached at the very beginning of that same period: philosophical explanations, though they can
be described as "pragmatic histories" or "genetic deductions" of ordinary consciousness, must never be confused with "natural histories" of
the same. Whereas the "genetic deductions" that constitute an actual
history of an event or institution begin and end with "facts of experience,"[52] the "deduction" of experience constructed by the transcendental
philosopher only concludes with something actual (the *explanadum*). It
always begins, however, with something freely invented—with a mere
"hypothesis," freely fabricated or "postulated" purely for the purposes
of philosophical explanation. Likewise, the "systematic order" grounded
upon such a principle, or, if you prefer, the "pragmatic history" derived
from such a starting point—in short, the entire *Wissenschaftslehre*—is a
philosophical *fiction*.

Some Tentative Conclusions

To what extent is Fichte's Jena *Wissenschaftslehre* actually compatible with
the proposed, "fictionalist" interpretation?
    On first glance, such an interpretation seems promising. It makes
sense, for example, of Fichte's frequently reiterated claim that the first
principle of his system (the "absolute I") *never occurs* within consciousness, except of course as freely "posited" by the philosopher for the
purposes of constructing his system,[53] a claim that fits rather neatly with
an admission of the purely *invented* or "fictional" character of all philosophical first principles. The latter admission would also appear to be
consistent with Fichte's occasional assertions concerning the merely "hypothetical" character of all purely philosophical concepts and principles,
as well as with his insistence that one enter his system (in this case, the
Wissenschaftslehre nova methodo) not by grasping a self-evident truth, but
by means of a "postulate."[54] (Admittedly, there are also other dimensions
to Fichte's use of the term "postulate," for a full understanding of which
one would have to consider the use of this term by both geometers and

other philosophers, most notably, J. S. Beck,[55] and these latter uses of the term "postulate" are much less easy to reconcile with a "fictionalist" interpretation of the same.)

In support of a fictionalist interpretation of the Jena *Wissenschaftslehre*, one might also appeal to Fichte's frank concession, in the Second Introduction to the *Wissenschaftslehre nova methodo* (and elsewhere) that his system "only postulates a series of original actions. It does not affirm that such a series actually exists." "The series of necessary actions of reason disclosed by *Critical* idealism possesses no reality except this: if one is to succeed in explaining what one is trying to explain, then one necessarily has to assume that these actions do occur."[56] "Reality for thinking," however, is precisely the kind of reality characteristic of fictions. When a fictional first principle (or explanatory postulate) is further "analyzed" by means of successive applications of the rational laws of identity and "reflective opposition" (Fichte's usual name for Maimon's "principle of determinability"), this produces precisely the sort of "necessity of thinking" that is, according to Fichte, the only kind of "reality" encountered within the *Wissenschaftslehre*.[57]

So, too, might one cite Fichte's occasional references to the "experimental" character of his entire enterprise as evidence in support of the proposed "fictionalist" interpretation of the *Wissenschaftslehre*[58]— though, here again, one must not forget that there are also other ways to interpret the idea of a "philosophical experiment." In any case, it is not impossible that this is indeed the way in which Fichte understood his own "experiment" in transcendental explanation and that this is what he had in mind when he insisted that every philosophical explanation begins with principles that are assumed purely "problematically."[59] Viewed in this manner, the *Wissenschaftslehre* presents us not with a "description" of anything actual, but with an *artfully constructed model* for understanding both consciousness and the world.

It might also be possible to demonstrate a close connection between the sort of "fictionalism" suggested here and Fichte's claims concerning the place of "construction" within philosophy. One of the more obvious facts about "fictions," after all, is that we have to *construct* them.[60] This topic, however, will not be explored on this occasion.

Finally, the Jena *Wissenschaftslehre* also fits the fictionalist paradigm of philosophy in the sense that the ultimate test or criterion for evaluating the system as a whole and thereby "establishing" the validity of the first principle of the same (the principle of subjectivity or the I as subject-object) does indeed seem to be the *suitability (Tauglichkeit)* of the latter for "unifying" or "systematizing" something. But the unity established by the *Wissenschaftslehre* is not simply—or even primarily—the unity among the "real sciences" and among our various cognitions, which is what both Maimon and Forberg described as the aim of philosophy. To be sure, Fichte sometimes emphasizes this goal and feature of his system (especially in *Ueber den Begriff der Wissenschaftslehre*), but the more significant unity established by the Jena *Wissenschaftslehre* is that of freedom and necessity, infinitude and finitude, *Tathandlung* and *Anstoß*. The systematic structure of the Jena *Wissenschaftslehre* can, in this sense, be considered Fichte's solution to Kant's third Antinomy of Pure Reason. As I have argued at length elsewhere, the basic "strategy" of Fichte's reconciliation of freedom and finitude is to show that each is presupposed by and derivable from the other. To be sure, this kind of "circular" systematic unity may not be precisely what Maimon and Forberg had in mind, but it *is* a kind of "unity."

I suggest, therefore, that it is at least possible to understand the entire *Wissenschaftslehre* as a kind of "just so" story (in Kipling's sense of the term), a story devised to show the following. *If* one begins by "positing" (or constructing) the fictional concept of the "absolute I" and then analyzes rigorously what is contained in this *construct*, constructing along the way any additional concepts that may be required for the purposes of this analysis (as in the first half of the *Wissenschaftslehre nova methodo*); and if one then "reassembles" the concepts previously isolated in this manner, thereby constructing within philosophical reflection a new, synthetic whole (for example, the "five-fold synthesis" of Part Two of the *Wissenschaftslehre nova methodo*): then one will eventually realize that the various concepts encountered along this path—and, more specifically, the fundamental notions of, on the one hand, "sheer freedom" and, on the other, "sheer limitation" (whether understood as sensible or as intelligible limitation, that is, as *Anstoß* or "feeling" or as *Aufforderung*) can be understood only as *Wechselbegriffe* or "reciprocal concepts." The apparent "opposition" between freedom and necessity, which is certainly one of the most conspicuous, and from the standpoint of transcendental philosophy, significant features of ordinary experience, will thereby be overcome *in theory*, if not in practice. Anyone willing to accept this "fictional explanation" will now see *rationally necessary, systematic/dialectical unity* where one previously saw only brute opposition and conflict.[61] What such a result will establish, of course, is not the *truth* of those principles that make such a systematic reconciliation of freedom and necessity possible, but merely, as Fichte put it 1793, the "necessary assumability" of the former[62]—necessary, that is, *if* one wants to "make sense" of one's own, profoundly divided being in the world.

Finally, a fictional interpretation of the Jena *Wissenschaftslehre* would also appear readily compatible with Fichte's constantly reiterated distinction between "philosophy" and "life," between the purely theoretical or "ideal" standpoint of philosophical speculation and the practical or "real" standpoint of every day. And it is also, of course, compatible with those passages in which he explicitly rejects the "anthropological" and the "psychological" interpretations of his system.[63]

What is the evidence *against* such an interpretation of the Jena *Wissenschaftslehre,* and precisely what would we have to *sacrifice* in order to accept such an interpretation?

"The Wissenschaftslehre is a *thoroughly real philosophy,* in which, by its very nature, there is no room whatsoever for any free imaginative fabrication [*Erdichtung*]."[64] This passage, from "A Comparison Between Prof. Schmid's System and the *Wissenschaftslehre,*" is echoed over and over in Fichte's Jena writings and signals what surely appears to be the most flagrant shortcoming of any "fictionalist" interpretation of his system, inasmuch as it is difficult to imagine how any system based upon merely fictional principles could ever claim to be anything more than a purely "formal" philosophy or system of thinking. The *Wissenschaftslehre,* however, as Fichte seems never to tire of insisting, begins with the exhibition within immediate intuition ("intellectual intuition") of something *real* and then proceeds to describe a *real* series of (necessary) acts of the mind somehow generated from or produced by this original intuition.

It thus seems that, if one accepts a purely "fictional" interpretation of the hypothetical/deductive method of the Jena *Wissenschaftslehre,* then one will have to reject Fichte's frequently reiterated claims concerning the "descriptive" character of his own method and the reliance of the same upon the evidence of direct, "inner intuition."[65] There thus seems to be a strong tension, if not an outright contradiction, between the "fictional" and the "phenomenological" interpretations of the Jena *Wissenschaftslehre.* From this, however, one should not simply conclude that our experiment has failed, for the "phenomenological" interpretation of the Fichte's methodology raises formidable problems that are not raised by the fictionalist interpretation.

In a recent essay stressing the phenomenological character of the *Wissenschaftslehre nova methodo,* Günter Zöller asserts, entirely in the spirit of Fichte's own comments, that the pure I is nothing but a "structure designed to address the methodological requirement of thinking the ground of experience in a manner consistent with the systematic commitment to freedom," that is, that it is simply "the pure form of consciousness." The various "acts" of this I that are derived in the course of the *Wissenschaftslehre* are therefore "not to be thought of as empirical-psychological events but as the structural conditions that govern all men-tal life."[66] This is surely accurate; but it is also, as we have seen, quite compatible with a "fictionalist" interpretation of the structures and acts in question. The difficulties begin when one tries to reconcile this claim with Zöller's (and, to be sure, Fichte's) broadly "phenomenological" characterization of Fichte's method of examining the aforementioned "structural conditions." The task, writes Zöller, is, after constructing the pure concept of the I, "to choose an experimental setting that lets the I engage in its original activity."[67] The philosopher thereby, as Fichte puts it, sets the original I "in motion"[68] and simply sits back to *observe it in its self-construction* and to *describe* what he thus "observes" in "inner intuition."[69] It is, however, quite difficult to understand what it might possibly mean for a "set of structural conditions" or a "pure form of consciousness" to *act* in any manner whatsoever—let alone how one might hope to "observe" (or to "intellectually intuit") these same mysterious "acts." Another, equally obvious, difficulty raised by this competing, "phenomenological" account of the "intuitive" method of the Jena *Wissenschaftslehre* concerns the universality of claims based upon "inner intuition." To be sure, Fichte always insists that the method of transcendental philosophy must not be confused with that of psychology or any other purely empirical or "observational" science; yet it is not always easy to see how such confusion can be avoided if one endorses a "phenomenological" reading of Fichte's method as a philosopher.[70]

If we reject the "phenomenological" account of the methodology of the *Wissenschaftslehre* then we shall also have to call into question Fichte's well-known claim that "idealism" is superior to "dogmatism" because its "object"—unlike the object of dogmatism—"actually appears within consciousness."[71] If idealism is indeed superior to dogmatism, its superiority cannot (on our fictionalist construal) lie in the "reality" of its starting point, which is no less "fictional" in character than the dogmatist's.

Finally, there appears to be no good reason to believe that the formal unity demanded by "the method of fictions" is achievable in only *one* way, or that there is one and only one fictional first principle that might be "suitable" for establishing the kind of systematic unity aimed at within philosophy. Thus it would seem that if we accept a "fictionalist" interpretation of the *Wissenschaftslehre* we shall also have to reject Fichte's claim that there can only be *one* true philosophy, which would seem to align him with the sort of systematic pluralism apparently advocated by Schelling in his "Philosophical Letters on Dogmatism and Criticism."[72] Fichte, however, strenuously rejected such pluralism and unequivocally affirmed that there can be only *one possible philosophy*.[73]

Suppose, then, that we simple drop any attempt to defend Fichte on the above points: how much will we really have *lost* thereby? To be sure, we will have to call into question certain of his familiar metaphilosophical claims, concerning, for example, the presence, within idealism, but not of dogmatism, of a "dual series of acts"—those of the observing philosopher and those of the "observed I."[74] We will also have to challenge his characterization of the *Wissenschaftslehre* as a system of "real thinking" and call into question his own "phenomenological" claim to have based his system upon the alleged evidence of "inner intuition."

Perhaps the *Wissenschaftslehre* simply cannot survive such radical metatheoretical surgery, but then again, maybe it would survive the operation in a new, improved, leaner, and more intelligible form. In any case, it is worth noting that the modifications in question are less concerned with the actual *content* of the *Wissenschaftslehre* than with Fichte's (and our own) "critical" or metaphilosophical interpretation of the epistemic and ontological status of philosophical principles and explanations.

Nevertheless, the claims that have to be rejected in order to subscribe fully to a fictionalist interpretation of Fichte's early philosophy are by no means unimportant ones. Indeed, they seem intimately rooted in the very "spirit" of the Jena *Wissenschaftslehre*. For this reason, I believe, we must conclude that our attempt to interpret the latter purely in the context of Fichte's scattered remarks on the subject of fiction and on the basis of Maimon's and Forberg's much more explicit and extensive discussion of the use of fictions in philosophy has been, if not a complete failure, then less than a success. However attracted Fichte may have been to certain aspects of this thoroughgoing philosophical fictionalism, and however keenly he may have appreciated the merely "hypothetical" or "fictional" character of some of his own key concepts and principles, he would never have willingly endorsed a characterization of the *Wissenschaftslehre* as nothing more than a "fiction."

The question, then, is how Fichte's qualified recognition of the fictional character of any philosophical explanation can be *reconciled* with his unqualified insistence upon the *reality* of his own philosophy. How can Fichte possibly defend his claim that the *Wissenschaftslehre* is a system of "real thinking" without falling prey either to psychologistic naturalism or to metaphysical dogmatism? A possible solution to this problem may be found by considering a central element of Fichte's thinking that we have entirely ignored hitherto:[75] namely, his unambiguous insistence upon the ultimately *practical*—indeed moral—foundation of all *belief*, including one's belief in the *reality* of oneself, others, and the world. Such purely *practical belief* is not based upon theoretical considerations. It is not grounded upon nor is it presupposed by any philosophical system (so long as the latter is understand as a merely fictional, explanatory hypothesis). Instead, all belief, and hence all claims concerning the "reality" or "actuality" of anything whatsoever—including the "reality" of philosophy itself—must be based entirely upon a practical ascription of *real efficacy* to one's own freedom, an ascription in turn rooted in a categorical sense of one's duty to limit one's own freedom out of respect for the moral law and in recognition of the freedom of others.[76]

Only by being identified or associated with practical freedom, the "actual" object of "real"—but wholly extra-philosophical—"intellectual intuition,"[77] does the otherwise purely "fictional" concept of the pure I acquire any sort of reality or actuality. To be sure, it still remains a "postulate" of sorts, but no longer in the purely theoretical sense of an explanatory hypothesis for fiction, but rather in the quite different sense associated with the "postulates of practical reason" in the Kantian sense. The reality of this postulated freedom can, in turn, be transferred to the entire system constructed upon this otherwise purely fictional principle, and thus it might be possible, after all, to reconcile Fichte's flirtation with a "fictionalist" conception of philosophy with his insistence that genuine philosophy must be a system of "real thinking" and with his insistence that there can be one and only one *true system of philosophy*. This strategy is best illustrated in the work which, along with the *Sonneklärer Bericht*, may be said to bring to a close the period of the Jena *Wissenschaftslehre: The Vocation of Man*, in which the correctly deduced "fictions" of Book Two obtain all of their reality from the "practical faith" of Book Three.

Notes

1. See Breazeale, "Inference, Intuition, and Imagination: On the Methodology and Methods of the First Jena *Wissenschaftslehre*." In *New Studies of Fichte's Foundation of the Entire Doctrine of Scientific Knowledge*, ed. Breazale and Rockmore, pp. 19–36 (Amhert, N.Y.: Humanity Books, 2001). Also see "Fichte's *nova methodo phenomenologica*: On the Methodological Role of 'Intellectual Intuition' in the later Jena *Wissenschaftslehre*," *Revue Internationale de Philosophie* (Brussels) no. 206 (1998): 587–616.

2. See, e.g., Günter Zöller, "An Eye for an Eye: Fichte's Transcendental Experiment," in *Figuring the Self: Subject, Absolute, and Others in Classical German Philosophy*, ed. Dave E. Klemm and Günter Zöller (Albany: State University of New York Press, 1997), pp. 73–95.

3. Zöller, p. 87.

4. It also appears, for one final time, in an unpublished manuscript from 1813 ("Aus einem Träume), which has yet to appear in any edition of Fichte's *Nachlass*, but will be included in one of the final volumes of the *Gesamtausgabe* of Fichte's *Werke*, ed. Reinhard Lauth and Hans Gliwitzkey (Stuttgart-Bad Cannstatt:

Fromman Holzoog, 1964 ff.), hereafter cited, by series, volume, and page number, as *GA*.

5. Salomon Maimon, *Philosophisches Wörterbuch, oder Beleuchtung der wichtigen Gegenstände der Philosophie, in alphabetischer Ordnung* (Berlin: Friedrich Unger, 1791); *Streiferein im Gebiete der Philosophie* (Berlin: Wilhelm Vieweg, 1793); *Versuch einer neuen Logik oder Theorie des Denkens, nebst angehängten Briefen des Philaletes an Aenesidemus*, ed. Bernhard Carl Engel (Berlin:Reuther and Reichard, 1912).

6. See Breazeale, "Reinhold über Maimon über den Gebrauch der Fikzionen in der Philosophie," in *Proceedings of the Bad Homburg Reinhold-Tagung*, ed. Wolfgang Schrader (Amsterdam and Atlanta: Rodopi, forthcoming).

7. According to Maimon, the realm of legitimate synthetic judgments a priori (and therefore the realm of "real thinking") is strictly limited to mathematics, for it is in mathematics alone that we are able to *construct* the objects of our universal judgments. In the case of judgments of experience, however, no such a priori construction is possible, and therefore the various "unities" produced within experience by our (subjectively necessary) application of the categories of the understanding to the manifold of sensations do not possess "objective truth." According to Maimon, Kant's answer to the *quid justi* concerning the employment of the categories illegitimately begs the *quid facti* concerning the *reality* of genuinely "objective" empirical judgment. However unavoidable (and hence "subjectively necessary") or useful it may be for finite intellects like ourselves to view our own empirical judgments *as if* they were (objectively) necessary and universal, such judgments are in fact instances of subjectively produced "Erdichtungen," "Täuschungen," "Figuren," or "Fictionen." For further development of this point, see, in addition to the entry on "Fiction (Erdichtung)" in Maimon's *Philosophisches Wörterbuch*, his essays "Über Täuschung," *Deutsche Merkur* (März, 1791): pp. 274–87; "Ueber Selbstäuschung," *Gnothi sauton, oder Magazin zur Erfahrungsseelenkunde* 8, St. 3 (1791): pp. 38–50; and "Einleitung zur neuen Revision des Magazins zur Erfahrungsseelenkunde," *Gnothi sauton, oder Magazin zur Erfahrungsseelenkunde* 3, St. 1 (1792): pp. 1–28.

See, too, "Ueber die philosophischen und rhetorischen Figuren," VI Abhandlungen of *Streifereien*, esp. pp. 270–71. Very much in the spirit of the entry on "fictions" in his *Wörterbuch*, Maimon here defines "Figuren überhaupt" als "Vorstellungsarten die in Beziehung auf ein Objekt nicht *ursprünglich*, sondern nach Gestetzen der *Einbildungskraft* in uns *hervorgebracht* werden" and then proceeds to interpret representations of absolute space and time and of things in themselves as instances of such "Täuschungen." "Diese Arten von Täuschungen," notes Maimon, "sind nicht nur dem gemeinen Manne eigen, sondern selbst Philosophen vom ersten Range mit demselben gemein. Die feinsten, darunter ein Leibniz, ein Kant, kennen die Natur dieser Täuschungen recht gut, und unterhalten sie bloß als nützliche *Fikzionen*, deren man sich in andern Wissenschaften mit glücklichem Erfolg bedient" (p. 271).

Note, too, the connection between Maimon's general theory of fictions and his account of "Schärmerei": "Die *Schwärmerei* ist ein Trieb der *produktiren Einbildungskraft* (das Dichtungsvermögen), Gegenstände die der Verstand, nach

Erfahrungsgesetßen, für *unbestimmt* erklärt, zu bestimmen" ("Zur höhern Er-harungsseelenkunde, I, Ueber die Schwärmerei," *Magazin zur Erfahrungsseelen-kunde* X, St. 2: p. 45). In a note to this passage Maimon expresses his agreement with Kant's theory of ideas, but he locates their ground in the imagination rather than in the reason.

The intimate connection between Maimon's skepticism and his "fictional-ism" (Skeptizismus und Fiktivismus) is duly noted by A. Zubersky in his *Salomon Maimon und der kritische Idealismus* (Leipzig: Meiner, 1925), p. 25, though Zuber-sky dismisses both "skepticism" and "fictionalism" as inconsistent with what he takes to be the true, positive direction [Richtung] of Maimon's thought.

8. "Fiction (Erdichtung) ist in der allgemeinsten Bedeutung eine Oper-ation der Einbildungskraft, wodurch eine nicht objectiv nothwendige Einheit im Manigfaltigen eines Objects hervorgebracht wird" (*Philosophisches Wörterbuch*, p. 36). All translations in this essay are my own.

9. *Kritik der reinen Vernunft*, A771/B799. Maimon's theory of fictions is not simply a revised version of Kant's theory of the ideas of reason. The difference between Kant and Maimon on this point is clearly expressed by Maimon himself: "Ich unterscheide mich also hierin von dem Herrn Kant, indem er die Categorien für *Verstandesbegriffe* halt, ich hingegen dieselben für *transcendentale Erdichtungen* der Einbildungskraft halte" (*Philosophisches Wörterbuch*, p. 20).

10. See my essay, "Fichte on Skepticism," *Journal of the History of Philosophy* 29 (1981): pp. 427–53.

11. According to Maimon, this simply reflects the fact that "the principles of higher mathematics . . . are mere fictions," *Streifereien*, p. 202.

12. *Streifereien*, p. 17. Maimon's many illustrations of this method of mathe-matical fictions include the so-called "method of tangents" and Wallis's "method of indivisibles" in calculus, Cavalieri's *methodus indivisibilium continuorum* in geom-etry, the concept of the cosine of a right angle, concepts of *maxima* and *minima*, and irrational numbers.

13. *Streifereien*, p. 203.

14. *Streifereien*, pp. 270–71. On this point, see also Maimon's "Anmerkun-gen zu" his translation of Pemberton's *Anfangsgründe der Newtonishcen Philoso-phie* (Berlin: Friedrich Maurer, 1793), pp. 197–201. "[D]ie Vorstellung einer zusammengeseßten Bewegung [ist] eine bloß *Idee* oder *Fikzion,* wozu man sich in der Darstellung immer nährern, die man aber nich völlig erreichen kann" (pp. 200–1).

15. *Streifereien*, p. 30.

16. *Streifereien*, pp. 29–30. See, too, p. 271: "*Monaden* sind bei Leibniz in der Philosophie der Natur keine reele Objekte, sondern bloß das was Differ-entialgrößen in der Mathematik sind, Gränzen der Verhältnisse." According to Maimon's interpretation, therefore, Leibniz does not really maintain that a body consists of monads, but simply suggests, in order to obtain a correct concept of the relation of bodies to one another and in order to determine the magnitude of this relation exactly, that we must dissolve these bodies into their infinitely small parts and then determine the relationship of the whole in terms of the

relationship between these parts. Such an infinite analysis can, to be sure, never really be accomplished. Thus it is no mere an *Idee*, in the Kantian sense, but an *Idee* "welcher wir uns in unserer Untersuchung über die Beschaffenheit der Körper und ihrer Verhältnisse zu einander, beständig nährer können. Leibniz spricht also (seiner exoterischen Lehrart ungeachtet) nicht von *Dingen an sich* als einfachen *Substanzen*, sondern bloß von *Fikzionen*" (*Streifereien*, p. 30).

17. *Streifereien*, pp. 30–31.

18. See, in addition to *Streifereien*, pp. 30–31, "Einleitung zur Realübersicht des Magazine zur Erfahrungsseelenkunde," *MzE* 10, St. 3 (1793): p. 140.

19. *Streiferien*, pp. 17 and 30.

20. *Streifereien*, p. 56. See, too, pp. 18–25.

21. See *Versuch einer neuen Logik* (Berlin: Ernst Felisch, 1794), p. 51: "Aus *Leibnitzens Schriften* wird es mir freilich schwer fallen, meine Erklärungen der Fundamentalartikel seines Systems zu erweisen. Aus dem *Geiste seiner Philosophie* hingegen könnte ich dieses allerdings erweisen, wenn sein *Geist* nicht zu *erhaben* wäre, um sich völlig *einkörpern* zu lassen."

22. Such a reconciliation between, on the one hand, Leibniz and Kant, and, on the other, skepticism and dogmatism, was one of Maimon's explicit goals. See *Streifereien*, pp. 29, 45–46, 56–58, and 188–89.

23. *Streifereien*, p. 56: "die als *Mittel zur Erfindung* in der *Mathematik* von größer Wichtigkeit sind, und in der *Philosophie es seyn können.*"

24. *Streifereien*, p. 31.

25. The aim of philosophy is "die vollkommensten systematischen Form einer Wissenschaft überhaupt [zu] erhalten," i.e., "das gröste mögliche Manigfaltige unter der höchste Einheit der Prinzipien in der vollkommensten systematischen Ordnung [zu subiumieren]" (*Streifereien*, p. 41).

26. *Streifereien*, p. 13.

27. *Streifereien*, p. 272.

28. "Eine Erscheinung *erklären*, heißt nicht bloß die *Bedingungen unter welchen*, sondern die Art, *wie* sie möglich ist, nach allgemeinen Naturgesetzen, angeben." "Einleitung zur Realübersicht des Magazin zur Erfahrungsseelenkunde," *MzE* 10, St. 3 (1793): p. 139.

29. [Gebhard Ulrich Brastberger], Review of Maimon's *Streifereien*, *Neue allgemeinen deutschen Bibliothek* 7, St. 2 (1794): pp. 352–57; [Gottlob Ernst Schulze], Review of Maimon's *Paradoxen*, *Neue allgemeinen deutschen Bibliothek* 8, St. 2 (1794): pp. 351–61. Brastberger's review was published in January 1794. Schulze's in mid-February. (Once again, I gratefully acknowledge the assistance of Erich Fuchs and Achim Engstler in dating these reviews and identifying the authors.) Maimon reprinted both of these hostile reviews, along with his own annotation and remarks, as a preface to his *Versuch einer neuen Logik, oder Theorie des Denkens*. The passages in question, along with Maimon's own defense of his method of fictions, may be found on pp. xxxiv–v and liv of Maimon's *Logik*. Unfortunately, the otherwise exemplary reprint edition of Maimon's *Logik* issued in the series of "Neudrucke seltner philosophischer Werke," sponsored by the Kantgesellschaft, omits these reviews (although it includes most of Maimon's

Anmerkungen to the same: Maimon, *Versuch einer neuen Logik,* ed. Bernard Carl Engel (Berlin: Reuther and Reichard, 1912).

30. K. L. Reinhold, "Ueber den Gebrauch der Fikzionen in der Philosophie," *Neue Teutsche Merkur* 3 (1794): pp. 262–78. This appeared anonymously in May 1794, about the time Fichte was preparing to move to Jena. Reinhold had earlier critized Maimon's remarks on fiction in his review of Maimon's "Berlin, b. Unger, *Philosophisches Wörterbuch, oder Beleuchtung der wichtigsten Gegestände der Philosophie in alphabetischer Ordnung,* 1 Stück 1791. 222 S.8," *Allgemeine Literatur-Zeitung* (Jena: Expedition, 1792), nr. 7 vom 7.1.1792, col. 49–56. Note that Reinhold never mentions Maimon by name in this article, which is plainly directed at Maimon.

31. The publication date of the *Versuch einer neuen Logik* cannot be established with certainty. Maimon did send a copy to Fichte in late August, however. (See Maimon's August 16, 1794 letter to Fichte.)

32. "Ich widerhole abermals meine Behauptung, daß die *Philosophie* nicht anders als die Wisenschaft von der bloßen *Form einer Wissenschaft* ist. Es liegt ihr so wenig an der (metaphysischen) Wahrheit der *Principien,* wovon sie ausgeht, als der *Resultate,* wozu sie endlich gelangt, an sich, sondern bloß an der Tauglichkeit der *Principien* als *Principien* zur Erhaltung der höchsten *möglichsten Vernunfteinheit. Fictionen* sind eben solche *Principien,* die an sich nicht wahr sind, aber dennoch zum Behuf der wissenschaftlichen Form angenommen werden. So wenig dem *Astronomen,* als solchem, daran gelegen seyn kann, zu bestimmen, ob die Sonne um die Erde, oder die Erde um die Sonne sich bewege, und, wenn er ja das letzte annimmt, dies von ihm nicht wegen der *objektiven Wahrheit* dieser *Hypothese* an sich, sondern blos deswegen geschieht, weil nur unter dieser Voraussetzung ein Weltsystem möglich, und die *Astronomie* eine *systematische Wissenschaft* ist; eben so wenig kann dem wahren *Philosophen* daran liegen, ob unsere Erkenntniß einen *Realgrund* außer dem *Erkenntnißvermögen* hat, der sich aus dem Erkenntnisvermögen selbst herleiten läßt, wie die *kritischen Philosophen* behaupten, und wenn er diesen beipflictet, so geschieht es bloß deswegen, weil dadurch die höchste mögliche *systematische Einheit* in unserer Erkenntniß erhalten wird, wodurch alles darin im genauesten Zusammenhange erklärbar ist. Dahingegen die Assertionen der Dogmatiker von den *Dingen an sich* ganz müßig sind, weil sich daraus nichts in unserer Erkenntniß erklären läßt.

"Die Erfindung der *Fiktionen* zur *Erweiterung* und *systematischen Ordnung* der Wissenschaften ist ein Werk der Vernunft. Die Vorstellung dieser Fiktionen als reeler Objekte ist ein Werke der *Einbildungskraft.* Dennoch kann selbst derjenige, der diese Vorstellung für falsch erklärt, dieselbe nicht zwar zum *Behuf der Wissenschaften an sich,* sondern ihres *praktischen Gebrauchs* wegen zugeben, wodurch er die Philosophie mit dem sogenannten *Bon-sens* aussöhnt" (*Versuch einer neuen Logik,* pp. xxxv–xxxvi, note d).

[I reiterate my claim that *philosophy* is nothing else but the science of the mere *form of science* as such. It is concerned neither with the (metaphysical) truth of the *principles* with which it begins nor with the *results* at which it finally arrives (considered for their own sake). Instead, it is concerned simply with the suitability of these *principles,* considered simply as *principles,* for producing the highest *possible degree of rational unity. Fictions* are precisely such principles: they are not true in themselves, but are assumed for the sake of scientific form. An *astronomer* cannot, as such, be expected to determine whether the sun revolves around the earth or the earth revolves around the sun; and if he assumes the latter, he does so not because of the *objective truth* of this hypothesis, considered in itself, but because only on this assumption is a system of the universe possible. Similarly, a genuine philosopher cannot be expected to determine whether our cognition possesses a *real ground* outside of our *faculty of cognition,* a ground that can be derived from this faculty (as the *Critical* philosophers maintain); and if he nevertheless adopts such a position, he does so only because this will produce the highest possible degree of *systematic unity* in our cognition, by means of which everything therein will be explicable in the most exact interconnection. The assertions of the dogmatists concerning *things in themselves* are, in contrast, quite superfluous, since nothing within our cognition can be explained thereby.

[The invention of *fictions* for the purposes of *extending* the sciences and providing them with *systematic order* is a work of reason. To represent these fictions as real objects is a work of the *power of imagination.* But even those who explain such a representation as false can still accept it—not, to be sure, *for the sake of science itself,* but on account of its *practical utility.* In this way philosophy can be reconciled with so called "common sense."]

33. "Meiner Meinung nach gehört zu einem *Vernunftprinzip* bloß *logische,* nicht aber *metaphysische Wahrheit.* Ich kenne kein anderes *Vernunftprinzip* als den *Satz des Widerspruchs.* Wenn also *Fiktionen* keinen *Widerspruch* enthalten, so können sie als *Vernunfprincipien* zur *Begründung* und *systematische Ordnung* der Erkenntniß gebraucht werden" (*Versuch einer neuen Logik,* p. liv, note u).

34. See *Streifereien,* p. 29.

35. It is also possible, and perhaps more likely, that Maimon simply revised his earlier view of mathematical fictions, in line with his new appreciation of the distinct roles of reason and imagination with respect to fictions. This in fact seems to have been the case. See *Versuch einer neuen Logik,* p. 206, where Maimon maintains that no real contradiction is involved in the fictional concepts of mathematics, so long as one remembers to treat such fictions merely as *methodological* devises and not as real concepts. "Das Methodus indivisibilium, die *unendliche Reihe,* die *Differentialrechnung* u.d.gl. führen nothwendig auf Widersprüche, wenn man sie für mehr als bloße *Methoden* betrachtet. Die *Einbildungskraft* treibt ihr Spiel mit ihnen, und stellt ihre *Fikzionen* als *reelle Objekte* vor. Die *Vernunft* aber kehrt sich daran nicht, und erklärt sie für das was sie wirklich sind, für bloße *Fikzionen.*"

36. An exception is M. Gueroult, *La philosophie transcendentale de Salomon Maimon* (Paris: Librarie Félix Alcan, 1929).

37. "Ja, aber dieses *ursprüngliche* Streben kommt nicht in's Bewußtseyn, weil es nicht vorgestellt ist. Eben so wie ein uspründliches Ich als Subjekt ausgenommen werden muß; so auch <ein> *ursprüngliches* Streben.—Es kann zur Erklärung, als eine Fiktion, wie Maimon sagt, allerdings angenommen werden" ("Practische

Philosophie," *GA* II/3, p. 192). See, too, the earlier remark in this same manuscript: "Ferner, wo bleiben die Fiktionen, denken einer Möglichkeit deßen, was nicht wirklich ist?—Gehort wohl nicht hieher, sondern in die Beziehung auf's absolute Ich" ("Eigne Mediationen über Elementar-Philosophie," *GA* II/3, pp. 160–61). ["Where, moreover, does this leave fictions—thinking of the possibility of something that is not actual? This certainly does not belong here, but [needs to be discussed] in conjunction with the absolute I."]

38. "Nur ist zu erinnern, und wohl einzuschärfen, *daß* diese Abstraktion gemacht worden, daß mithin der dadurch hervorgebrachte Begriff zwar ideale Möglichkeit (für das Denken), aber keine reele Bedeutung hat. Vernachtlässigt man diese Bemerkung, so erhält man eine lediglich formale Rechtslehre.—Es gibt keinen Stand der Urrecht, und keine Urrechte des Menschen. Wirklich hat er nur der Gemeinschaft mit andern Rechte, wie er denn, nach den obigen höhern Principien, überhaupt nur in der Gemeinschaft mit andern gedacht werden kann. Ein Urrecht is daher ein bloße *Fiktion,* aber se muß, zum Behuf der Wissenschaft, nothwendig gemacht werden" (*Grundlage des Naturrechts, GA* I/3, pp. 403–4).

But it must be remembered, indeed, it must be emphasized, that an abstraction has been made here [—namely, an abstraction from those limitations of primordial right that are required in every actual community of free beings], and thus that the concept [of primordial right] produced thereby, though it certainly possesses ideal possibility (for thinking), possesses no real meaning. If one neglects to note this, then one obtains a purely formal theory of right.—There is no state of primordial right, and there are no primordial human rights. In actuality, a human being has rights only in community with others, just as, according to the higher principles indicated above, a human being can be thought of only in community with others. A "primordial right" is therefore a mere *fiction;* yet it is one that necessarily must be fabricated for the sake of science.]

39. See Breazeale, "Fichte's Conception of Philosophy as a 'Pragmatic History of the Human Mind' and the Contributions of Kant, Platner, and Maimon," *Journal of the History of Ideas* (forthcoming).

40. "Die eigentl. Frage einer Kritik ist: wie kommen wir denn erst zu einer *Welt:* und der Vorstellung eines Verhälnisses: u. inwiefern haben *diese* Vorstellungen, u. alles, was durch weiteres Räsonnement auf sie gebaut werden könnte, Gültigkeit. Und darauf antwortet die Kritik: wir bringen sie durch das Verfahren unsers Geistes nach Gesetzen erst hervor. . . . Nun aber stellt Hrr Pl[atner] allerdings so etwas auf (u. weis sich viel damit). was ist es?—Es ist seine *pragmatische* Geschichte: u. eine dergl. will ich auch verzeichnen; nur aus den <ganz> umgekehrten Grundsätzen—*pragmatisch* wie es zu Stande kommt.—*Geschichte,* ist Fiktion, giebt den genetischen Gang des Vortrags. . . . Das, was Herr Pl. meint [als Logik].—Ist eine dogmatische Fiction.—Ich werde an derselben einen kurzen Abriß der kritischen Philosophie geben" ("Vorlesungen über Platners Aphorismen, Theil I," *GA* II/4, pp. 51–52).

[The proper question that critique addresses is the following: How do we first arrive at a *world* and at the representation of a relationship [between it and ourselves], and to what extent do *these* representations, along with all that is constructed upon them by means of further argument, have validity? And to this the *Critique* replies: we first produce these through the law-governed operation of our mind. . . . Herr Platner certainly proposes something similar (and employs it to illuminate much). What does he propose? It is his *pragmatic* history [of the human mind], and I too want to sketch something similar—*pragmatic*, with reference to how it comes about.—*History*, [this] is a fiction, indicating the genetic method of the presentation. . . . What Platner means by "logic" is a dogmatic fiction. In its place I will provide a short sketch of the Critical philosophy.]

41. "Wir wollen uns unsre Begriffe von bewußtlosen Vorstellungen mittheilen. Wir müssen sonach doch denke ich von ihnen *wissen,* sonst könnten wir nicht darüber reden.—. Wie kommen wir denn sonach zu diesem *Wissen.* . . . Wohl nicht anders, als daß wir aus dem mit *Bewußtseyn* vorhandnen auf sie schliessen: sie als einen Erklärungsgrund brauchen—wir können sie nur *setzen,* u. *setzen* sie. aber sie sind nichts wirkliches. . . . Eine dunkle Vorstellung ist eine Anschauung; . . . d.i. ein Handeln des vorstellenden, in welchem es seiner selbst nicht bewußt wird.—es wird auf sie nur *geschlossen.* Diese wird *begriffen,* d.i. es wird noch einmal, als auf eine Handlung des Ich darauf reflectiert: jezt ensteht, Bewußtseyn des Objekts, u. Subjekts, *völlige Vorstellung,* im Reinholdischen Sinne. . . . Aber die Begriff der Anschauung selbst is insofern eine Fiction: d.i., um die Vorstellung zu erklären, müssen wir so etwas voraussetzen" ("Vorlesungen über Platners Aphorsmen, Teil I," *GA* II/4, pp. 64–65).

[We want to communicate our concept of unconscious representations. Thus, I think, we surely must *know* about them, since otherwise we couldn't even talk about them. But how do we arrive at such *knowledge?* . . . Only in the following way: we infer these unconscious representations from those representations that are consciously present. We need the former as a ground of explanation. We can only *posit* them, and we do *posit* them. But they are nothing actual. . . . An obscure representation is an intuition; . . . , i.e., it is an act of the representing subject, in which it is not conscious of itself. Such an intuition is only *inferred.* This is [then] grasped conceptually, i.e., it is reflected upon once again, as an action of the I. There then arises consciousness of an object and a subject, a *complete representation* in Reinhold's sense of the term. . . . But the concept of intuition itself is, to this extent, a fiction. That is to say, it is something that we have to presuppose in order to explain representation.]

42. "Anschauung u. Begriff sind beisammen: Kant sagt Anschauung ohne Begriff ist blind, u. Begriff ohne Anschauung ist leer *i.e.* Ansch[auung] ohne Begriff würde nicht zum Bewustsein kommen; es kann also weder eine blinde Ansch[auung]. noch einen leeren Begriff geben. Nichts hat in der Philosophie mehr Unglück gestiftet als daß die Philosophen ihre Distinctionen, die sie in der Schule machen musten für wirkliche Dinge ansahen; denn der Philos[oph] muß oft unterscheiden, was in der Natur eins ist. Anschauung ist also eine Fiction, um etwas daran begreiflich zu machen" (K. C. F. Krause's Kollegnachschrift of the SS 1797 "Vorlesungen über Logik und Metaphysik," *GA* IV/1, pp. 197–98).

[Intuition and concept go together: Kant said that an intuition without a concept is blind and that a concept without an intuition is empty. I.e., an intuition without a concept would not come to consciousness; therefore, there can be neither a blind intuition nor an empty concept. Nothing has done more harm in philosophy than the fact that philosophers viewed those distinctions that they had to make within the context of their schools as actual things, for the philosopher frequently has to disassemble what is, within nature, something unitary. Intuition is therefore a faction, (introduced) in order to make something comprehensible.]

43. Like many other people in 1797, Forberg treated Schelling and Fichte as exponents of the same philosophical system, namely, the *Wissenschaftslehre*.

44. For a detailed account of these circumstances, see the editor's introduction to Fichte, *Introductions to the Wissenschaftslehre, and Other Writings,* ed. and trans. Daniel Breazeale (Indianapolis and Cambridge: Hackett, 1994), pp. xiii–xv.

45. Though Forberg never mentions Maimon by name, there can be no doubt that he was familiar with Maimon's proposal concerning the use of fictions within philosophy. The distinction between "the qualitative" and "quantitative" extension of knowledge was, for example, already proposed, in precisely these terms, by Maimon in his *Ueber die Progressen.*

46. Emphasis added.

"Oder hofft man durch die Voraussetzung des absoluten Ich etwas für die *Qualität* unserer Erkenntniß zu gewinnen?—Also etwa die systematische Einheit des Wissens? Den Knäuel, von dem sich, wie Erhard sagt, alle Wahrheiten abwinden lassen sollen? Das wäre nicht übel. Aber welche Rolle müsse dann das absolute Ich in den System spielen? Doch wohl die eines ersten Princips? Meinetwegen! Nur müsste man am Ende, wenn man mit dem Systeme fertig wäre, nicht etwa vergessen, daß eigentlich kein erstes Princip gefunden war, sondern daß bloß und allein desswegen, um das System zu Stande zu bringen, verfahren wurde, *als ob* eines gefünden wäre. Das absolut Ich wäre dann weiter nichts, als eine systematische Fiction, und nur so lange nöthig gewesen, als an dem Systems gebauet wurde. Ist der Bau vollendent, was indessen wohl nie der Fall seyn wird, so hat es gethan, was es thun sollte, und es wird entlassen. Die Idee des absoluten Ich hätte ungefähr dieselbe Function in der Metaphysik, wie die Idee eines verständiges Urhebers der Welt in dem Studium der organisirte Natur: so wie diese zwar selbst keine Entdeckung sondern blöße Fiction ist, aber doch uns zu Entdeckungnen leitet; so wäre jene, ohne selbst erser Ring der Kette zu seyn, doch zum Zusammenhängen der Glieder sehr behülflich. Beide wären nichts weniger als Erkenntnisse zu unsern Erkenntnissen, sondern blöße Methoden, die eine, Erkenntnisse zu finden, die andere, die gefundenen zu ordnen. Die Vernunft, wenn sie die höchste systematische Einheit des Wissens zum Zweck hätte, könnte nach einer gedoppelten Maxime zu Werke gegen. Sie könnte nämlich entweder voraussetzen, das Wissen richtet sich nach den Dingen, oder umgekehrt, die Dinge richten sich nach dem Wissen. . . . Beide Voraussetzungen blieben immer und ewig Voraussetzungen, und ließen sich nimmer beweisen, und sobald man den Versuch machte, sie zu beweisen, müsste sich sofort ihre Nichtigkeit entdecken. Aber sie ließen sich allerdings bestätigen, und zwar durch den Erfolg" (Forberg, "Briefe über die neuesten Philosophie," *Philosophische Journal einer Gesellschaft Teutscher Gelehren* VI/1 [1797]: pp. 78–79).

[Or does one, by presupposing the absolute I, hope to achieve something concerning the *quality* of our cognition—regarding, perhaps, the systematic unity of our knowledge? The skein, perhaps, from which, as Erhard says, all truths might be unwound? That would not be so bad. But in that case, what role must the absolute I play in the system? That of first principle? To be sure! At the end, however, once the system has been completed, one must not forget that no first principle was really discovered, and one must remember that one simply proceeded *as if* one had been discovered, and that one proceeded in this one simply in order to bring the system into being. In such a case, the absolute I would be nothing more than a systematic fiction, and it would have been necessary only while one was constructing that system. But once the system is complete (which, of course, will never be the case!), the absolute will then have served its purpose and can be dismissed. The idea of the absolute I would then have approximately the same function in metaphysics that the idea of an intelligent creator of the universe has in the study of organic nature: just as the latter is a mere fiction and not a discovery, though it leads us to make discoveries, so the latter, without itself being the first link in the chain, would nevertheless be very useful for connecting the parts. Neither of these would be new cognitions, but would simply be methods: the first, a method for discovering cognitions; the latter, a method for ordering the cognitions we have discovered. If reason takes as its aim the highest systematic unity of knowledge, then it can set to work by two different methods: it can presuppose that knowledge conforms to things, or, conversely, it can presuppose that things correspond to knowledge. . . . Both of these presuppositions always remain no more than presuppositions. They can never be proven, and as soon as one tries to prove them then one immediately discovers their nullity. The can, however, be confirmed: namely, through success.]

The text of Forberg's "Briefe" is reprinted in *Aus der Frühzeit des deutschen Idealismus. Texte zur Wissenschaftslehre Fichtes 1794–1803*, ed. Martin Oesch (Würzburg: Königshausen und Neumann, 1987) pp. 153–78.

47. See Reinhold Lauth, *Die Enstehung von Schellings Indentitätsphilosophie in der Auseinandersetzung mit Fichtes Wissenschaftslehre* (Freiburg and München: Karl Alber, 1975), pp. 211–28. See especially, pp. 224 and 228: "Fichte läßt sich von Forberg nicht auf einen Fiktionilsmus abdrängen, sondern verteidigt und erklärt die intellektuelle Anschauung der Wissenschaftslehre."

48. "*Ueber Ihren Gegensatz* der Transscendental- und der Naturphilosophie bin ich mit Ihnen noch nicht einig. Alles scheint auf eine[r] Verwechselung zwischen *idealer* und *realer* Thätigkeit zu beruhen, die wir beide hier und da gemacht haben; und die durch die neue Darstellung ganz zu heben hoffe. Die *Sache* kommt nach mir nicht *zum Bewußtseyn hinzu*, noch das *Bewußtseyns zur Sache*, sondern beide sind im Ich, dem *ideal = realen*, *realidealen*, unmittelbar vereinigt.— Etwas anders ist die *Realität der Nature*. Die letztere erscheint in der Transscendental Philosophie als durchaus *gefunden*, und zwar *fertig* und *vollendet;* und dies zwar

(gefunden nemlich) nicht nach *eignen* Gesetzen, sondern nach *immanenten* der *Intelligenz* (als ideal = realem) Die Wissenschaft, die durch eine feine Abstraktion die Nature allein sich zum Objekt macht, muß freilich (eben weil sie von der Intelligenz abstrahirt) die Natur, als *absolutes* setzen, und dieselbe durch eine *Fiction sich selbst contruiren* lassen; eben so wie die TransscendentalPhilosophie durch eine *gleiche Fiction,* das Bewußtseyn sich selbst construiren läßt" (Letter to Wilhelm Joseph Schelling, 15 November 1800, *GA* III/4, pp. 360–61).

[I am not yet in agreement with you *concerning your opposition* between transcendental philosophy and the philosophy of nature. This all seems to me to be based upon a confusion of *ideal* with *real* activity—a confusion of which we have both been guilty here and there, and which I hope to eliminate entirely in my new presentation [of the *Wissenschaftslehre*]. In my view, the *object* [*Sache*] does not *enter consciousness,* nor does *consciousness enter the object;* instead, both are immediately united within the I, which is *ideal-real* or *realideal.*—The *reality of nature* is a different matter. Within transcendental philosophy the latter appears as something *discovered,* and indeed as something *finished* and *complete*—albeit not in accordance with its *own* laws, but rather in accodance with the *immanent* laws of the *intellect* (as ideal-real). Any science which, through a fine abstraction, makes nature itself into its object must, to be sure (and precisely because it abstracts from the intellect), posit nature as something *absolute* and must, by means of a *fiction,* allow nature *to construct itself*—just as transcendental philospohy, by means of a *similar fiction,* allows consciousness to construct itself.]

49. See Schelling's letter to Fichte, 19 November 1800, *GA* III/4, p. 364.

50. See *GA* II/5, pp. 351–99. For an account of this text and of its relationship to the *Wissenschaftslehre nova methodo,* see my introduction to *Foundations of Transcendental Philosophy* (*Wissenschaftslehre Nova Methodo*) (hereafter abbreviated as *FTP*), trans. and ed. D. Breazeale (Ithaca: Cornell University Press, 1992), as well as Günter Meckenstock, "Fichtes Fragment, 'Neue Bearbeitung der Wissenschaftslehre,' " in *Der transzendetnale Gedanke: Die gegenwärtige Darstellung der Philosophie Fichtes,* ed. Klaus Hammacher (Hamburg: Felix Meiner, 1981), pp. 80–90.

51. "Das wirkliche Bewußtseyn ist; es ist ganz, und durchaus fertig, so wir nur wir selbst fertig sind, und Selbstbewußtseyn haben, mit welchem, als mit ihrem letzten Gliede, die Wissenschaftslehre schließt. . . . Dieses absolut vorhandene nun läßt sich zufolge unsrer Philosophie, im wirklichen Leben sich *behandeln und beurtheilen, gleich als ob* es durch eine urprüngliche Construktion, so wie die Wissenschaftslehre eine vollzieht, entstanden sey. . . . Dieses *gleich als ob* für ein kategorisches *daß,* diese Fiktion für die Erzählung einer wahren irgend einmal zu irgend einer Zeit eingetretnen Begebenheit zu halten, ist ein grober Misverstand. Glauben sie denn, daß wir an der Construktion des Grundbewußtseyns in der Wissenschaftslehre eine Historie von den Thathandlungen des Bewußtseyns, ehe das Bewußtseyn war, die Lebensgeschichte eines Mannes vor seiner Geburt, liefern wollen? Wie könnten wir doch, da wir selbst erklären, daß das Bewußtseyn nur mit allen seinen Bestimmungen zugleich ist; und kein Bewußtseyn vor allem Bewußtseyn, und ohen alles Bewußtseyns, begehren? . . .

"So sind alle Kosmogonien Versuche einer ursprünglichen Construktion des Universum aus seinen Grundbestandteilen. . . . Freilich glaubt der unwissenschaftliche Verstand, den man im Umfange des Gegebnen erhalten, und Forschungen dieser Art nicht an ihn kommen lassen sollte, eine Erzählung zu hören, weil er nichts denken kann, als Erzählungen. Läßt sich nicht aus der gegenwärtigen Annahme so vieler, daß wir durch unsre Gnosogonie eine Erzählung zu geben glauben, schließen, daß sie selbt nicht abgeneigt seyn würden, es für eine Erzählung zu nehmen, wenn sie nur das Siegel der Autorität, und des Alterthums darauf ruhte?" (*Sonnenklarer Bericht an das grösserte Publikum über das eigentliche Wesen der neuesten Philosophie, GA* I/7, pp. 249–50).

[Actual consciousness exists. It is a whole and is completely finished, just as we ourselves are finished and self-conscious—which is the final step, with which the *Wissenschaftslehre* concludes. . . . According to our philosophy, this absolutely present reality can, in turn, be *treated and judged* within actual life *just as if* it had arisen through an original construction, such as is accomplished in the *Wissenschaftslehre*. . . . It is a crude misunderstanding to take this "just as if" for a categorical "that," to take this fiction to be a narration of a true event that is supposed to have occurred at some time or another. Do you actually suppose that our construction of fundamental consciousness in the *Wissenschaftslehre* is intended as a history of the Acts of consciousness before there was any consciousness, the life-history of a man prior to his birth? How could this be our intention, since we ourselves explain that consciousness exists simultaneously with all of its determinations?

[All cosmologies are thus attempts to produce an original construction of the universe and all of its constituent elements. [. . .] Granted, the unscientific understanding, which is confined within the perimeter of the given and which does not admit inquiries of this sort, believes that it is listening to a narrative, since it can think of nothing else but narratives. Since so many people at present believe that we, in our gnoseogony, are providing a narrative, couldn't one conclude that they would not be disinclined to accept this narrative, if only it bore the seal of authority and antiquity?]

52. See Fichte's correspondence with Fessler, criticizing Fessler's "secret history" of freemasonry and discussing the issue of "public" vs "secret" history and the distinctive reasons why a mason (such a Fessler or Fichte) would have a special interest in the history of his order. According to Fichte, what is wanted here is something other than a usual, scholarly history. Instead, writes Fichte: "Seine Geschichte muß seyn eine *genetische Deduction* der bestehenden Mysterienfeyeren; so wie, z.B. eine Staatsengeschichte eine genetische Deduction der bestehended Staatsverfassung seyn muß.

"So stehet die Aufgabe.—Es sind mir gewisse Gebräuche und Formeln überliefert worden: ist ist unmittelbares Factum, wovon ich ausgehe. Wie sind *diese* so geworden" (*GA*, III, 4, p. 246).

Fichte then proceeds to criticize Fessler's "secret history" of secret societies in general and of freemasonry in particular for leaving out all the evidence that opposes the result at which Fessler knows in advance he wants to arrive and including only evidence that supports his preordained conclusion. As Fichte notes, "Ich will jede Wette eingehen, daß auf diese Weise ich gerade so gründlich und bündig meine Abstammung von Alexander dem Grossen darthun können" (*GA*, III/4, p. 248).

Fichte then refers Fessler to a passage in his own (Fichte's) lecture of 25 May 1800 (the sixth lecture on masonry), where he opposes the secret history of masonry to its public history and asks him to reflect "ob man nicht auf diese Weise der öffentlichen Geshichte durchaus glüklich ausweiche. Fiction gegen Fiction würde ich immer für die durchaus consequente und auf dem Wege der Geschichte unwiderlegbare, entscheiden: diese so einrichten, daß sie für den klügern Kopf zugleich *Allegorie* wäre; und dem, der es erräth, freimüthig das wahre Geheimniß, und wir wir alle zu unsern Kenntnissen gekommen sind gestehen" (Letter to Ignatious Aurelius Feßler, 28 May 1800; *GA* III/4, p. 248).

Fessler, in his reply to this letter, indignantly rejected Fichte's suggestion that a fiction cannot be refuted by history and points out that the people in the lodge do not think they are dealing with fictions there. See Fessler to Fichte, letter from the end of May or beginning of June 1800, *GA* III/4, p. 256.

In his response to Fessler, Fichte asserts that his remark about fictions versus history was never meant seriously! "Den Vorschlag einer durchgeführten Fiction that ich nicht im Ernste, sondern um Ihnen zu zeigen, wohin man meines Erachtens gerathen müste, wenn man nicht mit der reinen Wahrheit durchaus herausgehen wolle" (Letter to Fessler, 10 June 1800; *GA* III/4, p. 263). ["The proposal for a thoroughgoing fiction was not meant seriously, but only to show you what has to happen if one does not want to be accompanied (?) completely by the pure truth."]

In the accompanying list of "additional remarks" to Fessler, Fichte goes on to repeat his earlier views of what a "wahre Geschichte" of freemasonry must be like—"wenn sie *wahre* Geschichte, und nicht ein *Meinen* und *Wähnen*, also kurz—eine *Fiction* ist" (Letter to Fessler, 10 June 1800; *GA* III/4, pp. 265–66). ["[I]f it is a true history, and not an *opinioning* and *fancying*, in short, a *fiction*."]

53. See *GA,* I/3, pp. 254–56 (*EPW,* pp. 323–26) and *GA,* II/5, pp. 331, 335, and 338.

54. Though there are many passages in which Fichte talks about beginning philosophy by "seeking out" a first principle and emphasizes the "hypothetical" character of the same, this point is most clearly formulated in his lectures on *Wissenschaftslehre nova methodo,* which begin with an explicit postulate, in the form of a directive to the reader to "think the I."

55. For Fichte's reception of Beck's notion of beginning philosophy with a postulate," see *IWL,* pp. 29–30n.; *GA* I/4, p. 203n., and *IWL,* p. 189n.; *GA* I/7, p. 156n.

56. *FTP,* pp. 102–3; *GA* IV/2, p. 27; and Johann Gottlieb Fichte, *Wissenschaftslehre nova methodo. Kollegnachschrift K. Chr. Fr. Krause 1798–99,* ed. Erich Fuchs (1982), 2nd, improved ed. (Hamburg: Felix Meiner, 1994), pp. 22–23.

57. *FTP,* p. 103; *GA* IV/2, p. 27.

58. See, e.g.: *GA*, I/4, p. 209; II/3, p. 25; and IV/3, p. 339 (*FTP*, p. 101).

59. See, e.g.: *GA*, II/3, p. 24.

60. See "[Ankundigung: Seit sechs Jahren"] Public Announcement of a New Presentation of the *Wissenschaftslehre, IWL,* pp. 193–98; *GA*, I/7, pp. 159–62. Fichte's most detailed account of the "constructive" or "reconstructive" character of his philosophy is to be found in the *Sonnenklarer Bericht* (1801).

61. See my "Philosophy and the Divided Self: On the Existential and Scientific Tasks of the Jena *Wissenschaftslehre,"* *Fichte-Studien* 6 (1994): pp. 117–47.

62. "Das reflectirende Gang schließt, u. folgert allerdings: aber daraus nicht das Factum, sondern nur die nothwendige Annehmbarkeit derßelben" (*GA* II/3: 25).

63. Fichte's rejectiom of what would today be called "psychologism" begins with his criticism of Platner and continues in his criticism of the effort of Schmid and others to base philosophy upon an appeal to the "facts of consciousness." It becomes even more explicit and pointed in his writings of 1799 through 1801. See, e.g., "Antwortschrieben an Herrn Professor Reinhold" (1801) and " Aus einem Privatschreiben" (1800), where Fichte notes that unlike psychology, which deals with "facts of consciousness," which one simply discovers to be the case, the *Wissenschaftslehre* deals with "was man nur so vorfindet, wenn man sich findet [which one discovers to be so only when one discovers oneself]" (*GA* I/6, p. 387n.). See too " Neue Bearbeitung der W.L. 1800" GA II/5, p. 333.

64. "A Comparison between Prof. Schmid's System and the *Wissenschaftslehre,"* *GA* I/5, p. 261; *Fichte: Early Philosophical Writings,* p. 330. This was precisely the criticism that Reinhold leveled against Maimon's fictionalist conception of philosophy: that it would reduce philosophy to a purely "formal" science. (Maimon, in turn, had made a similar criticism of Reinhold's *Elementarphilosophie.*)

65. Regarding Fichte's description of the importance of "intuition" and "observation" in philosophy, see "Announcement of a New Presentation of the *Wissenschaftslehre,"* as well as the frequent comments on this subject in the lectures on "The Foundations of Transcendental Philosophy *(Wissenschaftslehre) nova methodo."*

66. Zöller, pp. 77 and 84–85.

67. Zöller, p. 79.

68. For a particularly clear account of the philosopher as mere observer of the original action of the I, see Fichte's introduction to the *Grundlage des Naturrechts.*

69. *GA* I/4, p. 213 (*IWL*, p. 41), and *FTP,* K, p. 28.

70. See Breazeale, "Fichte's *nova methodo phenomenologica:* On the Methodological Role of 'Intellectual Intuition' in the later Jena *Wissenschaftslehre,"* *Revue Internationale de Philosophie* [Brussels] no. 206 (1998): 587–616.

71. See "First Introduction" to the *Attempt at a New Presentation of the Wissenschaftslehre* (*GA* I/4, p. 191 [*IWL*, p. 141]).

72. On the disptute between Fichte and Schelling on this point, see my introduction to *IWL.*

73. For Fichte's defense of "one-sole-philosophy" conception of philosophy see "From a Private letter," *IWL*, p. 163n. Note that this same principle is explicitly affirmed by Kant is his *Rechtslehre* (*AA*, 6:207).

74. The "dual series" consisting of (1) the observed acts of the I and (2) the series of philosophical observations of the former series is discussed in the First Introduction to the *Attempt at a New Presentation of the Wissenschaftslehre.*

75. As Martial Gueroult writes: "Fichte semble hésiter entre les deux conceptions du principe comme fiction, ou du principe comme réalité. Mais au fond de sa pensée, c'est que le principe a une réalité métaphysique" (*La philosophie transcendentale de Salomon Maïmon*, p. 13). This claim is later glossed as follows:

> De Maimon également, Fichte dans sa première philosophie retiendra le caractère d'Idée du Moi, lequel ne peut jamais être réalisé effectivement dans notre conscience, tout en pouvant se réaliser comme concept, au moyen de l'intuition intellectuelle, dans la conscience philosophique. Ce concept, simple image, participe à la réalité du Moi, par l'activité dont il est issu, mais le Moi absolu, source de l'intuition intellectuelle, n'est pas lui-même une réalité distincte. Comme premier principe, il n'est posé séparément qu'à titre de concept dans la pensée du philosophe; dans la réalité naturelle il n'est qu'une Idée vers laquelle tend le Moi pratique, seul réel. C'est beaucoup plus tard seulement que Fichte se dégagera de cette conception ambiguë pour poser un Moi absolue existant actuellement par soi comme une réalité à laquelle nous fait participer l'intuition intellectuelle. La question du rapport entre le Moi absolute, l'Idée, l'intuition intellectuelle, et le concept ce trouve deja posée chez Maimon avec celle de l'entendement infini, du Moi indéterminé déterminable, fondment premier, et en même temps Idée. (Gueroult, p. 71)

76. See Breazeale, "Certainty, Universal Validity, and Conviction: The Methodological Primacy of Practical Reason within the Jena *Wissenschaftslehre.*" In *New Perspectives on Fichte*, ed. D. Breazeale and T. Rockmore (Atlantic Highlands, N.J.: Humanities Press, 1996), pp. 35–59.

Another, equally practical but ultimately less fundamental, source of our beliefs about what is actual is our actual encounter with the empirical limits of our freedom in the form of a brute *encounter* corresponding to the philosophical fictions of *Anstoß (Grundlage der gesamten Wissenschaftslehre)* or "feeling" (*Wissenschaftslehre nova methodo*). See my "Check or Checkmate? On the Finitude of the Fichtean Self," in *The Modern Subject: Conceptions of the Self in Classical German Philosophy*, ed. Karl Ameriks and Dieter Sturma (Albany: State University of New York Press, 1995), pp. 87–114.

77. Our practical certainty of the categorical imperative is described as a "real intellectual intuition" in the Second Introduction to *VWL* (*IWL*, p. 49).

Intellectual Intuition, the Pure Will, and the Categorical Imperative in the Later Jena *Wissenschaftslehre*

Yolanda Estes

I n the *Wissenschaftslehre nova methodo* and "Chapter One" of *Versuch einer neuen Darstellung der Wissenschaftslehre,* Fichte claims that philosophical self-reflection consists in self-reverting activity, which has the *form* of an intellectual intuition.[1] The transcendental philosopher infers that a *Tathandlung* or intellectual intuition (pure I-hood) underpins this conscious act of reflection and constitutes the immediate foundation of all mediate consciousness.[2] In the "Second Introduction" to the *Versuch einer neuen Darstellung der Wissenschaftslehre* (1797–1798) and in the *Sittenlehre,* Fichte calls nonsensible awareness of the ethical law a *wirkliche intellektuelle Anschauung,* that is, a real intellectual intuition, which he associates with immediate consciousness of freedom.[3]

In the *nova methodo,* Fichte identifies the philosophical concept of pure I-hood with the pure will and its determination as individuality through the *Aufforderung.* Moreover, the "Second Introduction" and the *Sittenlehre* imply that real intellectual intuition relates closely to pure I-hood. The *nova methodo* associates pure I-hood and real *(wirkliche)* intellectual intuition with the pure will and its determination as individual will by a summons to act freely, or an *Aufforderung.* This essay addresses, first, intellectual intuition *qua* philosophical reflection; second, intellectual intuition *qua* pure I-hood; and third, intellectual intuition *qua* immediate consciousness of freedom.[4] I attempt to clarify the relation between intellectual intuition, the pure will, and the *Aufforderung* in Fichte's later Jena *Wissenschaftslehre* without conflating the different types of intellectual intuition. Afterward, I suggest a way to mitigate tensions between my interpretation of intellectual intuition in the *nova methodo* and Fichte's discussion of the pure will and *Aufforderung* in the *Rechtslehre* and *Sittenlehre*.

Real intellectual intuition, philosophical self-reflection, and the philosophical concept of pure I-hood share structural features. Each form of intellectual intuition involves self-reverting activity, self-consciousness, and reflection on an intelligible I. By virtue of a non-sensible intuition of the ethical law, the moral subject views itself as an intelligible will, thereby distinguishing itself from its determination as a sensible being in the empirical world. Philosophical reflection involves an abstraction from empirical consciousness whereby the philosopher produces the concept of an intelligible I. The transcendental philosopher presupposes pure I-hood as an intelligible ground of empirical consciousness.

In grasping the ethical law, the moral subject becomes conscious of itself as a willing subject with a moral obligation. This immediate co-incidence of self-awareness and moral awareness involves a self-reverting activity. Consciousness of the ethical law enjoins an act of self-determination, and thus is itself a determinate self-reverting activity.[5] Moral activity consists in an autonomous determination of the will. In thinking of itself, the philosophizing subject forms the concept of the I, and this immediate coincidence of self-awareness and thinking activity also involves a self-reverting activity. If the philosophizing subject thinks of the I, it engages in this self-reverting activity, which is itself the concept of the I. Philosophical self-reflection involves a free determination of thinking activity. Pure I-hood, which the philosopher presupposes as the immediate consciousness underpinning all mediate consciousness, is the concept of pure self-reverting activity. The philosophical concept of pure I-hood refers to a being whose essence consists in free self-activity.

Despite these similarities, real intellectual intuition, philosophical self-reflection, and pure I-hood are not identical. Real intellectual intuition refers to the moral subject's act of self-determined willing. A *feeling* of an absolute "ought" gives rise to moral self-awareness, wherein the empirical subject recognizes itself as subordinate to the Categorical Imperative, and thus views itself in light of its capacity to act freely rather than in light of its empirically determined nature. Philosophical self-reflection refers to a deliberate act of abstraction performed by the philosopher, wherein the philosophizing subject becomes aware of its free thinking activity. Pure I-hood refers to a concept that the transcendental philosopher infers and postulates as the ground of consciousness. As the ground of consciousness, it is never an object of the philosopher's direct awareness.

By means of philosophical self-reflection, the philosophizing subject infers a formal characterization of the intelligible pure I, but in recognizing the ethical law, the empirical moral subject becomes conscious of itself as an intelligible I.

Both types of "philosophical" intellectual intuition retain a contrived character. Real intellectual intuition alone provides nonsensible consciousness of the real efficacy of the I. Hence, in the "Second Introduction," Fichte asserts that the ethical law provides the sole point of connection between philosophy and reality.

> It is only through the medium of the ethical law that I catch a glimpse of
> myself and insofar as I view myself through this medium, I necessarily
> view myself as self-active. In this way an entirely alien ingredient,
> viz., my consciousness of my own real efficacy, arises for me within a
> consciousness that otherwise would be nothing but a consciousness of a
> particular sequence of my representations.[6]

For this reason, intellectual intuition seems incomprehensible to the person who has not developed the facility for free practical activity.[7] Hence, in the *Sittenlehre*, Fichte claims that no philosophical concept of intellectual intuition is possible apart from the real intellectual intuition of freedom.[8] Intellectual intuition grounds the *Wissenschaftslehre*, but the *nova methodo* does not commence with real intellectual intuition or with the pure will. It begins with a preliminary definition of I-hood as self-reverting activity that results from following the summons: "Think the concept 'I' and think of yourself as you do this."[9] Fichte "deduces" intellectual intuition (that is, the pure will) as a hypothetical ground, which he subsequently "applies" to objective consciousness.[10] The pure will, employed in this manner, is a presupposition of the pure activity of the I that underpins all consciousness. The *nova methodo* employs the pure will as a hypothesis in order to discharge the central task of explaining how the I discovers itself as active. The I discovers itself through an intellectual intuition, so Fichte must explain how the I obtains a simple intuition of itself as determinate activity and freely determinable *Vermögen*.

> "How do I discover myself? Or—since thinking is an ideal act, which
> presupposes that its object is given—how am I given to myself?" In the
> previous section, we answered this question provisionally as follows: This
> act of thinking refers to an intellectual intuition {of myself as willing
> subject, and this intellectual intuition is immediate}. This must here be
> made more precise. What is {this} intellectual intuition itself, and how
> does it originate?[11]

Willing presupposes the concept of a goal, which requires an objective cognition. Since an objective cognition is impossible apart from willing, the account of consciousness in the *nova methodo* seems to degenerate into a vicious circle. Fichte introduces the pure will as a *hypothesis* (an explanatory ground) in order to explain the activity of willing by presupposing a will that contains a goal-concept within itself.[12] The *nova methodo* then shows how this concept is connected to sensibility as an appearance within empirical consciousness.

The transcendental philosopher *conceives* intellectual intuition by means of abstraction and infers that something resembling this concept grounds consciousness, but the real intuition of the I's activity only *appears* within a sensible context, wherein it occurs as an act of willing characterized as *ein Sollen, ein Fordern*.[13] An *Aufforderung* initiates the empirical I's real intellectual intuition of its intelligible self. Philosophical reflection copies this real intellectual intuition, from which the philosopher infers the concept of intellectual intuition that serves as the grounding principle of the *Wissenschaftslehre*.[14] Although this pure form of willing (the pure will) appears within actual consciousness as a determinate categorical command that expresses the ethical law, it is not employed in the foundational part of the *Wissenschaftslehre* as the Categorical Imperative. Consequently, in the *nova methodo*, Fichte explains:

> Pure willing, at this point, is not supposed to be anything more than the explanatory ground of consciousness; it is still a hypothesis, *not yet* an object of consciousness. {One should think of this determinacy of pure willing in the most indeterminate manner possible—as a mere hypothesis, as a *qualitas occulta,* or however else one may wish—since it does not appear within consciousness at all.} We posit it here only as if it were something. . . . Later on we will show how pure willing appears within consciousness; here we are concerned only with the consequences that follow when it is presupposed as the explanatory ground of consciousness.[15]

The *nova methodo presupposes* the pure will as a supersensible ground necessary for the possibility of empirical consciousness, but this "necessary" presupposition is "not yet" connected to reality or empirical consciousness. In other words, philosophy offers no evidence that a *Wissenschaftslehre* grounded in the pure will describes any system of real thinking. In order to demonstrate that the *Wissenschaftslehre* describes such a real system, and to show that it explains the possibility of the system of "representations accompanied by a sense of necessity," Fichte must explain how the pure will *appears* as a necessary feature of consciousness.

Feeling grounds everything that enters consciousness as necessary. The pure will must also be related to a feeling, in this case, to a feeling of obligation to remain within the sphere of the "ought," or *das Gefühl des Nichtdürfens*.[16]

Empirical willing constitutes the essential fact of consciousness, which is immediately conjoined with the sole "fact" of reason, that is, an awareness of the ethical law and freedom. The empirical will presupposes the pure will, or the determinable realm of the supersensible, for the empirical will is the determinate object of the pure will. All consciousness of empirical objects presupposes the empirical will.

> The empirical will is derived from the pure will and all other objects are derived from the object of the pure will. . . . Every act of thinking, every act of representing lies between and mediates original willing and limitation through feeling.[17]

All consciousness is sensible, but sensible consciousness follows from the pure will, which is itself supersensible, and thus, the pure will must be assimilated to the form of all sensible consciousness and discursive thinking, which is a movement of transition from determinability to determinacy.[18] In order to connect sensible experience to the pure will, it is necessary to disclose the determinable aspect of the transition from determinability to determinacy that arises when we think of the "ought."[19] The transition from determinability to determinacy associated with the pure will relates to consciousness through the thinking subject's discovery of itself as determined to determine itself. In other words, the pure will relates to consciousness insofar as the conscious subject recognizes its basic human character *(Bestimmung des Menschen)* as consisting in its obligation as a willing subject to be self-determining.[20] This movement from determinability to determinacy involves something intelligible (the pure will) in opposition to which the I discovers itself as a spiritual, but still determinate, being.[21]

As a determinate spiritual being, the I must grasp itself in opposition to some determinable mass or sphere, which must also be something intelligible. Feeling determines the I as an individual member of a determinable realm of rational being.[22] Both the determinate individual and the determinable sphere of rational being are *noumena*, which emerge within consciousness only through a feeling of self-imposed limitation of striving in response to an *Aufforderung*, or summons from another individual. Through the *Aufforderung*, the willing subject becomes aware of itself as an individual, viz., a determinate part of the determinable realm of rational being as such. Thus, there occurs a simultaneous recognition of the individual will as a determinate aspect of the determinable realm of rational being. The awareness of individual will requires awareness of another similar individual who solicits a determination within the sensible world through the outer organ (body) as an instrument of the will.[23] Belief in the objective reality of the sensible order arises for the I through its empirical act of willing the realization of the solicited sensible action and its consequent affirmation of the sensible order through which this action occurs.[24]

The *Aufforderung* solicits some specific free act, or self-limitation, in deference to the freedom of another individual. The supersensible realm of rational being appears to empirical consciousness only through a determinate embodied intelligence within a specific empirical context, viz., a contingent world of space, time, and matter. The supersensible *will* manifests itself to consciousness only within an act of empirical willing that refers to another individual's expectation of a determinate sensible action in the determinable sensible world. The act of empirical willing involves five elements: (1) a determinable world of rational being, (2) a determinate individual, (3) a determinable material world, (4) a determinate sensible object, and (5) a law that unites the determinable and the determinate as well as the sensible and supersensible. The sensible is given and the determinable is added by thinking, but the law uniting these elements is the content of an intellectual intuition.

Although each aspect of the intelligible world presupposes the others, no simultaneous recognition of willing, other rational beings, and the ethical law occurs apart from a particular sensible context and a specific encounter between free individuals, who become fully conscious of their nature only by means of mutual recognition of subjectivity. Practical activity involves a determination of the will. Any determinate activity presupposes something determinable that serves as a backdrop against which occurs the determination of the object of reflection, and thus the I cannot intuit its activity unless it feels itself as limited. The moral subject becomes aware of itself *as an I* insofar as it discovers itself as determined to be self-determining. This real intellectual intuition requires some original determining impulse, but since the will suffers no sensible constraint, something intelligible must limit it.[25]

The empirical I discovers its willing activity to be limited by another will. An *Aufforderung*, or a summons, from another rational being occasions intellectual intuition of the ethical law.[26] The summons determines the I as individual will within a determinable mass of rational being. The *Aufforderung* involves a specific encounter between two rational beings within a particular sensible context, which reveals the I's original goal-concept and initiates consciousness of the ethical law and thus the subject's discovery of itself as willing activity. The subject feels this limitation as an appeal for an act of self-determination, which expresses the super-sensible ethical law, formulated as a particular, but unconditional, command to treat another subject as an end in itself.[27] Insofar as it solicits self-determination for its own sake, the summons expresses the very essence of the Categorical Imperative and affirms both individuals' autonomies. By means of this encounter, the moral subject forms an Idea of the will it "ought to have within time," which constitutes a goal-concept determined by the ethical law.

> The pure will is merely the will that I ought to have within time. Answer to the question "who am I?" {I am the person I make of myself; my determinacy depends on my own free decision, which follows from the task of limiting oneself.} But who ought I to be? {This lies in my individuality.} Individuality is not determined by any being, it is determined by pure law: What I should become is something that is prescribed for all time. {This, as was already said above, is the ethical law.}[28]

Several objections could be raised against my association of the Categorical Imperative, intellectual intuition, and the pure will. First, the *Rechtslehre* includes an a priori theoretical deduction of society as a condition for the possibility of consciousness. Second, in the *Rechtslehre* the voluntary act of self-determination, which determines the pure will as individuality, seems to be a merely prudential act of self-determination, whereby the empirical individual limits its will in face of the *Aufforderung* because it recognizes that preserving its liberty to pursue its own interests depends on doing so. Third, the pure will fulfills a purely theoretical role as a "scientific hypothesis" in the *Wissenschaftslehre nova methodo*. Despite these serious criticisms, I believe my account of intellectual intuition is tenable if we attend carefully to the distinctions between the transcendental and empirical standpoints, the sensible and moral world orders, and the various parts of the *Wissenschaftslehre*.

From a morally neutral, empirical perspective, it is obvious that no individual can exercise its freedom and all individual goals are foiled without a mutually deferential limitation of individual willing. As empirical beings, it behooves us to defer to the wills of others in order to accomplish our goals and to receive an acknowledgment of our freedom. Nonetheless, the fact that prudence decrees a mutually deferential limitation of willing does not imply that Fichte referred to nothing more than a prudential self-limitation in his discussion of the original determination of the pure will.[29]

From a morally neutral, transcendental perspective, it is likewise obvious that the *nova methodo* employs the *Aufforderung* as a *qualitas occulta*. The fact, however, that the theoretical account of consciousness employs the summons as a "scientific" hypothesis does not negate Fichte's claim in the *nova methodo* that the Categorical Imperative is more than a practical principle and that the limitation of individuality is more than a theoretical principle. In section 18 of the *nova methodo*, Fichte summarizes the conclusions of his previous arguments.

> {From what has been said so far,} it must now be clear that:
>
> {A} No self-consciousness is possible apart from a consciousness of individuality.
>
> (B)} The "ought" or the categorical imperative, is also a theoretical principle.
>
> What forces us to assume the existence of other beings outside ourselves? {Whenever we think of something determinate we must also think of something determinable. We are thereby driven to the assumption that there is a world of other rational beings outside of ourselves. "I am a person." This means I am limited. This limitation is a duty, and individuality consists in being limited in consequence of a duty.[30]

If the determination of the pure will were simply prudentially motivated, then the deduction of the pure will in the *nova methodo* would imply that contingency and empirical desire ground consciousness. Likewise, if the pure will were nothing more than a "scientific" hypothesis, then the *Wissenschaftslehre* would rest on an arbitrary foundation. Reconciling these claims with Fichte's repeated assertions that the *Wissenschaftslehre* accords with dutiful acting would prove an imposing, and I believe, impossible task, thus rendering Fichte's explanation of how philosophical first principles are determined meaningless.[31] If prudential willing alone is fundamental to moral willing, then a morality of duty is an illusion, a futile wish. If the *Wissenschaftslehre* rests on some hypothetical principle that we are permitted to deny, then any attempt to formulate a *Wissenschaftslehre* is equally futile. In some sense, the capacity for dutiful acting, and the certainty of a principle one is obliged to accept, must be essential *primordial* aspects of the *Wissenschaftslehre*, or freedom and certainty simply do not arise in that system.

The *Aufforderung* seems to express an ethical imperative, because Fichte claims we feel it in empirical experience as an immediate awareness of an absolute "ought." It seems unlikely that Fichte would refer to a merely hypothetical imperative as an absolute *Sollen*, the same word used in the *Sittenlehre* to refer to the feeling accompanying ethical awareness.[32] Moreover, it seems unlikely that Fichte would say in the *Sittenlehre* that the *Aufforderung* expresses an absolute prohibition *(Verbot)*—namely, that it prohibits absolutely the use of others as mere means to accomplish our own ends, if it did not function as a practical principle.[33] Finally, a hypothetical imperative could not supply an original goal-concept entailing an act of willing. The need to introduce the pure will arises because willing requires a goal-concept and the latter presupposes cognition of an object, which in turn requires an act of willing. For this reason, it becomes necessary to postulate a kind of willing that contains its own object in order to explain empirical consciousness. A hypothetical imperative, in as much as it always seeks some empirical object, cannot satisfy this requirement.[34] The fact that some parts of the *Wissenschaftslehre* employ the determination of the pure will through the *Aufforderung* as something other than an expression of the supreme principle of morality does not imply that the pure will is *nothing more* than a theoretical principle or that the *Aufforderung* expresses *nothing more* than a hypothetical imperative.[35]

The pure will and the *Aufforderung* can be understood from the standpoint of philosophy or the standpoint of life.[36] At the philosophical standpoint, the philosopher assumes a purely theoretical perspective and infers the pure will according to the law of thinking that demands something determinable to be thought in opposition to what is determinate. At the standpoint of life, the empirical subject discovers itself as a divided being, insofar as it participates in the sensible world order and in the supersensible (or moral) world order; hence, the *Aufforderung* is subject to a dual interpretation within ordinary consciousness. For the moral subject, the *Aufforderung* expresses the Categorical Imperative whereas it appeals to the prudent self-interest of the sensible subject.

The transcendental philosopher introduces the pure will as a hypothesis in order to provide a theoretical account of consciousness. Viewing the pure will in this manner involves nothing specifically ethical. When employed in this capacity, the pure will represents neither a belief nor a practical imperative. The pure will, *qua* scientific hypothesis, is simply an explanatory concept that satisfies the laws of thinking and provides the basis for a philosophical theory of empirical consciousness.

For the empirical subject, *qua* naturally determined member of the sensible world order, the demand to limit individual willing is a hypothetical imperative, that is, a necessary, albeit prudentially motivated, condition for the pursuit of individual ends and, ultimately, happiness itself. This hypothetical imperative provides incentive for delineating a sphere of juridical obligations and thus for formulating a philosophical theory of right, a *Rechtslehre* that takes the summons as its first principle.

For the empirical subject, *qua* member of the moral world order, the *Aufforderung* expresses a categorical demand and a necessary condition for the realization of the "vocation of man" or the goal of reason in general. As the Categorical Imperative, it derives from no empirical observation *or* philosophical argument; it is a belief made evident through a real intellectual intuition and thus a mode of nonsensible immediate awareness. From the Categorical Imperative we can derive a sphere of duty in general; it provides the basis for a *Sittenlehre* or theory of ethics.[37]

Fichte refers to the dual role of the pure will in experience when he says of the determination of the pure will: "Considered as something sensible this determinate sum of determinability will turn out to be individuality; whereas thought as something supersensible it will turn out to be the ethical law!"[38] The *Sittenlehre* begins with what is universal in the summons, that is, with the *Aufforderung,* insofar as it is an expression of the Categorical Imperative. It does not concern itself with the individual but with reason in its individuality.[39] Ethics concludes with the idea of the world as it ought to be constructed by rational beings, that is, the goal of reason as such. Although the goal of reason is foremost in the individual consciousness insofar as the subject identifies with its moral vocation, the moral subject as an empirical individual also identifies itself as a member of a sensible world order, which is not what it ought to be.

In the sensible world, reason appears in many individuals; because conflicts can and do arise between the activities of these individuals, the unification of individual wills, which concludes the *Sittenlehre,* requires some means to ensure a restriction of individual wills. The task of the *Rechtslehre* consists in describing how to establish a juridical world, which limits individual wills, in order to accomplish the goal of reason. The *Rechtslehre* is both practical and theoretical insofar as it concerns a (juridical) world that "is brought about {by human beings through the joint efficacy of nature and reason.}"[40]

In the *Rechtslehre,* philosophy must take up the task of self-limitation expressed by the *Aufforderung,* but not insofar as the summons expresses the supreme moral principle. Although the Categorical Imperative offers the ultimate moral authorization for establishing a juridical world in order to realize the unification of individual wills as the goal of reason, the philosopher can by no means assume that every individual recognizes this practical sanction. The juridical world must arise within a sensible world of morally conscious individuals potentially, and sometimes actually, exercising their freedom in pursuit of both happiness and moral perfection in manners that often conflict, rather than in the supersensible realm of the pure moral will.

The *nova methodo* and the *Grundlage des Naturrechts* demonstrate the a priori necessity of other rational beings as a condition for the possibility of empirical consciousness, but the philosopher cannot assume that all members of the sensible world recognize or understand this theoretical necessity.[41] The *Rechtslehre* describes a postulate addressed by theory to freedom, that is, a juridical world that is the product of freedom and nature. If a theory of natural law is to obtain any real application, it must express some incentive that appeals to man as a natural being. Consequently, it is necessary to begin with a principle that all human beings, insofar as they are rational beings, but without regard for their level of moral development or philosophical understanding, can recognize, namely, the fact that the realization of individual goals and the recognition of individual wills depends on a mutual limitation of freedom.

The determination of pure will as individuality can be interpreted in three ways: (1) as a hypothesis and theoretical first principle of a general theory of consciousness; (2) as a hypothetical imperative and theoretical first principle of a theory of right; and (3) as a particular expression of the Categorical Imperative (conjoined with a real intellectual intuition of freedom) and first principle of a theory of ethics. From the perspective of the transcendental philosopher, who grasps each of these parts in relation to the entire *Wissenschaftslehre* they are not separate principles but different formulations of one principle applied to different parts of one complex philosophical system.

The transcendental philosopher, who understands both the transcendental and empirical standpoints, and who must be acquainted with his or her own divided nature at the level of ordinary consciousness in order to be a transcendental philosopher, understands all three roles of the pure will as well as the relations between the various theories based on the pure will as principle. As a hypothetical imperative, it provides an incentive to justice, which does not depend directly on any particular moral theory, but which makes the moral education of rational individuals within society possible. As a scientific hypothesis, it is not the only possible starting point for philosophy, but it is the only possible starting point that allows for a system of philosophical thinking consistent with dutiful action in Fichte's sense of the term. As real intellectual intuition, it provides an ultimate practical sanction for the claim that the *Wissenschaftslehre* describes any system of real thinking.

Notes

1. See *Wissenschaftslehre nova methodo (1796–98), Krause Transcript*, ed. E. Fuchs (Hamburg: Meiner, 1982), hereafter cited as *WLnm[K]*, p. 28; see the corresponding reference in *J. G. Fichte: Foundations of Transcendental Philosophy (Wissenschaftslehre) nova methodo (1796–1799)*, trans. D. Breazeale (Ithaca: Cornell, 1992), hereafter cited as *FTP*, p. 110. See also *J. G. Fichte Gesamtausgabe der*

Bayerischen Akademie der Wissenschaften, ed. R. Lauth, H. Jacobs, and H. Gliwitzky (Stuttgart-Bad Cannstatt: Frommann, 1964–), hereafter cited as *GA, GA* I, 4, pp. 521–23; see also the associated reference in *J. G. Fichte: Introductions to the Wissenschaftslehre and Other Writings,* ed. and trans. D. Breazeale (Indianapolis: Hackett Publishing Company, 1994), hereafter cited as *IWL,* pp. 106–8. Fichte asks one to think about oneself and attend to this very act of thinking. An attentive response yields the observation that thinking of oneself is possible only in relation to something else, and thus the act of thinking oneself always involves a wrenching of one's thought away from this other thing and toward the self. In other words, it involves a "self-reverting activity." The philosopher is fully conscious of this act, which has the *form* of an intellectual intuition. Intellectual intuition is a pure activity that the philosopher presupposes as the foundation of all consciousness but which does not appear *as such* in consciousness. Although the philosopher has no direct consciousness of this pure activity, he (or she) forms a concept of "pure I-hood," which resembles but is not identical to the act of self-reflection required to "think the concept of the I."

2. *WLnm[K],* section 1; *Wissenschaftslehre nova methodo (1796–1798) Halle Transcript,* in *GA* IV, 2 (hereafter cited as *WLnm[H]*), *WLnm[H],* section 1; *FTP,* section 1.

3. *Versuch einer neuen Darstellung der Wissenschaftslehre* (1797–1798), *GA* I, 4 (hereafter cited as *VWL*), pp. 219–20 (*IWL,* pp. 48–50). See also, *Das System der Sittenlehre* (1798), in *GA* I, 5 (hereafter cited as *SS*), *SS,* p. 60.

4. Fichte used the term "intellectual intuition" in several different senses. For a discussion of the different senses of "intellectual intuition," as the phrase is employed in the later Jena *Wissenschaftslehre,* see Daniel Breazeale, "Fichte's *nova methodo phenomenologica:* On the Methodological Role of 'Intellectual Intuition' in the Later Jena *Wissenschaftslehre," Revue International de Philosophie* [Brussels] no. 206 (1998): 587–616. Breazeale argues that Fichte employed the term "intellectual intuition" in reference to: (iA1) real intellectual intuition of freedom or intellectual intuition *qua* "fact of reason," (iA2) intellectual intuition as pure "I-hood" or "transcendental apperception," (iA3) intellectual intuition as freely produced "fact of consciousness," and (iA4) "inner intuition" as the method of philosophy. My discussion focuses on the first three forms of intellectual intuition considered in relation to the pure will and the *Aufforderung.* I do not address the fourth form. I address the relations among the first three forms of intellectual intuition. Moreover, I restrict my account of intellectual intuition, the pure will, and the *Aufforderung* to sections 13 to 18 of the *Wissenschaftslehre nova methodo.* Obviously the ultimate strength of my position depends on relating this analysis to the entire *nova methodo* as well as to the other Jena lectures and writings. Although I make no pretense to prove that some overarching conception of "The Jena *Wissenschaftslehre"* and its basic principle unifies Fichte's Jena writings, my interpretation of intellectual intuition assumes Fichte's philosophy remained more or less unified during the Jena period and implies a relationship between intellectual intuition, the pure will, and the *Aufforderung* in the lectures and writings of the later Jena period. For an example of other essays that attempt to sort out Fichte's puzzling use of the term "intellectual intuition," see Alain

Perrinjaquet, "'Wirkliche' und 'Philosophische' Anschauung: Formen der in-tellektuellen Anschauung in Fichte's *System der Sittenlehre* (1798)," *Fichte-Studien* 5 (1993): pp. 7–82; Alexis Philonenko, "Die intellektuelle Anschauung bei Fichte," in *Der tranzendentale Gedanke: Die gegenwärtige Darstellung der Philosophie Fichtes*, ed. Klaus Hammacher (Hamburg: Meiner, 1981), pp. 91–106; Jürgen Stolzenberg, *Fichtes Begriff der intellektuellen Anschauung: Die Entwicklung in den Wissenschaftslehre von 1793/94 bis 1801/02* (Stuttgart: Klett-Cotta, 1986).

5. *SS, GA* I, 5, p. 147. See also, pp. 83–86 of Perrinjaquet's "Some Remarks Concerning the Circularity of Philosophy and the Evidence of Its First Principle in the Jena *Wissenschaftslehre*,'" in *Fichte: Historical Contexts/Contemporary Controversies* (Atlantic Highlands: Humanities Press, 1994), pp. 71–95.

6. *VWL, GA* I, 4, p. 219 (*IWL*, p. 49).

7. *VWL, GA* I, 4, pp. 194–5 (*IWL*, pp. 18–20).

8. Fichte expresses this claim explicitly in the *Sittenlehre:*

Die einzige in ihrer Art, welche ursprünglich, und wirklich, ohne Freiheit der philosophischen Abstraktion, in jedem Menschen vorkommt. Die intellektuellen Anschauung, welche der Tranzendental-Philosoph jedem anmutet, der ihn verstehen soll, ist die bloße Form jener wirklichen intellektuellen Anschauung; die bloße Anschauung der inneren absoluten Spontaneität, mit Abstraktion von der Bestimmtheit derselben. Ohne die wirkliche wäre die philosophische nicht möglich; denn es wird ursprünglich nicht abstrakt, sondern bestimmt gedacht. (*SS, GA* I, 5, p. 60)

9. *WLnm[K]*, p. 28 (*FTP,* p. 110).

10. Self-reverting activity involves a movement of transition from a state of determinability to determinacy. See *WLnm[K]*, section 2, and *WLnm[H]*, section 2, *GA* IV, 2 (*FTP,* section 2). In the *nova methodo*, Fichte employs the "principle of determinability" to produce a detailed examination of the determinate and determinable aspects of the I, which is characterized in terms of its real (self-determining) and ideal (representing) activity. For the original discussion of the principle of determinability, see Solomon Maimon, *Versuch einer neuen Logik oder Theorie des Denkens* (Berlin: Ernst Felisch, 1794), pp. 310–4. For a detailed discussion of ideal and real activity in the *Wissenschaftslehre nova methodo*, see Günther Zöller's "Thinking and Willing in Fichte's Theory of Subjectivity," in *New Perspectives on Fichte*, ed. D. Breazeale and T. Rockmore (Atlantic Highlands: Humanities Press, 1996), pp. 1–17.

11. *WLnm[K]*, p. 141 (*FTP,* p. 290).

12. "The difficulty that faced us was actually this: to explain an act of willing without {presupposing} any cognition of the object {of this act—a pure act of willing—one that is present in itself—therefore something original and a condition for the possibility of all consciousness. Such an act must be possible, because this act of willing, even if it is considered only as an empirical one, already contains within itself cognition of an object.} The reason for the above mentioned difficulty lay in the fact that we considered empirical willing (i.e., the movement of transition from what was determinable to what is determinate) to be the only

kind of willing. This has now been denied; we have now postulated a kind of willing which does not presuppose cognition of an object, but which carries its object within itself and which is not based upon any act of deliberation {but which is original and is a pure act of willing—an act of willing which is determinate without any assistance from us as empirical beings.} Such a willing is a demand. All empirical willing first arises from this [pure] willing" (*WLnm[K]*, p. 143, and *WLnm[H]*, *GA* IV, 2, pp. 134–35 [*FTP*, pp. 292–93]).

13. "But how does this determinacy appear in this case? It is appropriate to talk about 'appearance' only in the context of sensible perception. How then does this determinacy appear within sensible perception? It appears there as an act of willing; according to what was said above, however, willing can be characterized as an 'ought' or as a demand. Therefore, this determinacy of the I would have to appear as a determinate, absolute ought, as a categorical demand" (*WLnm[K]*, p. 142 [*FTP*, p. 291]).

14. Freedom, which can only appear as individual empirical willing, constitutes the essence of the ethical law, the ground of consciousness and the sole point of connection between the sensible and supersensible worlds. Consequently, the ground of the *Wissenschaftslehre* in it entirety—and thus, the ultimate ground of its various parts, viz., *Rechtslehre*, *Sittenlehre*, and *Religionslehre*—must be at once a practical and theoretical principle as well as a principle capable of some sensible expression. The Categorical Imperative satisfies these criteria insofar as it serves as a practical and a theoretical principle and insofar as it obtains a sensible expression through other rational embodied beings. Many passages in the *Sittenlehre* address the role of moral freedom as a theoretical/practical principle, moral consciousness as the ground of all consciousness, and the relation between intersubjectivity, freedom, and the ethical law. For discussions of freedom and the Categorical Imperative as practical/theoretical grounding principle, see *SS*, *GA* I, 5, pp. 28, 77–78, 81–82, 94, and 161. For discussions of intersubjectivity, freedom, and the ethical law, see *SS*, *GA* I, 5, pp. 199–227, 233, 248, 251f., 260, 266, 269, and 274.

15. *WLnm[K]*, p. 144, and *WLnm[H]*, *GA* IV, 2, pp. 135–36 (*FTP*, pp. 293–94).

16. "Since this act of thinking is a necessary one, {and since everything that is necessary is grounded in a feeling,} the mediating link between it and willing must be supplied by a feeling of some sort. {Consequently, some feeling must lie between this categorical demand and this act of thinking.} What kind of feeling can this be? A feeling is a limitation of striving; accordingly, striving must extend beyond the sphere of striving that is originally determined by pure willing, and the limitation of striving by an act of pure willing would produce a feeling of prohibition, of not being permitted to go beyond this sphere, a feeling of being obliged {to remain} within this sphere of the 'ought' " (*WLnm[K]*, pp. 142–43, and *WLnm[H]*, *GA* IV, 2, p. 134 [*FTP*, p. 292]).

17. This passage reads in full:

> The empirical will is derived from the pure will, and all other objects are derived from the object of the pure will. Any time we attempt to explain consciousness,

we have to assume something that is first and original. This was the case in our previous account of feeling, and it is also the case in our present account of willing: {We have to assume an original act of willing, which is simply what it is}. Every act of thinking, every act of representing, lies between and mediates original willing and limitation through feeling. We are able to observe the {modifications of the} ideal activity, because ideal activity is the only thing we are able to intuit or grasp {and from this there arise the various states of consciousness, as well as what is sensible.} (*WLnm[K]*, p. 143, and *WLnm[H]*, *GA* IV, 2, p. 135 [*FTP*, p. 293])

Note also Fichte's claim: "Being and willing are the same thing merely viewed from two different sides." The sensible and the supersensible represent two reciprocal aspects of empirical willing. "I will": this statement expresses the supersensible aspect of willing, namely the thought of my own activity of self-determination. But I am never aware of myself as pure willing, i.e., willing "in itself" or "as such." I always will some specific determination—if only some specific determination of my own body—within the sensible world. "I will X." This expresses the sensible aspect of willing through which willing is completely concentrated on some determinate object within the determinable sensible realm. In this case my willing is directed at something external to me. *WLnm[K]*, p. 159, and *WLnm[H]*, *GA* IV, 2, p. 153 (*FTP*, pp. 318–9).

18. *WLnm[K]*, p. 144, and *WLnm[H]*, *GA* IV, 2, p. 136 (*FTP*, p. 294).

19. *WLnm[K]*, p. 146, and *WLnm[H]*, *GA* IV, 2, p. 138 (*FTP*, p. 297). Note that Fichte here refers to Immanuel Kant's *Second Critique*. Fichte claims that the thought of what is determinable in relation to the "ought" is contained in Kant's practical postulate: "I ought to do something; therefor what I ought to do must be possible." See *Critique of Practical Reason*, Pt. I, Bk. I, Chap. 1, section 6.

20. The I appears to itself as possessing a particular *Bestimmung*, i.e., as determined to determine itself. This original determination constitutes the essential goal, nature, or vocation of human beings as such and of each empirical individual as a sensible instantiation of reason in the world. In Fichte's words:

> How is the movement of transition of my pure willing from its determinability to determinacy related {to consciousness}? This is a transition that occurs without any help from us, for we ourselves first come into being by means of our movement. (I appear to myself as determined to determine myself in one way or another.) The Idea that we ourselves first originate within time is contained in this. The I here appears to itself as determined to determine itself in just the way it does determine itself, and the movement of transition is here thought of not as free, but rather as necessary. It is something discovered. This determinacy, which constitutes my basic character, consists in the fact that I am determined to determine myself in a certain way; it assigns me an "ought." Man's determinate nature or "vocation" [*Die Bestimmung des Menschen*] is not something he gives to himself; instead, it is that through which a human being is a human being. (*WLnm[K]*, p. 148, and *WLnm[H]*, *GA* IV, 2, p. 140 [*FTP*, p. 300])

21. *WLnm[K]*, p. 149, and *WLnm[H]*, *GA* IV, 2, p. 140 (*FTP*, p. 301).

22. "But [even] as a spiritual being, the I is still a determinate one, and what is determinable thereto [i.e., what becomes determined as this determinate spiritual being] must also be purely spiritual: a spiritual mass {or sphere}. (*Sit venia verbo*, this 'spiritual mass' will later reveal itself to be the realm of rational beings. The I is a determinate portion of this mass; as we shall see below, what is spiritual is divisible.) The I is reason—determinate reason. What is determinable in this case is reason as a whole (my generic essence). I myself am what is determinate {(through a feeling), as what is *posited in opposition* to this sphere} namely, I as an individual (for I posit a sphere of rational beings in opposition to myself)" (*WLnm[K]*, p. 149, and *WLnm[H], GA* IV, 2, p. 149 [*FTP*, pp. 301–2]).

23. For a more detailed discussion of Fichte's explanation of the body as an articulated instrument of the will, see *WLnm[K]*, pp. 159–61, and *WLnm[H], GA* IV, 2, pp. 153–57 (*FTP*, pp. 318–22).

24. *Ueber den Grund unseres Glaubens an eine göttliche Weltregierung* (1798), *GA* I, 5, p. 353, and *Aus einem Privatschreiben* (1800), *GA* I, 6, pp. 379–81.

25. Here again, we see a parallel between the real intellectual intuition and the philosophical concept of I-hood. In the *Grundlage*, Fichte asserts that the determinate self-positing activity underpinning all consciousness presupposes a determining impulse, which Fichte characterizes in terms of a sensible *Anstoß* or "check." For a more detailed discussion of Fichte's doctrine of the *Anstoß*, see Daniel Breazeale, "Check or Checkmate? On the Finitude of the Fichtean Self," in *The Modern Subject: Conceptions of Self in Classical German Philosophy*, ed. K. Ameriks and D. Sturma (Albany: SUNY Press, 1996), pp. 87–114.

26. "What does a 'summons to freedom' mean? This is a concept that would produce an action on the part of a free being—if, that is, such a concept were endowed with causal power. This concept is posited in relation to the action of a free being; i.e., they are posited in a relationship of dependence, in such a way that the concept is supposed to occasion the action {albeit without any compulsion, for then freedom would be sacrificed—and this is why we said 'if such a concept were endowed with causal power'}. Such an action, however, is [only] possible, and therefore, we have postulated it only hypothetically. When one becomes aware of the existence of another individual, then this is a concept of that individual which accompanies what is summoned; it is a concept that also includes the latter" (*WLnm[K]*, p. 179, and *WLnm[H], GA* IV, 2, p. 178 [*FTP*, p. 355]).

See also *Grundlage des Naturrechts nach Principien der Wissenschaftslehre* (1796), sections 1–3, in *GA* I, 3.

27. See pp. 145–46 of Robert William's "The Other in Fichte's Thought," in *Historical Contexts/Contemporary Controversies*, pp. 142–57. See also *SS, GA* I, 5, pp. 200–2.

28. *WLnm [K]*, p. 169, and *WLnm[H], GA* IV, 2, pp. 167–8 (*FTP*, pp. 337–8).

29. *SS, GA* I, 5, pp. 200–1.

30. *WLnm [K]*, p. 220, and *WLnm[H], GA* IV, 2, pp. 240–41 (*FTP*, p. 437). See also *SS, GA* I, 5, pp. 77–8; *WLnm [K]*, p. 169; and *WLnm[H], GA* IV, 2, p. 168 (*FTP*, pp. 338).

31. *VWL, GA* I, 4, pp. 191–6 (*IWL*, pp. 15–20). For a thorough discussion of the manner in which the first principle of philosophy is determined, see Daniel Breazeale, "How to Make an Idealist: Fichte's 'Refutation of Dogmatism' and the Problem of the Starting Point of the *Wissenschaftslehre*," *Philosophical Forum* 19 (1987–88): pp. 97–123. See also *Appelation an das Publikum* (1799), *GA* I, 5, p. 430, and *Ueber den Grund unseres Glaubens an eine göttliche Weltregierung* (1798), *GA* I, 5, pp. 351–52 (*IWL*, pp. 147–48).

32. *SS, GA* I, 5, pp. 66–7 and 145.

33. *SS, GA* I, 5, pp. 200–1.

34. *SS, GA* I, 5, pp. 81–2.

35. "{*Synthetic thinking* is the necessary connection of all our consciousness to *one* single point.

To think Synthetically of the 'ought' with which we are presently concerned means I am supposed to derive it from and to connect it with something determinable.} I must think of myself as obliged to do something; but, just as surely as I have to think of myself in this way, I must also think of something determinable. This [connection between the thought of the 'ought' and what is determinable] is synthetic. Moreover, the scope of Kant's practical postulate is too narrow, for he limits it entirely to belief in God and immortality; but we will see that consciousness in its entirety is included within this postulate. At the time he was writing the *Critique of Pure Reason*, Kant had not yet worked out all of this out with complete clarity. The first *Critique* is concerned only with sensible, objective thinking, and the I appears there not [as it is] for itself, but only as an accident. In the *Critique of Judgment* and the *Critique of Practical Reason*, however, the I is presented [as it is] for itself" (*WLnm[K]*, pp. 146–7, and *WLnm[H], GA* IV, 2, p. 139 [*FTP*, p. 298]).

36. See *GA* III, 3, pp. 103–86, and *Fichte: Early Philosophical Writings*, ed. and trans. D. Breazeale (Ithaca: Cornell, 1988), pp. 432–37. For a detailed discussion of the standpoint of philosophy and the standpoint of life, see also Breazeale, "The 'Standpoint of Life' and the 'Standpoint of Philosophy' in the Context of the 'Jena *Wissenschaftslehre*,'" cited above.

37. A moral theory of this sort might also be derived independently of any particular account of consciousness or theory of natural law. That is to say, one could accept this system of duties without understanding its metaphysical assumptions and without adopting any particular political theory. The possibility that this theory might also be part of a larger system, entailing its own particular metaphysics and *Rechtslehre*, would be beside the point for the individual moral agent.

38. *WLnm[K]*, p. 140 (*FTP*, p. 287).

39. *WLnm[K]*, p. 242 (*FTP*, p. 470).

40. *WLnm[K]*, p. 242, and *WLnm[H], GA* IV, 2, p. 264 (*FTP*, p. 471).

41. *WLnm[K]*, sections 16–18, and *WLnm[H]*, sections 16–18, *GA* IV, 2 (*FTP*, sections 16–18). See also *Grundlage des Naturrechts nach Principien der Wissenschaftslehre* (1796), sections 1–3, *GA* I, 3.

PART III

ESSAYS ON THE *SYSTEM OF ETHICAL THEORY, 1798*

Fichte's Reformulation of the Categorical Imperative in the *Wissenschaftslehre nova methodo* and *Das System der Sittenlehre*

Arnold Farr

Introduction

Consciousness reflects its own anxiety of possible nonbeing by a gesture of power. . . . This initial demand which considers itself a cry of victory governs all the ideal derivations which claim to attest the fecundity of consciousness. If I posit myself, I posit also my limits and my contingence at the same time as the basic determinations of life."[1] In *Freedom and Nature,* Paul Ricoeur suggests that we reread Fichte in reference to the above passage. Although Fichte is mentioned only once in Ricoeur's text, I think that it is of great significance that a contemporary philosopher of Ricoeur's status should suggest that we reread Fichte in light of his own philosophy of the will. Both Ricoeur and Fichte offer an analysis of a fundamental binary opposition or original duplicity[2] within the human subject that is at the same time a unity and constitutive of human consciousness as such.

The conflict between theoretical and practical reason in the Kantian philosophy merely reflects an original duplicity wherein human consciousness originates. The problem with Kant's philosophy is that while Kant attempts to show that there must be a unity of theoretical and practical reason, he never shows how human consciousness is constituted by this duality that is also a unity. Kant explains the nature of theoretical and practical reason as two distinct activities of reason, then attempts to unify them in a third principle (the principle of reflective judgment).[3]

Fichte, however, points out that Kant never explains external sensation (the objective side of consciousness).[4] Fichte will explain external sensation in terms of the structure of human consciousness, which requires an analysis of the possibility of consciousness. In his analysis of the structure of consciousness he will show that the split between theoretical and practical reason is nothing more than a distinction between two sides of one and the same consciousness.

In this essay I will show that Fichte's presentation of the Kantian philosophy requires a reformulation of the Categorical Imperative that makes it at once a theoretical as well as a practical principle, hence, demonstrating in a way that Kant never did the unity or equiprimordiality of theoretical and practical reason. In Fichte's philosophy, the Categorical Imperative has a constitutive as opposed to a merely regulative status. That is, the Categorical Imperative is not merely a principle whereby we regulate or determine our actions via the will; it is also the ground of consciousness. Not only am I made conscious of my duty through the Categorical Imperative; any consciousness whatsoever (even external sensation) has its origin in the Categorical Imperative, which lies at the origin of the formation of human consciousness.

Making Transcendental Philosophy More Transcendental

If the task of transcendental philosophy is to discover and explain the necessary conditions for any possible experience, one may say that Kant merely discovered the pieces to the puzzle while Fichte put the pieces together. That is, Fichte's more systematic presentation of the Kantian philosophy made possible a deeper analysis of the necessary conditions for human experience. Fichte, for example, shows how the tension between the laws of freedom (practical reason) and the laws of nature (theoretical reason) is necessary for the very constitution of human consciousness. Fichte does not merely explain the nature of our consciousness of duty, he explains the necessary conditions for any consciousness whatsoever (which happens to include consciousness of duty). The unity of theoretical and practical reason, that is, our consciousness of nature (external sensation) and our consciousness of duty, lies in a single unitary and originary structure that is the very ground of all human consciousness.

It is Fichte's task in *Das System der Sittenlehre* and the *Wissenschaftslehre nova methodo* to show how there is in human consciousness a unitary structure that is constituted by a necessary duality. He writes in *Das System der Sittenlehre*:

> Wie ein objectives jemals zu einem subjectiven, ein Seyn für sich zu
> einem vorgestellten werden möge—dass ich an diesem bekannteren
> Ende die Aufgabe aller Philosophie fasse—wie es, sagt ich, mit dieser
> sonderbaren Verwandlung zugehe, wird nie jemand erklaren, welcher
> nicht einen Punct findet, in welchem das objective und subjective
> überhaupt nicht geschieden, sondern ganz Eins sind.[5]

What has to be explained is two states of the I or two types of consciousness, of which neither without the other is possible. We must explain
how the I is able to make a transition from one state of consciousness
(objective consciousness) to another (subjective consciousness). How is it
that the I is at once subject and object? If this unified duality is explained,
then we have also explained consciousness in general.

In a letter to Niethammer of 6 December 1793, Fichte claims that
"Kant based the moral law upon a fact (which is correct if one understands it properly)."[6] He claims that "[t]here is only one original fact of
the human mind, a fact which is the foundation of philosophy in general,
as well as of its two branches, theoretical and practical philosophy."[7] The
task of the *Wissenschaftslehre* is to discover this original fact of the mind.
This fact cannot be a fact of consciousness, but rather, it is the ground of
all consciousness.[8] Hence, Fichte's question is "how is consciousness possible?"[9] Fichte states that "[a]ll consciousness is an immediate consciousness of our own acting, and all mediate or indirect consciousness provides
the condition for the possibility of this same acting."[10] We have not yet
answered the question "How is consciousness possible?" We have here
only a provisional answer, which needs to be made more precise. What
has to be explained is the reciprocal relation between the conditioned
and its condition. That is, "immediate consciousness must be explained
on the basis of mediate or indirect consciousness."[11] Also, immediate
consciousness is the condition for indirect or mediate consciousness.

According to Fichte, freedom is the condition for consciousness
of acting. However, "[f]reedom is possible only on the condition of a
concept of a goal; a concept of a goal is possible only on the condition
of cognition of an object; cognition of an object is possible only on the
condition of acting."[12] This passage suggests that there is a reciprocal
relationship between acting and cognition. This reciprocal relationship
indicates that the Categorical Imperative is not merely a practical principle wherein one is made conscious of one's duty, but that it is equally a
theoretical principle wherein cognition in general is grounded. This may
be explained by an analysis of the way in which the representation of an
object arises in consciousness (which is at once a theoretical and a practical issue). It is only through the activity of the I that the representation

of an object arises. This representation of an object, however, is made possible by a necessary degree of passivity in the I. That is, through its activity, the I encounters a limit, which not only restricts the I's activity, but is also an impetus for the I's activity.[13] It is through this encounter with a limiting force that the I becomes conscious of its activity; indeed, limitation is a necessary condition for consciousness of action.

Consciousness of a limitation is indeed consciousness of the representation of an object. In *Das Systen der Sittenlehre,* Fichte claims that "alles Bewusstseyn ist bedingt durch das Bewusstseyn meiner selbst."[14] My consciousness of any object is mediated or indirect consciousness, which is possible only on the condition that my activity is restricted by something. My consciousness of an object is conditioned by my perception of my activity. My perception of my activity is conditioned by the positing of a resistance as such.

How is my perception of my activity conditioned by the positing of a resistance as such? Without the positing of a resistance, no objective consciousness is possible. If no objective consciousness is possible, then consciousness of my own activity is not possible. If consciousness of my own activity is not possible, freedom is not possible to the extent that freedom requires consciousness which requires self-consciousness.

Two questions have been raised in the foregoing. First, how is something subjective or a concept determined by something objective or by being? Second, how is the objective being determined by the subjective?[15] The former is a problem for theoretical philosophy while the latter is a problem for practical philosophy. These two questions can only be answered by an examination of the dual nature of human consciousness, wherein subjectivity and objectivity are two sides of a single consciousness. With respect to the objective side of consciousness, we seek to show that there is a passivity within the I whereby the I feels itself to be affected by and even determined by something outside itself. With respect to the subjective side of consciousness we seek to show how the I is necessarily active and seeks to determine the external world, that is, it seeks to make all that is not-I conform to a concept that is produced by the I.

Through the subjective side of consciousness, the I is given a demand that everything that is not-I must conform to the will of the I. This demand presupposes the objective side of consciousness. The I must be conscious of something external to itself upon which it acts, that is, willing requires an object. But, the I is made conscious of that which it posits as external to itself only through its activity. While cognition of an object is the condition for acting, acting is the condition for cognition of an object. The I acts in order to bring about an alteration in some object that must be cognized by the I. It is only through the I's activity, however, that an object is made available.

Now this activity of the I is a free activity, which is not possible apart from the concept of a goal. Fichte claims that

> [f]reedom is a movement of transition from what is determinable to what is determinate, but [in order to accomplish such a movement of transition] I have to know what is determinate—i.e., I have to possess some concept of a goal. This, however, is possible only on the condition that there is cognition of an object of acting, and such cognition is in turn possible only if action itself occurs.[16]

What has to be explained now is the reciprocal relationship between the I's activity and its cognition, wherein each is the ground of the other. The I has within itself a drive toward absolute activity, which Fichte calls pure drive.[17] This pure drive is, however, merely the transcendental explanatory ground for something in consciousness and is itself beyond consciousness.[18] It is beyond consciousness because any object of consciousness must be a determinate object. That is, consciousness is always consciousness of something. Pure drive, insofar as it seeks to be absolutely independent, does not avail itself to consciousness. Fichte claims that "not the drive to have absolute material freedom, but, at least, the causality of that drive seems utterly cancelled."[19] That is, this freedom has no content and is merely formal. I posit myself as an I, however, only to the extent that I posit myself as causality. This contradiction is the necessary condition for self-consciousness (which is the condition for any consciousness whatsoever). The I's activity requires a unity of natural and pure drives. This is the I's original drive, which requires a unity of the pure and empirical conditions for consciousness. The I demands that it be independent of its material conditions. Nevertheless, these material conditions are necessary if the I is to exercise its freedom. But the demands of freedom require that the I strive to overcome all material limitation or influence. This demand can be given to the I only to the extent that the I finds itself originally limited.

As a result of the foregoing, the I's original state is at once determinate and determinable. It must be determinate insofar as the I exists at all. It must be determinable to the extent that the I must act efficaciously.

The Pure Will as the Categorical Imperative

In the *Wissenschaftslehre nova methodo,* Fichte claims that the pure will is the Categorical Imperative. He goes on to say, however, that the pure will will not be employed as the Categorical Imperative here, but will be employed for the purpose of explaining consciousness in general, while Kant employed it to merely explain consciousness of duty.[20] There are two questions that must be answered here. First, how is the pure will not employed as the Categorical Imperative here? Second, how is the pure will the same thing as the Categorical Imperative? The pure will is not employed as the Categorical Imperative here because it is a mere hypothesis, which does not appear in consciousness but must explain consciousness.

How is the pure will the Categorical Imperative? The pure will as the merely explanatory ground of consciousness is indeterminate. The pure will (which is supersensible) is the ground for empirical willing (which is sensible). Feeling mediates between pure will and sensible intuition. Feeling is an expression of the I's limitation, and it occurs when the I's striving encounters a limitation. That is, the I's activity is restricted; hence, empirical willing is the self-limitation of the I. Congruent with every act of self-limitation or self-determination is feeling, and vice versa. This feeling is the feeling of an "ought," which is produced by the union of will and desire. How is feeling produced by this union? Our answer must begin with an analysis of desire.

Fichte states that "[d]esire applies to all finite reason."[21] Desire presupposes a limit insofar as I can only desire that which I do not have. In this respect, desire is the impetus for all human activity. It is restricted by pure will insofar as pure willing restricts desire to a narrow sphere.[22] This sphere contains all that is permitted for the I. This is why for Kant and Fichte an "ought" implies "can." An ought arises only in the sphere of what is permitted for the I; that is, the pure will provides a sphere of possibility. In this respect, pure will is determinable and determinate. It is determinable to the extent that it is an undifferentiated mass from which something is determined. It is determinate insofar as it is an object of thought. Pure will must be thought to the extent that the I must be able to hold before itself in thought its possibilities for being from which a particular way of being is selected. The possibilities that the I holds before itself are determinate, since they are objects of thought. They are determinable because they are not yet empirically determined: they have not yet been instantiated in an empirical manifold.

The pure will demands that the I select from a field of possibility a particular way of being. The I "ought" to bring into being a particular manifold. A possibility for being becomes actual by an act of empirical willing. Something determinable must become something determinate. This transition from that which is determinable to that which is determinate must be mediately an act of empirical willing. Fichte claims, however, that "pure will can be thought only as a movement of transition from what is determinable to what is determinate."[23] This transition, the real act of wrenching something out of an undifferentiated mass, is an act of empirical willing. When I think about this act, I realize that I am already something determinate. Through empirical willing, I merely make a transition from one determinacy to another. This movement itself, however, is possible only to the extent that every point of determinacy is already situated within a field of determinability wherein a movement of transition must occur. This *movement* occurring between two determinate points within a field of determinability is pure willing. The selection of a point toward which this movement is directed is empirical willing. Pure willing is the pure form of willing, while empirical willing is a particular act of willing whereby an object is determined. The I knows itself as something determinate and as something determinable, hence, Fichte maintains that willing is also being and is, therefore, sensible. How do we make the transition from pure willing to empirical willing? It is by means of thinking that the pure will becomes sensible.

We have seen that what is original and absolute in the I is pure willing. Pure willing has a dual nature, however, since it contains both willing and limitation. In this respect, it is determined and is the Categorical Imperative. That is, the I must make what is supersensible in pure willing sensible through empirical willing. The pure will is the concept of a goal that is possible only by means of objective cognition.[24] This objective cognition is the result of reflection, which also reveals to the I its original limitation (which is the body), the object of the I's willing. That is, the body is the instrument whereby the will expresses itself. The demand that I do something is the demand that I do something with my body. Only through the body does the will become actual. The facticity of the I is the body, which as finite can only occupy one point in space at a time, but through willing is moved from one point in space to another through time.

This reflection whereby the I becomes aware of its original limitation is a necessary component of willing insofar as through reflection the I makes an inner copy of its outer limitation and cognizes itself in its determinacy. This ideal activity has a dual function. First, ideal activity (reflection) makes a copy of the I's outer limitation. The I, therefore, sees itself as something finite, determinate, as being. Second, ideal activity holds before the I something that it is not, but ought to be. The I has before it two images of itself, that which it is and that which it ought to be. The first image is empirically determined, while the latter is empirically indeterminate. The task of the I is to make the empirically indeterminate image of itself determinate. This is an impossible task due to the fact that empirically indeterminate image of the I is the I as absolute I, that is, free of material restrictions. Such an I is unthinkable.

Ultimately, the I is an infinite striving to overcome limitations that can never be completely overcome. It can only overcome particular limitations by wrenching itself away from one set of limitations and throwing itself into another. The perpetual act of self-determination is the original fact of the mind that Fichte mentioned in his letter to Niethammer. The I is not simply a fact but is an act. It is an act that perpetually alters its facticity, while it is at all times bound by facticity. This act requires cognition of the I's condition and cognition of an "ought" that the I strives to bring into existence. Hence, the categorical demand given to the I by itself is not only the ground of our consciousness of duty, but it is also the ground of our consciousness of our condition (which is the field or empirical manifold wherein our duty is exercised). An "ought" is always accompanied by consciousness of the conditions wherein this "ought" is to be actualized.

Freedom and Facticity

Although Kant knew that the application of the Categorical Imperative required empirical conditions, he did not show how empirical conditions are necessary for the formulation of the Categorical Imperative. For Kant, the Categorical Imperative is a pure formal practical principle whereby maxims that are to be employed in the sensible world get determined. For Fichte, the sensible world is not merely the domain where maxims that are determined by the Categorical Imperative are employed; it is a necessary condition for the formulation of the Categorical Imperative. That is, the pure will is necessarily limited to the extent that it is the pure will of a determinate being. The I is not merely a being but is an act that is also a being.[25] The I is simultaneously an act and a fact (Tathandlung). As a fact, the I is being. In Sartrean terms, the I has a certain "facticity."[26] The facticity of the I is discovered through an act of reflection wherein even the pure will is immured in facticity, since through pure willing I must make a transition from one form of facticity to another. The facticity of the I is nothing more than the I's original limitation (the being of the I). For the I to exist as an act, it is required that the I exist also as a fact. In every act of the I there is something determinate that acts. At all times the I is something that is determinable and determinate.

Self-determination is in essence the actual act of wrenching something determinate from a determinable manifold. Consciousness of this
act is consciousness not only of this particular act, but also of my ability
to perform such an act (that is, my freedom). Hence, in the act of self-
determination, willing and cognition form an absolute unity. Through
willing I act, but this act requires knowledge or cognition of my possibilities for acting.

From the beginning we have been concerned with the unity of
consciousness with respect to the conflicting activities within the I. Fichte
claims to show how consciousness must necessarily arise for an empirical
I. Consciousness must originate in willing and cognition simultaneously.
Fichte writes, "To be sure, consciousness arises from both, but the cognition from which it arises is a summons to engage in free activity, i.e., a
cognizance of the fact that a goal is given to us. At the same moment, an
act of willing is {immediately} connected with this cognition. Willing and
cognizing are united in this X."[27]

Consciousness is the unity of willing and cognition. My act of willing
is inseparable from my cognition of my condition. As a matter of fact,
willing is not possible without cognition, and vice versa. Willing is at once
act and thought. It is cognition of a goal that is given to me, cognition
of my power to actualize this goal, and the actual act of giving being to
the concept of a goal. This entire act of willing requires that I freely limit
myself.

I find myself, however, as something already determinate. Part of
my original determinacy is the demand that I determine myself. This
merely means that initially I find myself at a particular starting point in
an empirical manifold. Entailed in this starting point is the demand that
I initiate a new series. We may think of this in Heideggarian terms. The I
finds itself thrown into the world.[28] This notion may be amended so that
it takes on a more Fichtean meaning. The I does not merely find itself
thrown into the world, but it finds itself to be the one who is doing the
throwing. To merely say that the I finds itself thrown into the world is to
strip the I of its power over its own existence. In this event, the threat of
nonbeing looms large. It is through the "gesture of power" that Ricoeur
mentions that the I overcomes this threat. The I is thrown because it
throws itself. It wrenches something from a determinable manifold. This
is disclosed to the I in every moment of self-consciousness.

Again, who is this I that determines itself? We can only answer this
question by listing a set of determinations that occur simultaneously with
the power for further self-determination. The "I am this" with which one
may respond to this question also contains an "I am not that." The "I am

this" is itself riddled with numerous complexities. It has two distinct but unified sides. Contained in the "I am this" is the I that I am (a fact) and the I that I ought to be (the concept of a goal). This "ought" is contained in the "I am this" because I am also an act whereby this "ought" actually comes into being. It is necessary that we make a distinction between two possible uses of "ought" in the same manner that Fichte made a distinction between willing and wishing.[29] It is common to hear people speak of what they ought to do but to then acknowledge that they will fail to do it: for example, "I ought to go to the store today but I will wait until tomorrow." This is the weak sense of "ought."[30] It is of no real moral consequence whether I go to the store today or tomorrow. This type of "ought" does not entail any element of logical or moral necessity. The strong sense of "ought" is of moral consequence. How I handle my freedom or power of self-determination does make a difference in the world. Further, the strong sense of "ought" does not pertain to an act that can be delayed. I can put off going to the store but I cannot postpone my responsibility for self-determination.

The strong sense of "ought" is embedded in a summons. My awareness of the summons is the awareness that I ought to determine myself. This summons to freely determine myself is given to me along with a realm of determinability, that is, the realm of rational beings. Here we may return to our previous discussion about cognition and willing. Willing requires the presence of something determinable from which it makes something determinate. In this respect willing requires cognition insofar as the I cognizes something determinable.[31] But what is determinable becomes possible only by means of what is determinate. What is determinable and determinate are coterminous, as are willing and cognition. I cognize something determinable but something determinate is already contained within what is determinable. Cognition of something determinate is not possible apart from cognition of something determinable, however. The concept of individuality already presupposes something outside of or other than the individual. It presupposes a realm of individuals. Individuality is the instantiation of something determinate within an determinable realm. I am an individual only because I am "this" and not "that." The "that" which I am not is the field of determinability from which my "this" is wrenched. In this context, I am not "that" (an individual other than myself), nor am I the total realm of rational beings. This is nothing more than the I's recognition of its finitude (which is necessary if there is to be any consciousness of an "ought"). But, in a way, I am "that." I am a rational being. My knowledge of myself as a rational being is conditioned by my being cognizant of rational beings other than myself. This will be discussed in a later section.

The Categorical Imperative and the Originary Structure of Consciousness

The task of the *Wissenschaftslehre* is to explain the objective validity of representations.[32] We must begin by examining representations as they are found in consciousness. Hence, the objective validity of representations must be explained in terms of the laws of consciousness. Fichte advances beyond Kant to the extent that the *Wissenschaftslehre* explains how the coexistence of two distinct forms of representations (our feeling of necessity and our feeling of freedom) lie in a unitary structure wherein neither representation is possible without the other. This unitary structure (an act) is the ground of all consciousness. The concept of an "ought" implies limitations. Consciousness of limitations (object consciousness) requires an act whereby the acting agent is already in the process of extending these limitations. Hence, my consciousness of my duty is my awareness that I am this but I ought to be that.

In Kant's philosophy, the Categorical Imperative seems to be an auxiliary principle to the extent that it is absolutely necessary for morality but does not seem to be necessary for the very being of the I. For Fichte, the very existence of the I is unthinkable apart from an originary act wherein consciousness of duty is produced, but not merely produced, for this originary act entails the concept of a goal (an ought). This originary act is indeed an attempt to transform an "is" into an "ought" and an "ought" into an "is." The I must posit itself and all that is required for self-positing. In a passage that resonates with the quote from Ricoeur earlier, Fichte states: "The essence of reason consists in my positing myself; but I cannot do this without positing a world in opposition to myself, and indeed, a quite specific world."[33] Hence, consciousness harbors a duality that it must strive to overcome, but, nevertheless, cannot overcome if it is to have *Wirklichkeit*.[34] Our consciousness of possible nonbeing mentioned by Ricoeur is a threat that the I encounters from two sides. The I is threatened by nonbeing as long as it accepts something else as the source of its being. Therefore, the I seeks to posit itself absolutely. If it were possible for the I to posit itself absolutely, however, the threat of nonbeing would threaten the I from another side. Absolute positing means that there is nothing posited over against the I. If there is nothing posited over against the I, there is no space that cannot be penetrated by the I, nor is there anything upon which the I acts. The I in such a situation is indeed infinite, since it encounters no boundaries. This is problematic to the extent that if this situation occurs, the I loses its individuality; it can no longer be this or that. Hence, it becomes nothing. Further, without limitation, there is no self-consciousness; if there is no self-consciousness, there is no consciousness.

Kant seemed to be aware of this to the extent that he knew that the Categorical Imperative applied only to finite rational beings.[35] He never fully explained this, however. Further, Kant never showed how the unity of theoretical and practical reason must lie in the Categorical Imperative itself, and how the unity of theoretical and practical reason in the Categorical Imperative is the necessary condition for any consciousness whatsoever. One may retort that "if the Categorical Imperative is the ground for any consciousness whatsoever, is it not the case that I have argued not for the unity of theoretical and practical reason in Fichte's philosophy but for the primacy of practical reason, which suggests that there is a disunity?"

While Fichte does at times argue for the primacy of practical reason, it is important that one notice the context and the issues at hand where such arguments are made. This has already been explained in "The Theory of Practice and the Practice of Theory: Fichte and the Primacy of Practical Reason," by Daniel Breazeale. At the level of consciousness, in general, theoretical and practical reason are equiprimordial. Practical reason cannot be primary, because if we attempt to explain what we mean by practical reason, we must include in our explanation the concept of limitation. Practical and theoretical reason are so intertwined that the activity of one presupposes the activity of the other. This is Fichte's "law of reflective opposition."[36] To every activity, there must be posited simultaneously a passivity. Consciousness of what I ought to be is possible only on condition of consciousness of what I am. To posit myself as free is, indeed, to posit myself as limited. In the act of self-positing, form and content are inseparable. Hence, while the Categorical Imperative is indeed a formal principle, consciousness of this principle is not possible unless there is content, the positing of a determinate being and its task to fill out infinity: this is the Categorical Imperative.

The Task of Reason in the Individual

Once we have characterized the nature of the human I as striving to overcome all limitation, it may still not be clear how the moral law is manifest in the individual, particularly with respect to the relationship between the individual and others. It is in our attempt to address this problem that the merit of Fichte's treatment of the Categorical Imperative is disclosed. What is missing in the description of the striving of the I to overcome the limitations of an empirical manifold is the account of the I's self-limitation for the sake of the moral law. In "Some Lectures concerning the Scholar's Vocation," Fichte writes, "Man's final end is to subordinate to himself all that is irrational, to master it freely and according to his own laws."[37] This passage is echoed in the *Sittenlehre*.

> Die Selbstständigkeit, unser letztes Ziel, besteht, wie oft erinnert worden, darin, dass alles abhängig ist von mir, und ich nicht abhangig von irgend etwas; dass in meiner ganzen Sinnenwelt geschieht, was ich will, schlecthin und bloss dadurch, dass ich es will, gleichwie es in meinen Leibe, dem Anfangspuncte meiner absoluten Causalität, geschiet. Die Welt muss mir werden, was mir mein Leib ist.[38]

In both texts, Fichte states that such absolute self-sufficiency is not possible; it is, nevertheless, something that we must strive for and approximate. To subordinate the irrational to the rational is the supreme task of reason. Fichte (like Kant) focuses on reason in general, however. That is, no individual human I can represent the full embodiment of reason. When Fichte says that the I must be in harmony with itself, he is not just speaking of an individual I; he means that reason in all of its particular embodiments must be in harmony with itself. Therefore, the harmony of all rational beings is a condition of morality.

What we are approaching here is Fichte's theory of intersubjectivity and individuality. While Kant's philosophy may have contained a tacit theory of intersubjectivity, it was never worked out in the kind of detail that we get in Fichte. In Kant's formulation of the Categorical Imperative, it is assumed that there are rational beings other than myself. Fichte, however, attempts to show how the I's consciousness of itself as an individual presupposes an intuition of the realm of rational beings. The deduction of individuality is based on a feeling of limitation, or, more precisely, a demand that the I must limit itself. We have heretofore discussed limitation in terms of an object or objective consciousness as it is determined by its encounter with nature. For Fichte, however, the I is limited from two sides.[39] We have seen how the Categorical Imperative must be a theoretical as well as practical principle. We have not, however, discussed Fichte's particular formulation of the Categorical Imperative. It is on the basis of the equiprimordiality of theoretical and practical reason and the dual limitation of the I that Fichte reformulates the Categorical Imperative.

In the *Sittenlehre* and in the *Wissenschaftslehre nova methodo,* Fichte deduces both sides of the I's limitation and shows their unity. In this dual limitation lies the division between and the unity of theoretical and practical reason. Fichte writes:

Das Ich muss sich selbst als Ich finden, war die Behauptung, von welcher die soeben vollendete Betrachtung ausging. Von ebenderselben geht die gegenwartige aus; nur mit dem Unterschiede, dass dort auf das Leiden des Ich in jener Reflexion auf sich selbst, auf das Object der Reflexion, hier auf die Thätigkeit desselben, auf das subjective in der Reflexion, gesehen wird. Ein Ich muss Reflexionsvermögen haben, um das gegebene innerlich durch Freiheit nachzubilden. Wir haben die Thätigkeit des Ich in dieser Rücksicht ideale Thatigkeit genannt. Dass dadurch die Ichheit bedingt ist, ist ohne weiteres klar. Ein Ich ist nothwendig Intelligenz.[40]

Here we have ascended to one of the most difficult and important features of the later *Jena Wissenschaftslehre*. The passage above may be better understood in terms of the method that Fichte employs in the *Wissenschaftslehre nova methodo*. Fichte claims that in sections one through twelve, the method employed is an ascending method. In the middle of section thirteen he begins his employment of a descending method. With respect to this change in method he writes:

> Hitherto we have employed the word "I" to designate self-reverting activity; this will no longer suffice, however, for it serves only to distinguish rational beings from other, irrational objects. (Moreover, as we will see later, self-reverting activity can be ascribed to the organic products of nature.) Hence, [in order to obtain an adequate concept of the I] something else must be added: the thought of the self-reverting activity must be connected with this self-reverting activity.[41]

In the first sections of the *Sittenlehre* and the *Wissenschaftslehre nova methodo,* Fichte deduces the necessary conditions for the self-reverting activity of the I. That is, he deduces the conditions for self-consciousness or the feeling of limitation. Through self-reverting activity the I becomes conscious of its limitations or its passivity. The I, however, is also conscious of this self-reverting activity, and as such it is conscious of its freedom to engage in self-reverting activity. Hence, there arises in consciousness something that is determinate (the passivity of the I) and something determinable (the activity of the I).

If this self-reverting activity is to be thought, then it must become something determinate; that is, a transition must be made from activity to passivity. Let us recall what is going on here. Through self-reverting activity, the I becomes conscious of its itself as a finite, determinate object. The I opposes itself to a not-I, that is, other objects. The I, however, must be conscious of this activity whereby it opposes itself to other objects. To be conscious of this activity is to make it an object for consciousness;

hence, it must be determinate, limited. Therefore, the I experiences a dual limitation. It is the nature of this second limitation that is to be discovered through the descending method employed in the last few sections of the *Wissenschaftslehre nova methodo.*

We have already discussed the relation between the individual and the realm of rational beings. The summons by a rational being other than myself is the demand that I freely limit myself for the sake of reason in general. Consciousness of myself as an individual member of the realm of rational beings is consciousness of a limitation with respect to my supersensible nature. With respect to the dual limitation of the I, Fichte writes:

> At one extreme there lies the world of rational beings, {from which I select myself as an individual}; at the other, the world of sensible objects, {within which I express myself as an individual. Both are instances of determinability. The former is determinable as I-hood; the latter is determinable as an object.}[42]

With this passage we are now in a position to understand Fichte's formulation of the Categorical Imperative. We have here two different concepts of the I: the I as something sensible (an object) and the I as something supersensible (a member of the realm of rational beings). As a member of the realm of rational beings, I receive the summons to determine myself as an individual. As a member of the sensible world, I am called to express my individuality in the sensible world. Hence, due to the dual nature of the I, the Categorical Imperative is a dual command.

The first command is that the I be self-sufficient. The second command is that the I not interfere with the freedom of others. Fichte states it thus:

> 1. Dass ich alles, was mich bescrankt oder, was dasselbe bedeutet, in meiner Sinnenwelt liegt, meinem absoluten Endzwecke unterwerfe; es zu einem Mittel mache, der absoluten Selbständigkeit mich zu nahern.
> 2. Dass ich einiges, was mich doch, da es in meiner Sinnenwelt liegt, bescrankt, meinem Zwecke nicht unterwerfe, sondern es lasse, wie ich es finde. Beides sine unmittlebare Gebote des Sittengesetzzes: das erste, wenn man dieses Gesetz überhaupt, das zweite, wenn man es in einer besonderen Aeusserung betrachtet.[43]

Self-sufficiency is a requirement for reason in general. The individual is only a particular manifestation of reason in the sensible world and must exercise causality in the sensible world. The apparent contradiction in the above requirement can be overcome only if we consider the goal of reason in general (which is to be self-sufficient). The goal of self-sufficiency is nothing more than the demand that reason be in harmony with itself. The Categorical Imperative, then, is a demand for harmony. Therefore, individual bearers of reason must be in harmony with each other, that is, must have the same end. Thus, for the sake of the harmony of reason, every individual member of the realm of rational beings must recognize and respect the freedom of other members of the realm of rational beings. This requires that each individual limit his or her freedom for the sake of reason in general.

Fichte's notion of individuality and intersubjectivity as essential features of the Categorical Imperative makes more comprehensible the element of universal legislation in Kant's formulation of the Categorical Imperative. The notion of universal legislation is not based on a purely abstract notion of reason as constructed by some isolated subject, but rather, it is the intersubjective ground of self-consciousness. Recognition of the universality of reason and the moral law does not preclude consciousness of myself as a concrete individual, but makes such an awareness possible. While Kant's formulation of the Categorical Imperative was merely regulative, Fichte's formulation is constitutive to the extent that the finite human I has its very constitution in its dual limitation, which is the Categorical Imperative.

Notes

1. Paul Ricoeur, *Freedom and Nature,* trans. Erazin V. Kohak (Evanston: Northwestern University Press, 1966), pp. 464–65.

2. For an analysis of this notion of "original duplicity" as developed in Fichte's philosophy, see Günter Zöller's "Original Duplicity: The Ideal and the Real in Fichte's Transcendental Theory of the Subject," in *The Modern Subject: Conceptions of the Self in Classical German Philosophy,* ed. Karl Ameriks and Dieter Sturma (Albany: State University of New York Press, 1995), pp. 115–30.

3. The principle of reflective judgment is a reflective principle whereby we think of nature as if nature acts according to some purpose. According to this principle, nature is not governed by blind mechanical forces, but, rather, nature is a teleological system. This view is an attempt to bridge the gap between the laws of nature and the laws of freedom. See Immanuel Kant, *Critique of Judgment,* trans. Werner Pluhar (Indianapolis: Hackett Publishing Company, 1987).

4. In a letter of 4 July 1797 to K. L. Reinhold, Fichte writes:

It may be that Kant did not explicitly pose for himself the question of the origin of external sensation (though I am bold enough to believe that I have detected an answer to this question, especially in the introduction to the *Critique of Judgment*). But even if he did not pose the question, he gave it no thought at all and assigned it to the realm of questions which are absolutely unanswerable. (*Fichte: Early Philosophical Writings,* trans. Daniel Breazeale [Ithaca and London: Cornell University Press, 1988], hereafter cited as *EPW,* p. 420)

5. J. G. Fichte, *Das System der Sittenlehre nach den Principien der Wissenschaftslehre,* ed. I. H. Fichte (Berlin: Verlag von Veit und Comp, 1845), hereafter cited as *SS,* p. 1.

6. *EPW,* p. 369.

7. Ibid., p. 369.

8. "Our task is to discover the primordial, absolutely unconditioned first principle of all human knowledge. This can be neither proved nor defined, if it is to be an absolutely primary principle. It is intended to express an that Act which does not and cannot appear among the empirical states of our consciousness, but rather lies at the basis of all consciousness and alone makes it possible" (J. G. Fichte, *The Science of Knowledge,* ed. and trans. Peter Heath and John Lachs. [Cambridge: Cambridge University Press, 1982], p. 93).

9. J. G. Fichte, *Foundations of Transcendental Philosophy: Wissenschaftslehre nova methodo,* ed. and trans. Daniel Breazeale (Ithaca and London: Cornell University Press, 1992), hereafter cited as *FTP,* p. 283.

10. Ibid.

11. Ibid.

12. Ibid., p. 19.

13. This point is discussed in detail in Daniel Breazeale's essay "Check or Checkmate? On the Finitude of the Fichtean Self," in *The Modern Subject: Conceptions of the Self in Classical German Philosophy,* ed. Karl Ameriks and Dieter Sturma (Albany: State University of New York Press, 1995).

14. *SS,* p. 7.

15. *SS,* pp. 8–9.

16. *FTP,* p. 285.

17. *SS,* p. 144.

18. Ibid., p. 152.

19. Ibid., pp. 148–49.

20. *FTP,* p. 293.

21. Ibid., p. 295.

22. Ibid.

23. Ibid., p. 301.

24. Ibid., p. 309.

25. In the Second Introduction to "Attempt at a New Presentation," p. 84, Fichte states:

> The essence of transcendental idealism is as such, and specifically, the essence of transcendental idealism as presented in the *Wissenschaftslehre* is that the concept of being is by no means considered to be a primary and original concept, but is treated purely as a derivative one, indeed, as a concept derived through its opposition to activity, and hence, as a merely negative concept. For the idealist, nothing is positive but freedom, and, for him, being is nothing but a negation of freedom.

In this passage Fichte continues his polemic against the dogmatism that views being as something original from which everything else is derived. This view of being takes being to be merely a fact. This much is true, however: this is not an adequate understanding of the human I and human knowledge. The I is not originally a fact only, but an act. The I is indeed originally immured by facticity; however, it is also active.

26. J. P. Sartre, *Being and Nothingness*, trans. Hazel E. Barns (University of Colorado, 1956), pp. 620–21.

27. Ibid., p. 353.

28. "Thrownness" is the term used by Heidegger to refer to *Dasein's* facticity. Heidegger, however, states: "Thrownness is neither a 'fact that is finished' nor a fact that is settled." Martin Heidegger, *Being and Time*, trans. John Macquarrie and Edward Robinson (San Francisco: Harper and Row Publishers, 1962), p. 223.

29. *FTP*, pp. 262–63. In respect to wishing, Fichte states:

To be sure, what is wished for, as well as "wishing" itself, may be taken in two different senses. On the one hand, one may understand that one is wishing for something that does not depend upon oneself, even though one still wants it; or, on the other hand, one may wish for something that does depend upon oneself, though one does not want to take the trouble to bring it into being.

Wishing is a desire (for something) which is manifest in thought only. Willing is an act, or the manifestation of desire through an act. Thought is merely a component of willing.

30. The two senses of "ought" are my own construction. The weak sense of "ought" is found in common everyday discourse. It is akin to wishing as described by Fichte. It is a desire for a particular state of affairs but no action is taken to bring this state of affairs into being, or at least there is a delay in action.

31. *FTP*, p. 347.

32. Ibid., p. 79.

33. Ibid., p. 83.

34. *Wirklichkeit* is often translated as actuality or reality. Fichte uses *Wirklichkeit* instead of *Realität* (which also is translated actuality or reality) because the latter term refers to something that is fixed or static, while *wirken* stresses the act of production or bringing about of a state of affairs. This distinction was pointed out by Daniel Breazeale in a lecture given in the fall of 1992 at the University of Kentucky.

35. Kant writes:

A perfectly good will would thus be quite as much subject to objective laws (of the good), but could not be conceived as thereby necessitated to act in conformity with the law, inasmuch as it can of itself, according to its subjective constitution, be determined only by the representation of the good. Therefore no imperatives hold for the divine will, and in general for a holy will; the *ought* is here out of place, because the *would* [*das Wollen*] is already of itself necessarily in agreement with the law. Consequently, imperatives are only formulas for expressing the relation of objective laws of willing in general to the subjective imperfection of the will of this or that rational being, e.g., the human will. (Immanuel Kant, *Grounding for the Metaphysics of Morals,* trans. James W. Ellington [Indianapolis and Cambridge: Hackett Publishing Company, 1993], p. 24)

36. *FTP,* p. 125.

37. *EPW,* p. 152.

38. *SSPW,* p. 229.

39. In his essay "Check or Checkmate? On the Finitude of the Fichtean Self," Daniel Breazeale claims that in the *Sittenlehre* and in the *Wissenschaftslehre nova methodo* two different types of *Anstoß* are present to consciousness. He describes them thus:

[T]he original "system of feeling," thanks to which the I posits for itself an external, phenomenal world and posits itself as an internally and externally limited agent therein; and an immediately felt but nonsensible "summons" to exercise one's freedom and to do so in a manner that respects and recognizes the freedom of others, thereby affirming one's place in the supersensible or noumenal realm— again, not as an "absolute I," but as a limited (in this case, to be sure, a "freely limited") individual. (Daniel Breazeale, "Check or Checkmate?" p. 97)

40. *SS,* p. 217.

41. *FTP,* p. 302.

42. Ibid., p. 446.

43. *SS,* p. 230.

The Severity of the Moral Law in Fichte's *Science of Ethics*

Lon Nease

A man being pursued by a sword-wielding maniac frantically asks you to hide him. After you do so, the maniac approaches and asks where his prey is to be found. If you tell the truth, an innocent will die. But the alternative is to lie.

This dilemma was originally intended by Benjamin Constant, a contemporary of Kant, to show the extreme nature of Kant's deontological moral theory, according to which, the critic claimed, one would be bound by duty to tell the truth in this matter, since the duty of truthfulness is unconditioned. But, Constant maintains, this conclusion is unsatisfactory, and hence, so is the idea that our duty to speak the truth is unconditionally valid. Surely, then, we are obliged in some situations to tell "necessary lies" in order to prevent such horrible things from happening. Kant, it seems, has overstated the requirements of duty and understated the importance of considering contexts.

Kant himself took up the challenge and defended truth-telling in this extreme thought experiment. He retorted that we cannot fully know the results of our actions, and that we're not morally responsible for them anyway. Moreover, if one lied to the madman, Kant claims, then one *would* then be legally responsible for whatever consequences resulted. Kant sums up his response as follows: "Every man has not only a right, but the strictest duty to truthfulness in statements which he cannot avoid, whether they do harm to himself or others. He himself, properly speaking, does not *do* harm to him who suffers thereby; but this harm is *caused* by accident."[1]

In the *Science of Ethics,* Fichte gives a different answer to the dilemma that, I believe, while showing some of the similarities of his ethics to Kant's, also shows the more radical nature of his practical philosophy. Writes Fichte:

> Firstly, why are you obliged to tell the questioner *either* the truth *or* the *lie?* Why not the third, which lies between, that you owe him no answer, that he seems to have an evil intention, that you advise him to desist from it kindly, and that, if he will not do so, you are resolved to take the part of the persecuted, and to defend him at the risk of your own life? . . . This fact alone [that you avoid such a confrontation] is enough to show that the first object of your lie was not to save the life of your neighbor, but merely to escape yourself with a whole skin.[2]

There are a number of revealing things about this response: Fichte's keen awareness of the arbitrary nature of the dilemma, his insight into the psychological motivations of people's so-called necessary lies (and of course the inevitable Fichtean *ad hominem),* and the great demands that duty places on us according to Fichte (we should risk our lives to save a stranger and the soul of a madman rather than lie once, and all for the sake of duty).

It is this last aspect of Fichte's response and of his ethics as such— that the moral law is much more exacting than is ordinarily thought by most ethical theorists—that I wish to explore in this essay. Why does Fichte hold that "everything, life, honor, and all that is dear to man, is to be sacrificed to duty,"[3] and what are the implications of this view? To address these questions, I will examine Fichte's rejection of the notion of indifferent acts, the nature of the moral law, the modes of evading its strictness, and Fichte's criticisms of less demanding moralities.

Fichte's Rejection of the Notion of Indifferent Acts

Moral philosophers have traditionally categorized acts into three classes: obligatory, permitted, and impermissible. In addition, since the 1950s, greater attention has been paid to another type of action: the supereroga-tory act (one that is above and beyond the call of duty). This way of categorizing acts supposes that some situations call for an ethical choice (whether it be to act or to leave something undone) while other situations are ethically indifferent. Deciding what color socks to put on in the morning would be a good example of a morally indifferent situation, while considering whether or not to shoplift from the local supermarket when tight on cash would be a situation requiring an ethical choice. Those seemingly rare times when a person sacrifices himself for another are examples of an individual "spending" himself "above" what would normally be expected of him, above the simply obligatory; hence, "supererogation."

While it is a matter of debate whether Kant's ethics is compatible with this classification, Fichte rejects the distinction between moral and nonmoral situations *outright*. He writes, "[T]here are no indifferent acts at all. The moral law relates to all acts."[4] And, "to do more than I am commanded to do is impossible, since duty disposes of all my strength and all my time."[5] Thus, for Fichte, there are no acts that are merely permissible or supererogatory, and, hence, all acts are either obligatory or impermissible: "[T]he moral law embraces and determines absolutely all possible acts of freedom."[6]

Fichte, however, should not be understood as excluding the possibility of there being some actions that are more praiseworthy than others, of our being able to act in ways that surprise and inspire those around us. Indeed, for Fichte, we have a *duty* to set an example for others; a duty which, moreover, cannot be fulfilled in private, since "the highest *publicity* of our acts and principles is commanded of us."[7]

Nor should Fichte's extension of duty to include *all* acts be seen as necessarily requiring people to quit their jobs, give all their money to charity, and join volunteer efforts around the world. (I believe this is the conception that comes to mind for many who dismiss ethical theories deemed "fanatical" or "overly rigorous.") For instance, although I have a duty to care for the welfare of others as I do my own, this "does not mean that I am to do nothing else than seek opportunities to save persons' health and life—unless, such is my special vocation."[8] Fichte's ethics *is* very demanding, but, it recognizes that, given the present state of affairs in the world, there is a clear need for property, a form of government, a division of labor, and the arts. As the "determined part of my world . . . subjected to my purposes and intentions,"[9] property must be established and recognized by others within a state. Without reciprocal recognition of each other's property, no rational agent is guaranteed a sphere for acting that would be free from the interference of others. For this reason, it is our duty to erect a state and to become members of it (although ideally no such state would be needed if each acted in a dutiful manner).

We must each act to realize the moral law in the sensuous world, but, according to Fichte, without separate vocations, some tasks in society would be left undone. Each of us has different skills and dispositions that are *better* suited for some tasks than for others. So, it is our duty to reflect on our abilities and to choose a vocation which would best serve to make the moral law a reality, given these abilities.

Despite his insistence on relating each act to duty, there is for Fichte, nonetheless, an important role for the fine arts. By showing nature as everywhere free, the arts "lead man back into himself. . . . They tear him loose from given nature, and place him self-sufficient upon his own feet."[10] While not itself virtue, the aesthetical sense is a "preparation for virtue, and predisposes the soul for virtue."[11]

But then if duty does *not* require a dramatic upheaval of society or of an individual's role in it, in what ways is the moral law demanding?

Although Fichte describes numerous duties in the *Science of Ethics,* including ones such as a duty to *marry* and a duty to choose a career, which would ordinarily be considered *nonmoral* matters, an accurate list of Fichtean particular, determinate duties would in fact be an *infinite* list. For Fichte, duty applies to *every* act. Accordingly, the moral law even relates to the choice of music one listens to, the bath soap one buys, the speed at which one drives, the flavor of soda pop one drinks, and so on. "The moral law leaves no playground for arbitrariness. Under its rule there are no indifferent actions at all; in each position of your life each act is either moral or immoral."[12]

Thus, in choosing a flavor of soft drink at the supermarket, I need to determine whether the act of selecting a particular brand is moral, whether the act would lie in the infinite series of acts leading to complete autonomy from nature. Of course, treating as an ethical dilemma a seemingly subjective, aesthetic matter like selecting a flavor sounds odd to say the least. But there *are* reasons why it would be an ethical situation for Fichte. For one thing, the time I spend on such a choice will no longer be available for matters that we would more readily identify as ethical (bettering myself, helping others, and so on); hence, the choice is at least *mediately* related to duty. Thus, it could be that *any* choice of soft drink is, in fact, immoral; regardless of the brand I choose, I am failing to do what is moral at that time (which might be *not* to buy a drink at all, but to save my money for my education, more essential purchases, and so on). As Fichte says, "We must take away from ourselves, retrench our own expenses, become more economical, and labor more, in order to be able to do more charity."[13] Another consideration that would make the choice ethical is if I knew, for instance, that one company was responsible for unnecessary pollution of the environment; I might use my purchase as a means to effect a change in their actions.

The lesson here is that the ethics involved in a choice will not always be immediately between the different possible options involved in the choice; but the "direction" the act takes us is an ethical matter. That is, since the moral drive is an impulse to become completely autonomous, according to Fichte, each act either furthers this cause in the best possible way, or it does not. At any given moment, Fichte claims, there is one morally correct thing to do. "For each determined man there is in each point of his life a determined duty; to do something or to leave something undone."[14] It is the responsibility of each person to reflect on his options and their relation to the moral law, and reach a point of moral certainty in regard to them; each must seek the voice of conscience to determine the proper thing to do. It is our *duty* to reflect in such a manner.

As was made evident in the case of the sword-wielding madman, Fichte's ethics draws attention to the surrounding *context* of a choice; no choice is completely innocent, completely without ethical significance. One can think there are morally indifferent acts *only* if choices are artificially abstracted from their surrounding contexts and their relation to the ideal state of humanity. It is my foremost duty, my vocation as a human, to use all my energies to make such a harmonious, autonomous society of individuals actual. And although this end is unreachable (since we are *finite* rational beings and not God), this fact in no way lessens the ethical exigency of approximating the ideal. Thus, duty demands that we constantly relate our current state to this ideal state (both, of us personally and of humanity) and judge the former's inevitable lack in a dispassionate and honest manner.

The Nature of the Moral Law

For Fichte, the moral law does not *arise* as a limit to our activities when we encounter other rational beings. It is *constitutive* of our very existence; it is a priori, not a posteriori. But it is also a *regulative* ideal for us, since, in so far as we are conscious, we cannot actually achieve the ideal. This is because all consciousness requires limitation, a check on the subject's infinite activity. The moral law stipulates an impossible condition of the finite I as identical with the infinite I: "I am I." Nonetheless, it is our *duty* to strive to achieve this ideal freedom of all rational beings from the influence of matter; since all consciousness is consciousness of this primordial "ought."

Given this relation of the moral law to our existence (that our very consciousness is made possible through an ethical demand), it follows that "there are no indifferent acts at all."[15] This is because for an act to exist *for us* (and Fichte's idealism is interested in no other kind of existence), we must be conscious of that act; and hence, that act must be subject to the moral law. Not even the chance circumstances into which we are born alter this fact. For example, if many people cannot *in fact* choose their vocation in the proper, reflective manner due to the current social conditions, we are not released from the responsibility to do so. Instead, this fact requires that we labor to make the necessary conditions for an authentic choice *actual.* Fichte writes:

> It might be objected: "But the fewest men choose their own vocation, but have it selected for them by their parents, circumstances, etc., or, if they do select them themselves, they do so in advance of the proper maturity of reason, and before they are disposed to serious meditation and susceptible to the moral law." I reply, that this should not be so, and that each one who sees that it should not be so ought to work to make it otherwise.[16]

Thus, fulfillment of our duties may first require political action, indeed, *sustained* political involvement. But this does not entail a *violent* overthrow of the current regime, "for it is not at all your moral duty to realize the good without regard to the means; the good is to be realized through morality, and otherwise it is not good."[17] So, rather than acting *immorally* to achieve a *moral* form of government, or withdrawing from society because it is unjust, "I must regard the present condition of our need-state as a means to produce the rational state, and must always act with this in view."[18] Thus, although duty for Fichte does not demand the *overturning* of society (as we saw earlier), it does call for persistent effort to improve it from *within* the system, through my chosen vocation and, if necessary, through rational persuasion of the other members of the state.

Modes of Evading the Strictness of the Moral Law

As a supplement to his account of duty in the *Science of Ethics,* Fichte also describes three ways in which we frequently *evade* the burden and pervasiveness of the moral law. Aside from offering psychological insights, an examination of these will also help us to better understand Fichte's rejection of less demanding moral theories.

According to Fichte, one's duty, as it manifests itself in conscience, has a threefold determinateness: a feeling that *this* act is my *unconditional* duty *now.* It is *this* particular act (and no other) that I *must* do (as my duty, not as a counsel of prudence) at *this* moment (it cannot be put off until later). If one does not hold the concept of duty before oneself in a fixed, determinate manner, that is, if one does not adequately reflect on one's duty, then it will appear vague and indeterminate. This is not uncommon at all, according to Fichte: "By far the fewest men seize things determinately and closely defined. Objects only float vaguely before their minds as in a dream or as covered by a fog."[19] In this condition, it is one or more of the three determinate aspects of duty that fail to manifest themselves. Rather than recognize, for instance, that *this* particular act is my duty, we might take some other act to be our duty. While this mistake is made possible by an inadequate reflection, it is one for which we are nevertheless responsible; because "if we went honestly to work, we should be sure to find [this mistake] impelled and determined through some inclination or another, since we have already lost the true thread of conscience."[20] In fact, Fichte describes this as a form of self-deception (Sartrean *bad faith*, so to speak) "against which we cannot be too much on our guard."[21]

If the concept of my duty is lacking *temporal* determinateness in my reflection, then the command will appear as requiring obedience, but not necessarily at the present time. From this comes the thought that we can follow our selfish inclination now and intend to reform in the future. Fichte describes this way of thinking as wicked, lazy, and dangerous, because "if we have once learned postponing, we are very likely to continue it."[22]

Finally, my duty will no longer appear as an unconditional command if its form *as duty* does not become determinate; instead, it will appear as "good advice which we may follow if we so wish and if it does not cost too much self-denial, but which we may also, if necessary, trim a little."[23]

Fichte's Criticisms of Less Demanding Moralities

It is this third way of evading the severity of the moral law, the denial that duty is unconditional, that Fichte claims is the most likely to lead to a failure of fulfilling one's duties. In this mode of thinking, duty does *not* require us to make significant sacrifices. According to Fichte, some people, including moral theorists, claim that they "cannot live as the moral law requires, that the punctual practice of that law is an impossibility."[24] And thus, the ethicist J. O. Urmson has argued in the twentieth century that

[basic] duties must be, in ordinary circumstances, within the capacity
of the ordinary man. It would be silly for us to say to ourselves, our
fellow men, "This and that you and everyone else must do," if the acts
in question are such that manifestly but few could bring themselves to do
them, though we may ourselves resolve to try to be of that few.[25]

The inability of most people to live up to standards that are too high
would lead to disillusionment, according to Urmson, which in turn would
lessen the urgency of the notion of duty. Thus, Urmson concludes, "the
basic moral code must not be in part too far beyond the capacity of the
ordinary men on ordinary occasions."[26] As an example of an act that must
not be *demanded* of others (as if it were a basic duty), Urmson mentions
tending to strangers in sickness. "We are not entitled to reproach those to
whom we are strangers if they do not tend us in sickness,"[27] and so, Urmson argues, this sort of act must be considered *supererogatory,* not duty.

Clearly for Fichte, there are problems in this account of morality.
Most important, Urmson has assumed that fulfillment of duty requires
achievement of our acts' intentions (anything less being a ground for guilt
and reprimand). But duty, according to Fichte, asks no more than that of
which each of us are in fact capable: *trying* with all our might. "The moral
law requires only that we should exert all our powers, should do all we
can do; and why should we not be able to do what we can do?"[28] So, those
who deny that we are capable of doing our duty are really saying that they
do not want to sacrifice some pleasure or to undergo some pain that the
moral law requires. As Fichte puts it, "the truth is not, we *cannot* do our
duty, but we *will not* do our duty. We cannot make up our will to make
those sacrifices. It is our will, not our power to do, which is at fault."[29]

If we grant that the locus of morality is in the *willing* of an act and
not in its *consequences,* Fichte has a good point. But it seems clear that
Urmson and any theorist of a consequentialist bent would not grant this.
So, this takes us to Fichte's attacks on consequentialism, that "immoral
doctrine of morals, which generally pretends good ends to excuse bad
means."[30]

In the *Science of Ethics,* Fichte offers four basic criticisms of consequentialism: (1) The choice of good works to do or to leave undone is
not our choice at all; rather it is the moral law (as manifest in our conscience) that unconditionally binds us to do certain acts.[31] (2) Since our
understanding is finite, we cannot know what consequences will bring
about the greatest advantage for everyone involved.[32] (3) As we have
already seen, the end for Fichte does not justify the means. And, finally,
(4) consequentialism (like all material systems of morality) is a form of
materialism (what Fichte calls "dogmatism") since it "seeks some other

LON NEASE

end for duty than duty itself, thus [it] tries to reach beyond [duty] . . . [it] looks for the final ground of whatsoever is in and for the I, outside of the I."[33] For Fichte, a consistent dogmatism can admit no morality at all, since it will yield only a system of natural, deterministic laws; no freedom can be derived from it.[34]

The first and third criticisms would appear to beg the question, and the second, that we cannot know what would be of greatest benefit, is of questionable value, but the accusation of dogmatism goes straight to the heart of Fichte's rejection of consequentialism. As a form of dogmatism, however, it cannot be refuted at the level of theory; rather, because it is our duty to presume the priority of our feeling of duty itself according to Fichte, we must *reject* any heteronomous theory as immoral. As to whether or not this move of Fichte's is adequate, I cannot explore within the confines of this essay. Nonetheless, the ethical nature of his choice of starting points allows us to appreciate further the profound demand for Fichte of the moral law.

Let us return a moment to Fichte's account of how we evade the severity of the moral law and relate it to consequentialism. By treating the pangs of our conscience as simply *one* consideration among others to be weighed in making a moral decision, consequentialism indeed demotes the moral *law* to a moral *advice*. This is only possible, according to Fichte, if one has failed to reflect enough on duty; the concept of duty manifesting itself so indistinctly that material goods can appear to be on a par with it or even more fundamental. But "that morality which is not pure, which does not proceed altogether from the idea of duty, is no morality at all."[35] Consequentialism is, therefore, *immoral.*

The spirit of *compromise* in consequentialism (namely, its weighing of interests alongside the feelings of one's conscience) is also found in Urmson's call for a manageable moral code, an attempt to compromise between what most people are capable of and the demands of morality. By treating actions too demanding for most people as "supererogatory," Urmson delimits duty to what requires less sacrifice. Fichte finds this kind of move to be one of the greatest dangers to humanity, for

> if we have once persuaded ourselves that we can make a compromise with the strictness of morality, we shall likely remain all our lifetime making such compromises, unless some severe external concussion stirs us up to repent; and in so far indeed it is much easier to reform a sinner, than a conceited just man of the latter sort.[36]

For Urmson, demanding from ourselves and others that we tend to ill strangers is asking too much. Not so for Fichte. If this does ask too much, in the sense of being more than most will achieve, then that is cause for us to arouse ourselves and others to do such things, whether it be through exemplars or through censure. That is, the conditions that make possible such moral actions must be made *actual*. If my fellow man is less than ethical, then it is my duty to help make him better: "For the moral law absolutely binds me to infuse moral culture into him, and to assist in making him better."[37] But no such change will come about if morality is leveled down to what is currently done, currently to be expected from people. Urmson and other moral theorists like him are correct in calling some acts "supererogatory" and other acts "permissible," if they mean only to describe them from the standpoint of the current social standards. But if those standards are less than desirable, less than *ethical,* then treating them as our essential touchstone of morality must be out of the question.

Frequently, arguments in ethical theory appeal to "moral intuitions" of what is right and wrong. But upon closer examination, some of these prove to be expressions of the social standards of the time. Currently it might be empirically true that most people do little to help sick strangers and are unwilling to sacrifice themselves for others; they would not attempt to stop a sword-wielding madman hunting his enemy. And because of this, few would expect themselves or others to do these things. But this awareness of what others expect of us is very different from what *is* morally right or wrong; the latter awareness is our *conscience,* the only authority in the matter for Fichte.

There will always be supererogatory and permissible acts *as judged from our social expectations,* because there will always be a gap between our ethical achievements and the demands of duty, between our finite I and the infinite I. But despite this lack, we can draw closer to our unreachable goal. The effect of this will be to *constantly raise the standards* of our society, and of humanity as a whole; so that what counts as a supererogatory act today will become a duty tomorrow. As Fichte puts it, "it is absolute and general duty to promote and extend morality outside of us . . ."[38] It is the vocation of man as such to overcome this distinction between the moral law and our actual, finite activities. The moral law indeed demands categorically and always, but we must not compromise its severity at the cost of our own humanity.

Notes

1. Kant, "On a Supposed Right to Tell Lies from Benevolent Motives," in *Kant's Critique of Practical Reason and Other Works on The Theory of Ethics,* trans. T. K. Abbott (London: Longmans, Green, and Co., 1898), p. 364.

2. Fichte, *The Science of Ethics,* trans. A. E. Kroeger (London: Kegan Paul, Trench, Trubner and Co., 1907), pp. 304–5.

3. Ibid., p. 207.

4. Ibid., p. 164.

5. Ibid., p. 337.

6. Ibid.

7. Ibid.

8. Ibid., p. 297.

9. Ibid., p. 308.

10. Ibid., p. 368.

11. Ibid., p. 369.

12. Ibid., p. 280.

13. Ibid., p. 313.

14. Ibid., p. 176.

15. Ibid., p. 164.

16. Ibid., p. 288.

17. Ibid., p. 300.

18. Ibid., p. 252.

19. Ibid., p. 205.

20. Ibid.

21. Ibid.

22. Ibid., p. 206.

23. Ibid.

24. Ibid., p. 207.

25. J. O. Urmson, "Saints and Heroes," in *Moral Philosophy: A Reader,* ed. by Louis P. Pojman (Indianapolis: Hackett Publishing Co., Inc., 1993), p. 229.

26. Ibid., pp. 229–30.

27. *Moral Philosophy,* p. 230.

28. *Science of Ethics,* p. 207.

29. Ibid., pp. 207–8.

30. Ibid., p. 309.

31. Ibid., p. 285.

32. Ibid., p. 318.

33. Ibid., p. 184.

34. Ibid.

35. Ibid., p. 330.

36. Ibid., p. 208.

37. Ibid., p. 294.

38. Ibid., p. 329.

PART   IV

ESSAYS ON VARIOUS
TOPICS

Idealism and the Ground of Explanation: Fichte and Schelling, 1794–1797

Steven Hoeltzel

B ecause Schelling so restlessly covered such vast and varied conceptual territory during his many years of philosophical production,
it is customary to organize his thought into a series of consecu-
tive stages, each of which is dominated by some overarching issue or
approach that particularly preoccupied him for a time.[1] Based on the
content and character of his earliest publications, the first and (one
might say) least characteristically "Schellingean" of these stages is widely
regarded as a period of thorough allegiance to the radicalized transcendental idealism articulated in Fichte's contemporaneous writings.
Commencing in 1794, when Schelling first encountered Fichte's earliest
published writings on the *Wissenschaftslehre,* and terminating circa 1797,
when his enthusiasm for *Naturphilosophie* impelled him into conceptual
regions uncharted by Fichte's system, this relatively brief period is generally thought to precede the point at which Schelling really comes into
his own as a philosophical figure of quite some depth and originality.

This is not to say, however, that the writings from Schelling's early,
most conspicuously "Fichtean" period do not contain important antici-
pations of his subsequent, quite un-Fichtean philosophical development.
Recent studies indicate important elements of continuity that render
Schelling's notoriously "protean" philosophical trajectory much less dis-
continuous than it admittedly appears at first.[2] In particular, Schelling's
characteristic ambition to grasp and disclose a unitary, absolute ground,

on the basis of which the world in its entirety can be philosophically comprehended as an organized unity of ultimately identical nature and mind, is widely regarded as both a considerable source of his early attraction to Fichte's idealism, and, ultimately, an important motivation for his eventual attempt to go considerably beyond idealism of the strictly Fichtean sort.[3] And as recent commentators have noted, subtle but important indications that Schelling's fundamental philosophical interests and commitments are by no means identical to Fichte's can be found even in Schelling's seemingly most Fichtean early works.[4]

The present inquiry examines this issue in greater historical, conceptual, and methodological detail. Its goal is twofold. First, via a comparative examination of Fichte's and Schelling's earliest publications, it aims to pinpoint more precisely where and how Schelling first diverges from Fichte with regard to philosophical fundamentals. Second, with attention both to Schelling's basic early commitments and to Fichte's forceful 1797 critique of his position, this study explores the general ramifications of Schelling's commitments in the context of an idealism that seeks not only to construct informative a priori explanations of the genesis and structure of human experience, but to do so in the most philosophically radical way possible.

As we will see, Schelling enthusiastically endorses the explanatory goals, systematic methods, and substantive first principles of Fichte's project in his own first publication, *On the Possibility of a Form of All Philosophy*, in late 1794. Matters become complicated, even contentious, however, in Schelling's next two published works: *On the I as Principle of Philosophy, or On the Unconditional in Human Knowledge*, issued in the spring of 1795, and *Philosophical Letters on Dogmatism and Criticism*, printed in two parts in late 1795 and spring, 1796.[5] With specific reference to these essays, I will show that Schelling diverges, in a conceptually subtle but systematically momentous manner, from Fichte's characterization of the "absolute I" (*das absolute Ich*) as idealism's ultimate explanatory basis or "ground" (*Grund*). I will then show that this divergence and its important implications did not escape Fichte's notice: the "First Introduction" to the *Attempt at a New Presentation of the Wissenschaftslehre*, which Fichte published in early 1797, is clearly designed (in part) to forcefully distinguish his own conception of the absolute I from Schelling's competing variant, and to argue for the methodological superiority of the Fichtean approach to the subject.[6] After examining Fichte's critique, I close with some brief ruminations on the overall relationship between Schelling's developing project and the transcendental idealism of Fichte.

Fichte and Schelling, 1794

As indicated in the ground-breaking "Review of *Aenesidemus*," which Fichte published in February 1794, the radicalized idealism of the *Wissenschaftslehre* is a transcendental theory that purports to provide a philosophical explanation of the fundamental organizing structures informing any humanly possible experience of an objective world. Basic experiential structures are transcendentally explained insofar as their necessary pre- or proto-experiential conditions are philosophically disclosed, and the explanation is an idealist one insofar as the necessary conditions that the philosopher postulates comprise only proto-experiential states and activities of subjectivity, making no reference to the existence or operation of any object independent of the mind. As Fichte puts it in the "Review," according to the *Wissenschaftslehre*, "Everything which occurs in our mind can be completely explained and comprehended on the basis of the mind itself."[7] Following his critical predecessor, K. L. Reinhold, Fichte also insists (at least in his earliest philosophical writings) on strict systematic form in philosophy, demanding that every proposition contained in idealism's explanations of experience be grounded in and certified by a single, self-certifying first principle *(Grundsatz)*.[8] (These methodological issues are dealt with in detail in *Concerning the Concept of the Wissenschaftslehre*, published by Fichte in May 1794.)[9] Given the idealism of the *Wissenschaftslehre*, its *Grundsatz* must describe or embody an act of the mind that is totally presuppositionless, dependent upon no conditions intrinsic or extrinsic to the mind—in a word, absolute.

In 1790, Reinhold had proposed to ground transcendental idealism on a principle describing the internally differentiated organizing structure common to all instances of object-directed awareness: "In consciousness, the subject distinguishes the representation from both the subject and the object and relates it to them both."[10] Inspired by criticisms leveled against Reinhold in 1792 by G. E. Schulze,[11] Fichte's "Review of *Aenesidemus*" contains a denial that Reinhold's proposed *Grundsatz* could be philosophically foundational.[12] On Fichte's view, Reinhold's principle correctly describes a necessary structure of any world-related awareness.[13] Nevertheless, Fichte argues, the principle merely delineates this structure, and does nothing to *explain* the origination and original relation of the structure's basic, analytically separable elements: (1) the subject's foundational awareness of itself *qua* subject, and (2) its more built-up awareness of the object *qua* distinct from and related to itself.[14] Thus, Fichte pledges to explain what Reinhold's idealism (and by extension, Kant's) had everywhere presupposed: the being of subjectivity *qua* (1) immediately self-aware, and (2) mediately aware of an object putatively distinct from itself.

The *Aenesidemus* review contains only a maximally schematic anticipation of such an explanation,[15] but Fichte soon begins working out his transcendental account in much greater detail, in Parts I and II of *Foundations of the Entire Wissenschaftslehre,* published in September 1794 (but circulated in fascicle form beginning in the late spring). As the ultimate explanatory basis—indeed, as the "first, absolutely unconditioned principle [*schlechthin unbedingter Grundsatz*]"—of the entire *Wissenschaftslehre,* he singles out the "absolute self-positing" of the I. "*The I originally absolutely posits its own being.*"[16] The I originates its own being *as* I in a single, unconditioned act *(Tathandlung),* a seamless unity of spontaneous self-assertion and immediate self-apprehension—"I am."[17] Of course, this *Tathandlung*[18] is neither an act nor an object of fully fledged consciousness. Rather, it is *the* most foundational *("absolut-ersten")* element in the proto-conscious activity-structure that underlies and informs all determinate episodes of world-related awareness.[19] Fichte postulates additional a priori activities that ground further articulation of experience's organizing structure. Having achieved its own being *qua* I via the *Tathandlung,* the I then originally equips itself to encounter an object as distinct from itself by counter-positing a not-I to itself.[20] And in order that the posited I is not annihilated by the positing of the not-I as such, I and not-I are posited (by the I) as mutually limiting one another.[21] Parts II and III of the *Foundations* go on to derive increasingly determinate activities, which are postulated as necessary both to preserve the integrity of this abstract structure and, simultaneously, to ground increasingly determinate universal structures of human awareness. Definitive of this entire philosophical project is that, as its ultimate ground and foundation, "an absolute I is postulated as wholly unconditioned [*schlechthin unbedingt*] and incapable of determination by any higher thing."[22]

Like Fichte, Schelling aspires to base an exhaustive philosophical system upon the disclosure of an original ground *(Urgrund):* "an ultimate point of reality on which everything depends, from which all firmness and all form of our knowledge springs."[23] Indeed, in late 1794, *On the Possibility of a Form of All Philosophy,* his first published writing, he figures this project in terms almost indistinguishable from those employed in Fichte's writings from that year. (By the time he composed *On the Possibility,* Schelling had clearly studied the *Aenesidemus* review, the essay *Concerning the Concept,* and the first fascicles of the *Foundations.* He acquired the final part of the *Foundations* shortly after its appearance in summer 1795, but he had not read it as of early 1796[24]—by which time he had struck out on a philosophical path very much his own.) In *On the Possibility,* echoing Fichte, he criticizes Reinhold's contention that the "Principle of Consciousness" could function as philosophy's *Grundsatz*,[25] insisting instead that the only truly viable candidate for such status must exhibit "absolute unconditionality [*schlechthin Unbedingtheit*]."[26] As we shall see, Schelling's particular emphasis upon "absolute unconditionality" as the definitive mark of philosophy's ultimate explanatory ground, together with his quite strict interpretation of what such unconditionality entails, forms the basis of a notable philosophical divergence from Fichte's position in 1795 and 1796.

In 1794, however, there is no real evidence of robust divergence. Again like Fichte, Schelling enthusiastically maintains that the first principle of philosophy, one everywhere presupposed but nowhere thematized by Kant, is "nothing other than the originally self-posited I."[27] Then, essentially recapitulating the argument broadly outlined in Fichte's *Aenesidemus* review and considerably fleshed out in the first sections of the *Foundations*, Schelling registers two subsidiary *Grundsätze*, which, in concert with the first, originate the elementary subject-object structure by which every act of representation is informed. Subsidiary to the I's self-originating act of self-positing are two acts that it conditions: one, in which a not-I is opposed to the I, and another in which I and not-I are posited in such a way as not to cancel each other out.[28] Finally, in an unequivocal endorsement of Fichte's project, he exalts the *Wissenschaftslehre* (by name) as an endeavor from which humanity can expect "a science which operates solely by logic and which deals with nothing but what is posited by the I (by its freedom and autonomy)."[29] Upon the foreseeable completion of this science, he says, "One will know nothing except what is given by the I, and by the principle I = I."[30]

Schelling contra Fichte, 1795–1796

So far, so Fichtean, it seems, and Schelling's next publication, in early 1795, *On the I as Principle of Philosophy*, only strengthened the impression among its contemporary audience that Schelling intended to provide his service to philosophy primarily by acting as a kind of publicist for the *Wissenschaftslehre*. (This, after all, is the text that earned for its author the jocular designation "town crier of the I [*Marktschreier des Ich*]," and that such luminaries as Novalis and Friedrich Schlegel apparently looked into for help in understanding Fichte.)[31] Undoubtedly, there is much to support this sort of reading of *On the I*. Yet despite all of its surface similarities to the Fichtean doctrine, this text conceals a seemingly minor but

STEVEN HOELTZEL

in fact quite significant conceptual shift away from the precise manner in which Fichte figures the absolute I as idealism's explanatory ground. And because this shift occurs in the very foundation of idealism's explanatory architecture, it has tremendous philosophical consequences, which become strikingly apparent in Schelling's next published work, *Philosophical Letters on Dogmatism and Criticism*—and which arguably can be taken to foreshadow important later developments in his thought.

In *On the I*, Schelling again insists on the necessity of grounding a properly comprehensive and systematic philosophy in an unconditioned absolute. Once again, he locates this endeavor within the post-Kantian program, inaugurated by Reinhold and revolutionized by the *Wissenschaftslehre*, of advancing transcendental idealism by disclosing and mobilizing its ultimate presuppositions.[32] But here, in a manner anticipated by remarks which Fichte had made in Part I of the *Grundlage*,[33] he draws a supposedly exhaustive distinction between two mutually exclusive types of philosophical system—"dogmatism" and "criticism"—which are differentiated by their strictly opposed accounts of philosophy's ultimate, unconditioned ground.[34] Dogmatism, exemplified, of course, by Spinoza, is the system whose first principle is "a not-I posited as antecedent to any I"[35]—a position whose "very foundations" Schelling vows to "annul explicitly" in this piece.[36]

He purports to do this—indeed, to demonstrate dogmatism's outright inconsistency—by means of an appeal to the oxymoronic flavor that the concept of an unconditioned thing or object—an "*unbedingtes Ding*"—has for the philosophically cultivated German tongue.[37] This (supposed) *reductio* should entail that there is, in fact, only one viable philosophical system: the system of criticism, within which a radically un-thing-like, nonempirical I is "posited as antecedent to all not-I and as exclusive of any not-I."[38] This absolute ground, considered *as such*, is the principal subject of Schelling's interest throughout *On the I*. Qua absolute, and in keeping with Fichte's conception of unconditioned self-positing, the I is definitively characterized by Schelling as radically self-realizing. But in a move that will rapidly put Schelling at quite some conceptual distance from Fichte, the ensuing philosophical discourse "on the I" proceeds, not by charting the further specific determination that the absolutely self-positing I must undergo if experience is to occur, but by deducing from the I's absolute unconditionality additional abstract predicates, which Schelling takes to be entailed strictly and solely by its status *qua* absolutely unconditioned.

The I is absolute, Schelling maintains, insofar as it receives its own reality "solely through itself alone," and the subsequent investigation of the I "is now nothing but a plain development of this."[39] In order that the

I may retain its absolute status, he continues, it must not be the bearer of any predicates that are not conceived "through its unconditionality."[40] On this basis, he infers (through a series of deductions the steps of which I will not undertake to trace herein) that the I "is determined in its own being by nothing but identity."[41] Because only what is conditioned can be determined conceptually, and because sensuous intuition reveals only conditioned objects, the I can be grasped only in intellectual intuition.[42] The I is "simply unity" that "cannot contain any multiplicity."[43] It "contains all being, all reality."[44] It is infinite, indivisible, and immutable,[45] the one and only unconditional, of which everything that is, is "merely" a modification *(Accidens)*.[46] *Qua* "absolute power [*Macht*]," it is the immanent cause of everything that is.[47] The ultimate goal of all striving of the empirical self;[48] it is the sole occupant of the supersensuous world.[49]

As numerous commentators have pointed out, some of these propositions resound with an unmistakably Spinozistic tone.[50] And as the above discussion should indicate, there are apparent echoes of Spinoza in the manner by which Schelling derives them. Clearly, it is important to recognize Spinoza's influence in this connection; however, I think it equally important to avoid the attendant temptation to suppose that by characterizing idealism's absolute ground in such a seemingly Spinozistic manner, Schelling has necessarily drifted into a discourse whose basic terms and problems are more metaphysical than "critical."[51] Instead, I think it best (that is, more potentially instructive) to suppose that Schelling self-consciously arrives at and unfolds these ideas entirely within the context of a critical idealism, which aims to explain human experience on the basis of its ultimate transcendental ground. Because such an approach takes seriously Schelling's avowed commitment to a rigorously explanatory idealism of the (broadly) Fichtean sort, such an approach enables us to work out and assess the implications that Schelling's depiction of the *Urgrund* has within the context of just such a theoretical project. In addition, this enables us to assess whether, and to what extent, the fundamental problems that arise within Schelling's own account are fundamental problems for *any* suitably radical idealism.

An extended version of this essay might individually address the manifold propositions through which Schelling characterizes idealism's absolute ground, with an eye toward a more detailed comparison not only with Spinoza's position, but also with Fichte's conception of the absolute I. This would be an extremely interesting project—and no doubt a highly illuminating one—but in the present context, a much more general contrastive approach to the relationship between Fichte and the early Schelling will have to suffice. Before making the contrast in question, however, we should attend to the principal implications of

Schelling's treatment of the I in this early text. In particular, note that what Schelling here envisions as philosophy's ultimate explanatory basis seems to be entirely bereft of any determination or tendency that might provide transcendental philosophy with some kind of explanatory purchase in or upon the unconditioned *explanans* that Schelling postulates as the experienced world's absolute ground. Schelling follows Fichte in the postulation of an absolute, self-realizing ground—but he then figures that ground in such a way that, first of all, it is exceedingly unclear how such a ground could operate as, or otherwise provide, an informative explanation of the specific determinacies of experience. A self-realizing, simple unity certainly does not explain too many details. Moreover, because this ground, *qua* ultimate basis of "everything that is," is postulated as productive of *objectivity* in addition to finite subjectivity, without any explanation (or even any clear indication) of how the postulated production actually occurs, it seems somewhat arbitrary to conceive of this ground as somehow specifically subjective.

Of course, one might interject at this point that to insist upon such implications is to put considerably more explanatory stress on the absolute I than Schelling does himself—especially given that Schelling does discuss the absolute opposition of the not-I, albeit quite briefly, in *On the I*. In the course of this discussion, he maintains that "it would be incomprehensible how the whole science could be based upon one theorem," where the context indicates that the "one theorem" in question is the absolute I's unconditioned self-realization.[52] As Fichte had done in Part I of the *Foundations*, Schelling insists on the necessity of a second absolute act, one whereby a not-I is originally opposed to the I, an act for which "one cannot give any ulterior reason, just as one can give none for the I positing itself absolutely."[53] He makes the additional claim (in a footnote) that "the one immediately implies the other,"[54] but this contention receives neither elucidation nor argument, and I do not think that Schelling is philosophically entitled to it, for reasons I will now explain.

In Part I of the *Foundations*, Fichte had appealed to certain necessary "facts of empirical consciousness" as incontestable *explananda* that would authorize him to postulate a second, unconditioned act of opposition.[55] Moreover, in the immensely difficult "Deduction of Representation" that concludes Part II of the same work, he further undertook to demonstrate just how it is that an initially absolute I could find itself impelled (though not necessitated) to originally oppose a not-I to itself.[56] In *On the I*, however, Schelling does not employ either strategy—the first of which provides explanatory warrant for postulating an original opposition of the not-I by the I, and the second of which provides a way of understanding how further determinations of the I's activity can be grounded in tendencies intrinsic to the I's absolute act of self-positing. Schelling's silence on these matters proves to be a fateful omission: coupled with his strictly definitional depiction of the absolute I, it leads to a critical explanatory gap at the very heart of his version of the idealist project—a gap between the original act of the I's unconditioned self-realization on one side, and on the other side, the increasingly determinate acts that, in concert with the first, conflict and cooperate in the production of the necessary structures that inform our experience.

As we have seen, Schelling's insistence on understanding the pure I strictly and solely in terms of its absolute unconditionality leads him to figure its activity of spontaneous self-production as an activity bereft of internal differentiation, dependent upon nothing else, and entirely self-contained. As such, the activity that Schelling treats as idealism's ultimate ground can be neither characterized by, nor essentially connected to, *any* specific determinations or limitations. (This may be what Schelling means when he says that the *Urgrund* must be "not only unconditional, but absolutely unconditionable [*schlechthin unbedingbar*].")[57] Determination, limitation, and constraint are all bound up with conditionality, and hence cannot characterize Schelling's 1795 version of the absolute I. As a result, the connection between Schelling's absolute ground and the determinate world of finite subjects and objects must be radically contingent—and therefore philosophically inexplicable. To say otherwise would be to bind up idealism's unconditioned ground in limitation, determination, and necessity—all of which the Schelling of 1795 takes to be strictly excluded by the I's "absolute unconditionality." Given the explanatory resources provided by *On the I,* our limited experience of a world of determinate objects is separated from its absolutely unconditioned ground by a conceptual divide that theoretical philosophy simply cannot span. Philosophy aims to explain the emergence of differentiated experience out of the I's pure activity of unconditioned self-positing, but if the conceptual tools available to this endeavor are as meager as those with which Schelling seems intent to make do, it seems that no such explanation can possibly be given.

The problem, in the language favored by Schelling himself in his next publication, the *Letters* of late 1795 and early 1796, is the impossibility of explaining "the egress from the absolute [*das Heraustreten aus dem Absoluten*]."[58] This "egress" is the basic precondition of coming to world-related consciousness, the point at which "the original opposition in the human mind"—the bipolarity of subject and object, I and not-I—first unfolds out of the initially seamless identity of the unconditioned absolute.[59] Put another way, it is the moment at which individual consciousness of an objective world first emerges from an absolute ground that is postulated as necessarily free of any internal structure or differentiation, let alone the specific, bipolar subject-object structure necessary to any world-related awareness. To attempt to pinpoint a reason for this development is, in Schelling's view, to ask nothing less than "the riddle of the world, the question of how the absolute could come out of itself and oppose to itself a world."[60] Stated otherwise, it is the question, "Why is there a realm of experience at all?"[61]

Given the way in which idealism's absolute ground is figured in *On the I*—that is, as perfectly exclusive of the activities of limitation and determination necessary for the production of fully fledged empirical awareness—it is unsurprising that in the *Letters* Schelling declares the transition from seamless act of absolute self-realization to fully fledged empirical consciousness theoretically "unintelligible,"[62] contending that "No system can realize the transition from the finite to the infinite. . . . No system can fill the gap."[63] Moreover, the incredibly abstract and indeterminate nature of his favored systematic ground now requires him to radically revise his previous account of the relative stature of dogmatism and criticism. No longer is dogmatism charged with inconsistency owing to its commitment to an absolute object—a silence that speaks volumes about Schelling's evolving conception of his system's absolute basis. Instead, dogmatism is understood to be strictly parallel, if everywhere opposed, to criticism; and each system is figured as a necessarily one-sided standpoint on the ultimate reality that both of them presuppose.[64] Dogmatism postulates an absolute objectivity; criticism, an absolute I. Yet because both necessarily remain mired in finite possibilities of comprehension—the price of "egress" from the absolute—both necessarily fall short of attaining a cognitive grasp of this absolute, in which "all conflicting principles and all contradicting systems become identical."[65]

The only commitment to idealism that Schelling clearly retains in the *Letters* is not a theoretical but a practical one.[66] Given the theoretical insolubility of philosophy's ultimate question, he says, the dissolution of this question must be a matter of practice.[67] The dogmatist, unable to apprehend the absolute object in theory, languishes in "the utmost unlimited passivity."[68] Conversely, the critical philosopher aspires to "unlimited activity," striving to obtain through activity the absolute I-hood unattainable in thought.[69] Since there is no theoretical basis for deciding on one project or the other, Schelling maintains—in a remark that clearly anticipates a famous Fichtean dictum from the 1797 "First Introduction"—"Which of the two we choose depends upon the freedom of spirit which we have ourselves acquired."[70]

Strikingly, the absolute is regarded in the *Letters* as a self-contained, undifferentiated subject-object identity whose connection to our determinate forms of subjectivity is theoretically impenetrable, and whose nature is equally compatible, theoretically speaking, with dogmatism and with the critical system. It is denoted in the *Letters* simply as "the absolute," with no lingering implication that this concept bears any definitive marks distinctive of subjectivity. Still, as we have seen, the conceptual preparation for all of this can be clearly located within *On the I,* of 1795—perhaps the most seemingly Fichtean of all of Schelling's works.

Fichte contra Schelling, 1797

While some of Schelling's earliest readers may have failed to recognize crucial differences between the position of *On the I* and the properly Fichtean conception of idealism's absolute ground, this is by no means true of Fichte himself. In fact, part of Fichte's "First Introduction" to the *Attempt at a New Presentation of the Wissenschaftslehre,* published in February 1797, is clearly designed to function as a rejoinder to Schelling on precisely this issue.[71] In keeping with his usual practice, Fichte does not refer to his intended target by name. Still, clear responses to the *Letters* are manifest throughout Fichte's discussion of the relative merits of dogmatism and criticism, in which he argues that extra-systematic considerations of explanatory power suffice to establish the theoretical supremacy of idealism over dogmatism in a nonquestion-begging way.[72] Moreover, he specifically addresses the issue of the proper conception of idealism's explanatory ground, in a way that is clearly intended to show that his position is both distinct from and methodologically superior to the view adopted by Schelling in both the *Letters* and *On the I.*

For all of its profound systematic importance, the basic difference between Fichte's position and Schelling's is fairly simple. Fichte does not treat the so-called "first principle" of the *Wissenschaftslehre,* the radically spontaneous and internally undifferentiated *Tathandlung,* as the system's sole bearer of explanatory weight. To be sure, the *Wissenschaftslehre* is grounded, just as Schelling's project is, in an unconditioned subject-objectivity, a radically free act of immediate self-realization within which being and thinking are one and the same. But while this activity certainly provides idealism with the "keystone [*Schlußstein*]" of "the system of the human mind's permanent modes of acting,"[73] Fichte does not regard it as a self-contained quasi-entity, radically disconnected from the conditioned activities it supports. Instead, it is postulated and regarded as one moment—the founding moment—of a living totality, within which radical freedom necessarily coexists with radical limitation and determinacy.[74] For Fichte, it is this entire organic, dynamic totality of proto-conscious activities that provides human experience with its necessary and sufficient a priori ground.

Schelling, on the other hand, philosophically detaches the *Tathandlung* from this articulated activity-structure and figures the *Tathandlung* alone, as depicted in *On the I,* as the conceptual basis upon which an explanation of experience must be constructed. That is to say, given Schelling's conception of the philosophical project, the features definitive of "the absolute" exhaust the conceptual resources available to a genuinely radical a priori explanation of the genesis and structure of experience. The philosopher must somehow show that, and also how a simple, self-realizing unity can function by itself as a sufficient ground for all of the multifarious determinacy and strict regularity in our experience. It is not difficult to see why, in the *Letters,* Schelling deems this an impossible task. For as Fichte puts it in the "First Introduction," "The principle of sufficient reason [*der Satz des Grundes*] is certainly not applicable to completely free and lawless acting."[75] Where there is only a perfectly free activity, necessarily exclusive of all limitation and determinacy, there can be no ground for an explanation of anything at all. Any idealism which maintains otherwise, Fichte says, is an idealism which has become "transcendent."[76]

Fichte cannot mean that idealism becomes "transcendent" simply by postulating explanatory elements that cannot be met with in any humanly possible experience. In that case, his own idealism would be transcendent, whereas he assures us that his approach is strictly "Critical" or "transcendental."[77] It must be, then, that idealism becomes "transcendent" insofar as the ultimate explanatory ground which it postulates is insufficiently conceptually tied to those determinate features of experience that the postulation of that ground is supposed to explain. Clearly, Fichte believes that this is the case with Schelling's absolute.

Just as clearly, Fichte believes that despite all of its daunting abstraction and demanding argumentation, the *Wissenschaftslehre* evades such a charge. "Nothing determinate can be derived from what is indeterminate," he maintains, going on to offer a highly abbreviated contention to the effect that the ultimate explanatory basis of the *Wissenschaftslehre* is just determinate enough to explain that which requires and admits of explanation, and to do so in strictly idealist terms.[78] *Qua* idealism, the system "explains the determinations of consciousness by referring them to the acting of the intellect, which it considers to be something absolute and active, not something passive."[79] But because "completely free and lawless acting" is an insufficient basis upon which to ground any genuine explanation,[80] this intellect must be additionally conceived as necessarily subject to *intrinsic* determinations: laws entailing determinate modes of acting, and feelings manifesting determinate kinds of limitation—both, indicative not of the being of any structure or object extrinsic to the I, but simply of "the limits of its [the I's] own nature."[81] For Fichte, radical freedom and equally radical finitude necessarily conflict and cooperate in the origination of the I and its experience. Hence, the *Wissenschaftslehre*'s explanation of experience draws its basic conceptual resources not from one abstract element conceived in artificial isolation from the others, but on the dynamic a priori interrelation of them all.

In fact, Fichte argues that, given certain fundamental laws of thinking, no one of the proto-conscious activities comprising the basic explanatory fundaments of the *Wissenschaftslehre* can be so much as conceived to occur in separation from that element's counterparts (supposing, of course, that the various elements are conceived of properly). "Idealism demonstrates that what is purely and simply postulated is not possible except on the condition of something else, which in turn is impossible without some third something, etc. Thus none of the individual things it postulates is possible on its own."[82] Indeed, in his lecture notes from the winter semester of 1796 to 1797, Fichte argues specifically that "as surely as the I is posited at all, a not-I must be posited along with it."[83] If this contention is correct—a quite complicated question—then Schelling's conception of philosophy's fundamental explanatory problem is not only structurally quite different from Fichte's; it is also arguably incoherent.

I say "arguably" incoherent, because a demonstration of such incoherence would require more than a demonstration that Fichte's arguments for the above conclusions are in fact sound. It would also require a demonstration that Schelling's conception of idealism's absolute ground is sufficiently akin to Fichte's to warrant such a charge. For Fichte, the occurrence of the *Tathandlung* is both necessary in order for any experience to occur and sufficient to entail the occurrence of the other proto-conscious activities that, in concert with the *Tathandlung*, give rise to fully fledged experience. Schelling, on the other hand, seems to conceive idealism's ultimate explanatory ground quite differently in these early texts: as a necessary condition of our experience, but one whose existence or occurrence is not sufficient to entail the determinate mediations and limitations upon which our experience also depends. Such a position may have its problems—among them, a lack of clarity and a dearth of explanatory power—but it does not seem to be necessarily incoherent.

Then is such a position "transcendent," as Fichte contends? If we interpret this criticism according to my suggestion above, then we are compelled to answer this question in the affirmative—indeed, we are forced to do so by Schelling's own insistence in the *Letters* that the transition between unconditioned absolute and finite world of experience is theoretically unintelligible. Still, it is important that we refrain from concluding on this basis—with Schelling's most brilliant years of philosophical production yet to be considered—that his embrace of such a position in the *Letters* represents a philosophically fateful, irreversible step beyond the confines of a methodologically rigorous and theoretically fruitful idealism and into a "transcendent" or "metaphysical" position whose cogency and rigor must compare unfavorably to the *Wissenschaftslehre*. After all, to insist on the impossibility of an informative theoretical derivation of experience from idealism's absolute ground, as Schelling does in 1795 and 1796, is not to deny the desirability of possessing such a derivation. Moreover, any such insistence is inherently relative to one's estimation of the conceptual resources and explanatory strategies available at the time. Hence, such a judgment leaves open the possibility that an eventual enrichment of one's philosophical resources (be it the discovery of hitherto-unseen conceptual connections, the formulation of a productive new method, or what have you) may sanction a renewal of the explanatory endeavor.

Clearly, not long after writing the *Letters* Schelling did return to this project—the quest to provide a deeply illuminating philosophical account of human experience by rigorously demonstrating that and how this experience is ultimately grounded in an absolute even more abstract and presuppositionless than the self-enacting finite subjectivity grounding the idealism of Fichte. It may be that such an ambitious project is bound, either in practice or in principle, to become problematically "transcendent." But this is not a question to be decided solely on the basis of Schelling's earliest writings and Fichte's critique thereof.

Notes

This essay is a revised version of remarks presented to the fourth biennial meeting of the North American Fichte Society, held in March 1997. This version reflects the influence of a number of helpful comments and suggestions made by participants at the meeting, particularly Johannes Brachtendorf, Daniel Breazeale, Dale Snow, Michael Vater, and Günter Zöller.

1. For a quite recent example, see Andrew Bowie, *Schelling and Modern European Philosophy* (New York: Routledge, 1993), pp. 12–14.

2. Particularly notable in this connection are two recent studies: Dale Snow, *Schelling and the End of Idealism* (Albany: SUNY Press, 1996); and Bowie, *Schelling and Modern European Philosophy*.

3. In addition to the works cited above, see Joseph Esposito, *Schelling's Idealism and Philosophy of Nature* (Lewisburg: Bucknell University Press, 1977); and Alan White, *Schelling: An Introduction to the System of Freedom* (New Haven: Yale University Press, 1983). The secondary literature in German contains work addressed more specifically to the Fichte–Schelling connection; for example, Ingtraud Görland, *Die Entwicklung der Frühphilosophie Schellings in der Auseinandersetzung mit Fichte* (Frankfurt: Vittorio Klostermann, 1973); and Reinhard Lauth, *Die Enstehung von Schellings Identitätsphilosophie in der Auseinandersetzung mit Fichtes Wissenschaftslehre 1795 bis 1801* (Freiburg/Munich: Verlag Karl Alber, 1975). See also Xavier Tilliette, *Schelling: Une Philosophie en Devenir,* 2 vols. (Paris: Librarie Philosophique J. Vrin, 1970). Note, however, that the real scholarly point of departure for this essay is actually provided by recent work on Fichte. (That this is so will become clearer as we proceed.) In addition to material specifically cited elsewhere in the notes, my approach to the issues addressed herein is indebted to works such as Daniel Breazeale, "How to Make an Idealist: Fichte's 'Refutation of Dogmatism' and the Problem of the Starting Point of the *Wissenschaftslehre,*" *Philosophical Forum* 19 (1988): pp. 97–123; Dieter Henrich, "Fichte's Original Insight," trans. David Lachterman, in *Contemporary German Philosophy (1)* (University Park: Pennsylvania State University Press, 1982), pp. 15–53; Frederick Neuhouser, *Fichte's Theory of Subjectivity* (Cambridge: Cambridge University Press, 1990); Alexis Philonenko, "Fichte and the Critique of Metaphysics," trans. William Earle, *Philosophical Forum* 19 (1988): pp. 124–39; Robert Pippin, "Fichte's Contribution," *Philosophical Forum* 19 (1988): pp. 74–96; Günter Zöller, "An Eye for an I: Fichte's Transcendental Experiment," in *Figuring the Self: Subject, Absolute, and Others in Classical German Philosophy,* ed. David Klemm and Günter Zöller (Albany: SUNY Press, 1997), pp. 73–95. (This is not intended to be an exhaustive list, but rather to provide a general indication of the particular current of recent scholarship to which I am especially indebted.)

4. For example, see Snow, *Schelling and the End of Idealism,* pp. 47–49; and Esposito, *Schelling's Idealism and Philosophy of Nature,* pp. 37–39.

5. English translations of the three essays cited herein may be found in Friedrich Wilhelm Joseph Schelling, *The Unconditional in Human Knowledge: Four Early Essays (1794–1796),* trans. and ed. Fritz Marti (Lewisburg: Bucknell University Press, 1980). All three essays are likewise contained in a single volume of the German edition: Schelling, *Sämmtliche Werke,* ed. K. F. A. Schelling (Stuttgart/ Augsburg: J. G. Cotta, 1856–61), vol. I. In this paper, citations of Schelling's writings refer first to the volume and page number in the German edition, hereafter abbreviated as *W,* then to the page number in the quoted Marti translation, hereafter abbreviated as *UHK.*

6. Daniel Breazeale has shown that the "First Introduction" is designed in part as a critical reply to the broadly metaphilosophical claims Schelling makes in the *Letters* that pertain to the proper philosophical status and function of the *Wissenschaftslehre.* (See Breazeale's "Editor's Introduction" to *Introductions to the Wissenschaftslehre and Other Writings,* ed. and trans. Daniel Breazeale [Indianapolis: Hackett, 1994], hereafter abbreviated *IWL,* pp. xxviii–xxx.) I will not address

these issues in any real detail herein; instead, I will show that the "First Introduction" is *also* meant to furnish a reply to Schelling on a "first order" philosophical issue of tremendous systematic import.

7. *Johann Gottlieb Fichtes sämmtliche Werke,* ed. I. H. Fichte, eight vols. (Berlin: Viet and Co., 1845–46); rpt., along with the three vols. of *Johann Gottlieb Fichtes nachgelassene Werke* (Bonn: Adolphus-Marcus, 1834–35), as *Fichtes Werke* (Berlin: de Gruyter, 1971), hereafter abbreviated as *SW, SW* I, p. 15; *Fichte: Early Philosophical Writings,* ed. and trans. Daniel Breazeale (Ithaca, N.Y.: Cornell University Press, 1988), hereafter abbreviated as *EPW,* p. 69. Citations of Fichte's writings refer first to the volume and page number in *SW,* then to the English translation quoted. In quotations from the Heath-Lachs translation of the *Grundlage der gesamten Wissenschaftslehre* (*J. G. Fichte: Science of Knowledge* [Cambridge: Cambridge University Press, 1982], henceforth, *LH*), the term "self" has been replaced with the more appropriate term "I."

8. For more on the importance of Reinhold, in this connection and in general, see Daniel Breazeale, "Between Kant and Fichte: Karl Leonhard Reinhold's 'Elementary Philosophy,' " *Review of Metaphysics* 35 (1982): pp. 785–821. See also Frederick Beiser, *The Fate of Reason: German Philosophy from Kant to Fichte* (Cambridge: Harvard University Press, 1987), pp. 226–65.

9. *SW* I, pp. 29–66; *EPW,* pp. 94–135.

10. Karl Leonhard Reinhold, *Beyträge zur Berichtigung bisheriger Missverständnisse der Philosophen,* vol. I (Jena: Mauke, 1790), p. 267.

11. Gottlob Ernst Schulze, *Aenesidemus* (Berlin: Reuter and Reichard, 1911). An English translation of part of this work can be found in *Between Kant and Hegel: Texts in the Development of Post-Kantian Idealism,* trans. and ed. George di Giovanni and H. S. Harris (Albany: SUNY Press, 1985), pp. 104–35.

12. A helpful introduction to this historically and conceptually pivotal early work of Fichte's is provided by Daniel Breazeale, "Fichte's *Aenesidemus* Review and the Transformation of German Idealism," *Review of Metaphysics* 34 (1981): pp. 545–68.

13. *SW* I, p. 8; *EPW,* p. 63.

14. *SW* I, pp. 6–10; *EPW,* p. 62–65.

15. *SW* I, p. 10; *EPW,* p. 65.

16. *SW* I, p. 98; original emphasis. Here I depart from the considerably less literal Heath-Lachs translation: "The self begins by an absolute positing of its own existence" (*LH,* p. 99). Fichte's original reads: *"Das Ich setzt ursprünglich schlechthin sein eigenes Seyn"* (*SW* I, p. 98).

17. For further elucidation, see *SW* I, p. 97; LH, p. 98.

18. *Tathandlung* is Fichte's coinage for an activity, the performance of which does not presuppose but actually constitutes the being of its agent.

19. *SW* I, p. 91; LH, p. 93.

20. *SW* I, p. 104; LH, p. 104.

21. *SW* I, p. 110; LH, p. 110.

22. *SW* I, p. 119; LH, p. 117.

23. *W* I, p. 162; *UHK,* p. 71.

24. Schelling, letter to Niethammer, 22 January 1796, in *Materialen zu Schellings philosophischen Anfängen* (Frankfurt: Suhrkamp, 1975), pp. 139–42.

25. *W* I, p. 93; *UHK*, p. 42.

26. *W* I, p. 96; *UHK*, p. 44.

27. *W* I, p. 97; *UHK*, p. 45.

28. *W* I, pp. 98–101; *UHK*, pp. 46–48.

29. *W* I, p. 102; *UHK*, p. 48.

30. *W* I, p. 102; *UHK*, p. 48.

31. For more on Schelling's contribution to the early reception of the *Wissenschaftslehre*, see Snow, *Schelling and the End of Idealism*, p. 42 f.

32. *W* I, pp. 154–5; *UHK*, p. 66.

33. *SW* I, p. 119 f.; LH, p. 117.

34. *W* I, p. 170 f.; *UHK*, p. 77 f.

35. *W* I, p. 170 f.; *UHK*, p. 77 f.

36. *W* I, p. 151; *UHK*, p. 64.

37. *W* I, p. 170 f.; *UHK*, p. 77 f.

38. *W* I, p. 170 f.; *UHK*, p. 77 f.

39. *W* I, p. 177; *UHK*, p. 82.

40. *W* I, p. 179; *UHK*, p. 84.

41. *W* I, p. 178; *UHK*, p. 83.

42. *W* I, p. 181; *UHK*, p. 85.

43. *W* I, p. 182; *UHK*, p. 86.

44. *W* I, p. 186; *UHK*, p. 89.

45. *W* I, p. 192; *UHK*, pp. 92–93.

46. *W* I, pp. 192–3; *UHK*, p. 93.

47. *W* I, p. 195 f.; *UHK*, p. 95 f.

48. *W* I, p. 198 f.; *UHK*, p. 97 f.

49. *W* I p. 202; *UHK*, p. 100.

50. For example, see Snow, *Schelling and the End of Idealism*, p. 47 f.; Bowie, *Schelling and Modern European Philosophy*, Chapter 1; White, *Schelling: An Introduction*, pp. 1–13 *passim*.

51. For an example of the sort of reading according to which Schelling's position represents a relapse into "transcendent" metaphysics, see Esposito, *Schelling's Idealism and Philosophy of Nature*, p. 38. See also White, *Schelling: An Introduction*, pp. 1–4.

52. *W* I, p. 187; *UHK*, p. 90.

53. *W* I, p. 187; *UHK*, p. 90.

54. *W* I, p. 187; *UHK*, p. 90.

55. *SW* I, p. 104; LH, p. 104.

56. *SW* I, p. 227–46; LH, pp. 203–17. For a detailed treatment of this "Deduction of Representation," see Steven Hoeltzel, "Fichte's Deduction of Representation in the 1794/95 *Grundlage*," in *New Studies in Fichte's Foundations of the Entire Wissenschaftslehre*, ed. Daniel Breazeale and Tom Rockmore (Amherst, N.Y,: Humanity Books, 2001).

57. *W* I, p. 164; *UHK*, p. 72.

58. *W* I, p. 294; *UHK,* p. 163.

59. *W* I, p. 294; *UHK,* p. 163. Friedrich Hölderlin is an important influence on the way in which Schelling formulates this basic problem and treats some of its implications throughout the *Letters.* See Friedrich Hölderlin, *Werke Briefe Dokumente* (Munich: Hanser, 1963), pp. 490–91. For concise treatment of Hölderlin's influence in this connection, see Bowie, *Schelling and Modern European Philosophy,* pp. 25–29; and White, *Schelling: An Introduction,* p. 30. For much more detailed documentation, see Schelling, *Materialen zu Schellings philosophischen Anfängen* (Frankfurt: Suhrkamp, 1975).

60. *W* I, p. 310; *UHK,* p. 173 f.

61. *W* I, p. 310; *UHK,* p. 175.

62. *W* I, p. 310; *UHK,* p. 175.

63. *W* I, p. 314; *UHK,* p. 177.

64. *W* I, p. 298 f.; *UHK,* p. 166 f.

65. *W* I, p. 331; *UHK,* p. 189.

66. Here Schelling exhibits some important indebtedness to F. H. Jacobi. See Snow, *Schelling and the End of Idealism,* pp. 24–31 *passim.*

67. *W* I, p. 299; *UHK,* p. 167.

68. *W* I, p. 334; *UHK,* p. 191.

69. *W* I, p. 335; *UHK,* p. 192.

70. *W* I, p. 308; *UHK,* p. 173.

71. The "First Introduction" is also clearly designed as a rejoinder to a number of broadly metaphilosophical claims regarding the *Wissenschaftslehre* that occur in Schelling's *Letters,* claims I have not dealt with in any real detail here. (See Breazeale, "Editor's Introduction" to *IWL,* pp. xxviii–xxx.) My present concern is simply to show that Schelling's "first order" characterization of idealism's ultimate explanatory ground is also singled out for criticism within the "First Introduction."

72. See Breazeale, "Editor's Introduction" to *IWL,* pp. xxviii–xxx.

73. *SW* I, p. 20; *EPW,* p. 73.

74. For a detailed defense of this interpretive claim, see Daniel Breazeale, "Check or Checkmate? On the Finitude of the Fichtean Self," in *The Modern Subject: Conceptions of the Self in Classical German Philosophy* (Albany: SUNY Press, 1995), pp. 87–114.

75. *SW* I, p. 441; *IWL,* p. 27.

76. *SW* I, p. 441; *IWL,* p. 27.

77. *SW* I, p. 441; *IWL,* p. 26.

78. *SW* I, p. 440; *IWL,* p. 26.

79. *SW* I, p. 440; *IWL,* p. 25.

80. *SW* I, p. 441; *IWL,* p. 27.

81. *SW* I, p. 441; *IWL,* p. 26.

82. *SW* I, p. 448; *IWL,* p. 33.

83. *J. G. Fichte-Gesamtausgabe der Bayerischen Akademie der Wissenschaften,* ed. Reinhard Lauth, Hans Gliwitzky, and Erich Fuchs (Stuttgart-Bad Cannstatt: Frommann-Holzboog, 1964 ff.) IV/2, p. 35; *WLnm,* p. 123.

Fichte, Jacobi, and the Atheism Controversy

Curtis Bowman

acobi's sole contribution to the atheism controversy consisted of a letter written and sent to Fichte in March 1799 and then published in an amended form in the fall of that year. Now known simply as "Jacobi to Fichte," it came as quite a surprise to Fichte and quickly led to the composition of *The Vocation of Man*. In that work, Fichte attempted, among other things, to come to terms with Jacobi's criticisms. Although these writings make up Fichte and Jacobi's official exchange of views in the atheism controversy, we would be hard pressed fully to understand the nature and extent of their disagreement if we confined our attention to these two works, or even if we also took into account the many other writings published during the course of the controversy. This is the case for a plain yet compelling reason: the entire controversy presupposes a complex history of prior disputes and problems. An adequate understanding of the quarrel between Fichte and Jacobi requires, at a minimum, that we first go back to the pantheism controversy of the 1780s and then to Fichte's Kantianism of the early 1790s, especially as it reveals itself in his *Attempt at a Critique of All Revelation*. Only then we will be able to see that the atheism controversy brought to a head a conflict that had been many years in the making.

The relevance of the pantheism controversy for understanding Jacobi's reaction to the atheism controversy should be fairly obvious. It was in his dispute with Mendelssohn over Lessing's alleged Spinozism that Jacobi first articulated his philosophy of faith and the conception of

God that it was intended to support. And so this is where Jacobi developed at length the criticisms that he wielded in compressed form against Fichte in "Jacobi to Fichte." Thus we are on solid ground in looking to the 1780s for a greater understanding of certain aspects of the atheism controversy.

But how does Fichte's early Kantianism fit into the controversy? Answering this question requires showing that the conception of God found in the *Attempt* puts Fichte on a path that leads to his conflict with Jacobi. Prior to the formulation of the *Wissenschaftslehre*, Fichte subscribed to an orthodox reading of Kant's moral theology, to which he added the Critical concept of revelation developed in the *Attempt*. This view alone, as we shall see, was enough to raise Jacobi's ire. Its metamorphosis into the doctrine that appalled Jacobi (justifiably or not) during the atheism controversy served to make matters that much worse, and thus served to provoke his letter to Fichte.

Filling out the details of the exchange between Fichte and Jacobi is no easy matter. Inevitably, some inspired (if not tendentious) reconstruction is needed from time to time, primarily because documentation of many important matters is lacking. Furthermore, in the following reconstruction of their quarrel I have tried to occupy Jacobi's point of view in an effort to understand how and why he interpreted Fichte's writings in such a way that "Jacobi to Fichte" became his natural response to the atheism controversy. Therefore, it is not too important whether or not Jacobi correctly understood Fichte. (Fichte, as we know, certainly thought that Jacobi had misread him.) Rather, what matters here is how the history between the two men has to be read in order to account for their disagreement.

This interpretive constraint guides the strategy pursued throughout the rest of this essay.[1] First, I sketch out Kant's moral theology and Fichte's appropriation of it in the *Attempt*. The next thing to consider is how the *Wissenschaftslehre* demanded the reworking of this moral theology and how it produced the views that gave rise to the atheism controversy. (The role that F. K. Forberg's "Development of the Concept of Religion" played in the unfolding of Fichte's views will be discussed as well.) Finally, I briefly discuss Jacobi's response to the controversy, not only as it explicitly appeared in his letter to Fichte, but also as it *could* have appeared in the form of implications drawn from his philosophy of faith. Once the complexity of his response is seen from this standpoint, we can more adequately understand the negative assessment of the *Wissenschaftslehre* found in "Jacobi to Fichte."

The Kantian Background

Despite the prominent place that Kant's moral theology holds in his ethical thought, Kant's modern commentators have usually been embarrassed by or indifferent to it.[2] These attitudes are in marked contrast to those of his contemporaries. For many of them, for example, Karl Leonhard Reinhold, Kant's doctrine of the highest good and the postulates of practical reason was one of the chief selling points of the Critical philosophy.[3] Fichte also shared this enthusiasm in the early part of his career, for he imported Kant's moral theology, without significant modification, into his investigation of the concept of revelation.

The broad outlines of Kant's moral theology are as follows. Kant claims that the highest good—that is, that perfect proportion of happiness to virtue such that virtue is the cause of happiness—is, for any finite rational being whose will is determinable by the moral law, an end that is also a duty.[4] If, however, this end is to be one that we can rationally pursue, then it must be a real possibility for us. That is, we cannot rationally pursue that which we know to be impossible. The highest good, though, seems to be an object we cannot possibly attain: virtue is never completely acquired in a normal lifetime, because finite rational creatures such as ourselves are always subject to the blandishments of inclination (and thus are often tempted away from doing our duty). Furthermore, virtue does not seem to be causally connected with happiness, because it is an empirical fact that the virtuous are often unhappy; and so it is clear not only that virtue does not always cause happiness (although there might be *some* circumstances in which it is causally responsible for our happiness), but also that virtue often goes unrewarded. Given these facts about virtue, happiness, and the ways in which they are related, it seems that we have to conclude that the highest good is not a possible end of our actions. Since, however, it is actually demanded of us, Kant argues that we must postulate the two things required to guarantee its possibility: first, immortality, in which we are given the opportunity to perfect our virtue; and second, the existence of God, who guarantees that happiness exists and is produced in perfect proportion to virtue.

These two postulates of practical reason have been the subject of great debate, since it is not clear whether they are assumptions about the real possibility of immortality and God's existence or are intended to prove that we are actually immortal and that God actually exists. Different texts point to different interpretations.[5] In any event, the postulates are said to be the objects of a rational faith serving as the Critical substitute for the traditional natural theology that Kant had attacked to such dev-astating effect in the Transcendental Dialectic of the first *Critique*.

In his *Attempt at a Critique of All Revelation,* Fichte sensitively in-terprets Kant's doctrine of the postulates, although at times he, too, is unsure as to whether they establish only the real possibility of immortality and God's existence or actually prove that we are immortal and that God exists.[6] In every important respect, however, Fichte adopts Kant's posi-tion. Fichte claims, for example, that the requirement that we postulate immortality and God's existence follows from the fact that the highest good is an end that is also a duty:

> Through the legislation of reason, simply a priori and without relation to
> any end, a final end is proposed: namely, *the highest good,* i.e., the highest
> moral perfection united with the highest happiness. We are necessarily
> determined by the command to *will* this final end; but according to
> theoretical laws, under which all of our knowledge stands, we can cognize
> neither its possibility nor its impossibility. If we therefore wanted to
> hold it to be impossible, we would partly, even with regard to theoretical
> laws, be assuming something without a ground, and partly we would be
> placing ourselves in the self-contradiction of *willing something impossible;*
> or if we wanted just to leave its possibility or impossibility in its place,
> assuming neither the one nor the other, this would be a complete
> indifference that cannot coexist with our serious willing of this final
> end. So nothing remains for us but to believe in its possibility—i.e., to
> assume it not because we are forced by objective grounds but rather
> because we are moved by the necessary determination of our faculty of
> desire to will its actuality. If we assume the possibility of this final end,
> we cannot without the greatest inconsistency avoid also assuming all the
> conditions which alone make it conceivable for us.[7]

And, as Kant had argued, since the realization of the highest good lies beyond our powers, Fichte claims that we must postulate the necessary conditions that make it a possible end for us: "There must therefore be an *eternal God,* and every moral being must endure *eternally,* if the final end of the moral law is not to be impossible."[8]

> As a result of our moral determination to will the final end of the moral
> law, we are immediately dictated to believe that which we require with
> respect to the concept of God for the moral determination of our
> will: that a God *exists,* and that He is the *Only Holy,* the *Only Just,* the
> *Omnipotent,* and the *Omniscient One,* the supreme lawgiver and judge of all
> rational beings. That we must be *immortal* follows immediately from the

requirement on our finite natures to realize the highest good, a demand which they as such are not capable of satisfying, but *ought* to become more and more capable of doing, and must therefore be *able* to do.[9]

Fichte's *Attempt* abounds in similar statements, which is as it should be, given his enthusiastic adoption of Kant's moral theology.

As the passages just cited indicate, the conception of God that is said to follow from Kant's moral theology is a traditional philosophical one, according to which God is understood as omnipotent, omniscient, benevolent, eternal, and so on. This is so because these attributes are required for God to fulfill His role as the guarantor of the possibility of the highest good. Thus, presumably, God must be omnipotent so that no part of nature can escape or resist His power in His efforts to proportion happiness to virtue. Similar arguments can be constructed for His other attributes.[10] In short, God's perfections are said to be of infinite magnitude, so that nothing required for the real possibility of the highest good could possibly go unaccounted for, thereby ensuring us that we can rationally pursue it.

To this philosophical account of God, Fichte adds a Critical investigation of the concept of revelation. The motive behind his account of revelation (and thus of the *Attempt* as a whole) is said in the opening section to be the universality of the concept of revelation in human history. We encounter it everywhere, says Fichte, and so are led to wonder whether or not it is legitimate.[11] Such a motive is certainly sufficient to pique a theologian's interest in these topics, but it seems insufficient to move a philosopher. Yet Fichte denies that philosophy may look upon revelation as a mere curiosity. The philosophical motive for Fichte's account is more forceful than he lets on, and it arises from his commitment to Kant's moral theology.[12] If God is to guarantee the possibility of the highest good, then how we understand Him to do so is an important issue.

Since God is portrayed as a moral being in Kant's moral theology, the proper relationship between happiness and virtue must be brought about in a moral fashion. One way that this might happen is through revelation, but there are precise restrictions on what may qualify as revelation. There must first be a compelling reason for God's recourse to revelation. Fichte considers the possibility that a revelation might be required for the moral education of a people so mired in sensuous corruption that without it they will never become moral.[13] God could be revealed to them as a moral lawgiver so that their respect for Him might be transformed into respect for the law in accordance with which He unfailingly acts; revelation could thus act as a "counterweight to inclination," which would lift them out of their corruption and spur them on to virtue.[14]

Since, however, any revelation said to have issued from God must be of a suitably moral nature, its content must agree with morality, as must its mode of propagation.[15] Furthermore, the content of any purported revelation must conform to the demands of the moral law; otherwise, it cannot be considered a genuine revelation from God.[16]

Because Fichte's conception of revelation is an extension of Kant's moral theology, it possesses similar ambiguities and limitations. Whereas Fichte is undecided (as was Kant) about whether or not the postulates only concern real possibilities or are actual demonstrations of immortality and the existence of God, he never claims to be offering criteria for determining the authenticity of some representation alleged to be a revelation. Instead, he sets out the conditions in which a representation could *possibly* be a revelation from God. Hence, with regard to some appearance in the sensible world that is purported to be revelation, we can at most say "that *may* be revelation," not "that *is* revelation" (as long as there is nothing in it that contradicts the aforementioned restrictions).[17] Therefore, finite creatures such as ourselves must reach the following conclusion: "[W]e see with complete certainty at the end point of this investigation that there is absolutely no proof concerning the actuality of a revelation—neither for it nor against it—nor will there ever be; and that no being other than God Himself will ever know how the fact of the matter stands in itself."[18] So, at best, we can employ the concept of revelation negatively, sorting out possible from impossible revelations, but we can never maintain that a revelation has actually occurred.[19]

Fichte, like Kant, puts severe limitations on traditional religious concepts, refusing to allow them to contradict morality in any fashion. Both philosophers, regardless of their other differences, concur in thinking that religion is derived from, and thus limited by, morality. The consequences of the circumscription of religion by morality became the issue in the atheism controversy that prompted Jacobi's harsh attack on Fichte. But before turning to the dispute between the two men, we must look at the further elaboration of Kant's moral theology found in the opening phase of the controversy—that is, in Forberg's and Fichte's efforts to develop the concept of religion in what they took to be an appropriately moral fashion.

Fichte's *Wissenschaftslehre* and the Atheism Controversy

Fichte's "On the Basis of Our Belief in a Divine Governance of the World" was written in response to F. K. Forberg's "Development of the Concept of Religion." These essays, as is well known, constitute the official starting point of the atheism controversy. Both appeared in the November 1798 issue of the *Philosophisches Journal,* a publication Fichte co-edited with F. I. Niethammer. Fichte's essay was placed before Forberg's, despite the fact that Fichte was replying to Forberg. The superior positioning of Fichte's essay is not accidental, nor should it be seen solely as an expression of editorial prerogative; there is a philosophical motive at work as well. Fichte had, of course, already read Forberg's piece prior to writing the "Divine Governance" essay; and so his response attempts to prevent a false understanding of the relationship of religion to morality that his audience might acquire from reading Forberg.[20]

Exactly how one ought to approach Forberg's essay is a problem, for it is not clear that it is a philosophical work in the first place. It mostly contains the rhetoric and emotion of a sermon, and thus little of the rigor and dispassionate objectivity that one expects of a philosophical investigation: that is, it primarily consists of a series of fervently held convictions, offered to the reader in elevated language, and therefore lacking the efforts at justification normally found in a philosophical treatise. Hence it is an open question whether or not we should apply philosophical standards to it at all. It does, however, bear enough of a resemblance to some of Kant's views about the relationship of religion to morality to have warranted Fichte's attention. An ineffective presentation of Kant's moral theology (if, indeed, Forberg's essay is one) in a journal edited by Fichte was certainly something for him to worry about: the *Wissenschaftslehre* might have become tainted in the minds of some readers from the association of Forberg's work with Fichte's journal.

However we are to understand the literary genre to which Forberg's essay belongs, it is reasonable to assume that he had read and taken to heart Kant's moral theology, even though Kant is never explicitly mentioned by name. The tone of the essay is that of Kant's writings on religion and morality, minus the fearsome terminology of transcendental philosophy; and Forberg employs, in a condensed form, much the same progression of ideas as Kant does. Thus the essay begins with a brief sketch of past failures to answer religious questions in a satisfactory manner. Experience, he says, gives us no insight into a moral world-order; and the traditional proofs of God's existence, that is, the ontological argument, the cosmological argument, and the argument from design, are unconvincing. The ontological argument, for instance, fails for the very reason that Kant offered: existence is not a property that can be contained in any concept, be it the concept of a most perfect being or any other being, for that matter.[21]

If experience and philosophical speculation cannot establish the existence of a moral world-order, then, Forberg continues, conscience is the sole remaining source of conviction that can. Our belief in the triumph of virtue and the defeat of vice, he declaims, "arises solely from the *wish of the good heart that the good in the world may get the upper hand over the evil.* "[22] A wish, surprisingly enough, is supposed to be the origin of our belief in a moral world-order, that is, the origin of religion in general.

Forberg's tract is filled with references to this "wish" [*Wunsch*] of the good person for the eventual victory of good over evil. At times he virtually quivers with the excitement inspired by this eschatological expectation:

> Every well-meaning person, everyone to whom an interest in virtue is dear, wishes and must wish that he is not the only righteous person on earth, that everyone around him may pay homage to the good as he pays homage to it, that vice may little by little disappear from the face of the earth, and that a time may finally come in which only good people live peacefully and amiably alongside one another on the earth. This moment, if it ever arose, would be the moment of a universal rule of good over evil, would be the *golden age of the heart,* would be the *kingdom of right* on earth.[23]
>
> Therefore—it is the wish and aspiration of every righteous person to secure in the world the supremacy of good over evil and finally, where possible, to wipe evil from the face of the earth. All good people have the same wish and the same aspiration, and so arises a union of all good people for a *single* final end, and this union is the church, or "the congregation of saints on earth."[24]

Forberg doubtless numbers himself among those possessed by this wish. Although the letter of Kant's moral theology is absent, its spirit is present in Forberg's remarks, because, like Kant, he anticipates the realization of single final end in which (as the context of his remarks makes clear) virtue and happiness hold sway in the world.

Can, however, a mere wish support the sort of belief advocated by Forberg? It is difficult to see how it could. Wishing for a particular future cannot make it so, nor can it even give us a good reason for thinking that it will come to pass. Perhaps Forberg is not to be taken too literally; perhaps he is only speaking metaphorically, which would be quite appropriate in the context of an essay that reads like a sermon. Yet his talk of a good person's wish for a better future might be reconstructed in a Kantian fashion. If Forberg's good person who wishes for the victory of good over evil is understood as a metaphorical representation of Kant's person of good will motivated to act for the sake of duty alone, then such a person understands the will to be determinable by the moral law; thus such a believer accepts (or at least would in principle, if the proper reasoning were brought to bear) both that the highest good is an end that is also a duty and that the postulates of practical reason provide the necessary conditions for the realization of the highest good.

This Kantian reading of Forberg's rhetoric is not inherently implausible, but there is really no textual evidence to support it. That he constantly appeals to what the good person *wishes* is as a good reason as any for taking him at his word. If we accept that he should be read literally, rather than in the suggested metaphorical fashion, then Forberg repeats a common misreading of Kant's moral theology, according to which Kant invalidly infers the postulates of practical reason from our desire for the highest good. (More on this misreading is found in the following section.) To infer a moral world-order from our desire for it would obviously involve a fallacy. From this inference, however, Forberg draws various conclusions, including, for example, the claims that it is our duty to believe in God or a moral world-order (the two seem to be the same for Forberg, an identification that would be very un-Kantian, and for which he offers no justification), and that even the atheist has religion (given that practical belief and theoretical unbelief can co-exist).[25]

I do not want to suggest too strenuously that Forberg commits the fallacy just mentioned, because much of his essay is, as mentioned earlier, an exercise in exhortation; therefore, it is probably fairer to read his claims in a milder, less rigorous homiletic spirit. The point of a sermon, after all, is not to submit one's congregation to a bout of abstract philosophical reasoning, but rather to move them to act on the maxims of their faith. Since, however, Forberg's essay contains unorthodox ideas that were to be published in a philosophical journal, it is not surprising that Fichte decided to recast Forberg's essay in an appropriately philosophical form—in his case, naturally, that of the *Wissenschaftslehre*—in which even the appearance of such fallacious reasoning was to be studiously avoided.

Fichte's "Divine Governance" essay employs much the same reasoning as the *Attempt at a Critique of All Revelation,* but this time in the transformed context of the *Wissenschaftslehre.* The ordinary person, says Fichte, believes that providence is at work in the world, but how, he asks, is this belief arrived at? Drawing on his distinction between the standpoint of life and the standpoint of philosophy, Fichte argues that from the former point of view, that is, the ordinary one, the world is viewed as a self-regulating whole governed by the laws of the natural sciences. Thus the ordinary standpoint gives us no grounds for believing in a moral world-order created by a divine being.[26]

Instead, he argues, our belief in providence arises from the transcendental point of view of the *Wissenschaftslehre.* There we discover ourselves to be free. We do this by performing the act of intellectual intuition that the *Foundations of the Entire Wissenschaftslehre* of 1794 to 1795 offers as the starting point of philosophy:

> I discover myself to be free of any influence from the sensible world, absolutely active in and through myself, and thus I discover myself to be a power elevated above everything sensible. This freedom, however, is not indeterminate; it possesses an end of its own; instead, it posits it through itself. I myself, along with my necessary end, constitute what is supersensible.[27]

Whatever this end may be, Fichte argues, as he had done in the *Attempt*, it must be a real possibility for us, if we are to be asked to pursue it. Since it is demanded of us, we must assume that we can attain it.[28]

In the "Divine Governance" essay, Fichte does not explicitly tell us what this necessary end is, but he does provide several hints about what it could be. Given, however, his long-standing interest in Kant's moral theology, it makes sense to reconstruct his remarks about this end as related in some fashion to the highest good—that is, Kant's source of our belief in providence (understood in terms of the postulates of practical reason). We can thus draw on the overtly Kantian roots of Fichte's thoughts on these matters. "From a Private Letter" and "Concluding Remark by the Editor," two essays that follow the "Divine Governance" essay, helpfully expand on his initial reticence, but mostly by repeating in slightly different terms the same ideas of the earlier essay. Yet the following picture can be gleaned from Fichte's various efforts to explain his position.

The end of freedom is freedom itself, in the sense that any finite rational being that recognizes the demands of morality acts so as to place its own freedom and that of others under laws. Morality, in the Kantian scheme of things, is freedom subjected to laws, but not just any laws, and not just for any reason. Morality demands that we place freedom under laws (and these laws are said to be ultimately reducible to the moral law as it appears to us in the form of the Categorical Imperative) so that the realm of freedom (freedom being of absolute value for the Kantian and thus the end which we ought always to pursue) is both preserved and enlarged. In other words, to be moral is to be a free being that recognizes the absolute value of freedom and acts on this recognition through the self-imposition of law, thereby acting so as to produce a world of maximal freedom for all finite rational beings. This self-imposed restraint leads to greater freedom, for the self-imposition of law rationally orders our ends and produces circumstances in which the greatest number of ends can be satisfied. That is, this is a situation in which the freedom of every individual is respected, since freedom consists in a capacity to choose among a plethora of ends and to pursue the most effective means to these ends without interference.

Although this position is not explicitly contained in the writings under consideration here, it is a reasonable reconstruction of the views found therein (and, furthermore, is consistent with the larger context of the *Wissenschaftslehre* as a whole). Fichte uses language that suggests these ideas. He speaks, for example, of the end of reason, which is made real through the actions of a free being,[29] the necessary end of man in obeying the commands of duty,[30] and morality as the absolutely final end given to man by reason.[31] Thus, according to Fichte, to be a free being subject to various duties is to set ends for oneself, viz., those of morality, the attainment of which serves to maintain and promote the realm of freedom. It is in this fashion that one can coherently say that freedom is the end of freedom.

Fichte's end of freedom is very much like what Kant intends by the highest good, for the successful pursuit of this end would result in circumstances similar to those found in a world that has genuinely realized the highest good. If we are willing to subject our freedom to laws, then we have recognized, though usually in an implicit way, that morality is our overarching end. Insofar as we pursue morality, we develop the proper means for its realization, which include the development of the requisite dispositions for most effectively doing our duty when the occasion to do so arises. This, however, is to pursue our own virtue, that is, to develop those character traits that lead us willingly and gladly to act for the sake of duty. But the pursuit of virtue in the effort to develop the most effective means of doing our duty involves ordering our ends in a maximally consistent way and respecting the efforts of others to pursue their own ends. Therefore, as we pursue virtue, happiness will tend to come into existence, for happiness results from the satisfaction of our ends.[32]

The resemblance of this view to Kant's concept of the highest good is unmistakable. But such a view raises the issue of the prospects of success that one can expect in one's efforts to realize the end of freedom, for only under ideal conditions can we reasonably expect it to be realized as envisioned above. Much could interfere with our efforts to attain it. Kant was led to postulate the existence of God and the immortality of the soul to guarantee the possibility of the highest good. We should expect Fichte to do something similar; when he does so, however, he makes a startling claim:

> The end of reason can be actualized only through the efficacious acting of a free being; moreover, in accordance with a higher law, this end will quite surely be achieved through such acting. It is possible to do what

is right, and thanks to this higher law, every situation is arranged for this purpose. In consequence of this same arrangement, an ethical act infallibly succeeds and an unethical one infallibly fails.[33]

Kant always maintained that the highest good was a real possibility for us, but never that we could be assured of attaining it. So why does Fichte think that "this higher law," that is, the moral world-order, guarantees that our necessary end of reason will be attained?

Once again, Fichte is not especially forthcoming on an important point in the "Divine Governance" essay; therefore, how we are to view this guarantee is problematic. Reconstructing his reasoning at this point in his essay is crucial to a better understanding of his philosophy of religion, but in order to keep to the topic of this paper, I must have recourse to the explanatory constraint laid down in my opening comments. In what follows I shall restrict myself to how Jacobi most likely understood this guarantee, leaving aside the larger question of whether or not my remarks present the correct interpretation of Fichte's views. If we are to follow Jacobi's objections, then we must try to occupy his point of view, however mistaken it may have been. In this context, identifying the source of his criticisms is more important than accurately interpreting some portion of Fichte's philosophy of religion (yet it is possible, though improbable, that Jacobi understood Fichte exactly as Fichte understood himself in this matter).

In his letter to Jacobi of 30 August 1795, Fichte referred to the pure I of the *Wissenschaftslehre* as God. Presumably, he did this not only for Jacobi's benefit, but also because the identification of the two expressed an important philosophical insight in more familiar (though potentially misleading) terms.[34] One would think that Fichte came to regret this formulation later during the atheism controversy, because of the likelihood that it contributed to Jacobi's hostile criticisms in "Jacobi to Fichte." Jacobi, it seems, interpreted the I in something like the fashion sketched in the next two paragraphs.

The transcendental viewpoint of the *Wissenschaftslehre* reveals to us that the I, through its power of productive imagination, is the unconditioned ground of all that exists. Insofar as it posits itself absolutely, it is ultimately free and subject solely to the moral law, yet it posits within itself a not-I that is in contradiction to the I and thus subject to different laws, that is, laws of natural necessity. But this contradiction is not a permanent one, because the I can bend the not-I to its will, slowly yet surely approaching a world in which the I has made everything conform to the moral law in such a way that its freedom is not compromised.[35]

The "Divine Governance" essay inherits these ideas and applies them to the notion of a moral world-order. There Fichte expresses himself in a suitably popular form, but with the same intent as before: "Wherever we look, we see nothing but the reflection of our own inner activity."[36] That is, we discover nothing but the activity of the I, an activity that is ultimately in accordance with the end of freedom described earlier and thus guarantees that nothing will inexorably oppose our sincere efforts to realize it in the world. This would explain why Fichte thinks that the "higher law" mentioned earlier will infallibly lead, through our action, to the end of reason.

Furthermore, Fichte does not claim that God is the creator of the moral world-order that brings about the final end of morality, be that end the highest good or the end of freedom. (That is the sort of claim that Kant makes in his moral theology.) Instead, Fichte claims that God *is* the moral world-order, that God cannot be conceived apart from the moral world-order. In an incendiary formulation, he summarizes his recasting of Forberg's essays as follows: "This living and efficaciously acting moral order is itself God. We require no other God, nor can we grasp any other."[37] Such a passage is consistent not only with the view of the I developed in the *Wissenschaftslehre*, but it is also what one would expect from the author of the *Attempt at a Critique of All Revelation*. That is, the earlier work restricts us to a concept of God as a moral lawgiver whose actions are in conformity with the moral law. Any other conception of God is condemned as superstition. The later work (written under the influence of the appendix on transcendental idealism in Jacobi's *David Hume*)[38] eliminates the transcendent realm of things in themselves, which Kant required to limit knowledge in order to make room for faith, and replaces it with the self-positing I possessing absolute sovereignty over all things. So God, if we bother to use the term at all, can be nothing other than the moral world-order produced by the self-positing activity of the I.

This understanding of the relationships among the concepts of the I, God, and the moral world-order—leaving aside the (not inconsiderable) issue of whether or not Fichte truly held the view just sketched—accounts for Jacobi's negative reaction to the *Wissenschaftslehre*, as we shall see in the next section. The unpleasant events that unfolded after the publication of Fichte's and Forberg's essays do not concern us here. They are sufficiently well known to be passed over in silence.[39] How Jacobi's response to Fichte arose out of his thinking that went back to the pantheism controversy is the final issue that concerns us.

Jacobi's Response to the Controversy

Throughout his career, Jacobi consistently displayed hostility toward the sort of philosophical theology examined in the previous sections. The paradigmatic expression of this aversion is found in the pantheism controversy of the 1780s. We need not dwell on the details of his dispute with Mendelssohn over the proper interpretation of the Spinozistic remarks that Lessing made shortly before his death.[40] What matters is that we understand why Jacobi rejected what he took to be Lessing's atheistic pantheism.

To put the point briefly, Jacobi disagreed with Lessing's refusal to believe in an intelligent, personal creator of the world who existed apart from His creation. That is, Jacobi was an orthodox Christian believer, whereas Lessing was a pantheist of a Spinozistic sort. This, in a nutshell, is how Jacobi characterized the nub of their private disagreement.[41] He made very little effort in the later public dispute with Mendelssohn to justify his belief in God, offering, instead, his infamous *salto mortale* as his rationale (if it can be called one). In his later works, especially in *David Hume*, Jacobi goes to some lengths to develop a philosophy of faith that has as its conclusion a justified belief in the sort of God he worshipped.[42]

The views developed during the pantheism controversy serve as the foundation of Jacobi's subsequent criticisms of Kant and Fichte. He actually said very little about Kant's moral theology, but what he wrote on the matter was negative, which should come as no surprise to anyone familiar with his work. In his letter to Hamann of 4 September 1786, he writes, "I cannot possibly put up with Kantian faith."[43] Why he rejected it was briefly explained many years later in his 1801 essay *Über das Unternehmen des Kritizismus, die Vernunft zu Verstande zu bringen*. There he writes quite disparagingly of Kant's rational faith, saying that the postulates of practical reason are "mere subjective fictions" [*blosse subjective Fictionen*] and that only superstition can turn a dream into truth.[44] These sketchy remarks are probably best understood as an expression of the then-common complaint that Kant's postulates illegitimately inferred the existence of God and the immortality of the soul from a desire for their existence. Such a reading would make sense of Jacobi's complaint that Kant turns our dreams, that is, our mere subjective fictions, into truth.

The persuasiveness of this reading is increased once we recall that the same objection was more famously made by Thomas Wizenmann, who was a friend of Jacobi's. His open letter "An den Herrn Professor Kant" was published in February 1787 in the *Deutsches Museum*, when he was living in Jacobi's home, and so it is safe to assume that Jacobi was familiar with his argument. The core of Wizenmann's objections is as follows:

> For if it is supposed to be rational for a thinking person simply to assume and to believe in a God, in whose existence he lacks all grounds [to believe], merely because it is a need of his for the practical use of his reason; then it must also be rational for the lover simply to assume and believe in the love of a creature, in whose reality he lacks all grounds [to believe], merely because this belief is a need of his. But what should one call the condition of such a believer?[45]

We might aptly call the condition of such a believer "deluded," or perhaps something even less complimentary. The reality of something cannot be inferred from a mere desire for its existence.[46]

The influence of Wizenmann aside, Jacobi rejects Kant's moral theology (and thus Fichte's appropriation of it as well) because it merely provides us with a rational faith in a God Jacobi would never accept. This Kantian God is hardly the personal being Jacobi says is revealed to him in feeling [*Gefühl*], that form of cognition based not on inference or argument, but rather on the immediate perception of an object, whether that object is one in the external world or God Himself.

Fichte, as we have seen, adopts and initially supports Kant's moral theology. But the *Attempt* puts such constraints on the possible content of revelation that the traditional Christian revelation, the one that Jacobi supports, would be declared superstitious by anyone applying Fichte's criteria. (Think, for example, how the story of Abraham and Isaac and the notion of original sin fare when they are subjected to Fichte's criteria of the content of a revelation. They could not meet the moral requirements placed on potential revelations.) Furthermore, once those parts deemed unacceptable by Fichte were excised, the Christian revelation would be demoted from its position as the genuine word of God, reducing what little would be left to the status of being at best a real possibility. Such an outcome of Kantian-style moral theology was clearly unacceptable to Jacobi.

Fichte's transformation of Kant's moral theology into the idea that God is to be identified with the moral world-order resulted, as far as Jacobi was concerned, in a view that was even less acceptable. At least the Kantian view sees God as existing apart from His creation. Thus it is hardly surprising that in his letter Jacobi rejected Fichte's notion of God. This rejection rests on two things. First, there is Jacobi's conviction that feeling gives him insight into a personal God quite different from Fichte's. This the source of the claim found in "Jacobi to Fichte" that a God cannot be known, but only believed in.[47] Philosophical thought can in fact give us knowledge, but it leads to atheism—this is the lesson, as Jacobi would have it, of the pantheism controversy. Second, Jacobi rejects Fichte's distinction between the standpoints of life and philosophy: that is, he rejects the possibility of transcendental philosophy. This is consistent with his empiricism and his enthusiasm for the writings of David Hume and Thomas Reid. Without the aid of the intellectual intuition with which Fichte begins the *Wissenschaftslehre*, he cannot reach the conclusions of the "Divine Governance" essay.

In this essay I have really only gestured at Jacobi's views, and instead have devoted most of my efforts to setting out the background of the atheism controversy in the writings of Kant, Fichte, and Forberg. A more in-depth analysis of Jacobi's works of the 1780s and 1790s would be required to show that his philosophy of faith does not simply beg the question against Fichte. But the limited discussion presented here does allow us to see that Fichte's Kantianism, orthodox or transformed, naturally led to his conflict with Jacobi. Jacobi rejected the transcendental point of view and all that went with it, and thus he rejected the limitations that it placed on the concepts of God and revelation. So, of course, he considered the *Wissenschaftslehre*, if not Fichte himself, to be atheistic.[48] Fichte was naïve to have expected anything else. Perhaps the most perplexing aspect of the entire controversy is why Fichte was surprised by Jacobi's vehement rejection of his views. Jacobi was no Fichtean, and Fichte should have known that.

Notes

1. This constraint is explicitly invoked on only two occasions: first, in formulating an important claim in Fichte's "Divine Governance" essay, and then in reconstructing Jacobi's claims in "Jacobi to Fichte." Otherwise, it is tacitly assumed that the interpretations developed in this essay are offered from a point of view that would have been acceptable to all of the involved parties.

2. See, e.g., Lewis White Beck, *A Commentary on Kant's* Critique of Practical Reason (Chicago: University of Chicago Press, 1960), pp. 239–79. Beck sometimes seems positively pained by Kant's moral theology.

3. For a discussion of Reinhold's championing of Kant's moral theology, see Frederick Beiser, *The Fate of Reason* (Cambridge: Harvard University Press, 1987), pp. 232–36.

4. Kant, *Critique of Practical Reason*, in *Kant's gesammelte Schriften, herausgegeben von der Deutschen* [formerly *Königlichen Preussischen*] *Akademie der Wissenschaften* (Berlin: Walter de Gruyter [and predecessors], 1902–), vol. V, p. 122. This edition is henceforth referred to as *AK*.

5. Paul Guyer has convincingly argued that Kant, in fact, meant to prove that we are actually immortal and that God actually exists, even though there are places in his works indicating that he thought the postulates to be merely real possibilities. For Guyer's claims and documentation of relevant passages, see his "In praktischer Absicht: Kants Begriff der Postulate der reinen praktischen Vernunft," *Philosophisches Jahrbuch* 104 (1997): pp. 1–18.

6. The general tendency of Fichte's remarks on this subject is to assert, as Kant does, that we are justified in assuming that the soul is immortal and that God exists. Depending upon how one interprets this notion of an assumption, one can defend either reading of the modal status of the postulates. If it is sufficient for our practical activity to believe that the highest good is a real possibility because we also believe that the immortality of the soul and God's existence are themselves possible, then we would be limited to postulating their real possibility. If, however, the soul must be immortal and God must exist in order for the highest good to be a real possibility for us, then assuming the postulates would involve a belief in more than their real possibility, i.e., a belief in their actual existence. For Kant's use of the term "assumption," see *Critique of Practical Reason, AK* V, p. 11 n. Fichte addresses these issues, without ever fully resolving them, in various places. See, e.g., *J. G. Fichte-Gesamtausgabe der Bayerischen Akademie der Wissenschaften,* ed. Reinhard Lauth, Hans Gliwitzky, and Erich Fuchs (Stuttgart-Bad Cannstatt: Frommann-Holzboog, 1964 ff.), hereafter cited as *GA, GA* I/1, pp. 31–32, 105–6; and *Attempt at a Critique of All Revelation,* trans. Garrett Green (Cambridge: Cambridge University Press, 1978), hereafter cited as *ACR,* pp. 70–71, 154–5.

7. *GA* I/1, p. 19; *ACR,* p. 173 (translation altered). Although this passage was omitted from the second edition of the book, Fichte stood by the propositions expressed in it. For evidence of this continued commitment, see *GA* I/1, pp. 32, 104, 107 n.-108 n., 119; *ACR,* pp. 71, 152–3, 156 n.-157 n., 168.

8. *GA* I/1, p. 22; *ACR,* p. 61 (translation altered).

9. *GA* I/1, p. 79; *ACR,* p. 128 (translation altered).

10. For Kant's derivation of these attributes, see, e.g., *Critique of Pure Reason,* A814–5/B842–3; *Religion Within the Limits of Reason Alone, AK* VI, p. 139. For Fichte's derivation, see, e.g., *GA* I/1, pp. 19–23; *ACR,* pp. 60–63, 173–4.

11. *GA* I/1, p. 18; *ACR,* p. 39.

12. There can, of course, be other philosophical motives at work in Fichte's book, but the one offered here is an especially effective one. At the time of the publication of the *Attempt,* Kant had not yet published the *Religion* (and thus had not yet discussed the concept of revelation in the context of the Critical philosophy). Hence the necessity for Fichte to take up the issue of revelation in relation to the claims of moral theology.

13. *GA* I/1, pp. 51–69; *ACR,* pp. 100–17.

14. *GA* I/1, pp. 32–34; *ACR,* pp. 72–73.

15. *GA* I/1, pp. 75–76; *ACR,* pp. 124–25.

16. Claims to this effect can be found in many places. See, e.g., *GA* I/1, pp. 60, 76–77, 85; *ACR,* pp. 109, 125, 135.

17. *GA* I/1, p. 102; *ACR*, p. 151.

18. *GA* I/1, p. 106; *ACR*, p. 155 (translation altered).

19. This brief discussion of Fichte's *Attempt* should be supplemented by Hans Winter, *Die theologische und philosophische Auseinandersetzung im Protestantismus mit J. G. Fichtes Schrift* Versuch einer Kritik aller Offenbarung *von 1792* (Frankfurt am Main: Peter Lang GmbH, 1996), pp. 28–77.

20. *GA* I/6, pp. 384–385; *Introductions to the Wissenschaftslehre and Other Writings*, ed. and trans. Daniel Breazeale (Indianapolis: Hackett, 1994), hereafter cited as *IWL*, p. 173.

21. F. K. Forberg, "Entwickelung des Begriffs der Religion," in *Die Schriften zu J. G. Fichtes Atheismus-Streit*, ed. Frank Böckelmann (Munich: Rogner and Bernhard, 1969), pp. 43–46.

22. Ibid., p. 46.

23. Ibid., pp. 48–49.

24. Ibid., pp. 49–50.

25. Ibid., pp. 53, 56–57. Whether or not Forberg actually identifies God with the moral world-order is unclear. He seems to, but without explicitly saying so. His discussion of the relationship of God to the moral world-order (on p. 53) is ambiguous, intimating either that he takes the two to be distinct or that the concept of a God who rules the world through moral laws is a picturesque representation of a moral world-order that actually exists independently of a moral lawgiver. The initial paragraph of the essay (on p. 43) lends credence to the latter reading, since there Forberg formulates the philosophical concept of religion in terms of a practical faith in a moral world-order and then expresses this concept in terms of what he calls the "familiar, hallowed idiom" of living faith in the Christian concept of the kingdom of God. This supports (but does not confirm) the suspicion that Forberg's talk of God is metaphorical. Given, however, that he also claims (on pp. 56–57) that the atheist can have religion in the relevant sense (viz., through a practical commitment to bringing about the triumph of good over evil), it is clear that for Forberg ordinary belief in God is unnecessary for belief in a moral world-order—exactly the sort of claim that was ripe for the accusation of atheism.

26. For more on the distinction between these two standpoints, see Daniel Breazeale, "The 'Standpoint of Life' and the 'Standpoint of Philosophy' in the context of the *Jena Wissenschaftslehre* (1794–1801)," in *Transzendentalphilosophie als System: Die Auseinandersetzung zwischen 1794 und 1806*, ed. Albert Mues (Hamburg: Felix Meiner, 1989), pp. 81–104; "Philosophy and the Divided Self: On the 'Existential' and 'Scientific' Tasks of the Jena *Wissenschaftslehre*," *Fichte-Studien* 5 (1994): pp. 117–47.

27. *GA* I/5, p. 351; *IWL*, pp. 146–7 (translation altered).

28. *GA* I/5, p. 352; *IWL*, p. 148.

29. *GA* I/5, p. 353; *IWL*, p. 149.

30. *GA* I/6, p. 379; *IWL*, p. 167. It is also here that Fichte suggests that freedom is the end of freedom.

31. *GA* I/6, p. 413; *IWL*, p. 180.

32. This is one way of understanding Fichte's claim (in lecture I of "Some Lectures Concerning the Scholar's Vocation") that "only what is good makes us happy." That is, the failure to pursue virtue leads to a sort of moral chaos that hinders us from attaining our ends. See *GA* I/3, pp. 31–32; *Fichte: Early Philosophical Writings*, ed. and trans. Daniel Breazeale (Ithaca, N.Y.: Cornell University Press, 1988), pp. 150–1.

33. *GA* I/5, p. 353; *IWL*, p. 149.

34. Fichte, in F. H. Jacobi, *Auserlesener Briefwechsel* (Leipzig: Gerhard Fleischer, 1825–1827; Bern: Herbert Lang, 1969), vol. II, p. 209; *Early Philosophical Writings*, p. 411. This understanding of the I as an infinite self, i.e., a surrogate for God, has been challenged in many places. See, e.g., Daniel Breazeale, "Check or Checkmate? On the Finitude of the Fichtean Self," in *The Modern Subject: Conceptions of the Self in Classical German Philosophy,* ed. Karl Ameriks and Dieter Sturma (Albany: State University of New York Press, 1995), pp. 87–114; Thomas Hohler, "Fichte and the Problem of Finitude," *Southwestern Journal of Philosophy* 7 (1976): pp. 15–33.

35. This ideal is powerfully expressed in the many passages about progress and harmony found in "Some Lectures Concerning the Scholar's Vocation." See *GA* I/3, pp. 27–33; *Early Philosophical Writings,* pp. 145–53.

36. *GA* I/5, p. 349; *IWL*, p. 145.

37. *GA* I/5, p. 354; *IWL*, p. 151.

38. Jacobi, *Werke*, ed. F. Köppen and F. Roth (Leipzig: Gerhard Fleischer, 1812–1825; Darmstadt: Wissenschaftliche Buchgesellschaft, 1968), vol. II, pp. 289–310. It is here that Jacobi famously argues that Kant is not entitled to the thing-in-itself.

39. For a brief account of the controversy, see Wilhelm G. Jacobs, *Johann Gottlieb Fichte* (Hamburg: Rowohlt, 1984), pp. 65–81.

40. See, e.g., Beiser, *The Fate of Reason,* pp. 44–108.

41. Jacobi, *Werke,* vol. IV/1, pp. 58–59, 90. Jacobi's veracity in reporting Lessing's words is generally accepted. Mendelssohn, however, tended to attribute them to the latter's sense of irony, which implied that Jacobi had unknowingly been taken in by Lessing's banter. For Mendelssohn's claim about Lessing's irony, see Jacobi, *Werke,* vol. IV/1, pp. 114–15.

42. My reconstruction of Jacobi's philosophy of faith can be found in chapter four of my "Kant, Jacobi, and the Transition to Post-Kantian Idealism" (Ph.D. diss., University of Pennsylvania, 1993).

43. J. G. Hamann, *Briefwechsel,* ed. Walther Ziesemer and Arthur Henkel (Frankfurt am Main: Insel, 1955–1979), vol. VII, p. 3.

44. Jacobi, *Werke,* vol. III, p. 182.

45. Thomas Wizenmann, "An den Herrn Professor Kant," in *Materialien zur Geschichte der Critischen Philosophie,* ed. K. G. Hausius (Leipzig: Breitkopf, 1793; Düsseldorf: Stern-Verlag Janssen and Co., 1969), vol. II, p. 124.

46. It should be clear that Wizenmann has egregiously misread Kant, for the "need" referred to in the case of practical reason is not the same as the lover's need, i.e., desire, for the reciprocal love of a beloved. The need of practical reason

is to postulate the existence of God as a condition for the possibility of rationally pursuing the highest good, which must be possible, since it is an end that is also a duty. Whatever problems there may be with Kant's moral theology, a fallacious inference of God's existence on the basis of a desire for His existence is not one of them. According to Kant, we must postulate God's existence, whether or not we desire it, as long as we accept the claim that the highest good is an end that is also a duty. For Kant's response to Wizenmann (which takes the form outlined in this note), see *Critique of Practical Reason, AK* V, pp. 143–44 n.

47. Jacobi, *Werke,* vol. III, p. 7.

48. Ibid., pp. 45–46.

The Place of Aesthetics
in Fichte's Early System

Claude Piché

During his lifetime, Fichte published almost nothing directly concerned with art and aesthetics. The only document dealing with such questions appeared in 1800, although its draft dates from 1795. The document in question, as we know, is the article entitled "On the Spirit and the Letter in Philosophy." As a matter of course, this text bears little resemblance to, for example, Schelling's *Philosophy of Art* or Hegel's great *Aesthetics*. The fact that its title betrays no trace of aesthetic preoccupations, as well as its length—barely thirty pages—make it obvious that it cannot stand the comparison with, say, the ambitious undertakings of German Idealism. It does not even contain an outline of an aesthetic theory worthy of the name. Admittedly, it is an unfinished work. In adopting an epistolary style, Fichte's intention was to explicitly stress his reaction to Friedrich Schiller's *Letters on the Aesthetic Education of Mankind,* published as a series of articles in the journal *Die Horen* (1794 to 1795). Hence, the three letters, published by Fichte himself in 1800, betray the circumstances of their immediate purpose: Fichte's desire to position himself in relation to the aesthetic theory of Schiller. Evidently, Schiller did not take long to detect the critical intent of Fichte's text, which upset him to the point of refusing, in 1795, to publish it in his own journal. This being the case, how can one hope to take advantage of such a polemical piece of writing that, moreover, has the reputation of being highly complex? In what follows, I do not intend to offer a systematic interpretation of this text, but would simply like to unearth the few elements that are likely to provide an indication of what a Fichtean aesthetics would have looked like. In truth, the criticism contained in "On the Spirit and the Letter in Philosophy" is directed against Schiller from the perspective of an autonomous and original aesthetic theory, which belongs properly to Fichte. In this regard, his posthumous writings can be called upon to complete the picture.

In other words, I would like to suggest that the absence of a completed aesthetic theory within the works of Fichte can be related to contingent circumstances having to do with, among other things, his disappointment in Schiller's refusal to publish the first three parts of his text. As the *Wissenschaftslehre nova methodo* states: "Aesthetic philosophy is a principal part of the *Wissenschaftslehre*."[1] Thus there is no reason to believe that Fichte would have considered himself exempt from the task of proposing an aesthetic theory. As we shall see, he was not altogether satisfied with the developments in Kant's *Critique of Judgment*.[2] Fichte has a high opinion of aesthetics, not because it simply fills the gap between theory and practice, as suggested in Kantian philosophy,[3] but because art can be exploited in order to explore, on the basis of a remarkable affinity, the origin of philosophical discourse as such.

The Reaction to Schiller's Project of an Aesthetic Education

At first glance, Fichte's article "On the Spirit and the Letter in Philosophy" looks very much like a critique directed against both Schiller and aesthetics in general. In that Schiller is a dramatist, the charge against him is unmistakable. Before addressing the theoretical content of the *Letters on the Aesthetic Education of Mankind*, Fichte questions, in an allusive manner, Schiller's talent as an artist. When the time comes to give examples of good works of art, he contrives to mention the works of Schiller's great rival, Goethe. He quotes in a very laudatory style the *Tasso* and the *Iphigenie*, whereas his criticisms concerning works unsuccessful in hiding the mechanical aspects of their construction, or the "letter" behind the "spirit," are clearly, although allusively, directed against the author of *Die Räuber*.[4]

But even when Fichte turns his attention toward works of art that are the product of real genius, he does not seem ready to acknowledge unrestrictedly the educational benefits that can be drawn from art. In doing this, he touches upon the central thesis of Schillerian aesthetics. That a great artist is able to lead the spectator to the highest spheres of spirituality is not questioned; the problem is the following: this process of apprenticeships implies that the spectator falls beneath the "spell" *(Entzückung)* of the artist, that he literally falls "prey" *(Beute)* to him, who by the same token deprives him of his "freedom" *(Freiheit)*.[5] "The inspired artist does not address himself at all to our freedom. So little does he do so that, on the contrary, his magic [*Zauber*] begins only when we have given it up."[6] For the reader of Fichte's "Some Lectures Concerning the Scholar's Vocation," given in the summer of 1794, the above statement looks like a condemnation: in it one learns that the task of education in no way consists of an unconscious conditioning, of a kind of taming, but rather each individual must take charge of his or her own freedom. Given the conditions of the time, the class of scholars appeared to be the most appropriate *élite* to promote the cause of human emancipation. This is precisely why, in his lectures of 1794, Fichte could confer upon the learned, in the name of the education of mankind, the highest dignity.[7]

One must not, however, draw hasty conclusions: this characterization of the influence of the artist in no way means that Fichte refuses altogether the magic of art. He is willing to admit that the spirituality of the artwork "removes [man] from [the] influence [of the sensible world],"[8] so that when the moralist wants to open him to "the unploughed fields of our minds," he discovers that "half the work [has already been] done."[9] Three years after the writing of the article on the "Spirit" and the "letter," in 1798, the *System of Ethics* repeats this same phrase.[10] We find this reference to art and the artist in the last part of this work, in the chapters dealing with the duties of man according to his particular profession. It is astonishing to note that when considering contributions to the education of mankind, Fichte put the work of the artist on par with the task of the scholar and the moral educator of the people. This might come as a surprise, especially if we keep in mind the conclusions of "Some Lectures Concerning the Scholar's Vocation," but this statement, found in a book devoted specifically to the principles of morals, confirms the idea according to which Fichte's work betrays a great respect for aesthetics. Be that as it may, it does not seem that the criticism directed against Schiller's aesthetics in "On the Spirit and the Letter in Philosophy" is geared toward the dismissal of the principle, and subsequent project, of aesthetic education as such. Concerning the validity of such a project, both Schiller and Fichte agree.

It seems that we have to search elsewhere if we want to identify the real point of dissent between them. Could it be, perhaps, that the controversy involves purely theoretical questions pertaining to the structure of Schillerian aesthetics itself? An attentive reading of Fichte's article will reveal the fact that he stigmatizes in passing the play-drive (the key concept in the *Letters on the Aesthetic Education of Mankind*), which is, as we know, the establishing link between sensible and formal drive. Yet Fichte mentions the concept of play in his text only to characterize the merely mechanical aspect of an artwork, that which is unable to raise the spectator to the level of ideas.[11] In other words, a work apprehended as sheer play is simply void of spirit, meaning that play, in Fichte's opinion, can only relate to an unsuccessful artwork. This calls for a total reconsideration of an aesthetics based on the concept of play, and more so, as play reaches the status of a distinct and autonomous drive, as is the case in the *Letters on the Aesthetic Education of Mankind*.

Hence, it is for purely theoretical considerations that Fichte feels compelled to enter into a discussion with Schillerian aesthetics. Fichte felt invited to intervene, if only by the fact that Schiller had borrowed in an explicit manner some elements of the *Foundations of the Entire Science of Knowledge* (the concept of *Wechselwirkung*, namely) for use in his *Letters*. In order to illustrate the importance of the litigious point at issue here, I would like to introduce a recent thesis formulated by Dieter Henrich, according to which Schiller, without knowing it, directly challenged the Fichtean conception of aesthetics. In order to support this thesis, Henrich refers to the letter of a student of medicine at the University of Jena, David Veit. At the time of the debate, Veit was not a student of Fichte's, but they used to dine together, so that the opinion reported by Veit in a letter to his friend Rahel Levin most probably reproduces Fichte's reaction to Schiller's *Letters*.

> Consider this: many well educated donkeys are willing to pretend that Schiller's *Letters* are nothing more than Fichte's system presented in a nicer fashion; they could not notice that those letters are based on it, but that they nevertheless go their own way. Instead of the play-drive, says Fichte, he [Schiller] should have rather used "imagination."[12]

If this is a faithful report, we are in a position to assess the distance that separates both aesthetics. In fact, Fichte cannot accept Schiller's claim according to which there are in the human nature two radically independent drives (the sensible and the formal) that are mediated by a third: the play-drive. For his part, Fichte does not hesitate to distinguish three different drives (the practical, the cognitive, and the aesthetic) in "On the Spirit and the Letter in Philosophy," but he does not claim that they are independent of one another. On the contrary, they are mere ramifications of "the one indivisible primary force in man,"[13] so that none of them have a foundation of their own: we do not find in Fichte a plurality of *Grundtriebe*. Human being stems from a unique dynamic impulse; it is this "self-activity" that we find at the basis of the

Science of Knowledge that, in the realm of aesthetics, takes the form of an imagination envisioned in its "total freedom."[14] We can now understand the meaning of Fichte's remark, as reported by Veit: the center of philosophical aesthetics lies in the imagination, and not in the all too problematic play-drive. The *Foundations of the Entire Science of Knowledge,* to which Schiller refers, had already familiarized the reader with the important role assigned to imagination—through which every representation becomes possible. Fichte can see no other basis for a philosophical aesthetics than the productive imagination left to its own freedom. This is to say that he deliberately reserved a place for an aesthetic theory in his Science of Knowledge. Thus, bearing this in mind, it becomes clear to us why he could not forgive Schiller for having situated the aesthetic discourse on the level of a hybrid play-drive. For Fichte, then, replying to Schiller's *Letters* is a matter of philosophical duty.

Fichte's Own Aesthetic Theory

So far, our inquiry has revealed that Fichte did not raise any fundamental objections about the pedagogic virtues of art against Schiller. Over this point they both agree, although Schiller, for his part, tends to make of the aesthetic state not only a means of education, but an end in itself. The real debate concerns, as we have seen, purely theoretical questions, inasmuch as Schiller, according to Fichte, lacked discernment in his choice of elements taken from the Science of Knowledge: he should have realized that imagination is the cornerstone of aesthetic theory. But as far as Fichte is concerned, we have addressed only a few declarations that answer to Schiller. There may very well be an open space in his philosophy for an aesthetics; however, we do not yet understand why he feels that aesthetics constitutes, "a principal part of the Science of Knowledge." Further, in looking through his published works, we are even less sure if Fichte has at his disposal the theoretical means to develop such an aesthetics. There do exist, however, a few indications in this respect. For instance, the third section of his programmatic paper written in the spring of 1794, "Concerning the Concept of the *Wissenschaftslehre,*" clearly indicates that aesthetics is a component of the Science of Knowledge. In the section devoted to "practical philosophy," Fichte founds "a new fully determinate theory of the agreeable, the beautiful and the sublime.[15] What deserves to be noticed here is not so much the promise to provide the Science of Knowledge with further developments concerning aesthetics, but the fact that this projected aesthetic theory is "new." This amounts to saying that, despite the Kantian overtone of the three proposed themes, Fichte wants to innovate, or at least to revise Kantian philosophy. This proposition is confirmed by the manuscript of a course given in the summer and the fall of 1794, which was actually a continuation of his lectures on the "Scholar's Vocation." This manuscript deals with the "spirit" and the "letter" in philosophy, constituting the background of Fichte's article bearing the same title, even though its contents differ from the text sent to Schiller, drafted a year later in 1795. The manuscript shows beyond any doubt that Fichte clearly intended to renew aesthetic discourse, regarding, for instance, poetry. "According to *my* theory, which I do not have to prove here, the object of poetry is entertainment [*das Ergötzende*], the play of sensations in time."[16] What theory is it that he refers to here? A future theory or an already existing one? Fichte's posthumous writings allow us to shed light on these questions.

Before his departure from Zurich, Fichte spent the winter of 1794 working on a document entitled *Practical Philosophy,* in which he worked out the first elaboration of this part of the future Science of Knowledge. In it we find the questions pertaining to poetics developed to such a degree that it can be considered, in the very least, as a serious outline of this theory, to which he was to make allusions in class later in the same year.[17] Further, the manuscript comprises extensive developments that represent a first sketch of an autonomous aesthetics, that is, of an aesthetics cut loose from the theoretical yoke of the *Critique of Judgment.* For the sake of brevity, I shall limit myself to a few remarks in order to mark the distance taken from Kant's aesthetics. To begin with, one cannot but notice that the angle of approach through which Kant arrives at the problem of beauty, that is, the judgment of taste, is completely left aside. According to Fichte, the feeling of pleasure related to beauty has nothing to do with a "judgment."[18] Consequently, the faculty of judgment *(Urteilskraft)* is ostracized from his developments in aesthetics. As was to be expected, imagination becomes the main theoretical basis of this new aesthetics, insofar as it is considered as a productive faculty; this entails, in turn, a reorientation of the theory of the beautiful toward a theory of art. In other words, Fichte's turn is similar to what we find in Schiller: the philosophy of art becomes increasingly the sole field of aesthetics. The work of art becomes the center of interest precisely because it is the object of a creation. This inflection toward a theory of artistic production is, from the outset, in accordance with the new Science of Knowledge and its primacy of practical philosophy.

The fact that the Kantian problematic centered around judgment is put into abeyance implies that its correlate, taste, also loses ground. The *Critique of Judgment* reveals a marked difference between genius and taste, insofar as the act of production *(Hervorbringung)* is clearly opposed to judgment *(Beurteilung)*.[19] Fichte, being well aware of this distinction,[20] does not hesitate to base his theory on spirit and genius. Without doubt, he will be obliged to return to the problematic of taste,[21] but taste never represents more than a merely passive dimension of the aesthetic experience, as opposed to the active dimension clearly emphasized here. Because taste is a matter of judgment, it only fulfills a regulative function, whereas the genuine spontaneity of the spirit is instantiated in its whole range by the creative genius, which according to Fichte, overshadows the aesthetic dimension of external nature. This overshadowing is a direct consequence of the elimination of the problematic of judgment. Henceforth, natural beauty's appearances in Fichte's texts are scarce,[22] since original beauty, *das Urschöne,*[23] does not find expression in the external world. Archetypal beauty, in truth, can only be found in the deepest spheres of the human soul, where the artist discovers his raw materials and gives them aesthetic expression. The spectator need no longer wait passively to be surprised and overwhelmed by the contingency of natural beauty, as was the case in Kant. The aesthetic phenomenon takes place within the intimacy of the soul.

> Where is the world of the beautiful spirit? Within humanity, and nowhere else. In this way: the art of the beautiful [*schöne Kunst*] draws man back into himself and makes him feel at home. It tears him from the given nature and sets him free to be alone with himself. Throughout, the autonomy of reason remains our ultimate goal.[24]

From this remark taken from the *System of Ethics,* we can see just how far the artistic phenomenon contributes in returning the acting subject to itself and making it conscious of its sovereign independence toward the world. We realize in what sense an aesthetics based on the active faculties of creative genius and spirit coincides exactly with the orientation of Fichte's philosophy. Finally, we can understand why the faculty of judgment, with its mere regulative role, had to make room for the productive imagination.

Now that we have summarized the main elements of the Fichtean aesthetics as laid out in the Zurich manuscript *Practical Philosophy* (1794), we can return to the debate with Schiller, knowing that Fichte's reply can only be fully grasped in relation to his original aesthetic theory, the main ideas of which were quite well defined before the time of this debate. Naturally Schiller knew nothing of it, and in justifying his refusal to publish Fichte's article, he allowed himself to adopt the tone of a *Schullehrer.*

306

CLAUDE PICHÉ

> You entitle your article "On the Spirit and the Letter in Philosophy,"
> and the first three parts deal with nothing other than the spirit in the
> arts, which means, as far as I know, something totally different from the
> counterpart of the letter. Spirit as the counterpart of the letter, and spirit
> as an aesthetic property seem to me to be entirely different concepts.[25]

Doubtless, we cannot hold against Schiller his introduction of a clear distinction between spirit and letter in philosophy, and the concept of spirit—inaugurated by Kant—that we find in the realm of art. In fact, Schiller is aware of neither the contents of the manuscript *Practical Philosophy* nor the details of the course given by Fichte the year before, in which the concept of spirit—in the sense of the third *Critique*—was clearly related to philosophy. Consequently, Schiller did not suspect that, as is the case in art, there must be a place for spirit in philosophy. In reading the first three parts of the article and then refusing them, Schiller believed that Fichte condemns aesthetics in the name of the superiority of the philosophical concept. Yet the Science of Knowledge is aimed at nothing other than bringing the status of the artistic experience to the level of philosophical discourse, at least in regard to the depth of their origin in the human soul. This was indeed the global intent of the article; hence the necessity of correcting, at the outset, Schiller's misconceptions.

Astonished by the negative reaction of Schiller, Fichte offered further explanation in order to reveal the profound motivation of his endeavor, which was in no way aimed at the devaluation of art. "As far as *I* know, spirit in philosophy and spirit in the arts are as closely related as any subspecies of the same genus."[26] Art and philosophy originate from the same spirit, to which they have a privileged access. It is precisely this "kinship" *(Verwandtschaft)* that Fichte purported to demonstrate in his article. He added in his reply: "Isn't it likely that there would have to be within man an original tendency to philosophize? And what if the tendency in question were the drive to represent simply for the sake of representing—the same drive which is the ultimate basis of the fine arts, of taste, etc.?"[27] No doubt, Schiller was not prepared to face such an unexpected reply, especially since Fichte situated the artistic drive, that is, the "drive to represent simply for the sake of representing," at the lowest rank of the hierarchy of drives; below the practical and cognitive drives. Now, against all expectations he associates the aptitude for philosophy with the very drive occupying the third and lowest rank. Yet his reason for doing so is very good: the aesthetic drive is the most uninterested, and so the freest and closest to the spirit. In Fichte's view, art and philosophy rely on a faculty of imagination endowed with such a freedom that it can generate its own rules.

The pains Schiller takes in stressing the difference between artistic spirit and the spirit of a philosophical production are, in fact, intended to protect philosophy from the extravagances of the genius.[28] Fichte, for his part, does not sense any danger in allowing such a close affinity between the spirit at work in philosophy and the creative spirit in art, because imagination, which is productive in both cases, is not an arbitrary process. There is nothing unbridled about it and it cannot therefore be automatically associated with *Schwärmerey.* As if anticipating this very objection, Fichte told his students in his course on "the spirit and the letter" that there was no reason to be upset by the contiguity of art and philosophy, since a philosophy deprived of spirit and inventiveness would be, so to speak, an empty shell.

> For there are undoubtedly plenty of people who will readily grant everything that I said last time and will really understand and feel the truth of what I was saying, but will nevertheless make the following objection: "Spirit may certainly be needed in the fine arts, in literature, painting, music, etc., but what role does it have in philosophy?"[29]

If Schiller, by publishing the first three parts of Fichte's article "On the Spirit and the Letter in Philosophy," had encouraged him to write the rest—all in all the essay was to consist of nine or ten parts—thus bringing his initial project to an end, he would have been better able to figure out how serious Fichte was in claiming that philosophy and art share the same spirit and draw from the same source. It would then have been possible to examine in detail the reasoning with which Fichte relates purely aesthetic questions to problems pertaining to his conception of philosophy and the conditions of such a discourse. The text sent to the journal *Die Horen,* unfortunately, remained a fragment, cut off from the section devoted to the spirit at work in philosophy. Certainly, Fichte later came back, on some occasions, to this proximity between aesthetics and philosophy,[30] but the rich and fruitful reflection he had undertaken while distinguishing the spirit and the letter was never pursued. This is regrettable, precisely because he had initially intended to "determine" the very nature of the spirit in philosophy with the help of aesthetic theory, especially the aesthetic drive. "You find the basis for my classification [of the drives] unreliable because you have no idea of the full scope of what I have provisionally designated as the 'aesthetic drive,' and because you yourself classify and designate things differently."[31]

Without doubt, Fichte was well aware of, so to speak, the *differentia specifica* that prevails between art and philosophy. Art is nevertheless called upon to serve as a guiding thread, if not as a paradigm for philosophy, because of their common belonging to spirit as a *genus proximum*. Anyone interested in Fichte's philosophical discourse would profit in consulting the manuscript of his course dealing with the difference between the spirit and the letter, in which, contrary to the version sent to Schiller, the problem of the spirit in *philosophy* is directly addressed. One supposes that ignorance of this dimension of Fichte's thesis led Schiller to proffer a "precipitated judgment" on the Fichtean project. This would manifestly explain Fichte's tone in his retort: "*Zu welchem Stümper machen Sie mich!*"[32]

Philosophy and the Creativeness of Spirit

So far, we have seen that Fichte does not find anything to oppose to the pedagogic function of art. On the contrary, art raises man from the standpoint of ordinary life to the transcendental standpoint of philosophy. But art is thereby considered from the perspective of an aesthetic of reception, as we would say nowadays. Fichte, as is obvious, prefers to envisage art from the perspective of an aesthetic of production, because this vantage point allows attention to be drawn to the creative spirit common to art and philosophy.[33] In this manner art can become paradigmatic for philosophy.

The manuscript of the course on "the spirit and the letter" addresses directly the theoretical status of philosophy. More precisely, its purpose was to give a new account of the "whole essence of philosophizing." This preoccupation was not entirely new for Fichte, since in the spring of the same year (1794), he had systematically developed these questions in his programmatic text *Ueber den Begriff der Wissenschaftslehre*,[34] without however, exploiting the concept of "spirit" in all its consequences, although a note in section 7 clearly anticipates the future developments: "It becomes clear that the philosopher is no less in need of the obscure feelings of what is right and of genius than for example the poet or the artist; [he needs them] only in another way. The artist needs a sense for beauty whereas the philosopher needs a sense for truth, which doubtless exists."[35] In fact, this footnote mention of a special "sense" for philosophy remains, so long as it is not instantiated, a mere hypothesis. As we shall see, the demonstration of its existence will be provided a few months later in the course on "the spirit and the letter." But when he began to formulate the methodology of the *Wissenschaftslehre*, Fichte already possessed a relatively precise idea of what constitutes the essence of the philosophical activity: that which he himself tried to exert. Yet he does not claim that this idea is wholly original; on the contrary, he openly admits that his treatment of the concept of the "spirit" as well as the parallel he draws between the artist and the philosopher using the notions of "genius" and "spirit," are of Kantian inspiration.[36] If nothing else, he established an original link between two theses introduced by Kant, one from the first *Critique* and the other from the third. *The Critique of Pure Reason* issues a well known caution according to which one cannot expect to learn philosophy but, at best, to learn how to philosophize.[37] The step is small from this distinction to the one put forth in the *Critique of Judgment* between slavish imitation in art, the lot of an artist deprived of talent *(Nachahmung)*, and inspired imitation through which a genuine artist draws from the same original source as his model, which marks the work as that of a genius *(Nachfolge)*. No matter what Kant himself might have thought of this bringing together of philosophical originality and the originality that is specific to art,[38] it was most likely he who gave Fichte, who knew the third *Critique* so well, the idea of drawing such an analogy. It remains to be seen however if Fichte has the means at his disposal to concretize what in the programmatic text still appears to be an unfounded parallel between artistic and philosophical genius.

If the concepts of "genius" and "spirit" serve as the common denominator for art and philosophy, an inquiry into the extent to which Fichte remains faithful to the definitions of the third *Critique* and the extent he departs from them is essential. The reader is at first struck by a series of similarities to be found even in his choice of expressions. For Fichte, for example, spirit is the "vitalizing force in a work of art," and "spirit is therefore a faculty of the ideals."[39] This reminds us of the Kantian definition of spirit as the "faculty of presenting aesthetic ideas."[40] Moreover, as is the case in Kant, spirit and genius have a privileged relation, in comparison to all other faculties, to productive imagination.[41] But, notwithstanding these similarities in vocabulary, Fichte integrates these Kantian ideas into an entirely new framework, although the proposed readjustments are designed, in his eyes, only to attain a deeper understanding of what Kant really intended to say.

The concept of "feeling," for instance, had already gained a prominent role in aesthetics. One has only to reread the sentences of the programmatic writing referred to earlier: like the artist, the philosopher needs an "obscure feeling" in order to reach the truth. In the third *Critique*, feeling is no more than a sensible sign of the transcendental play of the faculties; this very concept, in the course on "the spirit and the letter," gains a new freedom as well as a revised meaning. It is no longer to be considered the result of a process that takes place at the level of the cognitive faculties of the mind; it becomes instead an element that provides the cognitive faculty known as imagination with activity orienting content. Compared with imagination and its product, that is, representation, feeling accesses the unknown territories that lay underneath our conscious representations. It is exclusively on the basis of such obscure feelings that productive imagination becomes capable of constituting images. The text of the course is very explicit in this regard:

> That which the imagination shapes and presents to consciousness is found in feeling. Feeling, which I neither can nor should explain at this point, is the material [*der Stoff*] of everything which is represented. Thus spirit as such, or productive imagination, may be described as a *capacity for raising feelings to consciousness.*[42]

It is obvious that the philosopher, as well as the artist, produces conscious representations, but both draw their materials from a deeply hidden source: feeling. Not content with describing the mechanism of imagination and the nature of its products from an external point of view, Fichte goes on to explore the *abyss* of the human soul from which the work of the genius emerges. Such is his reply to the *Elementar-Philosophie* of K. L. Reinhold who, in his search for an ultimate foundation, shows himself to be satisfied with a superficial "fact of consciousness."[43]

But the obscure feeling does not merely provide the raw material for the production of representations. Obscure feelings also maintain a reference, however vague, to the whole. For the spirit, feeling represents a first means of orientation. "The true inquirer philosophizes *with* this feeling [for the whole]."[44] In effect, this orientation remains at the level of what we are allowed to translate by "presentiment" *(Ahnung)* in English, that is to say at the level of a vague feeling of what ought to happen.[45] The programmatic writing gave us a taste of this principle in stating overtly that it is only on the basis of this feeling that the philosopher, groping along, progresses in the construction of his system.[46] Fichte then sees himself as obliged to bring under closer scrutiny the status of this feeling, if he is to succeed in his project of explaining what remained something like a postulate for the Kant of the third *Critique:* common sense *(Gemeinsinn)*. In fact, in the version of the text on "the spirit and the letter" sent to Schiller, Fichte proposes to solve, with the help of the feeling, the problem posed by this "universal sense," the problem implicit in the claim to universality presented by the work of art. Spirit, because of the nature of its sources, cannot express anything else but what is common to all. Because of its foundation in feeling, spirit becomes a principle of unity. "What the inspired [*Begeisterte*] finds in his breast lies in every human breast, and his capacity is the common capacity [*Gemeinsinn*] of the whole species."[47] This simply means that, for Fichte, the universal assent of rational beings does not come first from concepts, but rather from a very particular aspect of our sensibility. Even reason sees itself assigned to this unifying principle of feeling. "The spirit is one, and what is laid down by the essence of reason is the same for all individuals."[48] Thus the construction of the rational concept by the philosopher becomes a subsequent task. Immediate feeling must first trace the line of conduct for philosophy. In considering this idea we thereby reach the deepest ontological strata of Fichte's undertaking. In this respect, the manuscript of the course is quite eloquent: it is at the outset through feeling that the spirit, understood as this privileged being that genius is, is put into relation with the supersensible order of things.

> *Spirit,* in the *special* sense in which we certainly appear to be justified in denying spirit altogether to many persons, is the ability to raise to consciousness the deeper feelings underlying those other feelings which relate to the physical world. These deeper feelings relate to a supersensible world order, and the ability to raise them to consciousness may be termed the ability to convert ideals and ideas into representations.[49]

It goes without saying that the supersensible order rendered accessible through feeling in no way resembles a neutral ontological substratum. If we are entitled to characterize Fichte's idealism as an ethical idealism, it is because the moral vocation of man is made manifest to him or her through this feeling, which brings him or her into contact, albeit unconsciously, with "the laws of moral order, the spiritual harmony, [and] the unification of all in the kingdom of truth, and virtue."[50] Philosophy, as the activity of finite reason, deploys its system in the realm of the concepts, but this very reason cannot but find its raw material and its first orientation in feeling, which thereby becomes an indispensable principle of reality and unity. In Fichte's eyes, philosophical speculation must not be abandoned solely to the mediation of concepts.

Some commentators have argued that the title "On the Spirit and the Letter in Philosophy" was deliberately chosen by Fichte in order to echo Schiller's ironic remarks on the "spirit" and the "letter" in a footnote to the thirteenth of his *Letters on the Aesthetic Education of Mankind.*[51] For our part, we have discovered that Fichte was already working on this topic in the summer of 1794, well before the debate with Schiller. Thus the polemical aspect of Fichte's article should not be overestimated, as became clear with Fichte's agreement with the project of an aesthetic education. Undoubtedly, Fichte had to stress the originality of his aesthetics with respect to Schiller's and Kant's theories. But the main intent of his unfinished article was to provide a positive contribution through exposing the role of creative spirit in philosophy on the basis of an analogy with art.

The fact that feeling is considered as an original source, in philosophy as well as in art, clearly illustrates the extent of Fichte's move away from Kant's third *Critique*. Whereas in a judgment of taste, feeling plays the role of a mere sign originating in the free play of the cognitive faculties, it is envisaged by Fichte as immediate and irreducible. This is pertinent in relation to their respective conception of aesthetics; the contrast is even more acute with regard to their method of philosophy as a whole, especially when we are reminded that Kant vigorously rejects any philosophy based on feeling. One might well suspect the influence of Jacobi, although Fichte is by no means an advocate of the "nonphilosophy."[52] Indeed, we cannot characterize him, without further qualification, as a philosopher of *feeling*. The point of departure of philosophy might well be discovered at this level, but the whole task of elaboration and articulation of the system nevertheless remains to be fulfilled. This is the specific task of the philosopher: to make explicit the truth contained in these primary feelings, and render it accessible through the mediation of the concept. But in order to sustain and instantiate the truth of every step in the elaboration of the philosophical system, Fichte feels the need to have recourse to a second kind of immediacy: intellectual intuition.[53] With the help of this intuition, the human subject has the capacity to intuit him- or herself in his or her self-activity. Intellectual intuition literally gives direct access to the intellect, meaning that each step in the reconstruction of the system of the human mind can be corroborated by this intuition, which has a role similar to the intuition of space when considering geometric constructions.[54] This amounts to saying that in his Jena period Fichte draws upon two different metaphors in order to exemplify the procedures involved in the *Wissenschaftslehre:* the metaphor of the artist and the metaphor of the geometer. In the last analysis, he does not have recourse to only one kind of immediacy, but to both feeling and intellectual intuition. In fact, both are needed in that intellectual intuition touches upon the ideal activity of the subject while the feeling anchors the whole process in reality. Fichte sees a necessary complement between the clarity of intuition and the certainty provided by feeling. Whether or not the Jena *Wissenschaftslehre* succeeds in establishing the complementarity of these roles within a unique theoretical framework remains an open question. What is beyond all doubt, however, is that Fichte was determined to employ all possible means in order to circumvent the aporias linked with Kant's thesis, according to which philosophy cannot rely on any form of immediacy, but solely on a discursive process.

Notes

This text was first published under the title "L'esthétique a-t-elle une place dans la philosophie de Fichte?" in *Les Cahiers de Philosophie* (Spring 1995): pp. 181–202. I would like to thank Andrew Connochie for his careful revision of the English version.

1. *J. G. Fichte-Gesamtausgabe der Bayerischen Akademie der Wissenschaften,* ed. Reinhard Lauth, Hans Gliwitzky, and Erich Fuchs (Stuttgart-Bad Cannstatt: Frommann-Holzboog, 1964 ff.), hereafter abbreviated as *GA, GA* IV/2, p. 266.

2. Alexis Philonenko has argued that Fichte, in fundamental agreement with Kant's aesthetics, did not feel the urgency of developing this part of the *Wissenschaftslehre*. See his *La liberté humaine dans la philosophie de Fichte,* 2d ed. (Paris: Vrin, 1980), p. 99.

3. Considering the fact that aesthetics no longer plays the mediating role between nature and freedom that we find in Kant, Alain Renaut concludes that from an architectonic point of view aesthetics experiences a depreciation in Fichte's system. See *Le système du droit: Philosophie et droit dans la pensée de Fichte* (Paris: P.U.F., 1986), p. 99.

4. Günther Schulz attributes Schiller's refusal to publish Fichte's text to the rivalry that opposes them in their search for Goethe's friendship. See his paper "Die erste Fassung von Fichte's Abhandlung 'Über Geist und Buchstab in der Philosophie in einer Reihe von Briefen' 1795," *Goethe. Neue Folge des Jahrbuchs der Goethe-Gesellschaft* 17 (1955): pp. 114–41.

5. "Ueber Geist und Buchstab in der Philosophie," *Johann Gottlieb Fichtes sämmtliche Werke,* ed. I. H. Fichte, eight vols. (Berlin: Viet and Co., 1845–46); rpt., along with the three vols. of *Johann Gottlieb Fichtes nachgelassene Werke* (Bonn: Adolphus-Marcus, 1834–35), as *Fichtes Werke* (Berlin: de Gruyter, 1971), hereafter abbreviated as *SW, SW* VIII, pp. 275, 276, 300; trans. E. Rubinstein, "On the Spirit and the Letter in Philosophy," in *German Aesthetic and Literary Criticism,* ed. D. Simpson (Cambridge: Cambridge University Press, 1984), pp. 78, 79, 93.

6. *SW* VIII, p. 300.

7. *Einige Vorlesungen über die Bestimmung des Gelehrten, SW* VI, pp. 323, 328, 329.

8. *SW* VIII, p. 291.

9. Ibid., p. 300.

10. *SW* IV, p. 355.

11. *SW* VIII, p. 295.

12. David Veit's letter to Rahel Levin, 23 April 1795, quoted by Dieter Henrich in *Der Grund im Bewusstsein. Untersuchungen zu Hölderlins Denken (1794–1795)* (Stuttgart: Klett-Cotta, 1992), p. 332. Shortly thereafter, Rahel Levin was to host a literary salon in Berlin where Mme de Staël was invited during her visit to the Prussian capital in 1804. Cf. Reinhard Lauth, "Mme de Staëls Gespräch mit Fichte im März 1804," in *Vernünftige Durchdringung der Wirklichkeit* (Neuried: Ars Una, 1994), p. 251.

13. *SW* VIII, p. 278.

14. Ibid., p. 290.

15. *Ueber den Begriff der Wissenschaftslehre* (1794), hereafter abbreviated *BWL*, *GA* I/2, p. 71. See also D. Henrich, *Der Grund im Bewusstsein*, p. 335.

16. This sentence is taken from a preliminary sketch of the course on "the spirit and the letter." It bears the title, *Ich will untersuchen, wodurch Geist vom Buchstaben in der Philosophie ueberhaupt sich unterscheidet*, *GA* II/3, p. 303 (my emphasis); cf. p. 319.

17. *GA* II/3, pp. 221–23.

18. Ibid., p. 299.

19. Kant, *Kritik der Urteilskraft*, in *Kant's gesammelte Schriften, herausgegeben von der Deutschen* [formerly *Königlichen Preussischen*] *Akademie der Wissenschaften* (Berlin: Walter de Gruyter [and predecessors], 1902–), henceforth referred to as *AK, AK* V, section 48, p. 311.

20. *SW* VIII, p. 290.

21. Ibid., pp. 287, 290–91. See also *System der Sittenlehre* (1798), *SW* IV, p. 355; and *Ueber das Wesen des Gelehrten* [1805], *SW* VI, p. 396.

22. For example, see *SW* VIII, pp. 289–91. Also see *Über das Wesen des Gelehrten*, *SW* VI, p. 396. Concerning this last reference, it must be noted that nature in Fichte's thought is primarily associated with the sublime rather than with beauty—something thoroughly consistent with his doctrine. Indeed, the function of the sublime (the confrontation with the incommensurable in nature) is to return the subject to the self in order that it may realize the greatness of its moral vocation.

23. *GA* II/3, p. 319; cf. p. 207.

24. *SW* IV, p. 354.

25. Schiller's letter to Fichte, 24 June 1795, in J. G. Fichte, *Briefwechsel, GA* III/2, p. 333.

26. Fichte's letter to Schiller, 27 June 1795, *GA* III/2, p. 336; trans. D. Breazeale, *Fichte: Early Philosophical Writings* (Ithaca: Cornell University Press, 1988), p. 392.

27. *GA* III/2, p. 336.

28. In the letter with which he announced to Fichte his refusal to publish his article, Schiller draws attention to what he considers to be a confusion of genera:

> [A] philosophical work can entirely lack aesthetic spirit, and nevertheless be considered as an example of pure presentation of the spirit [*Geist*]. In truth, I do not see how you can, without a *salto mortale*, alternate from the one to the other, and I understand even less how you manage to find a connection between the spirit in the works of Goethe—whose name could hardly be expected considering the title of your article—and the spirit in Kant's or Leibniz's philosophy. (Schiller's letter to Fichte, 24 June 1795, *GA* III/2, p. 333)

29. *GA* II/3, p. 323; trans D. Breazeale, *Fichte: Early Philosophical Writings*, p. 199. In the 1798 edition of *BWL*, Fichte will have to respond to a similar objection; see *GA* I/2, p. 142.

30. See *Wissenschaftslehre nova methodo, GA* IV/2, p. 266: "and thus it follows that the philosopher has to possess an aesthetic sense, i.e., 'spirit.' " Cf. *Ueber das Wesen des Gelehrten, SW* VI, pp. 374, 376, 443.

31. Fichte's letter to Schiller, 27 June 1795, *GA* III/2, p. 338.

32. *GA* III/2, p. 337.

33. See James Engell, *The Creative Imagination: Enlightenment to Romanticism* (Cambridge: Harvard University Press, 1981), pp. 228–31.

34. *GA* I/2, p. 159.

35. Ibid., p. 142.

36. "I realize that I am here deviating from the opinion characteristic of even recent modern philosophy—unless one has correctly understood the hints given by the most brilliant thinker of all, i.e., Kant." *GA* II/3, p. 316. See also p. 325. Undoubtedly, in this passage Fichte had in mind the role of Kant's productive imagination in philosophical knowledge, and in knowledge in general, but one might certainly assume that the aim of the project that he intended to publish in *Die Horen* as a whole—the establishment of an explicit analogy between art and philosophy—was also of Kantian inspiration.

37. Kant, *Kritik der reinen Vernunft,* A 837/B 866. See also his *Nachricht von der Einrichtung seiner Vorlesungen in dem Winterhalbjahre, von 1765–1766, AK* II, p. 306.

38. It is well known that Kant refuses to use the notion of "genius" in the realm of science and of the "investigation of reason." See Kant, *Kritik der Urteilskraft, AK* V, section 47, pp. 310, 318.

39. *SW* VIII, pp. 274, 291.

40. Kant, *Kritik der Urteilskraft, AK* V, section 49, p. 314.

41. *GA* II/3, p. 316. Cf. Kant, *Kritik der Urteilskraft, AK* V, section 50, p. 319.

42. Ibid., p. 317.

43. Ibid., p. 310. See also "Recension des *Aenesidemus,*" *SW* I, p. 8.

44. *GA* II/3, p. 340.

45. Ibid., p. 336.

46. *BWL, GA* I/2, p. 142. See also *Sonnenklarer Bericht an das grosse Publicum, über das eigentliche Wesen der neuesten Philosophie* [1801], *SW* II, pp. 359, 362.

47. *SW* VIII, p. 292. This incorporation of the Kantian notion of "common sense" reveals how Fichte proceeds in order to "determine precisely" the themes that were only lightly touched upon by Kant in his third *Critique.* Already in the preface to the first edition of the programmatic writing, Fichte claims that the *Critique of Judgement* requires just such a process of elucidation. See *BWL, GA* I/2, p. 110. See also his letter to Schiller, 27 June 1795, *GA* II/3, p. 336.

48. *SW* VIII, p. 292.

49. *GA* II/3, p. 323.

50. Ibid., p. 318.

51. See, for instance, Xavier Léon, *Fichte et son temps,* vol. 1 (Paris: Librairie A. Colin, 1954), p. 349.

52. Cf. George Di Giovanni, "From Jacobi's Philosophical Novel to Fichte's Idealism: Some Comments on the 1798–99 *Atheism Dispute,*" *Journal of the History of Philosophy* 27 (1989): pp. 75–100.

53. Cf. here *GA* II/3, p. 330.

54. See the chapter entitled "Évidence géométrique et certitude philoso-phique chez Fichte" in my book *Kant et ses épigones: Le jugement critique en appel* (Paris: Vrin, 1995), pp. 129–89.

The Place of the *Vocation of Man* in Fichte's Work

Ives Radrizzani

Many leading experts agree that the *Vocation of Man*[1] plays a key role in the Fichtean journey. Martial Gueroult's thesis, formulated in 1930 and further developed in 1973,[2] admirably fixes the stakes for interpreting this text. According to Gueroult, this text marks a "decisive turning point," both in the life and in the thinking of the philosopher.[3] By seeking to come closer to Jacobi, Gueroult wrote, Fichte "seriously" modified "the meaning and the aspect of his doctrine" (82). By reducing knowledge to "a fantasy of empty images" Gueroult considered to be paradoxical, a completely arbitrary artifice to pave the way for the "'magic' wand trick, which, by introducing belief, restored reality" (84), Fichte completed an "about-face" (85), a "sudden tack" (86), which a "string of alibis" could not mask (85). According to Gueroult, Fichte "denies" intellectual intuition (87), and, by introducing the concept of a foreign force, makes the supersensible into "an actuality, that [exists] beyond the finite I" (94). In the *Vocation of Man*, Gueroult states, the *Wissenschaftslehre* passes "from a subjective basis to a transsubjective basis, from the ideality to the actuality of the absolute . . . from idealism to realism."[4]

It should be noted that in 1930, at the moment when he was defining the main lines of his interpretation of Fichte, Gueroult knew nothing of the *Wissenschaftslehre nova methodo,* the existence of which had perhaps been mentioned in the Medicus edition[5] but which was not published until 1937.[6] Nonetheless, the *nova methodo* is in one respect contemporary with the *Vocation of Man*. Fichte worked on the *Vocation of Man* in the second half of 1799 and taught according to the "new method" from 1796 to the beginning of 1799 (giving his last lecture on March 14).[7] It would therefore appear that the *nova methodo* clearly predates the *Vocation of Man*. Nonetheless, it must be stressed that in 1800 Fichte was planning to deliver this version of the *Wissenschaftslehre* to the printer[8] and that the *Crystal Clear Report*[9] of 1800 and even the *New Presentation of the Wissenschaftslehre*,[10] also of 1800, still closely reflect the *nova methodo*'s point of view. Clearly, editing the *Vocation of Man* did not incite Fichte to deny immediately the second version of the *Wissenschaftslehre*.

Hence the three following hypotheses: (1) Gueroult's reading is erroneous; (2) Fichte did indeed perform an "about-face," but actually did it in the *nova methodo;* or, finally, (3) Fichte was not aware of the changes taking place. As can be seen, the question of the interpretation of the *Vocation of Man* is directly linked to the question of its relationship with the *nova methodo*, and we will focus on clarifying this point here.

The *Vocation of Man* is without doubt one of the most difficult texts to interpret in the whole of Fichte's work. To be sure, the text is not difficult to read. It reads easily, and its great literary qualities have often been praised. But what does it mean? What message was Fichte trying to send? His contemporaries were quite perplexed. They were faced with a complete mystery.

Doubtless, Fichte provided clues. Nothing can be found in the text "which has not already been presented in other writings by the same author," he said in the very beginning of the Preface,[11] leaving us to think that the *Vocation of Man* would only be a formal variation on a well-known theme. It would appear, therefore, that some familiarity with the preceding works should allow us to put aside all doubts that might arise from reading it. Fichte nevertheless states further in the Preface that "those who only seek to repeat in a slightly different order formulas once learned by heart . . . will certainly find this book incomprehensible," suggesting that dependence on literal knowledge of his previous work, far from providing markers, runs the serious risk of generating confusion. Familiarity with the spirit of his work only results in finding the text of his previous works in another shape.

If it really consisted of nothing more than a straightforward formal variation, as Fichte claimed, then his contemporaries were not convinced. In addition, Fichte himself made a declaration that could be understood as denying this allegation. In a letter to his wife dated 5 November 1799, some days before completing the editing of the *Vocation of Man,* Fichte noted with satisfaction the progress made on matters of religion:

While editing this text, I considered religion more deeply than I have
ever done. . . . I do not believe that I would have come to this clear vision
and to this feeling in my heart without this accursed Atheism Controversy
and without the terrible consequences that have resulted from it,[12] to the
extent that the brutal methods used against me now have consequences
that both you and I can only welcome.[13]

This religious tone embarrassed his contemporaries. Could this be
called the same doctrine in a new disguise? And how should Fichte's comments be considered? For Baggesen at least, the about-face is complete.
For him, there was no doubt that Fichte had made a radical change of
course and was henceforth aligned with Jacobi's position.

I agree with every line [of the *Vocation of Man*], he wrote to Jacobi, but
only so far as each line refutes the entire *Wissenschaftslehre*. . . . This book
is in fact one of the most crazy and most intelligent works, one of the
most extravagant and of the most edifying, ever to have appeared in
the Republic of scholars. It is crazy to found science and to let it melt
into nothingness; it is intelligent, when one becomes aware of it, to
act as if one had long foreseen it . . . it is extravagant that, after having
presented to us in his way a popular exposition of his system, he should
address himself to the spirit to say to him: "You are a malicious spirit;
your knowledge itself is malice and derives from malice; and I cannot be
grateful that you have brought me along this road."[14] No adversary ever
used more violent insults against him. But it is also edifying to see an old
sinner make such a sudden conversion.[15]

For Baggesen then, Fichte rejects the results of the *Wissenschaftslehre* and
converts to Jacobi's beliefs.

Jacobi, for his part, was far from sharing these views. He also saw
Fichte's maneuver of rapprochement, but accused him of plagiarism,[16] as
he was not duped by the subterfuge and did not for one moment believe
in a "conversion." To his mind, the whole operation was nothing more
than an attempt to silence the critics who had sent him the famous Open
Letter[17] and, by this stratagem, to deny him the gain he expected to make
of it.[18] When Fichte began to talk like Kant and Jacobi and to pretend to
correct his theory by practice, this was no more than another sleight-of-
hand, making it evident that his entire thinking was no more than empty
hocus-pocus.[19]

The idea that the real aim was hidden also appears in the writings of
Christian Otto[20] and Jean Paul.[21] The latter even wrote: "The diplomats
have a code they call the destructive code [*vernichtende Chiffre*], because

it always means the opposite. [The *Vocation of Man*] is made of this destructive code for exoteric readers."[22] There is no point providing more of these quotes. I have only sought to record here the difficulties encountered by contemporaries in identifying the strategy followed in this work, which, paradoxically, was intended to be popular and intelligible to any reader capable of understanding a book.[23]

It is noteworthy that it was precisely while he was editing the *Vocation of Man* that Fichte began his meteoric career as a Mason in the Royal York Lodge of Friendship, which was to lead him to one of the most important positions in that venerable society, that of Grand Orator. I have described elsewhere the reasons that led Fichte to infiltrate this institution and the techniques he used to "neutralize" its orientation.[24] The *Philosophy of Masonry*,[25] published in epistolary form from the lectures Fichte gave to the Royal York Lodge, offers a perfect example of the Fichtean method of subverting rhetoric, in this case Masonic rhetoric, to make it conform to the spirit of the *Wissenschaftslehre*.[26]

A master in the art of simulation, Fichte, without any doubt, "encoded" his text in the *Vocation of Man,* to use Jean Paul's word. The problem is first to discover the code and second to gauge the impact of the advance made on the subject of religion. Let us therefore apply ourselves to discovering the strategy used by Fichte. The *Vocation of Man* consists of three parts: Doubt, Knowledge, and Faith.

Doubt

That the work should begin with doubt conforms perfectly to the lesson of the *nova methodo*. In fact, Fichte already cast doubt on the distinctive nature of humanity in this work. Describing philosophy as a method of justifying common sense, he demonstrated that it met one of man's fundamental requirements; man cannot in fact cling to an ingenuous trust in the truth of his consciousness but requires a well-founded truth:

> It is a good thing to have an ingenuous confidence in the dictates of
> one's own consciousness, but such is not the vocation of mankind;
> instead, it is mankind's destiny to strive constantly for well-grounded
> cognition. We are ceaselessly driven to seek well-grounded conviction;
> and anyone who has arrived at the point of philosophical doubt cannot
> be sent back along the path he has already traversed, but will always seek
> to resolve his doubts on his own.[27]

Thus, to doubt nothing would be to miss his vocation. The *Vocation of Man* opens with an experience whose universal validity speaks to every reader.

What is the content of this universal experience of doubt? The first book offers a poetically dramatized version of the third conflict of transcendental ideas in the *Critic of Pure Reason*.[28] Man is, in fact, described as torn between two antinomical concepts of the world, one based on the thesis of necessity and satisfying the intellect, the other based on the thesis of freedom and satisfying the heart. Man cannot, without denying a part of himself, adopt either of these theses and is caught between these conflicting demands: he therefore doubts. The autobiographical dimension of this "universal" experience of doubt has not escaped the attention of commentators.[29] Before discovering Kant[30] and reaching knowledge, Fichte himself experienced this dilemma.

Alexis Philonenko very astutely observed that the nature of doubt in the first book of the *Vocation of Man* did not correspond to the conflict between idealism and realism found in the *First Introduction to the Wissenschaftslehre* of 1797[31] (that is, in the Second Introduction of the *nova methodo*).[32] It should, nonetheless, be noted that this is not indicative of a change in doctrine, because this difference is due solely to the method employed in each work. In fact, the conflict between idealism and realism with which the *nova methodo* begins is the exact equivalent, in a shorter form, of the dialectic of systems, which was the backbone of the argument in the first version of the *Wissenschaftslehre*, the *Foundations*.[33] It was only relegated to the introduction because of the simplification in the method of exposition selected for the second version of the system.[34] This dialectic of systems results from the artificial method of philosophical reflection, however, and seems to belong to these "lengthy preambles in which the objections and extravagances of an unnatural and artificial understanding are anticipated," which are mentioned in the Preface to the *Vocation of Man*,[35] whereas the doubt of the first book is supposed to be produced by the ordinary course of natural understanding.

Knowledge

The reader cannot solve the dilemma alone. It is only thanks to the intervention of the Spirit, in the second book, that the reader manages to cast off doubt and attain the path of knowledge. Why Spirit? In what role does Fichte cast it; and what knowledge does it help gain? Does this Spirit, that commentators have not failed to link with Philonous in Berkeley's

Dialogue between Hylas and Philonous and with the Spirit of Goethe's *Faust*, not play the part of Kant in the Fichtean journey and especially the part played by Fichte himself at the beginning of the *nova methodo,* when he asks his audience to carry out a postulate? In my opinion, it is in the light of this parallel that the need to call on the Spirit becomes perfectly clear. In the First Introduction to the *nova methodo,* the postulate, which Fichte asks to be carried out in section 1,[36] is deliberately presented as the minimal basis required to develop a systematic philosophy, capable of satisfying man's inherent need for science.[37] The knowledge that is built on this base must therefore correspond to that which is required for man to progress on the path to his vocation. The completion of the postulate has the function of raising the listener or the reader to the philosophical viewpoint, however, and this elevation to the philosophical viewpoint assumes a break in the process of natural reflection and a dissociation between the series of I and that of the philosopher. But, so long as the reader of the *Vocation of Man,* according to the hypothesis, sticks to natural understanding, he cannot raise himself to the philosophical or transcendental viewpoint and remains immersed in the viewpoint of the common conscience. This is why the intervention of a third party, in this case the Spirit, is required.[38] Furthermore, this Spirit has no other aim than to lead the reader to an experiment similar to the one required by the postulate of section 1[39] and to bring him to admit that which, in the *nova methodo,* is presented as the cardinal proposition of transcendental idealism, that is, that "all consciousness is nothing but self-consciousness."[40] Consequently, the transition from the first to the second book and the intervention of the Spirit are meant to correspond to the elevation to the philosophical viewpoint.

There is doubtless elevation to philosophy, but to what philosophy? Must we conclude from this analogy that it is transcendental philosophy in its Fichtean formula, that is, the knowledge of the *Wissenschaftslehre,* that the Spirit in the second book of the *Vocation of Man* elevates the reader? This is generally what commentators have believed. But how should we understand the end of the second book and particularly the admirable summary that the I suggests for knowledge discovered by way of the Spirit?

> There is nothing permanent anywhere, neither outside me nor inside me, only an ceaseless change. Nowhere do I know of any being, not even of my own. There is no being. *I myself* know absolutely nothing and am nothing. *Images* are: they are all that exists, and they know about themselves in the manner of images . . . which do not represent anything, images without meaning and purpose. I myself am one of these images; no, I am not even that, but only a distorted image of these images. All

reality transforms itself into a marvelous dream, without a life which would be dreamed and without a spirit which would dream; into a dream which hangs together in a dream of itself. To *intuit* it is the dream; to *think* it (the source of all being and all reality which I imagine, of my being, my power, my purposes) is the dream of this dream.[41]

Why, at the end of the second book, does Fichte allow knowledge to dissipate into a pointless play of images that have neither meaning nor consistence? Was Baggesen right in claiming that each line of the *Vocation of Man* "refutes" the *Wissenschaftslehre*? And was this reduction of knowledge to a simple fantasy not, as Gueroult believed, anything other than a trick to make way for the jump into belief by a simple wave of a magic wand? If the knowledge developed by the Spirit in fact corresponded to the knowledge of the *Wissenschaftslehre*, Baggesen would be perfectly right to say that no enemy of Fichte ever spoke more critically of him. If this was Fichte's last word on theoretical knowledge, he must have been in real need of money, in 1800, to still nurture the project of publishing the *nova methodo,* and how illogical of him to write the *Crystal Clear Report* and the *New Presentation of the Wissenschaftslehre!*

But beware of the destructive code! What if it were the other way around? For my part, I believe that the useless and prenihilistic knowledge developed by Fichte with his consummate dialectic art of subtly using several parts of the *Wissenschaftslehre,* far from corresponding to the knowledge exposed in the *Foundations* and in the *nova methodo,* is only a pastiche of them. This "knowledge" in all its stupidity is not Fichte's *Wissenschaftslehre,* it is that of his enemies, or rather the fantastical knowledge to which Fichte's enemies thought to reduce the *Wissenschaftslehre,* an unnatural knowledge that was severed from the practical.

Gueroult was close to the solution in his admirable analysis in which he noted that, in the second book of the *Vocation of Man,* Fichte

not only leaves aside the practical philosophy, but also the practical part that constitutes an indispensable component of the system of knowledge. It would appear therefore that we are faced here with a purely theoretical [*bildende*] activity, i.e., with an intelligence that can be considered from the constant viewpoint of the W.L., as deprived by itself of contact with reality.[42]

As a first class connoisseur of Fichte, Gueroult noticed all the differences that separate the knowledge expounded in the second book of the *Vocation of Man* and the knowledge of the *Foundations* and of the *Outline.*[43] His mistake, which he shares with most commentators,[44] is that of simply wanting to identify Fichte's position with the one expressed in the second book. By being too literal, Gueroult missed the point, and when he wrote that "Fichte was right in the Preface to exorcise our memory and to incite us not to look in this book for what we thought we had read elsewhere,"[45] the words, by a cruel twist of irony, turn on him. As Jean-Christophe Goddard noted in the admirable introduction to his French translation of the *Vocation of Man*, Gueroult was right to mention that the exposition of theoretical knowledge in the second book starts with feeling, that is, with a limit to practical activity,

> but . . . there is no mention of this practical basis of feeling anywhere
> in the dialogue between the I and the Spirit [in the second book]. The
> attention focused on the I's reflection on feeling, sets aside the real basis
> of it, and leads therefore necessarily to the position . . . of thought as the
> only foundation of objectivity, i.e., to an absolute idealism, which cannot
> explain the original limitation of feeling and therefore posits the reality
> of the object only as transferred outside of the I by the subjective act of
> intuiting.[46]

This Berkelian style of idealism, which is denounced under the name of "dogmatic idealism" in the *Foundations*[47] and of "groundless idealism" in the *nova methodo*,[48] far from being the position of the Fichte of the *Vocation of Man*, is the very position from which he believed he should distance himself. Contrary to the commonly accepted interpretation, the Fichte of the *Vocation of Man* remains, on this point at least, faithful to the lesson of the *Foundations*, the most remarkable outcome of which was to demonstrate that the theoretical part only confers upon the principles of the system the modality of possibility, not that of actuality, which they first receive in the practical part. As a result, Fichte remains faithful to the lesson of the *nova methodo*, in which, basing himself on the results of the *Foundations*, he gave up the idea of presenting the theoretical and practical parts separately.

It remains to be explained why Fichte employed this strategy, which disturbed so many of his readers. The meaning of the structure of the work becomes clear once we see it as a reply to Jacobi's famous "Open Letter," sent to Fichte on 21 March 1799 and printed in early November of the same year,[49] exactly while Fichte was editing the *Vocation of Man*. This letter, written with the intent of coming to Fichte's assistance by giving him a timely support in the business of the accusation of atheism, while clearly distancing himself from Fichte's position,[50] was in fact a veritable philosophical assassination. The author of the *Wissenschaftslehre* was indeed praised to the heavens and endorsed as the "real Messiah of speculative reason,"[51] while Kant, the "John the Baptist of Königsberg," was relegated to the simple part of "forerunner."[52] At the same time, however, this philosophy of which Fichte was made the incarnation was ridiculed and damned, because of its very purity, as an irreducible solipsism, being forced, by a "chemical process," to destroy all that exists in order to create the world and the I.[53] The accusation of subjectivism in the example of the woolen stocking was the unkindest cut of all, a burlesque caricature of the *Wissenschaftslehre* of which Jacobi, by the way, was very proud:[54]

> Last winter, in a moment of mischief, I subjected the result of the Fichtean idealism into a form of comparison while in Hamburg. I chose that of the woolen stocking.
>
> To make the genesis and the constitution of a stocking into a representation other than the usual empirical representation, one only needs to unravel the wool and pull it along the skein of the identity of this object-subject. One can then clearly see how this individual was made: by a simple to and fro of the wool, which means that this thread is constantly limited in its movement and that it is prevented from continuing its striving for the infinite, without anything empirical intervening in the weft, without anything else interfering or being added.
>
> I add stripes, flowers, a sun, a moon and stars to this stocking that I am making, all possible kinds of design, and I know that all this is nothing more than a product of the productive imagination of the fingers, which hangs between the I of the textile fiber and the non-I of the knitting needles. Considered from the viewpoint of truth, all these designs and the stocking itself are nothing but naked thread. Nothing had entered into it, neither the needles nor the fingers; it alone is all this and in all this there is nothing but it; it is it entirely and it is only by its continuous movements of reflection over the needles that it has become this particular individual.[55]

The result of this speculative enterprise was summed up in this pithy formula: "From nothing, to nothing, for nothing, in nothing" *(aus Nichts, zu Nichts, für Nichts, in Nichts).*[56]

Now, what was Fichte's reaction? Was he annoyed by this gross disfiguring of his doctrine, which he clearly used as an inspiration in the *Vocation of Man?* The words that he puts into the mouth of the I, at the end of the second book, match those that the famous thread in the woolen stocking could have pronounced itself. As a skillful dialectician, far from taking umbrage at this mischief, which was to have serious consequences for the later fate of the *Wissenschaftslehre,* Fichte presented his thanks to the author on 22 April for having written *for* him a letter that could not, as far as he could see, be in any way *against* him and assured Jacobi that he "subscribed to it unconditionally almost from end to end."[57] What criticism this "almost" implies, the rest of the letter (which expresses in an indirect way, via the copy of an extract from a letter to Reinhold, what he apparently initially intended to write directly in a first draft)[58] proves this:

> I subscribe entirely to Jacobi's declarations [in his "Open Letter"]. He has a very intimate knowledge of the essence of speculation as of the essence of life. How is it, then, that he cannot coldly rise above them and relate them to each other. Why must he remain captive to the viewpoint of speculation to the extent that he is ashamed to formulate his objections to my system,[59] or, in an other mood, from the viewpoint of life, that he laughs like nobody else at speculation, whose value and meaning he knows, but that he curses and execrates it.[60]

In the parallel version of the draft, we read:

> I hardly know how and in which way we are opposed.—We are in agreement about science. We are also in agreement about life. . . . If the disagreement is not based on a complete misunderstanding, then it would necessarily turn on the question of knowing to what extent science can describe life. It is necessary to exactly indicate the point where they differ, on the basis of their concept.[61]

These two quotes, which are remarkable for many reasons, betray the deeper reason for the strategy used in the *Vocation of Man*. Fichte always believed in a close convergence of views with Jacobi, a subject that he cherished above all else and which recurs in all his correspondence with him.[62] Because of this convergence in which he believed, the "Open Letter," despite its appearance, could not have been written *against* him and could therefore only be a misunderstanding. The misunderstanding stemmed from a confusion, already diagnosed long before, between the viewpoint of speculation and that of life.[63] To clear up the misunderstanding, Fichte thought it judicious to play Jacobi's game, to adopt his viewpoint and his reproaches, in order to put the reply of the *Wissenschaftslehre* in a better light. The I who curses and execrates the Spirit, at the end of the second book, is not the I who takes the viewpoint of the *Wissenschaftslehre*, but the I who takes Jacobi's viewpoint, judging speculation from the viewpoint of life and not having "risen coldly" above speculation and life to discover the articulation of these two. If Fichte opted for this strategy, it was because he still believed that he could dissipate what he thought to be an unfortunate misunderstanding.

Faith

> Usefulness of science.—It is the vocation of man, who has tried and
> through trying failed [*in Irrtum kommen*]. The accomplishment eradicates
> these mistakes: negative usefulness.[64]

It is no accident that this quote, which strikingly summarizes the entire
project of the *Vocation of Man* and which provides a genuine key to its
interpretation, is extracted from a draft of the letter Fichte planned
to write to Jacobi in reply to the "Open Letter." This proves that the
Vocation of Man was, in Fichte's mind, his reply to the "Open Letter."
The knowledge of the second book has a "negative usefulness." In other
words, it has a pedagogical and dialectical function: it is a matter of
demonstrating what is false, to better highlight the truth. In the second
book, the presentation of false knowledge, or more exactly of a foreshort-
ened knowledge reduced to simple theory and faithfully reproducing
the position attributed to Fichte in the "Open Letter," is intended to
demonstrate that such knowledge must not be considered as the last word
of the *Wissenschaftslehre,* and, thereby, to protect it from accusations of
subjectivism. The function of the third book was to demonstrate to Jacobi
the true position of the *Wissenschaftslehre,* or, in other words, to enlighten
him about the link between speculation and life. The aim of the third
book was not to develop true knowledge, because more than one type of
knowledge does not exist. The one developed in the second book was in
a certain sense completely satisfactory; this is the reason why Fichte, in
the second book, was able to use major parts from the *Foundations* and
especially from the *Outline.*[65] As Philonenko remarked accurately, "the
knowledge described is not false, if one supports it."[66] The third book
was intended to provide the required support, the anchor in reality or in
life, which confers a real value onto purely theoretical knowledge. Just
as the transition to the second book signified elevation to the philosophical viewpoint, the transition to the third book was intended to signify
elevation to the viewpoint of the *Wissenschaftslehre.*

Up to that point, the general meaning of the *Vocation of Man*
seemed to conform to the lesson of the *nova methodo,* but is this precisely
the case in the third book, with the introduction of the practical foundation, which enacts a significant shift, or even a complete turn-about
in Fichtean philosophy, as certain commentators claim? This third book,
entitled Faith, accords a very important place to religious considerations.
But, is it not precisely in matters of religion that Fichte attained, while
editing this work, a clarity without precedent? What are the possible systematic repercussions? And why does the question of religion become so

important for him? These questions, I repeat, concern the interpretation of the *nova methodo* as well as that of the *Vocation of Man;* it is indeed hardly probable, for the above reasons, that a major change occurred between the two works.

In the *nova methodo,* Fichte explains that the second presentation of the system differs from the *Foundations* in that the first version intended to explain representation, while the second advances a step beyond and must provide the condition of what was the condition of the *Foundations.*[67] "With the *intelligible* world," the *nova methodo* provides "a firm substrate for the *empirical* one,"[68] thanks specially to the deduction of intersubjectivity. But the third book of the *Vocation of Man* has exactly the function of discovering a firm substrate for the empirical world; and in a general manner, Fichte's program in the Preface of this work is to "bring the reader from sensibility and to lead him to the supersensible."[69] There is clearly an analogy here, but how far does it go?

It is worth remembering that, for Gueroult, the *Vocation of Man* marks the transition from a subjective to a transsubjective viewpoint, or from the ideality to the actuality of the absolute, judging that Fichte would turn the supersensible into an actuality that exists beyond the finite I. In the same vein, Luigi Pareyson, without doubt one of the best commentators on the *nova methodo,* judges that the *Vocation of Man* marks the transition "from a philosophy of the I to a philosophy of the absolute that manifests a decisively religious character." The purpose would be not only to found "the sensible world on the moral law," but also "the spiritual world on an infinite *life,* on a supersensible reality."[70]

But does the problem not already appear in the *nova methodo,* when Fichte links explicitly the "main purpose of the new presentation" to the search for a firm substrate of the sensible world in the intelligible one? In what sense should we understand the term "substrate"? Does this term not announce a clear return to ontology? And does the idea of substrate not seem to be heterogeneous to the structure of the *nova methodo?* Indeed, the whole second part of this work is dominated by the construction of a fivefold synthesis. And within this synthesis, each term appears to have the same value: the sensible world, what is determinable in the real series, as well as the supersensible world, what is determinable in the ideal series. Fichte repeatedly insists that the fivefold synthesis must follow the model of a synthesis that is not linear but "like a circle."[71] The work ends with a general reciprocal influence, not only between the different components within both the sensible world and the supersensible world, but also between these two worlds. Does the structure of the fivefold synthesis not itself seem incompatible with the idea that one of the terms of this synthesis functions as the substrate of another term of the same synthesis?

329

It should be noted that the fivefold synthesis is first achieved at the end of the genetic process, at the moment where the speculation should coincide with the viewpoint of the natural consciousness. Although at the level of the natural consciousness, sensible and supersensible appear to be of equal value, this in no way precludes one being the substrate of the other at the transcendental level. But once again, in what sense should we understand this term? In the first part of the *nova methodo,* the methodological goal is to enumerate all the conditions required for the postulate at the beginning of section 1 and to conclude with the discovery of a supreme condition, an ultimate foundation of consciousness, the pure will. The pure will, which is "something purely intelligible," is the true root of consciousness, "which must be presupposed prior to all empirical willing and to all empirical cognition."[72] It is only to the pure will and, correlatively, to an intelligible world, which is posed with it, that "all other appearances are correctly connected,"[73] Fichte tells us.

It seems to me that, in the *nova methodo,* the pure will can be said to be "substrate of the intelligible world" only as an explanatory ground *(Erklärungsgrund).* As a transcendental condition of consciousness, it has the same status as the other conditions enumerated in the first part of the book, with the difference that it is the supreme condition. All terms deduced in the first part must therefore be connected to it in the artificial genesis of consciousness of the second part. If I am right, the preeminence of the pure will and, correlatively, of the intelligible world is an epistemological, not an ontological, one. In the transcendental ontology constructed on that supreme epistemological condition, intelligible and sensible worlds have an equal value, the one being determined by the other and reciprocally.

Let us return to the *Vocation of Man,* in which so many commentators thought they detected a radical change in Fichte's thinking. First observation: the elevation to what Fichte, in analogy to Jacobi, calls "faith" consists in the discovery of that which functioned in the *nova methodo* as the supreme condition of the consciousness, that is, the pure will. It is precisely the discovery of the pure will that disperses the fancies of subjectivism, which seemed to threaten the entire result of the knowledge at the end of the second book. It provides the required foundation, because it introduces by necessity that practical dimension missing in the second book. Indeed, in the will, I know that I will and I also will. And I would not know that I will if I did not will. Consequently, the will is the principle that allows us to go beyond representation, to which we remained captive in the second book.

There is once again a striking analogy with the *nova methodo,* but is there not nevertheless a profound change of course? Why did Fichte make this pure will an object of faith? Is this not an indication of a turn toward religion and of too great a concession to Jacobi? I think for my part that it is precisely by making the will an object of faith that Fichte was true to the lesson of the *nova methodo,* because one must not forget that the whole methodology of the *nova methodo* is based on a "postulate" and is not supposed to have any value for anyone, who could not carry out this postulate. "Every philosophy," Fichte tells us in the Second Introduction to the *nova methodo,* "presupposes something that it does not demonstrate on the basis of which it explains and demonstrates everything else."[74] The *Wissenschaftslehre,* like every other philosophy, is therefore finally based on a nonknowledge. This nonknowledge on which every knowledge depends is, in the *nova methodo,* the postulate of liberty. The term of "faith" is also to be found in that Second Introduction. According to Fichte, it is only the "faith in one's own self-sufficiency and freedom" that allows us to choose between idealism and dogmatism.[75] The idea that knowledge is ultimately based on faith implies in itself nothing religious, otherwise the whole *nova methodo* and every philosophical writing can be said to be "religious."

Once the supreme condition of consciousness and knowledge has been reached, Fichte turns to the deduction of the conditions for the applicability of this supreme condition. Thus, the voice that resounds inside me and that has led me to the discovery of pure will "does not only command me to act in general."[76] It is therefore a matter of demonstrating how the ability to act in any given concrete situation is linked to the duty stemming from the sentiment of pure will, which is the first step in the process of sensibilization of pure will and consists in the deduction of both the intelligible world and the sensible world as the sphere of my duty. The motive of this approach is the same as the one used in the second part of the *nova methodo,*[77] except that in the third book of the *Vocation of Man,* Fichte follows a simplified procedure. In fact, he can rely on the results of the second book, where he demonstrated that, from a purely speculative point of view, that is to say, without any practical basis, the sensible world and the supersensible world are "products of my act of representation,"[78] so that the accent in the third book is not so much on the deduction of these two worlds but on the benefit that their attachment to the practical foundation brings about in their deduction.[79] Transfigured by faith (to be understood in the meaning intended), the intelligible world and the sensible world are no longer simple fictions; because of my moral vocation, I am obliged to allow them an independent existence; the fancies of subjectivism and solipsism disappear; "empty speculation disappears like fog before the heat of the sun."[80]

The practical ontology developed on the basis of this postulate of my moral vocation—in agreement with the results of the *nova methodo,* in which the deduction of the intelligible world and of the sensible world was directly supported by its practical foundation—is of a perfectly tran-scendental nature and does not imply a "transsubjective basis" or a move beyond the perspective of the finite I or the introduction of an existing actuality beyond the finite I: "Everything that exists for me imposes its existence and reality on me only through this relation [namely my moral vocation], and only through this relation do I apprehend it. And for any other existence I have no organ at all."[81]

This deduction of the existence of the intersubjective world and of the objective world as the sphere of my duties, as a backdrop to my moral vocation, reveals a definite "religious" aspect, in the meaning defined by Fichte in the last pages of the *nova methodo,* in the chapter entitled "Deduction of the Subdivisions of the *Wissenschaftslehre.*" It in fact is grounded in the postulate of freedom, that is to say, in a "postulate that practical philosophy addresses to the theoretical realm, to nature, which, by means of a supersensible law, is supposed to accommodate itself to the goal of morality."[82] Fichte indicates, however, the principle of a purely "juridical" deduction of these two worlds "for the person who may never have thought about his own moral vocation (if there could be such a person), or, if he should have thought about it, has not the least intention of fulfilling it at any time in the indefinite future."[83] Such a "juridical" deduction, which by hypothesis, leaves moral vocation aside, and which must also be valid for he "who may never have thought about his own moral vocation" or who would deny it,[84] coincides with the "religious" deduction by basing the belief in the supersensible world and in the sensible world of anyone subject to the law, not, of course, he continues, on the "thought of his duties," but on the "demand of his rights." Al-ready in the *nova methodo* philosophy of religion and philosophy of right were presented as "closely related" together and as sharing "the same domain."[85] This assertion remained, however undetermined. While the third book of the *Vocation of Man* can be considered as an extension of the doctrine taught in the second presentation of the system, it thus adds an interesting specification that allows a better understanding of the link between the two parts of the "philosophy of the postulates" constituted by law and religion. This addition can certainly be attributed to the "clar-ification" of the concept of religion announced by Fichte to his wife.

The continuation of the third book, which lays out the program of adaptation of nature and society to the goal of morality required by the postulate of freedom, that is, the subjection of nature and the creation of a State of Law,[86] belongs to the philosophy of religion, in the meaning defined above. This part, which has no equivalent in the *Foundations* or in the *nova methodo,* despite having its foundation there, is, however, closely related to the *Lectures Concerning the Scholar's Vocation,* the two first lectures of which were dedicated to the deduction of man's universal goal.[87] In the *Scholar's Vocation,* man's inability to be satisfied with the world as he finds it and his need to strive for perfection were founded on the very essence of man as a mixture of the finite and the infinite. In the language of the *Foundations,* the absolute I, which is the principle of the system, cannot be restricted, because of its very absoluteness; but it cannot become aware of itself without positing itself within limits. As the absoluteness of the I cannot be suppressed, however, the I cannot posit limits without seeking to push them back in a demand for perfection.[88] From this Fichte concluded that "man's ultimate and supreme goal is complete harmony with himself and—so that he can be in harmony with himself—the harmony of all external things with his own necessary, practical concepts of them,"[89] though he noted that the achievement of this ultimate and supreme goal cannot constitute man's vocation, as it must remain "eternally inaccessible," "so long as man is not supposed to cease to be man and to become God."[90] This harmony to be achieved, namely, in the sensible category, the subjection of nature[91] and, in the supersensible category, the creation of a State of Law,[92] therefore takes on the status of a regulative ideal of pure practical reason, man's vocation being not to be perfect but to "perfect himself without end."[93] Fichte remains faithful to this concept in the *Vocation of Man.*

In the *Vocation of Man,* Fichte uses the difference between what he called, in the *Scholar's Vocation,* man's "ultimate and supreme goal" and his "vocation" to establish the second Kantian postulate of practical reason, that is, the immortality of the soul. The third book ends with the deduction of the third postulate concerning the existence of God. In my view, the development of this part of the philosophy of the postulates raises three questions: (1) Does this part of Fichte's teachings constitute an innovation, or does it belong to the program of philosophy developed by Fichte during his Jena years? (2) Is such a deduction compatible with a transcendental position, or must it be considered a relapse into dogmatism, from which Fichte, under the dominating influence of his time, was unable to extricate himself? Finally, (3) Is it necessary? Even if this part of Fichte's teaching were transcendentally founded, would it not be possible to bypass it, and wouldn't Fichte's Jena philosophy be entirely intelligible without this religious layer, as maintained for example by Luigi Pareyson?[94]

As already mentioned, Fichte, at the end of the *nova methodo,* reserves a place in the construction of his system for the philosophy of religion as part of the "philosophy of the postulates." Moreover, it has been noticed that Fichte, in the Kantian postulates, introduces an important asymmetry by strengthening the role of the postulate of freedom, which he made into the keystone of transcendental idealism, the copestone of the entire speculative edifice. What role should, therefore, be assigned to the two other postulates? Can they both be qualified as "postulates" in the same way, or should the term "postulate" be understood in two different ways? Finally, as the postulate of freedom encompasses consciousness in its entirety, is there a place alongside it for the postulates of the immortality of the soul and of the existence of God, or must these two be taken as parts of the first and be considered only as aspects of it?

Let it be noted that, in the *Wissenschaftslehre nova methodo,* Fichte charges Kant with unduly restricting the field of application of his practical postulates by limiting it solely to the immortality of soul and the existence of God. Nonetheless, Fichte, by extending it to consciousness in its entirety,[95] does not thereby put faith in God and immortality into question. On the contrary, in the First Introduction to the *nova methodo,* Fichte explicitly connects, on the one hand, the discovery of knowledge corresponding to the vocation of man and putting an end to doubt, and, on the other hand, the establishment of faith in God and immortality: "Skepticism can lead one astray concerning belief in God and immortality."[96] Thus, one already finds in the *nova methodo* the implicit idea that the overcoming of skepticism must allow us to support faith in God and immortality. And when, in section 13, he emphasizes that "we cannot consider any finite, rational, conscious being to be holy,"[97] he is directly echoing the chapter of the *Critique of Practical Reason* dedicated to the immortality of soul, in which Kant defines holiness as the "entire conformity of will to moral law . . . a perfection of which no rational being belonging to the sensible world is capable of at any moment of his existence." It is exactly on the point of this difference between will and "ought," however, that it is "practically necessary" to bypass, "in a *progression to the infinite,*" on which Kant established the postulate of the immortality of the soul.[98] So, when Fichte writes, in the *System of Ethics,* that faith in the possibility of promotion of the goal of reason and in the necessity of this progress toward improvement, is "if one looks closer, the belief in God and immortality,"[99] he remains perfectly faithful to the Kantian lesson.

Is the second postulate included in the first or should it be considered separately? In other words, does the postulate of the immortality of the soul include an element that is not part of the postulate of freedom? I do not think so; but in this case what status should be given in the transcendental system to the baroque hypothesis of a plurality of ever more perfect worlds that succeed each other after life on earth, which is a hypothesis defended in a curious way in the third book of the *Vocation of Man*,[100] the first outline of which can be found in *Lessons of Logic and Metaphysics*,[101] and that is also mentioned in the *Characteristics of the Present Age*?[102] That to Fichte's mind it cannot be a question of reincarnation or transmutation of souls is established clearly in several passages of the *Lessons of Logic and Metaphysics*.[103] Such a solution, which is based on a substantial concept of the I, is clearly rejected as being transcendent.[104] Since, as time is a product of the I, the I cannot posit a time in which it does not exist; it is therefore of all time and in all time. Consequently, from the transcendental point of view, it is an illusion of common sense to posit a time in which it would not exist and to introduce a break in its progression.[105] In addition, it is necessary, from a methodological point of view, to take note of the meaning of the third book. Knowledge was correctly defined in the second book and, as was seen from the deduction of the intelligible world and the sensible world, there is no point in returning to it. Suffice it to say that the knowledge of the second book, which lends itself to the accusation of subjectivism, takes on a new modality in the third book, as soon as it is linked to its practical foundation: from being purely possible, it becomes real. Therefore, we do not witness an extension of knowledge in the third book, which is also valid for the whole philosophy of the postulates. Since the plurality of worlds was not founded in knowledge or, to express it in the language of the *Wissenschaftslehre nova methodo,* does not belong to the conditions of possibility of consciousness, it belongs only to a statement of faith and not to one of knowledge; consequently, the plural worlds postulated could not have the same status as the sensible world and the supersensible world. Therefore it seems to me that the hypothesis of plural worlds means nothing other than the transposed image of the necessity for man to follow a goal that cannot be realized either on earth or within any time frame. If such is the case, the belief in the immortality of the soul is nothing other than the belief, for the I, in the possibility of achieving that goal of reason, which is necessarily imparted to it once it is freely engaged in the process of self-limitation. The combination of finitude and infinity can only be achieved at the end of infinite approximation, and hence the second postulate is included in the first. Namely, as soon as I posit myself as free, "I must take as a goal the promotion of the reign of reason, i.e., undertake something that will be effective in the future," but "I cannot at all posit it as effective and in consequence cannot resolve to achieve it without positing it as possible."[106] Henceforth, the postulate of freedom includes the postulate of the possibility of achieving the freedom, of "sanctification," which is a task that cannot be completed

in a finite period of time and which therefore implies the postulate of a
supertemporal persistence.

What now of the third postulate, relating to God? Is it in turn
included in the postulate of liberty, and, if this is the case, how can it
be distinguished from the two others? That the second and the third
postulates should be closely connected in Fichte's mind, in the writings
of the Jena period, is, in my opinion, revealed by a striking clue. He
uses the same argument in favor of the third that he used to support
the second: the belief in God is based on the belief in the possibility of
the coming of the reign of liberty. "God is revealed immediately by the
summons of moral law, because in this way it is posited that morality is
something possible, which is the same as saying: God exists."[107] Now, if
God is revealed "immediately" by the summons of the moral law, the third
postulate is also included in the first,[108] so that the atheism professed by
anyone obeying the moral law can only result from a speculative error,
which consists of "denying theoretically what he admits practically."[109]
That Fichte succeeds in systematizing and unifying the Kantian postulates
by adding an extension to the postulate of liberty, in such a way that they
are based on a single belief, seems to be demonstrated by the following
passage: "The true belief is the belief in the possibility of the realization
of the moral law; there is no other belief."[110]

What now of the *Vocation of Man*? The God of the third book, which
was a cornerstone for so many commentators, is characterized as a "will
which is in itself law."[111] He is the order and law of the supersensible
world. Order in the meaning of *ordo ordinans* and not of course of *ordo
ordinatus:* "That sublime will," writes Fichte speaking of God, "does not
go its own way separate from the rest of the rational world."[112] As order,
God is not extraneous to the supersensible world, transcending history,
or in some way overarching it from above and from all ages. He is the
living order, which coordinates "from the inside" the human community.
"Between it [that sublime will] and all finite rational beings there is a
spiritual bond, and it itself is this spiritual bond of the world of reason. . . .
It is the general mediator between all of us."[113] The resurgence of the
problem of the substrate allows us to establish easily the parallel with
the *nova methodo*. The God of the third book of the *Vocation of Man*
occupies exactly the place devoted to the pure will in the *nova methodo* and
coincides with it. As such, God assumes the link among all the individual
I's, in so far as each individual I is founded on the pure will. Thus, the
third postulate is already included in the first.

But is this sublime equation not obtained at the cost of a serious
ambiguity? Was not pure will declared "substrate of the intelligible world"

only as an "explanatory ground," that is, in a strictly epistemological sense that excluded any ontological connotation? However, does not the identification of pure will with God lead us imperceptibly from the epistemological level to the ontological level? To meet this objection, it seems to me that it is appropriate to insist once more on the status of the argument developed in the third book: the idea of a bond between all human enterprise, of a harmony between the diverse particular vocations that criss-cross, in short, the idea of a moral order, is simply part of the argument of belief and not of knowledge. The practical ontology based on this argument of belief remains perfectly transcendental, and thus God can only be said to be the transsubjective basis of the human community as a transcendental idea of practical reason. Like the deduction of the intelligible world and the sensible world, as well as the deduction of the postulate of the immortality of the soul, the deduction of the postulate of the existence of God can be considered to be part of the analysis of the requirements for the moral vocation posited with the postulate of liberty. That postulate is as necessary as the postulate of liberty and therefore necessarily included within it as a condition of the coming of the reign of liberty. It, therefore, may also be qualified as an "explanatory ground."

Conclusion

I have tried in this study to prove that the philosophy of religion as the pendant to the philosophy of right in the "philosophy of the postulates" was already developed by Fichte during the Jena period, even if he did not dedicate a particular work to it. The originality of this philosophy of religion, which is heavily inspired by Kant, mainly consists in the systematization and unification of the Kantian postulates, by virtue of the extension of the postulate of liberty, the importance of which Fichte himself emphasized.

In conclusion, it is possible, in my view, to prove that the *Vocation of Man* belongs entirely to the philosophy of the Jena period and that it reveals no significant systematic change. As soon as the strategy Fichte used to uncover the indispensable link between the theoretical and practical moments of the system becomes clear, it is simple to rediscover the point of view already expounded in the *Foundations* and further developed in the *Wissenschaftslehre nova methodo*. A strictly transcendental interpretation of the practical postulates of the immortality of the soul and of the existence of God imposes itself, and thus permits the perfect inscription of the religious point of view in the system of the Jena period without implying the slightest systematic change. I would go even further: the *Wissenschaftslehre nova methodo,* which, as first philosophy, serves to provide the foundation of the diverse particular disciplines, which are organically linked to it, must also serve to provide, as section 13 proved, the foundation of a purely transcendental philosophy of religion, as it is developed in the *Vocation of Man,* with a prophetico-pedagogical accent, which is linked to the popular character of the writing. Consequently, no "conversion" to Jacobi, no romantic mysticism, no recourse to a "transsubjective basis," no turning from idealism to realism can be found in the *Vocation of Man;* we discover there instead a living and graphic presentation of the main results of the *Wissenschaftslehre,* as they are exposed particularly in the *Wissenschaftslehre nova methodo.*

Notes

I wish to express my gratitude to the Fondation du 450e anniversaire of the University of Lausanne, whose financial support allowed me to take part in the 1997 meeting of the North American Fichte Society in Milwaukee, and to my friends Peter Tallon and Yolanda Estes for their assistance with the translation.

    1. The texts cited in this essay are, for the text in English, *The Vocation of Man,* trans. Peter Preuss (Indianapolis: Hackett, 1987), hereafter abbreviated as *VM,* and for the original German text, that in *J. G. Fichte-Gesamtausgabe der Bayerischen Akademie der Wissenschaften,* ed. Reinhard Lauth, Hans Gliwitzky, and Erich Fuchs (Stuttgart-Bad Cannstatt: Frommann-Holzboog, 1964 ff.), hereafter abbreviated *GA.* Cf. *GA* I, 6, p. 187 ff.

    2. M. Gueroult, *L'évolution et la structure de la doctrine de la science* (Paris: Les Belles Lettres, 1930), 2 vols. (rpt. Olms, 1982); from the same, "La Destination de l'Homme," in M. Gueroult, *Études sur Fichte* (Paris, Aubier Montaigne, 1974), pp. 72–96.

    3. Gueroult, "La Destination de l'Homme," p. 72.

    4. Gueroult, *L'évolution et la structure de la doctrine de la science,* pp. 379–80.

    5. Fritz Medicus, ed., *Fichtes Werke,* vol. VI (Leipzig: Meiner, 1912), p. 627.

    6. "Wissenschaftslehre nach den Vorlesungen von Hr. Pr. Fichte," the publication of a "Kollegnachschrift," called the "Halle manuscript," after the place of its discovery, in J. G. Fichte, *Nachgelassene Schriften,* vol. II, ed. Hans Jacob (Berlin: Junker und Dünnhaupt, 1937); this text, referred to below as *A,* was republished in *GA* IV, 2. A second notebook, in Krause's handwriting, was discovered in 1980 and published in J. G. Fichte, *Wissenschaftslehre nova methodo. Kollegnachschrift K.Chr.Fr. Krause 1798/99,* ed. Erich Fuchs (Hamburg: Meiner, 1982); it is referred to below as *B.* An English translation appears in *Fichte, Foundations of Transcendental Philosophy: (Wissenschaftslehre) nova methodo (1796–1799),* trans.

and ed. Daniel Breazeale (Ithaca and London: Cornell University Press, 1992), hereafter abbreviated as *FTP.*

7. See *FTP,* p. 474 (*B* 244).

8. See Fichte's letter to his editor Cotta, 16 August 1800, *GA* III, 4, p. 287.

9. J. G. Fichte, *Sonnenklarer Bericht an das größere Publikum über das eigentliche Wesen der neuesten Philosophie. Ein Versuch, die Leser zum Verstehen zu zwingen, Berlin, Realschulbuchhandlung,* 1801, *GA* I, 7, p. 183 ff.; *A crystal clear report to the general public concerning the actual essence of the newest philosophy: An attempt to force the reader to understand,* 1801, trans. John Bottermann and William Rasch, *Philosophy of German Idealism,* ed. Ernst Behler (New York: Continuum, 1987).

10. J. G. Fichte, *Neue Bearbeitung der W.L.,* 1800, *GA* II, 5, p. 331 ff.

11. *VM,* p. 1; *GA* I, 6, p. 189.

12. This is a reference to the loss of his chair at the University of Jena, following the Atheism Controversy.

13. *GA* III, 4, p. 142.

14. *VM,* p. 64; *GA* I, 6, p. 251.

15. Jens Immanuel Baggesen's letter to Friedrich Heinrich Jacobi, 22 April 1800, *Fichte im Gespräch—Berichte der Zeitgenossen,* 7 vols., ed. Erich Fuchs (Stuttgart-Bad Cannstatt: Frommann-Holzboog, 1978–1992), hereafter cited as *FG,* vol. 2, pp. 328–29.

16. See Jacobi's letter to Jean Paul, 16 March 1800: "[Fichte] should not have plagiarized me" (*er hätte mich nicht bestehlen sollen*).

17. Jacobi's letter to Fichte, 3–21 March 1799, *GA* III, 3, pp. 224–81; for a partial English translation, see "Open Letter to Fichte," hereafter cited as "Open Letter," trans. Diana I. Behler, in *Philosophy of German Idealism,* ed. Ernst Behler (New York: Continuum, 1987).

18. See the note entered by Jacobi in early 1800 in his *Denkbücher:* "Fichte has sought, with his *Vocation of Man,* to abort the fruit of my letter" (*FG* VI.2, p. 514); a similar formulation is found in the letter to Jean Paul, 13 February 1800, *FG* II, p. 292.

19. See *FG* II, p. 309.

20. In a letter to Jean Paul, 27 April 1800, Christian Otto wrote that, in the *Vocation of Man,* Fichte sought to "surreptitiously introduce" (*einschwärzen*) his system (*FG* II, p. 331).

21. See, for example, Jean Paul's letter to Paul Émile Thiériot, 23 February 1800, in which the *Vocation of Man* is described as "idealistic hocus pocus," which Fichte used to "hide [*verstecken*] his *casa santa* in the broad doctrinal framework of common sense" (*FG* II, p. 298).

22. Jean Paul's letter to Karl August Böttiger, 11 March 1800, *FG* II, p. 303.

23. See the Preface of the *Vocation of Man, VM,* p. 1 (*GA* I, 6, p. 189).

24. See the introduction to J. G. Fichte, *La philosophie de la Maçonnerie et autres textes,* trans. I. Radrizzani and Fawzia Tobgui (Paris: Vrin, 1995), pp. 7–54.

25. J. G. Fichte, *Philosophie der Maurerei: Briefe an Konstant* 1802–1803, published as "Incertum" in *GA* I, 8, p. 407 ff.

26. Another example, which appears later in Fichte's works, is the subversion of the nationalist rhetoric in the *Addresses to the German Nation;* see my essay "La Science de ses adversaires, 'Ist Fichtes Modell des Kosmopolitismus pluralistisch?'" in *Fichte-Studien* 2 (1990): pp. 7–19.

27. *FTP,* p. 81 (*B* 6).

28. See Immanuel Kant, *Kritik der reinen Vernunft,* A 444–451; B 472–479.

29. Gueroult, "La Destination de l'Homme," p. 76; Alexis Philonenko, "La position systématique dans la *Destination de l'homme,*" in: A. Mues (Ed.), *Transzendentalphilosophie als System—Die Auseinandersetzung zwischen 1794 und 1806,* ed. A. Mues (Hambourg: Meiner, 1989), p. 335.

30. Concerning the revolution experienced by Fichte on his discovery of Kant, see especially Fichte's letter to Weisshuhn, August-September 1790 (*GA* III, 1, pp. 167–68), as well as A. Philonenko's commentary, "Traduction et commentaire de la lettre à F.A. Weisshuhn," in *Approches de Fichte,* numéro spécial de la *Revue de Théologie et de Philosophie,* ed. I. Radrizzani, vol. III (1991): pp. 229–43.

31. J. G. Fichte, "Versuch einer neuen Darstellung der Wissenschaftslehre," *Philosophisches Journal einer Gesellschaft Teutscher Gelehrten* V, no. 1 (1797) (*GA* I, 4, 183 ff.); "First Introduction to the Wissenschaftslehre," in J. G. Fichte, *Introductions to the Wissenschaftslehre and Other Writings,* trans. and ed. D. Breazeale (Indianapolis and Cambridge: Hackett, 1994), hereafter abbreviated as *IWL,* p. 1 ff.

32. A. Philonenko, "La position systématique," p. 334.

33. J. G. Fichte, *Grundlage der gesammten Wissenschaftslehre als Handschrift für seine Zuhörer* (Leipzig: Gabler, 1794) (*GA* I, 2, p. 249 ff.); "Foundations of the Entire Science of Knowledge," trans. Peter Heath, in Fichte, *Science of Knowledge,* trans. and ed. Peter Heath and John Lachs (Cambridge: Cambridge University Press, 1982).

34. Concerning the transition from the *Foundations* to the *Wissenschaftslehre nova methodo* and concerning the changes linked to the simplification in the method of exposition, see my book *Vers la fondation de l'intersubjectivité chez Fichte—Des Principes à la Doctrine de la Science nova methodo* (Paris: Vrin, 1993), pp. 81–115, more particularly p. 87.

35. *VM,* p. 1 (*GA* I, 6, p. 189).

36. *FTP,* pp. 110–11 and 119 (*B,* pp. 28–29, 34).

37. *FTP,* pp. 81–82 (*B,* p. 7).

38. I do not share A. Philonenko's opinion on this point. He claims that "Fichte was not particularly well-inspired in introducing the Spirit," as this notably "devalues results in that they were affected by the mediation of a fictitious genius," adding that it was "without necessity" that Fichte projected "in an intellectual exteriority" what finally was only a dialogue with himself ("La position systématique," pp. 338–39).

39. The Spirit, at the beginning of the second book, leads the I to say: "What I see and feel, I know immediately and simply; I know it just because it is so, without mediation and transmission by way of another sense." Cf. *VM,* p. 28;

GA I, 6, p. 216. This is a "formulation of the intellectual intuition," according to A. Philonenko in his *L'oeuvre de Fichte* (Paris, Vrin, 1984), p. 95).

40. *FTP,* p. 381 (*B,* pp. 192–93):

> We are engaged in the presentation of the central thought {of transcendental idealism}: all consciousness is nothing but self-consciousness. As part of our presentation of this point, we must provide a genetic demonstration that—and how—the sort of consciousness with which we are ordinarily familiar flows from our consciousness of ourselves.

VM, p. 29 (*GA* I, 6, p. 216): "The immediate consciousness of yourself and your determinations would . . . be the necessary condition of all other consciousness."

41. *VM,* pp. 63–64 (*GA* I, 6, p. 251).

42. Gueroult, "La Destination de l'Homme," p. 86.

43. "Outline of the distinctive character of the Wissenschaftslehre with respect to the theoretical faculty," in Fichte, *Early Philosophical Writings,* trans. and ed. Daniel Breazeale (Ithaca, N.Y.: Cornell University Press, 1988), hereafter abbreviated *EPW,* p. 243 ff. (*GA* I, 3, p. 137 ff.).

44. See, for example, Edith Düsing, "Sittliche Aufforderung: Fichtes Theorie der Interpersonalität in der *WL nova methodo* und in der *Bestimmung des Menschen,*" in *Transzendentalphilosophie als System—Die Auseinandersetzung zwischen 1794 und 1806,* ed. A. Mues (Hamburg, Meiner, 1989), p. 191:

> [In the *Vocation of Man,* Fichte] grants henceforth an exclusive value to practical philosophy and radically depreciates speculation. Such a separation of theory and practice marks a revolution in the internal structure of Fichtean thought. This appears in a particularly impressive way at the end of the second book of the *Vocation of Man* by the mise hors jeu of the position of a theoretical idealism, as a position which loses itself in the complete unreality of representations and in a fantasmagory and inconsistency of the I, which can only experience itself as the "dream of a dream."

The same idea is already formulated by Wolfgang Janke, in the chapter "The Transition from Knowledge to the Absolute" in *Fichte—Sein und Reflexion—Grundlagen der kritischen Vernunft* Berlin: De Gruyter, 1970), pp. 207–22, especially pp. 213–14.

Alexis Philonenko must be mentioned for having been the first to defend a new interpretative approach, laying the foundations for an accurate understanding of the *Vocation of Man;* see *L'oeuvre de Fichte,* p. 87 ff. The interpretation that Jean-Christophe Goddard proposes of this work in the introduction to his translation derives directly from Philonenko's work.

45. Gueroult, "La Destination de l'Homme," p. 84

46. Jean-Christoph Goddard, "Introduction," in J. G. Fichte, *La destination de l'homme,* trans. Jean-Christophe Goddard (Paris: Flammarion, 1995), p. 16.

47. *GA* I, 2, p. 310.

48. *FTP,* pp. 100 and 299; *B,* pp. 20 and 147.

49. See *GA* III, 4, p. 142, n. 2.

50. See Jacobi's letter to Schenk, 13 February 1799: "I must break off, in order to write to Fichte concerning his *Apologie.* This will not be easy, because I will finally have to have to come out against him on the subject of his philosophy" (*FG* VI.1, p. 340); this testimony can be completed by that of Nicolovius, written the next day:

> In his *Apologie* . . . [Fichte] publicly invokes Jacobi's support. Jacobi will reply, but the reply will not be published [N.B.: the decision to publish the "Open Letter" was taken much later]; the reply will point out the analogies and the differences that exist between them, and will show that they are like two lines converging on a point, but that they have a completely different point of departure and that they are directed toward a completely different goal." (Letter to Schlosser, 14 February 1799, *FG* II, p. 53)

Jacobi's position regarding the *Wissenschaftslehre* was determined after reading the article on truth that Fichte published in Schiller's review, *Die Horen* ("On Stimulating and Increasing the Pure Interest in Truth," in *EPW,* p. 223 ff.; *GA* I, 3, p. 83 ff.); on that point, see my essay "Jacobis Auseinandersetzung mit Fichte in den *Denkbüchern,*" *Fichte-Studien* 14 (1998): 43–62.

51. "Open Letter" (*GA* III, 3, p. 226).

52. "Open Letter" (*GA* III, 3, p. 227).

53. "Open Letter" (*GA* III, 3, pp. 233–34).

54. There are in Jacobi's work two other versions of the comparison of the Fichtean system to a woolen stocking: in the *Denkbücher* (*FG* VI.1, p. 242), and in the letter to von Dohm, 13 December 1797 (*FG* I, p. 472).

55. "Open Letter" (*GA* III, 3, pp. 235–36).

56. "Open Letter" (*GA* III, 3, p. 234).

57. Fichte's letter to Jacobi, 22 April 1799, *GA* III, 3, p. 334.

58. The text entitled "Fichte an Jacobi" appears on the reverse side of a sheet carrying the beginning of a text against Heusinger. The publishers of the *GA* propose for it a date in spring 1799, specifying, in fact, May or June. It appears improbable, however, that Fichte could have begun a letter to Jacobi at the time that used nearly all the expressions taken from the letter to Reinhold copied in the letter dated 22 April. I am inclined to think it more likely to be a draft of the letter of 22 April.

59. See "Open Letter" (*GA* III, 3, p. 232).

60. *GA* III, 3, p. 334.

61. *GA* II, 5, p. 194.

62. The idea of a convergence *(Übereinstimmung)* of views appears as early as Fichte's first letter to Jacobi, 29 September 1794 (*GA* III, 2, p. 202). It can be found notably in the letter dated 30 August 1795, in which Fichte expresses his surprise at the "striking uniformity" of their philosophical convictions (*GA* III, 2, p. 391) and in the letter dated 26 April 1796, in which Fichte speaks of "complete agreement" (*GA* III, 3, p. 18).

63. The reproach of a confusion between the two viewpoints of speculation and life, or, in other words, between the series of the philosopher and that of the I, is already clearly formulated in the *Second Introduction to the Wissenschaftslehre:*

> From the viewpoint of life, within which I appear only as something empirical, *I must* think of something as a thing-in-itself, i.e., as present independently of me as an empirical [I]. I have no knowledge of the activity in which I am engaged when I think in this manner, precisely because it is not a free activity. It is only from the philosophical viewpoint that I am able to infer the presence of this activity within my thinking. A failure to make clear the distinction between these two different points of view may explain why the clearest thinker of our era [Jacobi] . . . did not accept the transcendental idealism that he grasped so correctly, and indeed, believed that he had succeeded in destroying it merely by providing an exposition of it. For he supposed that the manner of thinking that is characteristic of idealism is also required within life. (*IWL,* p. 68; *GA* I, 4, p. 236)

See also *Rückerinnerungen, Antworten, Fragen* (March–April 1799):

> Philosophy, even completed, cannot provide a sensation. This sensation is the only real inner principle of life. Kant . . . has already said this. . . . Jacobi has also said the same thing, independently of Kant, while believing that he was in disagreement with him. . . . I too have said the same thing in as intelligible a way as possible, right from the very first expression of the concept of my system. (*GA* II, 5, p. 120)

64. *GA* II, 5, p. 194.
65. Cf. Gueroult, "La Destination de l'Homme," pp. 83–86; A. Philonenko, *L'oeuvre de Fichte,* p. 96.
66. A. Philonenko, *L'oeuvre de Fichte,* p. 96.
67. *FTP,* p. 182; *B,* p. 72.
68. *FTP,* p. 314; *A,* p. 149.
69. *VM,* p. 1; *GA* I, 6, p. 189.
70. L. Pareyson, *Fichte—Il sistema della libertà* (Milan, Mursia, 1976), p. 406.
71. *FTP,* p. 446; *B,* p. 227.
72. *FTP,* p. 307; *B,* p. 152.
73. *FTP,* p. 304; *A,* p. 143.
74. *FTP,* p. 95; *B,* p. 17.
75. *FTP,* p. 95; *B,* p. 17.
76. *DH* 162; *GA* I, 6, p. 261.
77. *FTP,* pp. 297–98 (*B,* p. 146):

> I must think of myself as being obliged to do something; but, just as surely as I have to think of myself in this way, I must also think of something determinable. . . . What is determinable . . . would not exist apart from the task of thinking the "ought"; nor could such a task exist apart from the "ought" itself. . . . Something determinable

must necessarily be posited, and, from this, all the objects of consciousness will be derived, as mediated—that is, as produced by means of an immediate consciousness of the "ought."

78. *VM*, p. 76; *GA* I, 6, p. 262.

79. The affirmation that the existence of the sensible world rests on faith is so old that it already appeared in the essay on language published in the March/April 1795 issue of the *Philosophisches Journal;* cf. "Von der Sprachfähigkeit und dem Ursprung der Sprache": "From the point of view of philosophical reason, we cannot say, there *is* a world. I can only feel what is outside me, and in this respect can only *believe* it. It is therefore a total article of faith to say, that there are things outside me" (*GA* I, 3, p. 112).

Concerning the deduction of the intelligible world, I cannot agree with E. Düsing's interpretation, which, continuing the interpretative line begun by Gueroult, claims that, compared with the *nova methodo,* a "new concept" of intersubjective relationships makes its appearance in the *Vocation of Man* because of a transforming of the part played by speculation (Düsing, "Sittliche Aufforderung: Fichtes Theorie der Interpersonalität," p. 192). The "interposition of a metaphysical layer" might have led Fichte to prefer the vertical to the horizontal axis in the relationship to the *alter ego* (Düsing, p. 193). For my part, far from seeing a "surprising turn" (*überraschende Wendung,* p. 193) in the foundation of the intersubjective world on belief and the clue of the devaluing of interhuman relationships or again a metaphysical twist, I see nothing more in this passage from the third book than the restating of the viewpoint argued in the *nova methodo.*

80. *VM*, p. 77; *GA* I, 6, p. 263.

81. *VM*, p. 77; *GA* I, 6, p. 263.

82. *FTP,* p. 471; *B*, p. 243.

83. *VM*, p. 78; *GA* I, 6, p. 263.

84. *VM*, p. 78; *GA* I, 6, p. 264.

85. *FTP,* p. 471; *B*, p. 242.

86. See *VM*, pp. 79–91; *GA* I, 6, pp. 265–76.

87. *Some Lectures concerning the Scholar's Vocation,* hereafter abbreviated *SV,* in *EPW,* pp. 145–61 (*GA* I, 3, pp. 27–41).

88. *SV,* pp. 147–9; *GA* I, 3, pp. 29–30.

89. *SV,* p. 150; *GA* I, 3, p. 31.

90. *SV,* pp. 159–60; *GA* I, 3, p. 40 (see also *SV,* p. 152; *GA* I, 3, p. 32).

91. See *SV,* p. 152 (*GA* I, 3, p. 32): "Man's final end is to subordinate to himself all that is irrational, to master it freely and according to his own laws."

92. See *SV,* pp. 156 and 159–60 (*GA* I, 3, pp. 37 and 40).

93. *SV,* p. 152; see also *SV,* p. 160 (*GA* I, 3, pp. 32 and 40).

94. According to L. Pareyson, "Fichte's thinking between 1793 and 1799 constitutes a complete whole, an enclosed entity, a system: the system of liberty" (*Fichte—Il sistema della libertà,* p. 403), a thesis even appearing in the title of his

book. Note that, from L. Pareyson's point of view, contrary to M. Gueroult's thesis, the passage on the "philosophy of the absolute" does not, in fact, mark the passage to "another philosophy" (p. 407); it is simply that from the *Vocation of Man* onward, the finite would no longer be "absolutized, but recovers its true proportions as consciousness of the absolute" (p. 406).

95. *FTP*, p. 298; *B*, p. 146.

96. *FTP*, p. 81; *B*, p. 6.

97. *FTP*, p. 295; *B*, p. 145.

98. Kant, *Critique of Practical Reason*, AK V, p. 122.

99. J. G. Fichte, *Sittenlehre*, *GA* I, 5, p. 305.

100. *VM*, pp. 97–99; *GA* I, 6, pp. 282–84.

101. *GA* IV, 1, p. 167.

102. *GA* I, 8, pp. 388–89.

103. See for example *GA* II, 4, pp. 334, 342; and *GA* IV, 1, p. 166. See also *GA* IV, 1, pp. 441–42.

104. *GA* II, 4, p. 342. See also *Characteristics of the Present Age:* "Man remains to all eternity exactly as he exists here, as a necessary phenomenon of the earthly vision, but he cannot in all eternity become what he has never been and is not, i.e. a *thing in himself*" (*GA* I, 8, p. 212).

105. See *GA* II, 4, p. 341, and IV, 1, p. 165.

106. *GA* IV, 1, p. 160. It can be noted that, in the text quoted, this argument is developed by Fichte to support the third postulate. That this argument also applies to the second postulate is proved by the following quote: "The belief in our survival is based on action. All our action is inscribed in temporal succession. We begin with the hope of achievement and could not begin without this hope" (*GA* II, 4, p. 333).

107. *GA* IV, 1, p. 162.

108. See also *GA* IV, 1, p. 432: "I find within myself the task of being moral, and thereby I also find divinity."

109. *GA* IV, 1, 161; see also, in the continuation of the text, the following:

> Theoretical disbelief is an error of understanding, a lack of intelligence. Speculative disbelief has indeed an unfortunate influence on our peace of mind, it is however not absolutely blameworthy, because it does not bear prejudice on true moral value, which consists uniquely in action; it is only an improper thing.

110. *GA* IV, 1, p. 161.

111. *VM*, p. 106; *GA* I, 6, p. 292.

112. *VM*, p. 106; *GA* I, 6, p. 292.

113. *VM*, pp. 106–7; *GA* I, 6, pp. 292–93.

Fichte, Representation, and the Copernican Revolution

Tom Rockmore

We gain insight into a theory, any theory, by understanding the conceptual context in which it arose, including the problem to which it responds, the error(s) it is intended to correct, the idea it is meant to develop, and so on. Fichte intended his theory to carry forward and complete Kant's critical philosophy. The premise of this essay is that Fichte's relation to Kant, arguably misunderstood by both Kant and Fichte, is crucial to understanding Fichte's own position and post-Kantian German idealism.

Kant's problem can be depicted as the analysis of representation. His critical philosophy turns, as he indicated in a reference to Copernicus, on what has been called the Copernican Revolution. Perhaps the safest characterization of the post-Kantian period is as a collective effort to complete Kant's Copernican Revolution. In comparison to Kant's understanding of his critical philosophy, Fichte presents a very different reading, arguably faithful to its spirit if not to its letter, but incompatible with other readings of its spirit.

Fichte's protean position, which is initially presented in the *Grundlage der gesamten Wissenschaftslehre*, later undergoes a series of important changes. The reasons include his disputes with philosophical contemporaries, but also his continuing efforts to work out his own philosophical theory. A quick survey of his position in the Jena period shows the difference between the deduction of representation *(Vorstellung)* in the Jena *Wissenschaftslehre*, and his treatment of it in later publications in this period, concluding with the *Vocation of Man,* where he presents a revised version of the same problem.

Representation

To understand Fichte's theory of representation requires a survey of its origins in Kant's theory. Any account of the nature of Kant's critical philosophy needs to consider three main factors: representation, the Copernican Revolution, and deduction. Kant's critical philosophy turns on representationalism, or the problem of representation. In a famous letter to Marcus Herz toward the beginning of the critical period, Kant describes the key to that future science in the form of a question: "What is the ground of the relation of that in us which we call 'representation' [*Vorstellung*] to the object?"[1]

Proper translation is crucial to understanding the nature of the theory. *Vorstellung* can be rendered into English indifferently as presentation or representation. If it is translated as presentation,[2] then the critical philosophy is misconstrued as a mere phenomenalism.

There is a distinction between a mere phenomenon, which appears but does not refer beyond itself to anything else, and a representation, which by definition refers beyond itself to something else, such as an object that appears through it.[3] Kant's problem is not merely the analysis of the phenomenon, but rather, as he clearly states, the analysis of the relation of the representation to the object. When Fichte employs the same term, he is not concerned with a mere phenomenalism, but rather with an analysis of representation. The difference between Kant and Fichte is not their common concern with representationalism, but the difference in their analyses of it.

The Copernican Revolution

Kant's approach to representationalism is well known. In a famous footnote, he compares his approach to Copernicus's transformation of geometry.[4] Although Kant never uses the term "Copernican Revolution," his theory is for this reason said to rest on a Copernican Revolution.

We can distinguish among a Copernican Revolution, Copernicus's theory, and Kant's theory. As understood here, a Copernican Revolution makes claims to know dependent on the subject. Through his introduction of a heliocentric theory to replace the geocentric ptolemaic theory, Copernicus explained the apparent motion of the planets through the retrograde motion of the subject. His kinematic theory, which still presupposed the circular planetary orbits of the Ptolemaic theory, later led to the explanation of planetary motion through Newtonian mechanics.

According to Kant, through a change in the relation of knowledge to the subject, Copernicus advanced a mere hypothesis, which made possible Newton's theory, in which it was finally demonstrated. Kant suggests that a similar change in perspective will be proven, using Cartesian language, apodictically, presumably in the form of the future science of metaphysics. According to Kant, he has proven this theory in the body of the book.

Kant's conception of proof presupposes his seminal distinction between dogmatic and critical forms of philosophy. A dogmatic philosophy merely asserts what it does not demonstrate; a critical philosophy demonstrates what it asserts. Kant claims that his theory differs from all prior theories in asserting *and* also proving its cognitive claims.

Kant's alleged proof rests on his contention that there are two and only two possible ways to understand the relation of the representation to the object. Earlier philosophies that made claims to knowledge dependent on an independent object ended in skepticism. In making knowledge depend on the subject, hence through a Copernican turn, Kant famously suggests that we can know only that which we ourselves produce.[5] Kant's own analysis of the problem of knowledge requires that he demonstrate the relation of the representation to the object, more precisely that he demonstrate that and how the subject produces the object of experience and knowledge.

Deduction in the Critical Philosophy

There is a distinction between independent objects, or things in themselves, which stand outside experience and cannot be known, and representations, which are given as phenomena within experience. In claiming that the subject must in some sense produce (from the German *herstellen,* "to produce") the object as a condition of knowing it, Kant contends that as a necessary condition of knowledge the subject must produce the representation, which relates to an object outside experience.

It is well known that Kant's proof depends crucially on his deductions of the pure concepts of the understanding. The critical philosophy stands or falls on their success. "Deduction" is used, not in the familiar mathematical way but in a juridical sense. Kant needs, as he puts it, to answer, not the question of fact *(quid facti)* but the question of right *(quid juris)* with respect to the employment of the categories.[6]

Kant's deductions are notoriously obscure. They have been discussed at length and in detail in an enormous literature, which has not led to an agreement on many of the questions raised about them.[7] This is not the place to consider the difficulties of Kant's deductions.[8] Suffice it to say Kant contends that his Copernican hypothesis is conclusively demonstrated in his critical philosophy. He explicitly says that to change any part of his system of pure reason at all will produce contradictions, not only in the system, but, more important, in human reason.[9]

Improving Kant

This controversial claim was not widely accepted. Among his contemporaries, it was accepted only by Maimon, who held that any attempt to improve the critical philosophy would only weaken it. It was implicitly rejected even by Kant himself. Kant, who distinguished between the ideas in his theory and the style in which it was expressed, admits that his style could be improved. Though he claims that nothing in his system could be changed, he himself introduces changes in the second edition of the *Critique of Pure Reason,* as concerns, for instance, the deduction of the pure concepts of the understanding.

Later German idealism can be understood as an effort to carry through and complete Kant's Copernican Revolution in philosophy.[10] Kant's theory appears incomplete; for he is unable to describe how the subject, in fact, produces its object as a condition of knowing it. He comes closest to an account in a well-known passage in the discussion of schematism, where he describes it as "an art concealed in the depths of the human soul, whose real modes of activity nature is hardly likely ever to allow us to discover, and to have open to our gaze."[11]

The difficulty of how to go further than Kant in carrying out his project was inadvertently resolved by Kant himself. In his revised formulation of the venerable distinction between the spirit and the letter of a theory, he arguably intended only to provide for a better interpretation of the critical philosophy.[12] Although Kant certainly believed that different readers should reach similar interpretations of the work as a whole, his expectation was not borne out in practice. Fichte, Schelling, and Hegel, the main post-Kantian German idealists, each carry the critical philosophy beyond Kant in different ways, since each perceived its spirit differ-

ently. The later German idealist theories are incompatible with the letter
of the critical philosophy and incompatible with one another; though
perhaps compatible with its spirit, later German idealism seems simply
to turn the critical philosophy inside out.

Fichte and the French Revolution

Fichte famously insists on his fidelity to, and comprehension of, Kant.
At a time when the claim to be the only one to understand Kant was
widespread, it is noteworthy that Fichte's own claim was accepted by the
young Schelling and the young Hegel. Yet although the spirit of Fichte's
theory is generally Kantian, it certainly violates the letter and perhaps
even the spirit of the critical philosophy at crucial points.

None is more crucial than the conception of the subject. Kant's
theory of knowledge is, as Husserl clearly saw, anti-psychologistic.[13] Kant
is concerned with the conditions of the possibility of knowledge whatsoever (*überhaupt*); he is only incidentally concerned with the conditions of
human knowledge. His conception of the subject as an original synthetic
unity of apperception is a transcendental logical concept that responds
to a precise analysis of the conditions of knowledge. His conception of
subjectivity as the highest point of the understanding, even the highest
point of the critical philosophy,[14] is not consistent, but rather inconsistent, with the idea of an individual human being.

Between Kant and the post-Kantians falls the great French Revolution, still the most important single event of modern times. Philosophy,
which officially claims to be independent of society, but indispensable for
the good life, is often influenced, even deeply influenced by historical
events. The French Revolution, which swept away the French monarchy,
revealed the fragility of institutions that seemed to belong to reality itself.
An effect of the realization that human institutions are brought into being and depend on human beings was a shift in the analysis of knowledge
from a general to a more closely human perspective.

English empiricism has always had an anthropological basis. Bacon,
Locke, Hume, and Mill provide theories of human knowledge. With
some exceptions, until the French Revolution, continental philosophers,
such as Descartes and Kant, typically analyze the conditions of knowledge
in independence of human being. After the French Revolution, continental philosophers, with some exceptions, increasingly replace epistemological constructions of the subject with human beings as the real
subject.

Post-Kantian German idealists are deeply marked by the French Revolution, none more so than Fichte. His defense of the Revolution, even against Napoleon, is well known. Fichte's theory, as early as its initial formulation, reflects a revised conception of the subject as a human being.[15] This conception is incompatible with the letter, perhaps even with the spirit of the critical philosophy, but central to his own theory.

The Deduction of Representation in the Jena *Wissenschaftslehre*

Despite Kant's confidence in his work, post-Kantian German idealists were motivated by their conviction that the deduction of the categories was unsuccessful. Fichte contends that Kant fails to prove that or how representations obtain objective validity since he mistakenly substitutes induction for deduction.[16] Hegel regards the deduction of the categories as authentic idealism and as the speculative principle that Fichte carried further than Kant.[17] He sees Fichte's contribution as, in fact, deducing the categories Kant only claimed to deduce.

The Kantian problem of representation is a central theme in Fichte's theory. The "Review of *Aenesidemus*," in which he is generally thought to formulate the bases of his own theory, already concerns the idea of representation. Fichte notes that in his revision of Reinhold's theory of representation, he returns to the resources of the critical philosophy. Fichte here proposes that "the representation is related to the object as the effect is related to its cause and to the subject as the accident is related to the substance."[18] In a single sentence, this is the theory that Fichte immediately develops under the general heading of the *Wissenschaftslehre*.

In Fichte's initial statement of his position in the *Grundlage der gesamten Wissenschaftslehre*, the shift in the idea of the subject is already visible. He begins by elaborating three fundamental principles that, from the vantage point of the subject, comprise its interaction with the contents of experience. In elaborating the principles governing experience and knowledge through the subject, Fichte works out Kant's suggestion that subjectivity is the highest philosophical principle.

The theoretical part of the discussion closes with a revised deduction of representation. Kant and Fichte employ the word "deduction" very differently. Kant's theory of representation concerns an analysis of the conditions of the possibility of experience and knowledge of objects whatsoever. Consistent with the theory sketched in the "Review of

Aenesidemus," Fichte's theory of representation concerns a description of how we in fact experience and know objects.

This difference is consistent with Kant's and Fichte's rather different types of theory. An analysis of the conditions of possibility supposes that the subject is not a finite human being. How finite human beings must know cannot be deduced; at most, how they do know can be described. Although Fichte continues to employ the term "deduction" here and in other writings, in the shift from a view of the subject as a mere epistemological principle to a view of the subject as a real human being he cuts his ties with deduction in the Kantian sense.

The discussion in the theoretical part of the Jena *Wissenschaftslehre* culminates in a detailed summary of the discussion, followed by the Deduction of Representation. In the summary, Fichte accounts for representation through the assumption that the self, or subject, is unlimited. The subject needs to understand the possibility of representation as a fact in its mind through an account of the laws of its own nature.

Kant's deduction of the categories is motivated by his effort to understand the relation between appearances, or objects given in experience, and what can be thought but does not appear.[19] Fichte's deduction, which is consistent with his analysis of the fundamental principles governing interaction from the perspective of the subject, presupposes *inter alia* that there is nothing higher than the self;[20] that in philosophy we start from the self that cannot be deduced;[21] and that deduction is a direct, genetic demonstration focused on the self.[22]

Fichte's deduction is a complex argument in no less than eleven steps.[23] Suffice it to say informally that, starting from the hypothesis that the self, or subject, is active, Fichte maintains that we can understand the subject as what is left when all objects have been eliminated by the power of abstraction, and the not-self is that from which abstraction can be made. Either can be considered as determined by the other, and conversely. The deduction concludes with the claim that whether the subject is in fact finite, or determined, or infinite, hence determining, it is reciprocally related merely to itself. According to Fichte, theoretical philosophy can go no further.

Representation in the Later Jena Period

The deduction of representation in the Jena *Wissenschaftslehre* is focused and detailed. Fichte pursues this theme, although in increasingly less detail, in other writings from the Jena period. In the "First Introduction to

the *Wissenschaftslehre,*" he defines experience as the "system of representations accompanied by a feeling of necessity" and claims that philosophy
must "furnish the ground of all experience."[24] This is the task of the
Wissenschaftslehre.[25] Dogmatists, who are limited to a mere causal analysis,
are unable to explain representation. This can be explained from the
idealist perspective only, which distinguishes between the double series
of the real and the ideal, although philosophy consists in this deduction.[26]
The intellect functions according to necessary laws.[27] With an eye to
Kant, Fichte writes that a critical philosopher must "really deduce the
system of the necessary modes of operation, and with it concurrently the
objective representations created thereby, from the fundamental laws of
the intellect."[28]

Fichte studies this theme again in the "Second Introduction to the
Wissenschaftslehre," where he asks about the source of the system of representations accompanied by the feeling of necessity.[29] Here, breaking with
Kant, he introduces the idea of intellectual intuition on the grounds that,
since my representation is mine, to reject intellectual intuition is equivalent to rejecting sensory intuition.[30] Intellectual intuition is presented,
not as a fact, but rather as an inference through a train of reasoning.[31]

Though denied by Kant, Fichte's claim that self-consciousness is the
basis of consciousness[32] is consistent with a reading of the critical philosophy as not merely a hypothesis, but as a proof of knowledge, which,
hence, requires consciousness of consciousness, or self-consciousness.
In a later reflection on the obscure philosopher Schulz, Fichte notes
that, for Kant, Schulz, and himself representation requires three factors
(factors parenthetically already given in the "Review of *Aenesidemus*") including a relation to an object in sensory intuition, to a subject, and the
union of both in a concept.[33]

Fichte further continues his concern with representation in the
series of manuscripts known as the *Wissenschaftslehre nova methodo.* This
text is noteworthy for the relatively little attention accorded directly to
representation. In passing, he notes that the *Wissenschaftslehre* does not
generate new cognition, but observes the activity of the human mind;
the *Wissenschaftslehre* presents "a genetic understanding of the origin of
our representations."[34] Imagination is a productive power that grasps
representations, or representations of relations.[35] Unlike, say, the Jena
Wissenschaftslehre, where representation is a central theme, the direct consideration of the deduction of representation is reduced to less than a
page in this enormous series of manuscripts. In a rapid passage, Fichte
notes that Kant begins with representations, but fails to show why or how
we have them; on the contrary, the *Wissenschaftslehre* shows that repre-

sentations depend on the acting of the subject, thereby explaining what Kant fails to show, that is, the primacy of practical reason.[36]

Representation in the *Vocation of Man*

In examining Fichte's writings in this period, it is clear that representation, which is central to the critical philosophy and to the *Wissenschaftslehre,* quickly recedes in importance in later writings. This suddenly changes in the *Vocation of Man,* at the end of this period. Here the theme of representation is again brought to a kind of focus, although in a more diffuse way than in the Jena *Wissenschaftslehre,* and without the earlier attention to deduction. This text presents the elements of a different view of representation. Here Fichte perhaps comes as close as he ever does to making sense of Kant's Copernican claim that the subject produces its object as a necessary condition of knowledge.

This text is misdescribed by Fichte as merely popular,[37] since it is certainly more than that. The revised account of representation appears in the second section on knowledge, which follows from the account of doubt and leads up to that of faith.

Fichte bases his discussion of knowledge, hence representation, on self-consciousness. The link between his analysis and Kant's Copernican Revolution is clear, since a critical theory must not only account for knowledge of an object, or consciousness,[38] but knowledge of knowledge, or self-consciousness. Unlike Kant, Fichte argues, not that knowledge and experience of objects are one and the same, but rather that perception is an affection of oneself.[39] The object is a mere posit.[40] For Kant, so for Fichte there is no knowledge of things in themselves but of consciousness of consciousness of things.[41] Our knowledge of the external world rests on the principle of causality, but our knowledge of the principle itself rests, not on deduction, but on the immediate grasp of general principles.[42] In a passage that restates the contours of the position advanced in the Jena *Wissenschaftslehre,* Fichte writes:

> My consciousness of the object is merely an unrecognized *consciousness of my production of a representation of an object.* I know of this production only because I myself am that which produces it. And thus all consciousness is immediate, is but a consciousness of myself, and therefore perfectly comprehensible.[43]

Following Kant's distinction between sensation and perception, Fichte maintains that, on the basis of an object, the existence of which is not experienced, but posited, the subject produces what it knows, that is, its cognitive object, through the activity of its mind. He sums this up in writing:

> You perceive then that all knowledge is merely a knowledge of yourself; that your consciousness never goes beyond yourself; and that what you assume to be a consciousness of the object is nothing but a consciousness of the fact that you have *posited* the object—posited it necessarily, in accordance with the inner law of your thought, at the same time as the sensation.[44]

Consciousness, which is consciousness of an object, is consciousness of ourselves, or self-consciousness.[45] Self-consciousness, then, is immediate and consciousness is mediate.[46] Knowledge does not concern reality; it merely concerns appearance, and there is something real lying beyond mere appearance.[47]

The views of representation that Fichte presents in the Jena *Wissenschaftslehre* and *The Vocation of Man*, at opposite ends of the Jena period, are similar. The main difference is that, at the end of this period, Fichte abandons any pretense of a deduction, which is central to Kant's vision of philosophy. As he continues down the road of realizing the spirit of the critical philosophy, he diverges ever further from its letter.

Conclusion: Fichte, Representation, and the Copernican Revolution

Fichte's claim to be the only one who really understood Kant largely rests on his reworking of the Kantian conception of representation. This essay has traced Fichte's treatment of this conception in the writings of his Jena period. The legitimacy of Fichte's endeavor is justified by his appeal to the spirit of the critical philosophy, which, not surprisingly, since there are no guideposts, was interpreted in different ways by the post-Kantian idealists.

I would like to close with four points. First, it is clear that in Fichte the fate of pure reason turns out not to be triumphant but tragic: for Fichte replaces reason in the Kantian sense, which is self-demonstrating, by practical reason, and then later, in *The Vocation of Man*, by faith. In that sense, not only does Fichte turn against Kant by turning Kant inside out, but he also turns the spirit of Kant against Kant himself.

Second, if there is a residual sense in which Fichte is still foundationalist, it is clearly not foundationalism in the Kantian sense. Kantian foundationalism is deductive. Fichte, on the contrary, is not concerned with deduction in the Kantian sense, but with rather a description of the intrinsic logic of experience from the perspective of the subject, a view very close to Hegelian phenomenology.

Third, although Kant's views of subjectivity and deduction are compatible, in Fichte's theory they quickly become incompatible in his reinterpretation of the subject as a human being. In discarding any semblance of deduction at the end of the Jena period, Fichte loses little or nothing that is not already lost in the shift to a new version of subjectivity. Yet the price of this shift is the loss of a central element in Kant's claim to scientific philosophy.

Finally, the importance of Fichte's transformation of the subject in the wake of the French Revolution cannot be overemphasized. His new version of subjectivity influenced numerous later philosophers, including Hegel[48] and Marx,[49] and more distantly Heidegger. As we move further into the new century, perhaps the most important philosophical task remains, as it remained after the French Revolution, to rethink the theory of knowledge and philosophy in general from the perspective of the real human subject.

Notes

1. To Marcus Herz, 21 February 1772, in Immanuel Kant, *Philosophical Correspondence, 1759–99,* ed. and trans. Arnulf Zweig (Chicago: University of Chicago Press, 1967), p. 71.

2. See, e. g., Chisholm's translation of *The Vocation of Man* (Indianapolis: Bobbs-Merrill, 1956) and Heath and Lach's translation of the Jena *Wissenschaftslehre* (J. G. Fichte, *The Science of Knowledge, with the First and Second Introductions,* ed. and trans. Peter Heath and John Lachs [Cambridge: Cambridge University Press, 1982]).

3. See Immanuel Kant, *Critique of Pure Reason,* trans. N. K. Smith (London and New York: Macmillan and St. Martin's, 1961), B xxvii, p. 27.

4. Ibid., B xxii, p. 25.

5. Ibid., p. 20.

6. See ibid., B 116, p. 120.

7. See, e. g., H. J. de Vleeschauwer, *La déduction transcendentale dans l'oeuvre de Kant* (Antwerp: De Sikkel, 1934–37), 3 vols.

8. See, e. g., Stephan Körner, *Categorical Frameworks* (Oxford: Blackwell's, 1980).

9. Kant, *Critique of Pure Reason,* B xxviii, B 34.

10. See Tom Rockmore, *Hegel's Circular Epistemology* (Bloomington: Indiana University Press, 1986).

11. Kant, *Critique of Pure Reason,* B 180–81, p. 183.

12. See ibid., B xliv, p. 37.

13. See Edmund Husserl, *Logische Untersuchungen* (Tübingen: Max Niemeyer Verlag, 1980), 3 vols.

14. See Kant, *Critique of Pure Reason,* B 134, p. 154.

15. See Tom Rockmore, "Fichte, le tournant subjectif et le rêve de Descartes" (Actes du colloque de Poitiers, Octobre 1994), in *Les Cahiers de philosophie,* ed. Jean-Luc Solère, CNRS, Printemps 1995, pp. 301–12.

16. See *Fichte: Foundations of Transcendental Philosophy (Wissenschaftslehre) nova methodo,* ed. and trans. by Daniel Breazeale (Ithaca: Cornell University Press, 1992), p. 80.

17. See G. W. F. Hegel, *The Difference Between Fichte's and Schelling's System of Philosophy,* trans. H. S. Harris and Walter Cerf (Albany: SUNY Press, 1977), p. 79.

18 . "Review of *Aenesidemus,*" in *Fichte: Early Philosophical Writings,* ed. and trans.by Daniel Breazeale (Ithaca and London: Cornell University Press, 1988), p. 72.

19. See Kant, *Critique of Pure Reason,* B xxvii, p. 27.

20. Fichte, *The Science of Knowledge,* p. 224.

21. See ibid., p. 262.

22. See ibid., pp. 239, 269.

23. See Tom Rockmore, "Fichte on Deduction in the Jena *Wissenschaftslehre,*" in *New Essays in Fichte's Foundation of the Entire Doctrine of Scientific Knowledge,* edited by Daniel Breazeale and Tom Rockmore, Amherst: Humanity Books, 2001, pp. 60–77.

24. Fichte, *The Science of Knowledge,* p. 6.

25. See ibid., p. 7.

26. See ibid., pp. 16–22.

27. See ibid., p. 21.

28. Ibid., p. 22; translation modified.

29. Ibid., p. 31.

30. See ibid., p. 39.

31. Ibid., p. 40.

32. See ibid., p. 41.

33. See ibid., p. 47.

34. Ibid., p. 380.

35. See ibid., p. 399.

36. See ibid., pp. 162–63.

37. See Fichte, *The Vocation of Man,* p. 3.

38. See ibid., p. 37.

39. See ibid., p. 47.

40. See ibid., p. 48.

41. See ibid., p. 51.

42. See ibid., p. 55.

43. Ibid., p. 56; translation modified.

44. Ibid., p. 57.

45. See ibid., p. 75.

46. See ibid., p. 79.

47. See ibid., p. 82.

48. See Tom Rockmore, *Cognition: An Introduction to Hegel's Phenomenology of Spirit* (Berkeley and Los Angeles: University of California Press, 1997).

49. See Tom Rockmore, *Fichte, Marx, and German Philosophy* (Carbondale: Southern Illinois University Press, 1980).

Notes on Contributors

Curtis Bowman is a visiting assistant professor of philosophy at Haverford College.

Johannes Brachtendorf is a privatdozent on the faculty of Catholic philosophy at the Eberhard Karls University in Tübingen.

Daniel Breazeale is a professor of philosophy at the University of Kentucky.

Klaus Brinkmann is an associate professor of philosophy at Boston University.

Yolanda Estes is an assistant professor of philosophy and religion at Mississippi State University.

Arnold Farr is an associate professor of philosophy at St. Joseph's University in Philadelphia.

Steven Hoeltzel is an assistant professor of philosophy and religion at James Madison University.

C. Jeffery Kinlaw is an associate professor of philosophy at McMurry University.

Jean-Christophe Merle is a research assistant at the Eberhard Karls University, Tübingen.

Lon Nease is completing his Ph.D. in philosophy at the University of Kentucky.

Angelica Nuzzo is an associate professor of philosophy at Brooklyn College, City University of New York.

Claude Piché is professeur titulaire at the University of Montreal.

Ives Radrizzani is a privatdozent at the Ludwig Maximilians University, Munich, and an editorial associate on the Fichte and Schelling editions of the Bavarian Academy of the Sciences.

Janet Roccanova is an instructor in philosophy at the University of Kentucky.

Tom Rockmore is a professor of philosophy at Duquesne University.

F. Scott Scribner is a visiting assistant professor of philosophy at the University of Hartford.

Hans-Jakob Wilhelm is an adjunct professor of philosophy at the New School University.

Robert R. Williams is a professor of Germanic studies, philosophy, and religious studies at the University of Illinois at Chicago.

Günter Zöller is a professor of philosophy at the Ludwig Maximilians University, Munich.